# Shakesp
# minor

D0377323

JUN -- 2000

# notes

summaries and critical commentaries about the
minor plays of william shakespeare, including

henry VI, parts 1, 2, 3 • titus andronicus
king John • the merry wives of windsor
all's Well that ends Well • coriolanus
troilus and cressida • timon of athens
pericles • cymbeline • henry VIII

**Cliffs Notes**

INCORPORATED

LINCOLN, NEBRASKA 68501

**Editor**

*Gary Carey, M.A.*
*University of Colorado*

**Consulting Editor**

*James L. Roberts, Ph.D.*
*Department of English*
*University of Nebraska*

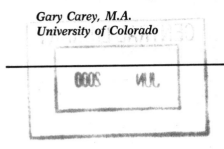

ISBN 0-8220-0059-8
*Henry VI, Parts 1, 2, 3* Notes © Copyright 1985; *Titus Andronicus* & *King John* Notes © Copyright 1983; *All's Well That Ends Well* & *The Merry Wives of Windsor* Notes © Copyright 1985; *Troilus and Cressida* Notes © Copyright 1964; *Coriolanus* & *Timon of Athens* Notes © Copyright 1981; *Cymbeline* & *Pericles* Notes © Copyright 1982; *Henry VIII* Notes © Copyright 1984 by C. K. Hillegass. All Rights Reserved. Printed in U.S.A.

1991 Printing.

## ACKNOWLEDGMENT

Authors of the following Notes on Shakespeare's minor plays are: *Henry VI, Parts 1, 2, 3,* W. John Campbell, Ph.D.; *Titus Andronicus* & *King John,* Evelyn McLellan, Ph.D.; *All's Well That Ends Well* & *The Merry Wives of Windsor,* Denis Calandra, Ph.D.; *Troilus and Cressida,* James K. Lowers, Ph.D.; *Coriolanus* & *Timon of Athens,* James E. Vickers, M.A.; *Cymbeline* & *Pericles,* James F. Bellman, Ph.D., and Kathryn A. Bellman, J.D., Ph.D.; *Henry VIII,* W. John Campbell, Ph.D.

The Cliffs Notes logo, the names "Cliffs" and "Cliffs Notes," and the black and yellow diagonal-stripe cover design are all registered trademarks belonging to Cliffs Notes, Inc., and may not be used in whole or in part without written permission.

Cliffs Notes, Inc.        Lincoln, Nebraska

# CONTENTS

# Shakespeare's
# Life and Background

*M*any books have assembled facts, reasonable suppositions, traditions, and speculations concerning the life and career of William Shakespeare. Taken as a whole, these materials give a rather comprehensive picture of England's foremost dramatic poet. Tradition and sober supposition are not necessarily false because they lack proved bases for their existence. It is important, however, that persons interested in Shakespeare should distinguish between *facts* and *beliefs* about his life.

From one point of view, modern scholars are fortunate to know as much as they do about a man of middle-class origin who left a small country town and embarked on a professional career in sixteenth-century London. From another point of view, they know surprisingly little about the writer who has continued to influence the English language and its drama and poetry for more than three hundred years. Sparse and scattered as these facts of his life are, they are sufficient to prove that a man from Stratford by the name of William Shakespeare wrote the major portion of the thirty-seven plays which scholars ascribe to him. The concise review which follows will concern itself with some of these records.

No one knows the exact date of William Shakespeare's birth. His baptism occurred on Wednesday, April 26, 1564. His father was John Shakespeare, tanner, glover, dealer in grain, and town official of Stratford; his mother, Mary, was the daughter of Robert Arden, a prosperous gentleman-farmer. The Shakespeares lived on Henley Street.

Under a bond dated November 28, 1582, William Shakespeare and Anne Hathaway entered into a marriage contract. The baptism of their eldest child, Susanna, took place in Stratford in May, 1583. One year and nine months later their twins, Hamnet and Judith, were christened in the same church. The parents named them for the poet's friends, Hamnet and Judith Sadler.

Early in 1596, William Shakespeare, in his father's name, applied to the College of Heralds for a coat of arms. Although positive proof is lacking, there is reason to believe that the Heralds granted this request, for in 1599 Shakespeare again made application for the right to quarter his coat of arms with that of his mother. Entitled to her father's coat of arms, Mary had lost this privilege when she married John Shakespeare before he held the official status of gentleman.

In May of 1597, Shakespeare purchased New Place, the outstanding residential property in Stratford at that time. Since John Shakespeare had suffered financial reverses prior to this date, William must have achieved success for himself.

Court records show that in 1601-02, William Shakespeare began room ing in the household of Christopher Mountjoy in London. Subsequent disputes over the wedding settlement and agreement between Mountjoy and his son-in-law, Stephen Belott, led to a series of legal actions, and in 1612 the court scribe recorded Shakespeare's deposition of testimony relating to the case.

In July, 1605, William Shakespeare paid four hundred and forty pounds for the lease of a large portion of the tithes on certain real estate in and near Stratford. This was an arrangement whereby Shakespeare purchased half the annual tithes, or taxes, on certain agricultural products from parcels of land in and near Stratford. In addition to receiving approximately ten percent income on his investment, he almost doubled his capital. This was possibly the most important and successful investment of his lifetime, and it paid a steady income for many years.

Shakespeare is next mentioned when John Combe, a resident of Strat- ford, died on July 12, 1614. To his friend, Combe bequeathed the sum of five pounds. These records and similar ones are important, not because of their economic significance but because they prove the existence of William Shakespeare in Stratford and in London during this period.

On March 25, 1616, William Shakespeare revised his last will and tes- tament. He died on April 23 of the same year. His body lies within the chancel and before the altar of the Stratford church. A rather wry inscrip- tion is carved upon his tombstone:

> Good Friend, for Jesus' sake, forbear
> To dig the dust enclosed here;
> Blest be the man that spares these stones
> And curst be he who moves my bones.

The last direct descendant of William Shakespeare was his granddaughter, Elizabeth Hall, who died childless in 1670.

These are the most outstanding facts about Shakespeare the man, as apart from those about the dramatist and poet. Such pieces of informa- tion, scattered from 1564 through 1616, declare the existence of such a person, not as a writer or actor, but as a private citizen. It is illogical to think that anyone would or could have fabricated these details for the pur- pose of deceiving later generations.

In similar fashion, the evidence establishing William Shakespeare as the foremost playwright of his day is positive and persuasive. Robert Greene's *Groatsworth of Wit,* in which he attacked Shakespeare, a mere actor, for presuming to write plays in competition with Greene and his fellow playwrights, was entered in the *Stationers' Register* on September 20, 1592. In 1594 Shakespeare acted before Queen Elizabeth, and in 1594-95 his name appeared as one of the shareholders of the Lord Chamberlain's Company. Francis Meres in his *Palladis Tamia* (1598) called Shakespeare "mellifluous and hony-tongued" and compared his comedies and tragedies with those of Plautus and Seneca in excellence.

Shakespeare's continued association with Burbage's company is equally definite. His name appears as one of the owners of the Globe in 1599. On May 19, 1603, he and his fellow actors received a patent from James I designating them as the King's Men and making them Grooms of the Chamber. Late in 1608 or early in 1609, Shakespeare and his colleagues purchased the Blackfriars Theatre and began using it as their winter location when weather made production at the Globe inconvenient.

Other specific allusions to Shakespeare, to his acting and his writing, occur in numerous places. Put together, they form irrefutable testimony that William Shakespeare of Stratford and London was the leader among Elizabethan playwrights.

One of the most impressive of all proofs of Shakespeare's authorship of his plays is the First Folio of 1623, with the dedicatory verse which appeared in it. John Heminge and Henry Condell, members of Shakespeare's own company, stated that they collected and issued the plays as a memorial to their fellow actor. Many contemporary poets contributed eulogies to Shakespeare; one of the best-known of these poems is by Ben Jonson, a fellow actor and, later, a friendly rival. Jonson also criticized Shakespeare's dramatic work in *Timber: or, Discoveries* (1641).

Certainly there are many things about Shakespeare's genius and career which the most diligent scholars do not know and cannot explain, but the facts which do exist are sufficient to establish Shakespeare's identity as a man and his authorship of the thirty-seven plays which reputable critics acknowledge to be his.

# the plays

1590-92

# henry VI
# parts 1, 2, 3

# A BRIEF SYNOPSIS OF THE TRILOGY

## Henry VI, Part 1

Part 1 deals primarily with the conflicts between **Lord Talbot,** general of the English armies, and **Joan la Pucelle,** more commonly known as Joan of Arc. Talbot has been in France leading the English attempts to gain the French crown, a goal which Henry V placed high among his priorities. Talbot is shown to be an excellent soldier and very loyal to the English crown. When the play opens, Henry V has just died, and messengers arrive at Henry's funeral to announce that the English have suffered losses in France. **Charles, the French Dauphin,** took advantage of Henry V's critical illness to raise a fearsome army against the attacking English forces. In addition, Joan of Arc lent hope to the French armies since she was apparently gifted with visionary powers.

As a result, dissension immediately arises in England between the **Duke of Gloucester** (young Henry VI's uncle and Protector of England) and the **Bishop of Winchester** (also known as Henry Beaufort); their disputes arise from personal ambition to influence the young king and gain control of the throne. Moreover, there is additional disagreement between **Richard Plantagenet** (the future Duke of York) and the **Earl of Somerset** (also known as John Beaufort), who will don, respectively, the symbols of the white rose and the red rose as the disastrous Wars of the Roses begin. It is Richard Plantagenet's goal as a Yorkist to wrench the crown away from the Lancastrian Henry VI and restore the Yorkists to the throne.

Meanwhile, after military victories, the youthful Henry VI is taken to France in order to be crowned King of France. He tells Somerset and York to resolve their differences by being friendly toward one another; thus, York is made Regent of France and, along with Somerset, is ordered to supply Talbot with the necessary supplies to win the English/French battle.

Due to the feud between Somerset and York, however, each man attempts to discredit the other by failing to send Talbot the required assistance. Talbot and his son struggle valiantly against the stronger French army at Bordeaux, but after many skirmishes they are killed. Accordingly, the English armies suffer defeat and enormous losses, but they converge in one last attempt to rout the French. During this battle, York takes Joan of Arc prisoner and berates her as a strumpet and a she-devil. Shortly thereafter, Joan is condemned and burned at the stake.

In a sub-plot, we learn that the **Earl of Suffolk** convinced Henry VI to take **Margaret of Anjou** as his wife; she had no dowry (virtually unheard of in those days—especially for a woman who would marry a king), but she had courage and spirit, and this made for a promising combination in their offspring. Suffolk realized that his success in bringing Henry and Margaret together set him up for a more advantageous position with the king. It was an excellent opportunity for him to rule the young Henry and, indirectly, the whole country.

Part 1, then, covers a period of about eighteen years, from Henry's infancy to his proposed marriage to Margaret of Anjou.

## Henry VI, Part 2

Suffolk returns to England with Margaret of Anjou and a peace treaty; the latter is ironic for when Suffolk returns to England, he finds Henry surrounded by a number of threatening lords who are attempting to undo the kingdom and set themselves up as virtual dictators. Gloucester, the good Lord Protector, deeply regrets both the marriage and the peace treaty, but he remains bound to his duty as a loyal subject. More important than anything else to Gloucester is his maintaining absolute protection of the royal authority.

Only the Nevilles—the new **Earl of Salisbury** and the **Earl of Warwick**—are prepared to support Gloucester, and very soon, several English nobles put aside their animosity for one another in order to join forces against Gloucester. For example, **Cardinal Beaufort** (formerly Bishop of Winchester), Somerset, and York cooperate with Suffolk and Margaret against Gloucester, the Lord Protector: once they can get rid of Gloucester, they think that they will be able to accomplish their individual, greedy goals. Gloucester has been an obstacle to them all. This, then, is the main story of Part 2: the destruction of Gloucester and the collapse of order after his death.

Gloucester's enemies are unable to turn the king or the English people against him, so they decide to murder the Lord Protector. Anarchy follows: Suffolk is banished and will soon be murdered, York is hiding in Ireland and gathering his rebellious armies, and Cardinal Beaufort dies. There is also an entire act of this part of the trilogy (Act IV) devoted to the rebellion of Jack Cade, a romantic who has been encouraged by York. Cade organizes a mob, scorns all authority other than his own, is lifted into power by a fickle mob and is soon tossed out of power by them. The play concludes with the flight of Henry and Margaret after their defeat by York and his three sons at St. Albans. Royal authority is lost in the smolder of heated factions against the crown.

## Henry VI, Part 3

Part 3 is considered to be the least successful play of the trilogy primarily because it is one long array of fighting and feuds. It chronicles the final phase of Henry's reign, a time of great anarchy for England and a time of great struggle between the fierce Queen Margaret and the equally fierce house of York. Shakespeare seems to have built Part 3 around the idea that disloyalty and faithless ambition serve no purpose other than to create chaos and disharmony.

York is shown to be unscrupulous, but perhaps the best candidate for the throne. He has argued his case in both Parts 1 and 2 as the legitimate heir to the throne and as England's best hope for peace. He offers Henry a compromise: Henry may remain king for the rest of his life provided that he recognize the Yorks as the legitimate heirs to the throne upon his death. Margaret rejects this proposal angrily, and the fighting begins again. She and her ally Lord Clifford capture York and behead him, leaving behind his young sons who are clearly unfit to rule. York's son Edward, who is king at the moment, sends Warwick to France to request in marriage the hand of Lady Bona, the sister-in-law of the king of France. Shortly thereafter, however, Edward falls in love with Lady Grey and creates enemies of King Lewis of France, Warwick, and Edward's own brother Clarence. All of the latter join forces with Margaret in an effort to dethrone Edward, and the fighting begins again.

The result of this turmoil is that England is confronted with a situation in which the crown has been violated by both sides: the choice between Henry and Margaret or Edward is equally treacherous. The country is ripped to pieces.

The major focus of Part 3 is to trace the events of the final phase of Henry's reign and to show the evolution toward the reign of Richard III. Richard is the strongest of York's sons, though by no means admirable. He opens Part 3 by hurling Somerset's severed head to the floor and then, midway through the play, he reveals his own bloody plans for the throne. At the end of the play, Richard kills Henry and becomes King Richard III. He is a cruel, unsuitable king and is no solution to England's woes. But we have seen in Act IV of the third part of the trilogy that Edward's queen is able to flee the war and escape to a hiding place; she is pregnant with the infant Elizabeth, who will eventually marry Richmond and, by so doing, will unite the houses of York and Lancaster into a union of peace and harmony.

## LIST OF MAJOR CHARACTERS

### Henry VI

Infant king at the beginning of Part 1; son of Henry V and the grandson of Henry IV; Henry belongs to the House of Lancaster, the "red roses," and he is killed at the end of Part 3.

### John, Duke of Bedford

Uncle of Henry VI; younger brother of Henry V; Regent of France.

### Humphrey, Duke of Gloucester

Uncle of Henry VI; younger brother of Henry V; Lord Protector of England while Henry is an infant; is arrested for treason and murdered in Part 2; Humphrey by name.

### Henry, Duke of Exeter

Great-uncle of Henry VI.

### Bishop of Winchester (Cardinal Beaufort)

Great-uncle of Henry VI; very ambitious; becomes Cardinal Beaufort; uses religion to suit his own purposes; lifelong enemy of Gloucester, he conspires in the Lord Protector's death and dies unrepentant; illegitimate son of John of Gaunt; prelate of the Church.

### Richard Plantagenet

Son of the late Richard, Earl of Cambridge; becomes Duke of York; belongs to the House of York, the "white roses." He claims to be the rightful heir to the throne occupied by Henry VI; he is killed in Part 3; his sons Edward and Richard become kings after his death, thus restoring the Yorkists to the throne.

### John Beaufort

Earl of Somerset; later Duke of Somerset; illegitimate; supporter of Henry VI.

### Earl of Salisbury

Military leader of the English armies in France alongside Lord Talbot; killed in Part 1.

### Earl of Warwick

Named Richard Neville; son of the Earl of Salisbury; known as "the king maker," he supports the Duke of York's attempts to capture the throne.

### Lord Talbot

A central figure in Part 1; general of the English armies in France; opponent of Charles the Dauphin and Joan of Arc; killed in Part 1.

### Edmund Mortimer

The Earl of March; uncle of Richard Plantagenet; spends most of his adult life in jail after his supporters try to place him on the throne as the rightful heir; the Duke of York will pledge to carry out Mortimer's request that the Yorkists have the throne restored to them.

### Sir John Fastolfe

A cowardly soldier who deserts Talbot's army in France; the early editions of *Henry VI* call him Sir John Falstaff, but he should *not* be confused with the Falstaff of *Henry IV* and *The Merry Wives of Windsor*.

### Charles, the Dauphin

Dauphin of France, made king during Part 1; initially skeptical about Joan of Arc's visionary powers, he eventually welcomes her, but fails to save her from being burned to death.

### Lewis XI

King of France in Part 3.

### Reignier

Duke of Anjou; titular King of Naples; father of Queen Margaret, who marries Henry VI.

### Joan la Pucelle

Joan of Arc; French peasant whose vision inspires her to protect France from the English; burned at the stake by the English in Part 1.

### Margaret

Daughter of Reignier, Duke of Anjou; marries Henry VI.

### Eleanor

Duchess of Gloucester; condemned as a witch.

### Margery Jordan

A witch.

### Lady Grey

Queen of Edward IV; afterward, mother of Elizabeth (*not* Elizabeth I).

### Earl of Suffolk

He arranges for Henry VI's marriage to Margaret of Anjou; becomes the king's favorite, and in Part 2 he is elevated to the rank of duke; named William de la Pole; falls in love with Margaret in Part 2, and ultimately he dies at sea, the victim of pirates.

### Lord Clifford

A supporter of Henry VI and Queen Margaret; killed by the Yorkists in Part 2.

### Young Clifford

Son of Lord Clifford; becomes Queen Margaret's favorite in Part 3; determined to avenge the death of his father.

# THE HISTORICAL BACKGROUND

Shakespeare's *Henry VI, Parts 1, 2, & 3* cover the events leading from the beginning of Henry VI's reign in 1422 until his death in 1471. By the end of Part 3, Shakespeare has led us to the midway point in the Wars of the Roses (1455–87). In *Richard III,* he focuses on the latter years of these Wars—that is, from the attainder and execution of George, Duke of Clarence, in 1478 to the defeat of Richard III at Bosworth Field in 1485. That war, a prolonged, intermittent conflict between the two noble houses of Lancaster and York, was closer to Shakespeare and his contemporaries than are the Napoleonic wars to the present generation.

On the throne of England when Shakespeare wrote, Elizabeth I ruled; she was the granddaughter of Richmond, the first of the Tudors, who, it was firmly believed, was the God-chosen savior of an England long torn by dissension and civil war. Throughout the sixteenth century, in particular, England had reason to fear civil strife as well as foreign invasion, and thus Elizabethans manifested a keen interest in the historical events of the preceding century. As has now been well established, Shakespeare's generation viewed history as a mirror in which could be read lessons important to ruler and subject alike. Moreover, the chronicle histories which provided materials for Shakespeare's "history plays" were written with a Tudor bias, presenting and interpreting characters and events from the point of view accepted as orthodox in sixteenth-century England.

Since Henry VI reigned in the period immediately prior to the Wars of the Roses and during the first years of these Wars, it is desirable to review briefly the story of this epoch which lasted for thirty-some years, during which many princes, many members of the nobility, and at least 100,000 commoners were slain. This was the dynastic struggle between the house of York and the house of Lancaster. Actually, the Lancastrians never adopted the red rose as their symbol, for it was used first by Henry Tudor (Richmond) in 1485, but because of historical precedent, a red rose is associated with the Lancastrians.

At the head of the White Rose party was Richard Plantagenet, third Duke of York, whose claim to the throne was an impressive one. On his mother's side of the family, he was descended from Lionel, Duke of Clarence, the elder brother of John of Gaunt—from whom the Lancastrians were descended. Unfortunately for Richard, however, Parliament had declared for the younger line, which had the advantage of uninterrupted descent through the males.

Richard of York (that is, Richard Plantagenet) was able to capitalize upon Henry VI's notorious weakness as a ruler and on his many misfortunes. Following Jack Cade's Rebellion (1450), Richard was hailed as a popular champion, particularly because of his opposition to the Duke of Somerset, who conducted affairs for King Henry. There was even a proposal that Richard be recognized as heir to the throne, the first suggestion of the devastating quarrel which became later known as the Wars of the Roses. Taking some liberty with history, Shakespeare dramatized the origin of these two hostile parties in *Henry VI, Part 2* and continued the story of these events into *Part 3*, wherein the Yorkists emerged triumphant.

By the year 1453, when Henry VI became quite ill, the Duke of York had succeeded in getting control of the government, and he was appointed "Protector and Defender of the Realm" by Parliament in 1454. But the king recovered late in the next year, and York was replaced by his rival, Somerset. York did not remain quiet for long. When a council was summoned to make provisions "for the safety of the king against his enemies," the duke led a force of his supporters in a march on London. Somerset, joined by the king and a host of nobles, led an army from London to meet the threat, and the two forces met at St. Albans. The Wars of the Roses had begun. Somerset was killed, and Margaret of Anjou, Henry's energetic queen, emerged as head of the Lancastrian party. During the next four years, England experienced a period of restiveness before warfare broke out again. Although York was supported by the powerful Earl of Warwick, head of the house of Neville, the Yorkists were defeated and York himself fled to Ireland.

King Henry's government, now controlled by Margaret and her council, proved anything but efficient. Faced with poverty and disaster, the average Englishman yearned for the return of Richard of York. In June 1460, Warwick and Edward, Richard's eldest son, moved on London and were joined by Richard, who again claimed the crown (October, 1460). This time, Parliament ruled that the head of the house of York should be heir to the hapless Henry VI. But Margaret was not to be repressed. She succeeded in mustering a strong force in the north and met the Yorkists at Wakefield. In this battle, Richard lost his life. And, since Edward (his son) was just a youth of eighteen, Warwick became the head of the White Rose party. In the next year, the Yorkists were defeated in the second Battle of St. Albans. Nevertheless, Warwick did manage to join forces with Edward and to occupy London. Thus, Margaret eventually lost the fruits of her victory. Young Edward, son of Richard, was declared king by the citizens and by the lords of Yorkshire, and this time, he did not hesitate to take the throne, although this did not constitute a legal election.

Subsequent events worked in Edward's favor. Margaret's Lancastrian forces were defeated near Towton in York on March 29, 1461. Henry VI and his son Edward fled to Scotland. By 1464, the Yorks' Edward was full master of England. Nevertheless, his position was jeopardized by his marriage to Elizabeth, a widowed daughter of Richard Woodville. Warwick, his chief supporter, was enraged, not only because the Woodvilles were of Lancastrian connection, but because Warwick himself had all but completed a plan for the English monarch to marry the sister-in-law of Louis XI of France. Edward IV further aggravated matters by favoring his wife's relatives at the expense of the Nevilles. Meanwhile, Henry VI had returned to England in 1464 and had been placed in the Tower of London (1465). Not long afterward, however, the king was released, and Edward IV was forced to flee to Holland. But because of the support of Charles of Burgundy, Edward was able to assemble a force and return to England. Once more the unfortunate Henry was imprisoned, and Warwick's army was defeated, Warwick himself being slain. To cap all this, the Lancastrians suffered a devastating defeat at Tewkesbury on May 4, 1471. Margaret was taken prisoner and her son, Edward, the young Prince of Wales, was put to death. Henry VI was reported to have died "of pure displeasure and melancholy," but in all probability, Edward IV ordered that he be put to death.

# THE SHAKESPEAREAN BACKGROUND

The three five-act parts of *Henry VI* date from the earliest phase of Shakespeare's career. Shakespearean critics have divided this career into four major periods: (1) *apprenticeship* to the London theater (which began with Shakespeare's arrival in London around 1586 and lasted until he joined the Lord Chamberlain's Men in 1594); (2) *growing mastery,* from 1594 to 1599, when the Globe Theatre was opened; (3) *maturity,* during which time the great tragedies were written; this period began with the acquisition of the Globe Theatre and continued until the acquisition of the Blackfriars Theatre in 1609; and (4) *the final retrospect,* from 1610 until Shakespeare's death in 1616.

The *Henry VI* plays belong to the first of these four periods, along with *Titus Andronicus, The Comedy of Errors, Two Gentlemen of Verona, Richard III, Love's Labour's Lost,* and probably *King John.* Shakespeare learned very early in his career that it was valuable to use history as a basis for his plays. He was not so much interested in teaching history, however, as in presenting it poetically in the form of stories. The genre of the history play was extremely popular when Shakespeare arrived in London. It was an outgrowth of the English people's deep faith in their monarchy (at that time, Elizabeth I was on the throne). In his book *Shakespeare's History Plays,* E. M. W. Tillyard describes how the Tudor chroniclers believed that their monarch was the only one capable of maintaining peace and justice in the kingdom. Divine Providence was ultimately responsible for selecting the correct monarch, and citizens were convinced that the history of their country would unfold within this system of Providence. The monarch was someone whom they looked up to for guidance and direction, and this is one of the reasons why Shakespeare often used royalty as subjects for his plays: historical figures almost always found a receptive audience in the England of his time. The Tudor success was seen as the final happy ending of the Wars of the Roses and the beginning of a new era in England. *Henry VI* and *Richard III* are sometimes referred to as "the Tudor epic" since they are set in this period of the Wars of the Roses. *Richard II* (set in the period of Richard's reign from 1377 to 1399) and the *Henry IV* plays chronicle the beginnings of the English civil wars; and *Henry V* seems a bit of an afterthought. *Henry VIII,* considered to be Shakespeare's last play, has essentially nothing to do with the other history plays, nor does *King John,* which is widely acknowledged to be one of Shakespeare's weakest dramas; it is rarely performed on the stage, and when it is, audiences are usually unimpressed.

Shakespeare disliked the style and manner of the history plays which were in vogue at the time of his arrival in London, and he decided to adapt history to his own vision of the world, highlighting the personal and human drama of his subjects and focusing on the conflicts which tormented royalty. It made little sense to him to see royalty glorified beyond all means of recognition; if audiences were unable to identify with a drama, then there was no point in presenting it to them. Shakespeare was not concerned with publishing his plays, but rather with the successful staging of them for his contemporaries. It is for this reason that the English director Michael Langham argues that Shakespeare should be seen on the stage before he is read and studied: his dramas speak directly to the heart, and the communication comes to life when one sees the plays in the flesh.

Shakespeare returned to historical subjects throughout his career, with a history play (*Henry VIII*) as his last dramatic work. His subjects include King John (a Plantagenet), Richard II (also a Plantagenet), Henry IV (a

Lancastrian), Henry V (also a Lancastrian), Henry VI (another Lancastrian), Richard III (a Yorkist), and Henry VIII (a Tudor). Shakespeare's history plays capture the evolution of the British monarchy from the Middle Ages (Plantagenets) through to the Renaissance (Tudors). They were not written in chronological order; the *Henry VI* plays came first, followed by *Richard III, King John, Richard II,* the *Henry IV* plays, *Henry V,* and *Henry VIII.* There is a total of ten history plays in the Shakespearean canon.

Because the *Henry VI* plays belong to Shakespeare's earliest period of writing, when we compare them with what will come later, we discover that they are less poetic and, dramatically, less satisfying. But as a trilogy, they can be very effective on the stage and constitute an impressive epic sweep. Scholars still debate the exact dates of their production and the order in which they were written. The important point is: Shakespeare was able to turn Henry's disastrous reign into a flowing, intelligent drama which is not devoid of interest. Henry's reign was a complicated one; as a weak king, he was surrounded by dozens of people determined to take advantage of him and to accomplish their own goals at his expense. Shakespeare uses only that information from the period which serves to highlight his drama. He is not concerned with total accuracy or with including all of the historical details from the period. Rather, his is a selective approach to history and, because of this method, we are not weighed down with subject matter that is irrelevant to the primary drama. Most significantly, it is the *crown of England* which interests Shakespeare, *not* Henry VI as a man or ruler. To be sure, Henry VI is often at the center of the action, and the trilogy focuses on the events during his reign, but it is the crown, and the English people's unshakable faith in the crown as a symbol of stability in their country, that Shakespeare is concerned with in this trilogy. Each of the three parts may be treated as an entity since each deals with a separate struggle for the crown. And as each struggle is resolved, Shakespeare sketches the beginnings of a new effort to dethrone Henry VI, and this new effort becomes the subject of the next part. Shakespeare apparently thought that Henry VI was not fit to serve as king, and the trilogy depicts the various weaknesses which expose him to the many and varied assaults on his throne.

When reading *Henry VI,* it is helpful to recall the historical events which occurred in the years prior to Henry's reign. His ancestor Henry IV had come to the throne after the murder of Richard II, and through his immense prestige as a "conquering hero," Henry IV succeeded in earning the confidence of his people. They felt that Henry IV was the man to safeguard their country, and this made it very difficult for Richard II's heirs to protest his murder. When Henry V became king, England had entered into an intensely patriotic period which paralleled Henry V's near-success at claiming the crown of France for England. *Henry VI, Part 1* begins at the moment of Henry V's death—a time when Henry VI is still an infant and the country is being run by Gloucester, the Lord Protector. Due to the absence of a mature king, the gates of protest are flung open for challengers to the throne. This sets the stage for the evolution of Henry VI's monarchy and for the drama at hand.

# CRITICAL COMMENTARIES

## HENRY VI, Part 1

### ACT I

The play opens in Westminster Abbey at the funeral of Henry V, once the shining Prince Hal, "this star of England." Henry V leaves behind him the boy Henry VI, who is too young to reign. Several of the principal characters of this trilogy are present at the funeral, including Humphrey (the good Duke of Gloucester), who is an uncle of Henry VI and has been designated to reign in Henry VI's place as Lord Protector until Henry is old enough to assume an active role. Also present is another of Henry VI's uncles, the Duke of Bedford, who is Regent of France; also present is Warwick, who (as an earl) has significant influence in the kingdom and is known as "the king maker." In addition, there is a great-uncle of Henry VI, Henry Beaufort (who will soon become the Cardinal of Winchester), and others.

The Duke of Bedford and the Duke of Gloucester bemoan the passing of their late king: "England ne'er lost a king of so much worth." As early as the first speech of the play, then, Shakespeare sets the tone for trouble: a beloved king has died, and there is no one to take his place. Henry V was virtuous, was an excellent soldier, and was a fearless competitor: "He ne'er lift up his hand but conquered." Now the throne risks being conquered by outsiders. The Duke of Exeter (another great-uncle) suggests that some wicked "French sorcerers" conspired to bring about Henry V's end, and this prepares us for the eventual role played by Joan la Pucelle (more commonly known as Joan of Arc, or the Maid). Winchester states that part of Henry's glory was due to the Church, which aided Henry's victories because Henry always fought "the battles of the Lord." Gloucester, however, retorts that the Church had *nothing* to do with Henry's glorious reign. Rather, the churchmen did not pray sufficiently—if at all—for the king; they wanted a monarch who was an "effeminate prince," one whom they could dominate. Shakespeare sets Gloucester up, therefore, as being the defender of the throne, of the royal family, and of the country: Gloucester will become the prime obstacle for several ambitious nobles, and this struggle will unravel dramatically in Part 2 of the trilogy. Gloucester represents a set of beliefs contrary to those held by such people as Winchester. Whereas Gloucester is the Lord Protector of England and has the country's best interests at heart, many of his peers seek to aggrandize themselves at the expense of the monarchy. They wish to have influence at the royal court and see their personal, ambitious desires brought to fruition. A major conflict, then, is drawn in this first scene: there will be a struggle between opposing factions for the monarchy. The old order will be called upon to defend itself from those who see themselves as legitimate heirs, those who feel that they should be on the throne.

Bedford finally puts an end to the arguing and calls upon the ghost of Henry V to keep the realm from "civil broils"—or else "our isle be made a nourish of salt tears." A messenger enters then with news from France: the English have suffered enormous losses and have been defeated at Rheims, Orleans, Champagne, and other French towns in their quest for the French throne. The English losses, he says, were due to a lack of manpower and money—not because of any French "sorcery"; moreover, the English soldiers are aware of various divisive factions at work back in England. They realize that there is confusion in the court and that the English generals do *not* have the necessary support at court in order to make victory possible. The messenger warns the nobles to resolve their petty arguments and realize that many human lives are at stake abroad: "Let not sloth dim your honours new-begot." He says that "England's coat is half cut away." Bedford proclaims his patriotism and states his intention to fight for "the cause"; he says that he intends to conquer France for England ("Wounds will I lend the French.").

Another messenger enters and announces that Charles, the Dauphin of France, has been crowned king in Rheims and that the Bastard of Orleans is with him, as well as the Duke of Anjou. The nobles are seemingly unanimous in their desire to fight France, but Gloucester and Bedford exchange sharp words about Bedford's true dedication to the cause. The seeds of dissent are present, then, even in an otherwise "unified" cause.

A third messenger enters with the news that Lord Talbot, general of the English armies, has been overthrown: he was surrounded by a French army of 23,000 men, almost four times the size of the English army (6,000 soldiers). Talbot fought valiantly for three hours and would have won, but Sir John Fastolfe "played the coward" and fled the battle scene, damaging morale and bringing about a general massacre. Talbot was wounded (a spear in his back) and taken prisoner, but his life was spared; most of his men, however, were slaughtered. Bedford vows to revenge the act by wrenching the Dauphin's crown: he will take ten thousand soldiers with him to France and aid the weak forces of the Earl of Salisbury. Exeter recalls the oath which they all took to the late King Henry: "To quell the Dauphin utterly/ Or bring him in obedience to your yoke." Gloucester hastens to the Tower so that he can examine the artillery available, stating that he will proclaim young Henry the new king of England. Exeter says that he plans to go to Eltham, where Henry VI is, so that he can prepare for the king's safety. When Exeter is gone, Winchester is left alone. He reveals his plan to steal the young king and "sit at [the] chiefest stern of public weal." In other words, he wishes to have power over everyone.

The scene shifts to Orleans, France, where the Dauphin (Charles) is in conversation with the Duke of Alençon and Reignier (Duke of Anjou). Charles is pleased that fate is on the side of the French and that they have defeated the English. Spontaneously, he and Reignier decide that there is no point in waiting to attack the English again: "Let's raise the siege; why live we idly here?" Talbot has been captured and only the "mad-brained Salisbury" remains. Thus, they sound the alarum, but, later, they are surprised to find themselves driven back by the English. Charles concludes that his men are cowards; they abandoned him amidst the enemy. They discuss the English courage and audacity.

Just as they are about to leave the English behind them, the Bastard of Orleans enters with news: he has brought with him "a holy maid," Joan la Pucelle, or Joan of Arc, who has been allegedly ordained by heaven to raise the siege against the English and drive them out of France. Seemingly, the maid is gifted with prophecy exceeding even that of "the nine sibyls of old Rome." Charles consents to speak with her, but he first decides to test her skill: he asks Reignier to stand in his place as Dauphin. When Joan enters, however, she identifies the trick immediately: "Reignier, is't thou that thinkest to beguile me?" She then insists on speaking privately with the Dauphin.

Joan tells Charles how she was seated in the field one day and was greeted with a vision from "God's mother" (Mary). Mary instructed Joan to leave her "base vocation" and save her country from calamity. Charles agrees to take Joan to battle with him and, if she is successful, he will place all his confidence in her word. But first, he challenges her to a duel; if, in single combat she "vanquishes" Charles, he will know that her words "are true." They spar with swords, and Joan bests him. Charles is impressed: "Thou art an Amazon. . . . 'Tis thou that must help me. . . . Let me thy servant and *not* sovereign be." Joan argues that France must fight till the end and never surrender. She predicts that England's glory is at an end because Henry V is dead. Reignier urges haste; she must drive the English from Orleans "and be immortaliz'd."

The scene moves once again to London; as is typical of the *Henry VI* plays, Shakespeare jumps back and forth from country to country. In London, Gloucester arrives to survey the Tower of London, but is told by the guards that he is unable to enter: Winchester (Henry Beaufort) has forbidden it; Gloucester and his people have been blacklisted by

Winchester. This is the first unmistakable proof that we have that Winchester intends to seize control of the kingdom, despite *any* possible consequences. Winchester enters then and gloats in the presence of Gloucester, who boldly calls Winchester a "manifest conspirator" and states that Winchester sought to murder Henry V. Gloucester insists on being allowed in the Tower or else he vows to drive Winchester back.

A skirmish breaks out between their men, and the mayor arrives, demanding that everyone return home. His officer commands them to put away their weapons—or be executed. Winchester warns Gloucester to be careful, and Gloucester warns Winchester that he will stamp Winchester's hat (his religious symbol) beneath his feet. The conflict between the two men is drawn: Winchester, as a representative of the Church, desires power, and he will try to impose himself through the authority of the Church, even if his intentions have nothing to do with religion or God. Gloucester, on the other hand, is the rightful Protector of England, and he is prepared to bring force to bear whenever necessary in his attempts to protect both Henry VI and the English people. Thus, it is clear that religion, law, and politics all disappear into the background as personal ambition and a drive for power consume Winchester. Even the mayor himself exclaims that Winchester is "more haughty than the devil."

At Orleans, in France, Salisbury welcomes Talbot back to the action, asking him questions about his treatment while he was a French prisoner (Talbot was released from jail through an arrangement with the Duke of Bedford, who exchanged another prisoner for Talbot). Talbot says that he was publicly humiliated by the French, exposed in the market place and mocked as the "terror of the French,/ The scarecrow that affrights our children."

As the two men are talking, Salisbury is shot from somewhere in the town; one of his eyes is destroyed and he dies. Then a messenger announces that the Dauphin has joined forces with Joan la Pucelle and that the French are gathering strength.

Talbot drives back the Dauphin, then Joan enters, driving back some Englishmen. Joan and Talbot duel, while Talbot curses her, claiming that she is a witch and that he will send her back to "him thou serv'st." They exchange more sharp words, and she taunts him to action. Then she announces that she will rescue Orleans. She dares Talbot to follow her and attempt to overtake her army. Her confidence is unfailing: she believes that divine strength is on her side. Talbot is confused by her; he believes that her "witch powers" are responsible for defeating the English. He bemoans the fact that the English soldiers lack courage and that Joan will reclaim Orleans—despite his efforts to hold her back. In the next scene, Charles confirms that Joan has indeed recovered Orleans.

Act I, then, sets up the major conflict of the play; it is a struggle for power on a number of levels:

(1) personal ambition (that is, Gloucester vs. Winchester);

(2) monarchic ambition (Gloucester attempting to protect the young king's interests); and

(3) international ambition (England at war with France).

Chaos and disorder reign in the place of a stable monarchy, and this idea will be further developed as the drama unfolds.

## ACT II

This act opens outside Orleans with a French sergeant instructing his sentinels (guards) to alert him if there are any signs of the English. Talbot enters with Bedford and Burgundy; the Duke of Burgundy's father has been murdered by the Dauphin, and this has caused Burgundy to become an ally of the British. The three men discuss the French army's brazen attitude of celebration, and Talbot suggests that they enter the city, where the French lie asleep.

The French sentinel sounds the alarum, and the French soldiers are clearly caught off-guard. Charles scolds Joan for deceitful planning; he claims that she flattered the French with minor gains, but set them up for major losses. She replies that her powers cannot work *all* of the time, that they are unable to prevail when she is *sleeping*. She blames the attack on unreliable watchmen.

The next day, Talbot orders that the body of Salisbury is to be brought to the marketplace so that the French can see *why* Talbot revenged Salisbury (". . . hereafter ages may behold/ What ruin happened in revenge of him."). The English armies, we learn, having fought all night, successfully revenged themselves on their enemies. And it seems now that Joan and the Dauphin fled the scene when they realized how serious a threat the English actually were.

But there is a French plan afoot to recapture Talbot: the Countess of Auvergne invites him to visit her castle, and Talbot accepts. Burgundy and Bedford fear chicanery on the part of the Countess, but Talbot decides to see her anyway. Before going, he whispers something in his captain's ear.

Once inside the castle, Talbot becomes the Countess' prisoner: she wishes to prevent him from causing any more damage to the French. Talbot does not take her seriously. Through a refined manipulation of irony, he dodges her insults and succeeds in alerting his men. She quickly acquiesces and apologizes for her abuse of him. The sudden strength of Talbot and his men makes her realize with whom she is dealing.

Back in London, Richard Plantagenet (who will become the Duke of York) meets with Warwick ("the king maker"), the Duke of Somerset, the Earl of Suffolk, and others in the Temple Garden. An argument has taken

# SELECTED YORK-LANCASTER GENEALOGY

YORKS

LANCASTERS

Richard, Earl of Cambridge

m.

Anne Mortimer

Lionel, Duke of Clarence

*(brothers)*

John of Gaunt, Duke of Lancaster

Cardinal Beaufort *(great uncle of Henry VI)*

Humphrey (Duke of Gloucester)

John (Duke of Bedford)

Henry IV (1399-1413)

*(son)*

3 generations

2 generations

Richard Plantagenet, Duke of York (killed, 1460)

m.

Cicely Neville

Katherine of France m.

Henry V (1413-22)

Henry VI (1422-61) and (1470-71)

m. Margaret of Anjou

Edward, Prince of Wales (1453-71)

Earl of Salisbury

Richard Neville, Earl of Warwick, "The King Maker"

m. Anne Neville

Edward IV (1461-70) and (1471-83)

George, Duke of Clarence (executed, 1478)

Edmund, Earl of Rutland (killed, 1460)

Anne m. Henry Holland, Duke of Exeter

Richard, Duke of Gloucester; later Richard III (1483-85)

place inside the Temple Hall between Richard and Somerset, and the group has withdrawn into the garden where things are more private. Somerset calls upon Warwick to decide who is right in the argument, but both Warwick and Suffolk decline to pass judgment since they feel unequipped to assess the subtle points of the dispute. Their argument concerns the throne of England, which will eventually be the cause of the Wars of the Roses: Richard Plantagenet and his followers choose a white rose as their symbol, while Somerset and his group opt for a red rose. Warwick dons a white rose and sides with Plantagenet. Suffolk takes a red one. Already, in this initial discussion, there is a clear suggestion of the bloodshed and sorrow ahead. Somerset warns: "Prick not your finger as you pluck it off,/ Lest bleeding you do paint the white rose red." The Yorks, on the side of Richard Plantagenet, are set against the Lancasters, supported by Somerset. The young king Henry VI is conspicuously absent from this colloquy; this shows to what extent the future of the English monarchy is being decided by factions which do not involve the king directly. Henry is brought into the conflict only because of his bloodline, and it is not significant that he appear at this point in the play. Rather, it is the *crown* of England which is of importance, *not* the *person* of the young king. But Henry's ultimate weakness as a ruler is already foreshadowed in his absence from this serious debate.

A lawyer present at the discussion claims that Somerset is wrong in his belief that the "red roses" are the legitimate heirs to the throne of England. He sides with Plantagenet and the white roses. Warwick interrupts and informs Somerset that he is in error about Plantagenet: the latter's grandfather was Lionel, Duke of Clarence, third son to Edward III, King of England. This royal link surely justifies Richard's claim to the throne. Shakespeare, however, errs in the genealogy of Richard since there are actually four generations between Plantagenet and Lionel. But the lineage *is* genuine, and Richard does have a legitimate claim to the crown. Somerset argues that Richard's father was executed for treason, but the young Plantagenet counters with: "Condemn'd to die for treason, but no traitor . . . I'll note you in my book of memory/ To scourge you for this apprehension." The scene ends with Warwick declaring his allegiance to the white rose faction.

Richard meets then with his aging uncle, Edmund Mortimer, Earl of March, in the Tower of London, and Mortimer relates his story to Richard in a weak, dying voice: Henry IV, grandfather to the present king, deposed his nephew Richard, Edward's son, who was also the first-born son and the lawful heir to the throne. The Percies of the North found this usurpation unjust and attempted to advance Mortimer to the throne, reasoning that he was the legitimate heir to the throne since Richard II had no children.

Mortimer reasons that he was, by birth, derived from Lionel, Duke of Clarence, the *third* son of King Edward III, whereas Henry IV was the son of John of Gaunt, the *fourth* son of Edward III. But when Henry V came to the throne, Mortimer was thrown in jail. Thus, Mortimer now pronounces his nephew Richard Plantagenet to be his heir, but warns him to be careful in his attempt for the monarchy: "Be thou politic./ Strong-fixed is the house of Lancaster/ And like a mountain, not to be remov'd." Mortimer dies, and Richard vows to revenge his lineage.

Act II advances the plot by explaining in detail the reasons behind Richard Plantagenet's rebellion: he believes himself to be the rightful heir to the throne and shall proceed to confront the Lancasters with this fact.

## ACT III

The act opens at the Parliament House in London during an open conflict between Gloucester and Winchester about a bill, which Gloucester attempts to submit and which Winchester rips apart. Gloucester accuses Winchester of having designs on the king: "If thy thoughts were sifted,/ The King, thy sovereign, is not quite exempt/ From envious malice of thy swelling heart." Winchester retorts that his uncle, Gloucester, seeks to be the only one in the kingdom with power over Henry VI. Then Warwick speaks up in favor of Gloucester: "Is not his Grace Protector to the King?"

At this point, Henry enters and attempts to reconcile the two men in a speech which depicts him as a precocious young man (in point of actual fact, Henry would be only five years old). Henry pleads for family unity and peace, and he hints that this kind of internal struggle augurs badly for the country: "Believe me, lords, my tender years can tell/ Civil dissension is a viperous worm/ That gnaws the bowels of the commonwealth."

The mayor enters and a skirmish follows: the supporters of Gloucester and Winchester have begun stoning one another and have wrought havoc in the town. Significantly, Henry calls upon Gloucester, *not* Winchester, to quell the strife: it is as if he has greater trust and faith in his Lord Protector.

Henry's first speeches portray him as a weak and fearful king, and although he is young, he is of royal blood and is expected to emulate the greatness of his ancestors. But from the very beginning, he shows no signs of strength or power; he defers to others and laments his sorrowful plight: "O, how this discord doth afflict my soul!" It should be remembered that the conflict in the streets between Gloucester's and Winchester's men has nothing to do with the Wars of the Roses, yet eventually, both conflicts will combine into a rising torrent of terror and bloodshed.

Winchester and Gloucester strike a begrudging agreement, and the skirmish is called off. When the two factions leave, Henry is offered a scroll by Warwick, and he re-establishes Richard Plantagenet to his royal bloodline, thereby making Richard Duke of York. Richard pledges an ironic allegiance to the young king: "Thy humble servant vows obedience/ And humble service till the point of death." In other words, Richard will remain faithful until Henry's death – at which point, he intends to assume the throne himself.

Gloucester suggests that Henry leave for France in order to be crowned king, and Henry reveals his dependence on his uncle: "When Gloucester says the word, King Henry goes." Exeter, in a monologue, predicts that the feigned love of the peers for one another will break out into vicious dissension: "Till bones and flesh and sinews fall away,/ So will this base and envious discord breed." He predicts that an oldtime prophecy uttered in the time of Henry V will come true – namely, that Henry V would *win* all and that Henry VI would *lose* all. This is another indication that the reign of Henry VI promises to be less than glorious.

Back in Rouen, France, Joan is in disguise; she plans to enter the city with four soldiers dressed like peasants. Her plan succeeds, and once inside the gates, she reasons that it will be possible to give notice to the French troops and that Charles will be able to launch an attack. This capture of Rouen has no basis in historical fact: the city actually remained under English control until 1449, eighteen years after Joan of Arc had been burned there.

Once inside the city, Joan sets a torch ablaze and flashes it for Charles to see. She is elated at the possibility of conquering the English inside the town and at restoring French rule to Rouen: "Behold! this is the happy wedding torch/ That joineth Rouen unto her countrymen,/ But burning fatal to the Talbotines!" Charles and his men storm the city, and Talbot flees, promising revenge and blaming the French treachery on Joan, "that witch, that damned sorceress."

Talbot invites the Frenchmen to fight the battle on the field, but Alençon refuses. Talbot then beseeches Burgundy to help restore the town to the English. Burgundy replies, "My vows are equal partners with thy vows," but this vow will soon prove to be devoid of meaning since Burgundy will betray the English and commit himself to supporting his native Frenchmen. Bedford, who is dying, resolves to remain close to the front so as to inspire courage in his soldiers. Talbot and Burgundy leave to gather their forces in preparation for a renewed attack on the French. Once again, Fastolfe flees camp in order to save his life. Left alone, Bedford dies.

Talbot and Burgundy re-enter with the news that Rouen has been taken from the French: "Now will we take some order in the town." It seems that Joan, Charles, and the Bastard had all fallen asleep.

The scene shifts to Joan and the two men, somewhere between Rouen and Paris; they are discussing the fall of Rouen to the English. Joan says that they should not be worried about it: "Let frantic Talbot triumph for a while/ And like a peacock sweep along his tail./ We'll pull his plumes and take away his train,/ If Dauphin and the rest will be but rul'd." She recommends order and discipline, and Charles agrees to support her. She vows furthermore to sway the allegiance of the Duke of Burgundy; Talbot, she says, would be weakened by such a desertion.

In an impassioned, persuasive speech to Burgundy, Joan argues the virtues of her homeland under threat by a foreign invader: "See, see the pining malady of France!/ Behold the wounds, the most unnatural wounds,/ Which thou thyself has given her woeful breast." She convinces Burgundy to support the French effort against the English. As with the recapturing of Rouen, this episode did *not* take place as such in reality: Burgundy's abandonment of the English did not take place until several years after Joan's death. But in the play, Joan uses patriotism as a leverage to lure Burgundy back into the French camp: "When Talbot hath set footing once in France/ And fashion'd thee that instrument of ill,/ Who then but English Henry will be lord/ And thou be thrust out like a fugitive?" Burgundy is portrayed as a man entranced by the language of persuasion; he does not appear as one who is invincible in his convictions or whose allegiance to a group of people is unbending. Whatever suits his needs of the moment is what determines Burgundy's affiliation. Shakespeare weaves a touch of irony into Joan's response to Burgundy's conversion: "Done like a Frenchman: turn, and turn again!"

At the palace in Paris, Talbot takes a break during his war activities and presents himself to the king. He says that he is the epitomy of loyalty through and through; he is proud to recite the sites of his conquests in France: fifty fortresses, twelve cities, and seven walled towns of great strength. Henry has grown older than the last time we saw him, but he is still a young king; Shakespeare does his best to hurry the aging process so that we are not dealing with an irresponsible youth. Instead, we are dealing with a vulnerable young adult. Henry lauds Talbot for his many years of devotion to the country, and in recognition of Talbot's faithfulness to the royal family, Henry elevates him to the rank of Earl of Shrewsbury. The act ends with a minor skirmish between Vernon and Basset—the former is a supporter of Richard Plantagenet, while the latter is faithful to Somerset. The skirmish serves to remind us, symbolically, that the Wars of the Roses are imminent and that the York-Lancaster conflict is nowhere near to being settled.

## ACT IV

As the act opens, Henry is being crowned by Winchester in Paris. Fastolfe enters with the news that Burgundy has betrayed the English, and Talbot, in turn, rails at Fastolfe for having deserted the English forces at the battle of Patay. Henry banishes Fastolfe, on pain of death, and Fastolfe scurries from the room.

The letter from Burgundy, which Fastolfe brought with him, discloses Burgundy's new allegiance to Charles, "the rightful king of France." Henry, in his naiveté, orders Talbot to confer with Burgundy about the desertion and to chastise him for his conduct—another sign that the young king has little understanding of the politics of power.

York (Richard Plantagenet) and Somerset bring their quarrel to the king, who addresses them as "good cousins both." Henry commands a peace between them. He claims that there is no room for argument among the English, particularly as they are in France and must present a facade of unity. In an attempt to reconcile the two factions, Henry plucks a red rose and puts it on his uniform, claiming that "Both are my kinsmen, and I love them both." Then he sends the Duke of York (Richard Plantagenet) off to be a regent in France and instructs Somerset to provide auxiliary support to York's forces.

Outside the gates of Bordeaux, Talbot announces that the French should give themselves up to the English and proclaim Henry their king. Talbot is then met head-on by a general who asserts that the town is well fortified and prepared for a fight. Talbot discovers that the general means business: an enormous troop of Frenchmen descend on the meager English forces. Motivated by his feud with York, Somerset has refused to send the horses which Talbot requires.

Sir William Lucy blames the English slaughter at Bordeaux on the discord between York and Somerset: "Whiles they each other cross,/ Lives, honours, lands, and all hurry to loss." He rages at Somerset for withholding necessary support from Talbot: "The fraud of England, not the force of France,/ Hath now entrapp'd the noble-minded Talbot." Somerset dispatches the horsemen, but it is too late: the English are losing the battle and nothing will help.

In an emotional scene between Talbot and his son John, Talbot orders the young boy to flee the battlefield lest he be killed. The son refuses to abandon his father, so the two remain together in their fight for England's victory. After a number of skirmishes, the two of them are slain, and the English suffer tremendous losses. In a mocking, naturalistic style, Joan permits Sir Lucy to remove the corpses of the two Talbots: "For God's sake, let him have them;/ To keep them here,/ They would but stink, and putrefy the air." Sir Lucy proclaims that their ashes shall become a phoenix which shall cause holy terror.

## ACT V

In London, Gloucester tells the king of the pope's message—that peace must be achieved between England and France so that the bloodshed can end. As a means to this end, Gloucester informs the king that the Earl of Armagnac, a man of great authority in France, has offered his only daughter to Henry as his future wife. Henry summons the royal ambassadors and promises to go along with their advice on the matter.

Winchester enters, dressed as a cardinal, and Exeter remarks that Henry V's prophecy is about to be fulfilled: "Henry the Fifth did sometime prophesy/ If once he come to be a cardinal,/ He'll make his cap co-equal with the crown." In other words, Winchester has advanced one step further in his quest for absolute power.

Henry informs the group of ambassadors that he shall indeed marry the Earl of Armagnac's daughter. He sends as a symbol of agreement a jewel for the French woman. In a brief aside, Winchester establishes his contention to be inferior to none, especially to Gloucester: "I'll either make thee stoop and bend thy knee,/ Or sack this country with a mutiny."

On the plains of Anjou, a scout announces to Charles (the Dauphin) and Joan that the English armies are headed in their direction and shall presently launch an attack on the French. Joan requests help from the spiritual bodies on whom she has depended, but when they appear before her, she finds them unwilling to cooperate with her. This means trouble for France, and Joan prepares for defeat: "See, they forsake me! Now the time is come/ That France must vail her lofty-plumed crest/ And let her head fall into England's lap." Burgundy and York (Plantagenet) fight hand to hand, and the French soldiers flee the scene, leaving Joan in York's power. They exit, and Suffolk and Margaret enter. Suffolk, who is married, admires Margaret of Anjou's beauty. She is a daughter of the King of Naples, and Suffolk decides to win her for Henry. The only problem is that her father is poor, but Suffolk wagers that the youthful Henry will nonetheless be drawn to her beauty. Her father agrees to the proposition provided he be allowed to enjoy peace and quiet in the territories of Anjou and Maine.

At Anjou, York orders that Joan be brought forth. He heaps insults on her, and she denies her earthly lineage. In fact, she denies *all* blood relationship with her shepherd father. Her forefathers, she says, were "kings,/ Virtuous and holy; chosen from above . . ./ To work exceeding miracles on earth." She denies that she ever had anything to do with "wicked spirits." She tells York and the others that they—and not she—are "polluted . . . and stained . . . and corrupt." She has been "chaste and immaculate" since infancy. And when the English will not listen to her defense, Joan announces that she is pregnant and defies them to murder not only her but "the fruit within [her] womb." The English scoff, but Joan is adamant. The child's father, she says, is Reignier (who will soon become the father-in-law of Henry). York tells Joan that her "words condemn thy brat and thee." Joan is led away, but not before she utters a curse upon

England: "May never glorious sun reflex his beams/ Upon the country where you abode."

Winchester (Henry's great-uncle) announces that a peace treaty has been struck between England and France. York, outraged at the idea of surrendering everything that England has fought for, foresees with grief the loss of France. Charles (the Dauphin) is insulted at Henry's suggestion that he be named viceroy to the King of England and that he become a liege to the English crown. Alençon, however, advises Charles to accept the truce in order to bring peace to an otherwise torn-apart country, adding that Charles can always break the truce when it serves his purposes. So Charles accepts the proposal.

At the palace in London, Suffolk spares no effort to persuade Henry to marry Margaret. Gloucester reminds Henry that he is already engaged to someone else, a lady of esteem and a daughter of a man whom England cannot afford to offend—the influential Earl of Armagnac. Exeter argues that Armagnac is wealthy, whereas Margaret's father is poor; surely it would be more advantageous to marry a woman of wealth. But Suffolk prevails, and Henry decides in Margaret's favor. He asks Suffolk to sail for France and bring her back to be his queen. Part 2 of the trilogy will begin with the arrival of Margaret in England.

Suffolk, left alone at the end of Part 1, acknowledges to himself that he has won an important victory with the king. He realizes that he now has power in the royal circle and can set himself up as someone to be reckoned with: "Margaret shall now be queen, and rule the king;/ But I will rule both her, the king, and realm." Alongside the other nobles in pursuit of this influence (Gloucester, Winchester, and Plantagenet, the rebellious Duke of York), Suffolk completes the tableau of a vicious, bitter struggle in the making. Part 2 will advance this struggle to the point of action and will show even further the disintegration of a weak king's monarchy into a state of growing chaos.

# HENRY VI, Part 2

## ACT I

Part 1 of *Henry VI* was centered largely around the conflict for power in England and Joan la Pucelle's role in the defense of France against the English; Part 2 is devoted to an examination of the mounting conspiracy against the extremely unselfish and noble Gloucester and the resultant chaos which ensues after his murder.

The play opens in a stateroom at the palace in London. Suffolk has arrived back in England with the new queen-to-be, Margaret of Anjou, who will not only come to despise Henry, but will actually take matters in her own hands and rule the kingdom as she pleases. At this point in the drama, however, Margaret meets Henry for the first time, and he is instantly infatuated with her "beauteous face."

As a part of the marriage contract, a peace treaty with France is announced, one which calls for an eighteen-month period of peace. Moreover, England will relinquish to Margaret's father, the King of Naples, the duchy of Anjou and the county of Maine, and Henry agrees to marry Margaret despite the fact that she has *no* dowry. These terms of marriage are *extremely* unsatisfactory to Gloucester, Henry's uncle, who is so stunned that he drops the marriage contract on the floor while he is reading it in disbelief. But King Henry is quite happy with his new bride and, as a gesture of appreciation, he elevates Suffolk to the rank of duke. At the same time, the Duke of York (Richard Plantagenet) is relieved of his title as Regent of France until the eighteen-month period of truce is over.

In particular, Gloucester resents the fact that his own brothers, King Henry V and the Duke of Bedford, worked so hard to conquer France for England, only to have their efforts now tossed aside by an inexperienced youth smitten with love:

> O peers of England, shameful is this league,
> Fatal this marriage, cancelling your fame,
> Blotting your names from books of memory,
> Razing the characters of your renown,
> Defacing monuments of conquer'd France,
> Undoing all, as all had never been!
>
> (I.i.98–103)

The nobles then discuss amongst themselves the pro's and con's of their king's marriage: Cardinal Beaufort (formerly Winchester), a great-uncle of Henry's, is critical of Gloucester's opposition to the king; Warwick reminds them of his personal efforts on the battlefield, which helped to win Anjou and Maine for England, and he is clearly infuriated that Henry has frivolously given them over to the King of Naples. York has no sympathy for France and holds Suffolk in disdain: "For Suffolk's duke, may he be suffocate,/ That dims the honour of this warlike isle!" The situation, then, is this: Henry has opted for a marriage based solely on physical attraction; his marriage has no monetary or political advantages, and Henry's nobles (with the exception of Suffolk, who sees personal gain in the marriage, and Cardinal Beaufort, whose attitudes always fall on the opposite side of the coin from Gloucester's) are dissatisfied with the conjugal union. Gloucester prophesies that England will lose France entirely before long.

Beaufort attempts to persuade the other nobles that they should not trust Gloucester because of his "smoothing words" and his "flattering gloss"; obviously, he has designs on the throne. Accordingly, Buckingham suggests that they get rid of Gloucester, and Beaufort leaves immediately to put matters in motion. Somerset, however, warns the nobles that Cardinal Beaufort is not to be trusted either: "His insolence is more intolerable/ Than all the princes in the land beside." Basically, the situation develops because of a conflict between pride and ambition; none of the nobles is exempt from these emotions, and survival will depend on a combination of integrity and strength.

The Earl of Salisbury then appeals to Warwick and to the Duke of York, asking them to put the public good before personal gain and to stamp out the ambitions of Somerset, Buckingham, Suffolk and Cardinal Beaufort: they should respect and "cherish Duke Humphrey's [Gloucester's] deeds/ While they do tend the profit of the land." So there are now two opposing factions, even if only tenuous: Beaufort, Suffolk, Somerset, and Buckingham, who oppose Gloucester and support Henry's marriage, versus Salisbury, Warwick, and York, who support Gloucester. York supports Gloucester because it is convenient to do so: were he to support Beaufort, Suffolk, or anyone else, he would have more obstacles in *his* way to the crown. As it is, Gloucester is a known commodity and is more easily handled than a completely new "regime." This is what prompts York to say in a monologue:

> A day will come when York shall claim his own;
> And therefore I will take the Nevils' [Warwick's and
>      Salisbury's] parts
> And make a show of love to proud Duke Humphrey;
> And when I spy advantage claim the crown,
> For that's the golden mark I seek to hit.
>
> (I.i.239–43)

Note that York has *no love* for Henry, whom he calls "proud Lancaster," and who, York says, holds the sceptre "in his childish fist."

For the first time, we meet Gloucester's wife, Eleanor, a woman who will cause a great deal of trouble for both her husband and for the country. She is an ambitious woman, anxious to be queen, and she intends to push Gloucester closer and closer to the throne:

> What seest thou there? King Henry's diadem [crown],
> Enchas'd with all the honours of the world?
> If so, gaze on, and grovel on thy face
> Until thy head be circled with the same.
>
> (I.ii.7–10)

As Duchess of Gloucester, Eleanor provides a parallel to the ambitious Margaret: her husband becomes an instrument of her own desires and, as a human being, he counts for little—in her estimation. Gloucester is aware of this trait in his wife, and he beseeches her to dispense with it: "O Nell, sweet Nell, if thou dost love thy lord,/ Banish the canker of ambitious thoughts!" The fact that she will do precisely the opposite of what her husband wishes should tell us something of her love for him. He is no more than a means to an end, and this fact reinforces the tragedy of Gloucester's position: Gloucester does *not* wish to be king, yet he wishes to prevent others from obtaining the crown. He tells Eleanor of a dream he had in which "on the pieces of the broken wand/ Were plac'd the heads of Edmund Duke of Somerset,/ And William de la Pole, first Duke of Suffolk." Eleanor interprets her husband's dream as meaning that whoever attempts to harm Gloucester will have his head cut off. Eleanor then relates a dream wherein Henry and Margaret kneeled before her and placed the crown on *her* head. Gloucester scolds her openly for such presumptuousness.

Gloucester is called away to Saint Albans, and in his absence, Eleanor receives Sir John Hume, a priest, whom she will entrust with her secret desire to use witches and spirits in her quest for the throne. Hume is a flatterer and does not hesitate to accept Eleanor's money for his "services," even though unbeknownst to her, Hume has *already* been hired by Suffolk and Cardinal Beaufort to work *against* her. Eleanor, meanwhile, asks Hume whether he has conferred with Margery Jordan, a "cunning witch," and Roger Bolingbroke, a "conjurer." Hume replies that they have promised to bring Eleanor in contact with "a spirit" who will answer her questions.

Inside the palace, Queen Margaret and Suffolk encounter a group of petitioners, one of whom incorrectly assumes that Eleanor is accompanied by Gloucester—and not by Suffolk. He wishes to present complaints to Gloucester, their Lord Protector, about certain goings-on in the township. They are surprised and somewhat fearful when Suffolk glances at the names of the men charged with the complaints: one of the complaints is directed against Suffolk himself for "enclosing the commons of Melford"; another is directed against Thomas Horner for claiming that the Duke of York is the rightful heir to the throne, etc. The queen rips up the supplications and chastises the petitioners for wanting to be "protected" by Gloucester. It is clear that *she* is among those who would do away with the Lord Protector.

In a speech to Suffolk, Margaret questions the English system of monarchy whereby Henry must still defer to a Protector; in particular, she dislikes the fact that she herself is "subject to a duke." She is also critical of Henry's religious devotion and of the fact that he is not more courageous and more manly. She delineates the other nobles whom she holds in disdain (Beaufort, Somerset, Buckingham, and York), but none of them bothers her as much as does Eleanor, Gloucester's wife: "Shall I not live to be aveng'd on her?" Suffolk tells Margaret that he has laid a snare for Eleanor and that, though they dislike Beaufort, they must join forces with him and the other nobles in bringing about the downfall of Gloucester;

"So, one by one, we'll weed them all at last,/ And you yourself shall steer the happy helm."

The king enters, surrounded by his nobles, and an argument develops immediately over who should be appointed to the regentship of France — York or Somerset. Gloucester states that it should be the king's decision and no one else's. Immediately, several of the nobles and Margaret, as well, heap insults on Gloucester. Margaret drops her fan and, when Eleanor refuses to pick it up, Margaret boxes her on the ear. A few nasty quips are tossed back and forth between the women before the king interrupts them. Suffolk then introduces Horner, a man whose apprentice (Peter) has stated that Horner said that York felt he was the rightful heir to the throne. York denies such a claim and asks for Peter's execution. Gloucester says that he believes that Peter's charge casts some doubt on York's reputation; York, therefore, should *not* be chosen Regent of France. The king thus chooses Somerset in his place. A combat is then scheduled between Thomas Horner and his apprentice, Peter, the two who are involved in the alleged claims made by York.

Meanwhile, in Gloucester's garden, the witch Margery Jordan meets with the two priests, Hume and Southwell, as well as with Roger Bolingbroke, a scholar and a conjurer. Eleanor is seated in her chair, and a spirit is conjured up, one who welcomes their questions. First, they ask what shall become of the king, and they are told that the king will outlive a certain duke who would depose him and that this duke will die a violent death. The spirit reports further that Suffolk will die "by water" and that Somerset should "shun castles," that he will be safer on sandy plains. The spirit vanishes as York and the Duke of Buckingham arrive on the scene. Eleanor and the others are arrested, and York congratulates Buckingham on being so efficient.

## ACT II

At St. Albans, an argument breaks out amongst the various political factions: Gloucester versus his uncle Beaufort (Winchester), Margaret versus Gloucester, and so on. This scene makes for exceedingly poor drama since there is neither poetic stamina to the verse nor is there any suspense about plot development. In fact, it is often annoying and tedious. These nobles are grown men who have been fighting since the beginning of Part 1, and it seems highly unlikely that their feud would continue for so long without some form of violence or royal ultimatum. In short, there is nothing new on any front — simply more of the same. In fact, Henry sums up the situation quite nicely: "How irksome is this music to my heart!"

Buckingham arrives to report that Eleanor (Gloucester's wife) has conspired with witches *against the state* and has been arrested. Gloucester is dismayed and hurt, and he states that if his wife is guilty, he will banish her from his household. Henry decides that he will return to London in the morning and look into the matter more carefully.

In London, York (Plantagenet) relates his claim to the throne in a conversation with Salisbury and Warwick. The scene is best read with a family genealogy on hand; it resembles those sections of the Old Testament which flow with "he begat so and so," and another person "begat so and so," etc. Warwick, known as "the king maker," sees York's point of view: "'Till Lionel's issue fails, his [John of Gaunt's] should not reign./ It fails not yet, but flourishes in thee [that is, York]." When he is finished, York tells Salisbury and Warwick to tolerate Suffolk and Winchester and the others until they have "snared" Gloucester; then, as they meet the king's wrath, York will seize the throne. Warwick says that he will make York king, and he proclaims his fidelity to the rightful king: "Long live our sovereign Richard, England's king!" Richard Plantagenet, Duke of York, promises to reward Warwick well.

In a Hall of Justice in London, Henry assembles various members of state (his queen, York, Salisbury, Gloucester, etc.) for the purpose of banishing Gloucester's wife, Eleanor, from England. Margery Jordan, Hume, Southwell, and Bolingbroke are also brought in. Eleanor is banished to the Isle of Man, and the four others are sentenced to be executed. This is a major blow to Gloucester, who is now torn between his loyalty to his wife and his loyalty to his kingdom. He recognizes his wife's wrongdoings, and he believes that the hardship of his remaining Protector to the king would be too stressful, given the circumstances. So he resigns his position, with the ready encouragement of Margaret, and Henry gives him permission to go with Eleanor to the Isle of Man. Henry then states that he will be his own "Protector" and that God will be his "hope and guide."

York, meanwhile, is eager to have the combat begin between Thomas Horner and his apprentice, Peter Thump. It is a scene of mild comedy because Horner and his neighbors arrive drunk. Peter slays his master, but just before he falls dead, Horner utters: "I confess, I confess treason." This reflects badly on York since suspicions are now even more strongly aroused concerning Peter's testimony that York has ambitions for the throne.

In a street scene, Gloucester watches as Eleanor is escorted to the place where she must do three days' penance before beginning her term of exile. Eleanor, barefoot in a white sheet, scorns her husband for allowing her to be treated so basely. She warns him about his death, which she says is imminent, and she relates the names of all those who have "lim'd bushes to betray thy wings." In a moment of surprising naiveté, Gloucester answers that he is safe. He says that he is absolutely guiltless, and he would have to do something truly vile before anyone would attempt to kill him: "All these [men] could not procure me any scathe/ So long as I am loyal, true, and crimeless." He advises his wife to remain quiet and to expiate her sins through patience. Eleanor is led away by Stanley, and she proudly tells him to lead the way: "I long to see my prison."

## ACT III

Act III is the beginning of Gloucester's final downfall. It opens at the Abbey at Bury St. Edmunds with the king and his entourage at Parliament. The king notes that Gloucester is not present, an unusual characteristic of the former Protector. Margaret attempts to sour Henry on Gloucester: "Will ye not observe . . . How insolent of late he is become,/ How proud, how peremptory, and unlike himself?" Suffolk claims that Gloucester instigated Eleanor's treasonous acts and that he desires the downfall of the king. Beaufort and York each voice complaints about Gloucester. Henry, however, will have nothing to do with their gossip. He remains faithful to Gloucester.

Somerset arrives with the news that all is lost in France. Gloucester enters, and Suffolk arrests him for treason. This is an unsteady scene with little dramatic development; there was no "scene of decision" to arrest Gloucester before his arrival, and Suffolk's dramatic action to do so comes as a complete surprise. Gloucester defends himself systematically against their charges and, in doing so, he gains much sympathy from us. He shows no signs of moral or ethical weakness, nor is there any evidence in the play to support the accusations levied against him. Suffolk pronounces that Gloucester shall be put under the control of his old nemesis, his uncle, Cardinal Beaufort (Winchester), and this is a moment when Henry's spinelessness comes through very clearly: he makes absolutely *no* attempt to defend his former Lord Protector, nor does he substantiate his earlier claims that Gloucester is "virtuous, mild, and too well given/ To dream on evil." Henry is clearly an impotent pawn whose usefulness as a king is limited by his inexperience and his lack of courage.

In a long and searing speech, Gloucester exposes the motivation of his enemies, pointing the finger at each of them for their vicious plotting: "Beaufort's red sparkling eyes blab his heart's malice,/ And Suffolk's cloudy brow his stormy hate. . . ." Gloucester shows himself to be astute of judgment and wise in the ways of human psychology. He knows that Henry will never survive in their midst, but he is prepared to die in order to defend the principle of truth: "Good King Henry, thy decay I fear."

When Gloucester is taken away, Henry hastens to give the nobles total liberty for taking action against Gloucester: "My lords, what to your wisdoms seemeth best,/ Do or undo, as if ourself were here." He is, to the end, a grief-stricken wimp. He knows that Gloucester's enemies are about to do him wrong, yet he cannot muster sufficient courage to act against them. After he leaves, his wife, Margaret, assesses her husband's abilities as a king: "Henry my lord is cold in great affairs,/ Too full of foolish pity." The problem of Gloucester, in effect, can be understood from both sides: on the one hand, Gloucester has been a strong protector of Henry and the country, so it is clear why Henry feels so close to his uncle; on the other hand, Gloucester has been an obstacle to the nobles in their quest for greater authority, and from their point of view, no advances are possible until he is out of the way. Henry is guilty of weakness and of a lack of insight, while the nobles are guilty of devising various plans for bloody violence. When all is said and done, we have a microcosmic vision of evolution and survival: the strongest and most conniving of the court is the one who will dominate the rest of them. Margaret, York, Beaufort, and Suffolk agree unanimously that Gloucester *must* die.

A messenger arrives from Ireland to report that rebels are killing the Englishmen in that country and that help is badly needed. Cardinal Beaufort (Winchester), who quickly assumes the power which Gloucester once possessed, nominates York (Plantagenet) to serve as the nation's leader against the rebels. Suffolk confirms Beaufort's recommendation, adding that they represent the will of the king: "Our authority is his consent,/ And what we do establish he confirms." The nobles exit, leaving York behind. In a long monologue, York vows to carry out his *own* plan: the men whom he has been given to conquer the Irish rebels are *precisely* the forces needed to seize the English throne: "'Twas men I lack'd and you will give them me." While he is in Ireland, he says, he intends to stir up a "black storm" in England which will not cease to rage until "the golden crown" sits on his head. He has chosen John Cade of Ashford as the one to incite a rebellion in England. Cade is a headstrong Kentishman who will act for York under the name of John Mortimer, whom he resembles. York plans to use Cade to fire York's popularity with the commoners. If Cade is caught, it is highly unlikely that he will confess to the nature of York's plan. Thus, with Gloucester dead, only Henry VI will stand between York and the throne.

In the next scene, the murderers of Gloucester run through a room in the palace, reporting to Suffolk that the deed is done. When the king enters, ignorant of Gloucester's death, he orders that Gloucester be summoned and that a fair trial to judge his treason be held. Suffolk returns, pale and trembling, with the news that Gloucester has been found "dead in his bed." Henry faints, and Margaret shouts: "Help, lords! the king is dead!" When Henry is revived, he pierces Suffolk with accusations that the latter is a vicious, evil man: "Hide not thy poison with such sug'red words./ Lay not thy hands on me; forbear, I say! Their touch affrights me as a serpent's sting." The first prophecy of the sorcerers, then, is fulfilled: that is, a king (Henry) *did* outlive a duke (Gloucester), who died a violent death.

In a long and hypocritical speech, Margaret bemoans the death of Gloucester, claiming that she will now be looked upon as an accomplice in his murder. She tries to win Henry's faithfulness to her, but she gets nowhere with him. She concludes, "Ay me, I can no more! Die, Margaret!/ For Henry weeps that thou dost live so long."

Warwick enters to report that Gloucester was murdered by Suffolk and Beaufort (Winchester). The citizens have formed a mob and are lusting for revenge, regardless of their object. Henry asks Warwick to examine Gloucester's corpse in an effort to determine *how* he was killed. Warwick then wheels the deathbed into the king's room for all to behold. What they witness is a ghastly, sordid sight which proves that the duke was indeed murdered:

> His face is black and full of blood,
> His eyeballs further out than when he liv'd
> Staring full ghastly like a strangled man;
> His hair uprear'd, his nostrils stretch'd with struggling.
>
> (III.ii.168–71)

Warwick exchanges harsh words with Suffolk, accusing him of involvement in the murder and promising to "cope" with him. Salisbury enters to report that the crowd outside demands the death of Suffolk. Henry replies that his thoughts have centered more and more on Suffolk as the murderer. Suffolk is thus banished from the country. This is the first time that Henry asserts himself powerfully as king; it demonstrates the depth of his love for Gloucester and, in an indirect way, it shows that he is capable of enforcing his will when moved to anger. Left alone, Margaret and Suffolk declare their love for one another and bid each other painful farewells.

Vaux, a gentleman of the court, arrives to report that Cardinal Beaufort (Winchester) is on the point of death: "For suddenly a grievous sickness took him,/ That makes him gasp and stare and catch the air,/ Blaspheming God and cursing men on earth." In Beaufort's bedchamber, the Cardinal confesses to having conspired toward the murder of Gloucester, but when the king invites him to make a signal of hope concerning life after death, Beaufort makes no sign. He dies unrepentant.

## ACT IV

By the end of Act III, Shakespeare has gotten rid of Gloucester, Eleanor, Suffolk, and Beaufort—four pivotal characters surrounding the king. Now we are left with York (Plantagenet) and his supporters, and the king and his entourage. The conflict of personal ambition gives way to that of a more sustained struggle for the throne. It is at this point that the Wars of the Roses occupy the forefront of the action, with the white roses of the house of York in opposition to the red roses of the house of Lancaster.

Suffolk, who was banished in Act III, disguised himself in rags and left the country onboard a ship. Pirates at sea captured the ship and beheaded him for his evil doings, thus fulfilling another aspect of the sorcerers' prophecy. A gentleman close to Suffolk returns with his remains to England, where the Queen or Suffolk's friends, he assumes, may revenge his death.

The beginning of the York protests (the faction of the white roses) takes place in Scene 2, at Blackheath, with various supporters of Jack Cade: George Bevis, John Holland, Dick the Butcher, and Smith the Weaver, along with Cade himself. Cade announces that his father was a Mortimer and his wife a Plantagenet; therefore he is heir to the throne of England. And as he declaims about how he will rule the kingdom when he becomes king, Sir Humphrey Stafford enters and instructs Cade and his followers to drop their plans. The king will be merciful, he claims, and Cade will not suffer if he gives up his plan to revolt. Cade has been speaking to his men as if he were Sir John Mortimer, but Stafford knows his true identity and scoffs at his intentions: "Villain, thy father was a plasterer,/ And thou thyself a shearman." Stafford and his brother realize that they cannot stop Cade from proceeding, so they order that the king's army be brought in to overcome the rebel and his supporters. Cade is not worried: he stands for liberty, and he will not be deterred. In the fight which ensues, both the Staffords are slain, auguring well for the rebellion. Cade dresses himself in one of the Staffords' armor, and he and Dick the Butcher and their followers leave for London to free all the prisoners.

At the palace in London, the queen is caressing Suffolk's severed head just as the king walks in with a supplication from the rebels. Henry decides to talk directly with Jack Cade instead of having the rebel's supporters put to death. A messenger enters and announces that Cade's men are savagely destroying anything in their path, that they have captured London Bridge, and that Cade intends to crown himself in Westminster. Moreover, the fickle mob has joined forces with Cade and "they jointly swear/ To spoil the city and your royal court." Henry and Margaret flee to Killingworth until an army can be raised to defend them.

The Cade rebellion is in full force, with its men running all over London. The rebels capture the Tower of London, and Cade, disguised as Mortimer, claims that he is "lord of the city." Absolute chaos is the result, with men being murdered for any reason whatsoever. Cade orders that both London Bridge and the Tower of London be set on fire; he orders the burning "of all the records of the realm." The melee resembles a proletariat revolution, where everything is "by and for the people." As Cade says, "Henceforward all things shall be in common."

As a representative of Henry, Buckingham proclaims a royal pardon to the populace; if they will abandon Cade and his rebellion, Henry will *not* punish them. The mob then shouts out in favor of the king, showing their fundamental fickleness. After Cade makes a speech to them, however, they swing back to his side. This see-sawing continues for a while, and then Cade flees, disgusted with them all. Buckingham offers a thousand crowns to anyone who brings him Cade's head.

At Killingworth Castle, Henry regrets aloud that he is a king and *not* a subject. Buckingham enters with a repentant mob, and Henry "redeems" Cade's followers and praises them for having decided to support the monarchy.

It is learned that York is back from Ireland with a force of heavily armed Irish soldiers. Their intention, supposedly, is *not* to overthrow the king, but to get rid of Somerset, whom they believe to be a traitor. Henry asks Buckingham to meet with York and "ask him what's the reason of these arms." He instructs Buckingham to tell York that Somerset has been sent to the Tower, and that he will release Somerset once York's troops have disbanded.

Cade finds himself in a country garden in Kent after having been in hiding for five days. The proprietor of the garden, Alexander Iden, comes upon him and, after a brief discussion, they begin to fight. Iden slays Cade and drags him to a dunghill, "which shall be thy grave." He cuts off Cade's head and prepares to show it triumphantly to the king, leaving Cade's body "for crows to feed upon."

## ACT V

The act opens in some fields between Dartford and Blackheath. York and his army of Irishmen plan to "pluck the crown from feeble Henry's head." Buckingham arrives and asks York why he has assembled such a great army in a time of peace and in a location so close to the court. York is outraged, but he quells his anger and replies that his purpose is to get rid of Somerset, whom he considers to be seditious and a threat to Henry. Buckingham reports that Somerset is already in the Tower as a prisoner, so York abruptly and surprisingly dismisses his army. The two men are then greeted by the king, who is scarcely able to say a word before Iden enters with Cade's head. Iden is knighted for his efforts and, at this point, the queen enters with Somerset. York discovers the ruse and is furious with Henry for being so dishonest: "False king! why has thou broken faith with me,/ Knowing how hardly I can brook abuse?/ King, did I call thee? No, thou are not king,/ Not fit to govern and rule multitudes." This is the first time that York has openly declared his hostility to Henry: "Thy hand is made to grasp a palmer's staff/ And not to grace an awful princely sceptre." He informs Henry that, by heaven, Henry shall rule no longer over him who is the rightful heir. Somerset makes a move to arrest York for treason, but York demands that his sons be present; they will bail him out of his present situation. His sons, Edward and Richard, arrive and vow to defend their father. York asserts openly to all present that *he* is king, and he requests that Warwick and Salisbury be brought to him.

Warwick enters, but he does not bow before the king, and Henry realizes that the Nevilles do *not* support him. Salisbury states his belief that York is the rightful heir to the throne. Henry calls for Buckingham and requests that he arm himself. This leads directly to the Battle of Saint Albans.

At Saint Albans, Warwick challenges Clifford of Cumberland to fight with him. York also wishes to slay Clifford and does this in short order. Clifford's son sees what has happened and swears that he will spare "no York" in battle (young Clifford will reappear in Part 3 of the trilogy).

Richard (York's son) and Somerset begin fighting, and Somerset is killed. Margaret and Henry arrive on the scene, with Margaret urging that they flee. Henry seems indecisive and unable to decide whether to fight or flee: it is a classic psychological phenomenon described by Freud as the fight/flight syndrome. Ultimately, Henry opts for flight, a suitable option for a hopeless fighter.

The play ends when Salisbury arrives on the scene from the battle. Despite his age, he has fought valiantly and is a fitting model for younger soldiers in the camp. Young Richard Plantagenet helped him three times during the battle, and Salisbury pays tribute to him. But he cautions that they have not won *yet,* and York adds that the Lancasters should be pursued before the writs go forth. The spirit of battle is re-ignited by Warwick:

> Saint Albans battle won by famous York
> Shall be eterniz'd in all age to come.
> Sound drums and trumpets, and to London all;
> And more such days as these to us befall!
>
> (V.iii.30–33)

The play ends on this note of optimism for the Yorks: they are the legitimate heirs to the throne, and they intend to make this a reality. In Part 3, we shall witness the conclusion to this pursuit.

# HENRY VI, Part 3

## ACT I

Part 3 of this trilogy might aptly be subtitled: "Crown, crown, who's got the crown?" The English crown is taken and won several times throughout the drama, and it is sometimes difficult to remember precisely *who* is on *which* side of the struggle.

The play begins as the Duke of York, his sons (Edward and Richard), and Warwick have returned to Parliament in London, and Warwick wonders how Henry escaped from the Yorkists after the Battle of Saint Albans. York explains that Henry slyly stole away during the battle and deserted his men, who were soon slaughtered.

York's sons then recount their triumphs in battle, and each brags about whom he killed; Richard proudly displays Somerset's head. As we said earlier in these Notes, Part 3 is not the most theatrically satisfying of the three dramas; it is a panorama of egos, challenges, and bloody fights-to-the-death, and, on stage, this often makes for tiresome, difficult scene changes.

Young Richard has gained the approval of his father by beheading Somerset, York's longtime enemy, and Warwick vows that he will kill Henry unless Henry renounces his crown in favor of York and his heirs. Warwick then escorts York to the throne, just before the entrance of the king, Clifford (Margaret's favorite), Northumberland, Westmoreland, Exeter and others. Henry immediately realizes that York, backed by Warwick, means to have the throne, and when Northumberland and Clifford impulsively vow to avenge their fathers' deaths at the hands of York, Henry stops them, reminding them that the people of London support the rebels. For his part, Henry says that he refuses to fight "in the parliament-house" (another sign of weakness in this appeasing, peace-seeking young king). Instead of using weapons, Henry says, "frowns, words, and threats/ Shall be the war that Henry means to use." Then he states that *his* right to the throne comes from his father, King Henry V, who seized France. He asserts that York is merely the son of a duke and the grandson of an earl. Warwick, in turn, accuses Henry of having lost France, but Henry retorts that it was the Lord Protector (Gloucester) who lost it – and not Henry – because Henry was but an infant of nine months when that happened.

York's sons urge their father to "tear the crown" from Henry's head; they are willing to fight. Henry grows impatient; he threatens a war which will "unpeople" his realm before he allows his crown to be taken from him, arguing that *he* is the true heir to the throne. York, in turn, argues that Henry IV rebelled against Richard II and got the throne "by conquest." Henry admits that this is true, but he does so *only* in an aside. Openly, he maintains that Henry IV was Richard II's *heir.* Thus, what might otherwise have seemed like a very straightforward matter is converted into an impossible imbroglio, resolvable only on the battlefield.

At this point, Exeter, who had been on the king's side earlier, decides that York is the "lawful king." Clifford, however, refuses to kneel to York, the man who killed his father. Warwick demands that Henry resign and, in order to appear more threatening, he stamps his foot, and soldiers appear, ready to take away the prisoners. Henry, seeing that he is outnumbered, begs Warwick to allow him to remain king for at least the rest of his life.

York *agrees* to this idea, but *only* on the condition that Henry name him and his sons as *direct heirs*. He does so, and Westmoreland, Northumberland, and Clifford chastise the king for disinheriting his only son (calling him a "faint-hearted and degenerate king"), and then they depart to inform Queen Margaret. Henry regrets his decision to compromise, but he is more concerned about the present—not the future. He wants to take an oath to cease the civil war. Again he repeats his wish to be treated as king and sovereign by York and his followers, and so York pledges his loyalty and returns to his castle. Warwick, however, stays behind in London with his soldiers to guard the city. Seemingly, the houses of York and Lancaster are reconciled.

Exeter and Henry are ready to depart when they see Margaret and young Prince Edward approaching. She rails against Henry for what she considers to be an extremely foolish concession on his part. And Edward, of course, questions Henry's decision; as Henry's son, he has just lost his claim to the throne. Henry replies that he had *no choice:* he was forced by circumstances to act as he did. Margaret warns him that he has forfeited his safety and honor, and she refuses to see him again until their son is restored as Henry's heir to the throne. She announces plans to enlist the aid of the northern lords in the fight against the Yorkists, and although Henry begs them to stay, young Edward vows not to see his father until such time as he, Edward, returns victorious from the battlefield. Henry can do nothing but let them fight, while he tries to regain the favor of Westmoreland, Northumberland, and Clifford.

On a plain before Sandal Castle near Wakefield, York enters to hear his sons arguing. Edward urges him to seize the crown now, and young Richard explains that the oath which their father took has no meaning since it did not take place before a magistrate. His argument with his brother, he says, arose over who should plead the case to York; both believe that their father is the rightful heir, and both wish to see him disregard his oath *not* to claim the throne during Henry's lifetime. York is convinced of the truth of his sons' arguments, and so he dispatches them to gather support for an uprising. He is interrupted, however, by a messenger who warns him that Margaret and "all the northern earls and lords" plan to lay siege to the York castle. Moreover, Margaret and Edward have 20,000 men with them, so they present a very real threat to the Yorkist position. York decides to keep his sons with him and sends his brother Montague to London to warn the nobles of the upcoming events. York's uncles, Sir John and Sir Hugh Mortimer, arrive and set off to meet the queen in the field. They have only 5,000 men in contrast to Margaret's 20,000, but Richard is nonetheless confident of success ("A woman is general; what should we fear?").

An alarum sounds, and York's young son Rutland enters with his tutor, looking for a means of escape. Instead, they are captured by Clifford, and the tutor is taken away by soldiers. Rutland begs for his life, but he is cruelly slaughtered by Clifford as an act of revenge for York's having murdered Clifford's father. This only serves to intensify York's eventual wrath, of course.

York enters, tired and faint, mourning the death of both his uncles and the success of Margaret's army. Unable to escape or fight, the exhausted York is taken prisoner by Northumberland and Clifford, but he vows that success will ultimately come from his death. As Clifford, the queen's favorite, prepares to execute York, Margaret stops him in order to insult York with one final humiliation. She has him led to a molehill and taunts him about his desire to rule England, and she mocks his "mess of sons" who are incapable of helping him now. Then she offers him a handkerchief soaked in Rutland's blood, and she puts a paper crown on York's head, saying, "Off with the crown; and with the crown, his head." Then she orders York's execution. Before Margaret and Clifford stab him, York tears off the crown and curses her. Then he is beheaded, and his head is set on the gates of the castle so that it "may overlook the town of York."

## ACT II

Several days later, York's sons, Edward and Richard, march onto a plain in Herefordshire, fearful of their father's fate, which is as yet unknown to them. A messenger dashes in with the story of York's humiliation and his murder, and Edward dissolves into grief. Richard, however, is fired with anger and calls for revenge. Then Edward rallies and claims the title of Duke of York. But Richard encourages his brother to demand more — demand Henry's *throne*.

Warwick and his men enter and are told of York's death. Warwick, however, has already heard about it and says that he gathered together an army in London and marched to Saint Albans for the purpose of intercepting Queen Margaret. He had been told that she intended "to dash" the pledge given by York concerning Henry's right to reign during York's lifetime. Since Margaret intends to nullify York's oath in favor of her own son's succession, Warwick committed himself to defending the oaths taken by Henry and York. But when his soldiers were assembled, Warwick discovered that they were not really interested in fighting, even with the promise of higher pay. He conjured several reasons: the king's gentleness or rumors of Margaret's fierceness, or the fear of Clifford.

Richard derides Warwick for retreating, but explains to Warwick that it is only out of frustration that he is critical of Warwick ("In this troublesome time, what's to be done?"). Warwick tells the young men that the queen, Clifford, and Northumberland have gone to London to defy the king's oath to deliver his throne, eventually, to Richard's heirs. Thirty thousand soldiers have gone in support of them, and Warwick urges York's sons to try to assemble at least 25,000 men in an attempt to counterattack Margaret and claim the throne. Richard and Edward promise to help, and Edward is assured by Warwick that in every borough they pass through on their way to London, he will be named king. Those who do not support him will forfeit their heads.

Margaret and Henry arrive at York Castle with the Prince of Wales (Edward, their son), Northumberland, and Clifford. Margaret delights in showing York's impaled head to Henry, but Henry pleads to God that this bloody deed was not his fault. Clifford reminds the king that York made him disinherit Edward, his son, but Henry argues that perhaps the crown is not his to give, because it was "ill-got." Margaret then urges Henry to steel his "soft courage" and give Edward his promised knighthood *immediately*. Henry obeys her.

A messenger enters to warn of the enormous Yorkist march and of the Yorkists' gaining men as they progress toward London. Clifford and Margaret urge Henry to withdraw from the battlefield because of his indifference to war, but the Yorkists enter, and York's son Edward immediately challenges Henry to surrender the crown. Henry tries to speak, but he is shouted down by an exchange of insults. Both sides part ways and group their troops for battle.

Edward, Warwick, and George (another of York's sons) withdraw from the battlefield in Yorkshire since the ranks of their soldiers are broken and "Edward's sun is clouded." Richard (York's son) enters to report the death of Warwick's brother at the hands of Clifford, and this sufficiently angers Warwick, Edward, and George to return to the battle. Revenge *must* be sought.

Henry enters alone, having been forced by Margaret and Clifford to leave the battle; they told him that they were more successful in battle if he was absent. Henry sits down and reflects on his condition, as he has done in other parts of this trilogy; he wishes that he were a "homely swain" rather than a king. As he sits alone, a young man enters, one who has just killed his father by mistake in battle; and moments later, a father enters who has mistakenly killed his son. Henry cries out in anguish, and he sympathizes with them deeply, but his horror of this kind of slaughter is impotent, suggesting Henry's fundamental inadequacy throughout the battle. Despite his desire to help bring peace to England, there is not much he can do to influence matters. Margaret, Edward, and Exeter urge Henry to escape with them since the battle has turned against them. Henry, indifferent to his safety, does as he is told.

A wounded Clifford enters, sensing a Lancastrian defeat, and faints. The Yorkists arrive and hear a groan from Clifford as he dies. Warwick has the Duke of York's head removed from the castle gate and has it replaced with Clifford's. He announces that they will proceed to London for Edward's coronation and then he will depart for France, where he will ask the king for the hand of Lady Bona, sister of the French queen, for Edward. This will assure French support for the Yorkist efforts. Edward then names Richard as the Duke of Gloucester, and George as the Duke of Clarence.

## ACT III

This act opens in a forest in the northern part of England, where two gamekeepers are hiding themselves under a thick bush; they are stalking a deer. A disguised Henry enters, carrying a prayer book and counting his sorrows. One of the keepers recognizes the king and makes a move to capture Henry, but he is stopped by the other so that they may hear more of the king's story, which Henry relates aloud to himself. He confesses that Margaret and his son have gone to France for aid, but he fears that she will be unsuccessful. The keepers corner him and lead him away to the authorities. They state that their loyalties lie with King Edward.

Lady Grey appears before King Edward in order to win back the lands of her husband, who was slain in battle at Saint Albans in the cause of the Yorkists. Edward's brothers comment upon the exchange between their brother the king and Lady Grey, in which he attempts to woo her as his queen in exchange for the lands. Edward is pressing his suit to marry her when he is interrupted by a messenger, who announces that Henry VI has been taken prisoner. Edward orders that Henry be taken to the Tower while he and his brothers question the man who arrested him. Richard stays behind and, in a long soliloquy, he reflects on his desire that Edward should produce *no heirs* if he marries Lady Grey; if there are no heirs, this would make it easier for Richard to claim the throne after Edward's death. He bemoans his unsightly, hunchbacked appearance and vows to do whatever is necessary in order for him to become king.

In France, Margaret secures an audience before King Lewis. He listens to her eloquent plea for help against the Yorkists, then he asks her to be patient. Warwick enters suddenly with his request that Lewis' sister-in-law, Lady Bona, be allowed to marry Edward, the new King of England. Lewis asks Margaret to leave him alone with Warwick. Warwick immediately assures King Lewis that Edward is honorable in his love and is the rightful King of England. Lady Bona, who is present, agrees to the marriage proposal, and so Lewis informs Margaret of his change of heart: he has opted to help a *strong* monarch (Edward) instead of a weak one (Henry). He will not be able to do anything political for her.

A messenger enters with letters for Margaret, Lewis, and Warwick, which contain news of King Edward's sudden marriage to Lady Grey. An enraged Warwick renounces King Edward and returns to Henry VI's side.

He tells Margaret that he is her "true servitor," and he vows to "replant Henry in his former state."

At this point, the machinations of the plot resemble the melodramatics of a soap opera. Warwick volunteers to land French soldiers on England's coast in an effort to unseat King Edward. Thus, the messenger is sent back to England to announce the imminent arrival of French forces. Lewis vows to send 5,000 soldiers with Warwick and a fresh supply with Henry's son Edward, the Prince of Wales. Warwick, to further prove his loyalty, gives his eldest daughter in marriage to Henry's son, ending the act on a firm note that he and King Lewis seek revenge on Edward, who would mock England's throne and who would renounce a proposed marriage to a lady of the French court. Furthermore, Edward's fickle choice of wife has made Warwick look ridiculous.

## ACT IV

In London, Gloucester (Richard, the hunchbacked son of Plantagenet) and Clarence (George, Richard's brother) argue over their brother Edward's marriage to Lady Grey. Clarence confronts Edward, who has just entered, with the fact that France and Warwick will not willingly submit to such humiliation as Edward has dealt them. Gloucester warns Edward that a "hasty marriage seldom proveth well," but he says that he does not ultimately oppose his brother's marriage to Lady Grey. Montague (Warwick's brother) and Lord Hastings warn Edward that England *must* be prepared to fight. In addition, both Clarence and Gloucester are jealous of the wives whom Edward has bestowed on his new wife's brother and son. Discontent reigns in the house of York. Clarence even announces his decision to leave the court and find a wife for himself. The queen (Lady Grey) tries to intervene and make peace among the brothers, and Edward warns them that they *must* bend to his will—or experience his *wrath*.

The messenger from France enters with the message from Lewis, Margaret, and Warwick regarding the imminent arrival of French troops on English soil. Edward is not unduly upset; he states that he will meet them in war. Clarence then decides to marry Warwick's younger daughter (thereby joining Warwick's camp), and he challenges his supporters to go with him. Somerset follows him. Gloucester (Richard) remains behind, but not for love of Edward; instead, for love of the crown. Edward announces that preparations for war are to begin immediately.

Warwick welcomes Clarence and Somerset into his camp and vows that Clarence shall marry his younger daughter. He then informs them that King Edward's camp may be easily taken. Only three watchmen guard the king, who has vowed not to sleep until either he or Warwick is killed. He has chosen to stay in the field with only a small guard ("carelessly encamp'd") since " 'Tis the more honor, because more dangerous."

Warwick, Clarence, Oxford, Somerset, and several French soldiers enter, and Edward's watchmen, followed by Richard and Hastings, flee when they realize they are outnumbered. Edward is brought out of his tent, and Warwick announces that Edward is not the Duke of York and seizes the crown from him. He orders that Edward be conveyed to Warwick's brother, the Archbishop of York, and that the rest of them shall march to London to seat Henry once again on his rightful throne.

Queen Elizabeth (the former Lady Grey) has heard that Edward was taken prisoner, and she tells this news to Rivers, her brother, revealing that she must be strong since she carries Edward's heir. She asks Rivers to help her escape in order to save the unborn child.

Gloucester (Richard) meets with Hastings and Sir William Stanley in a park in Yorkshire where he hopes to rescue Edward, his brother. Edward is encountered along with his huntsman, and he is told that he is to go to Flanders for his own safety; his huntsman is to accompany him. Warwick, Clarence, Somerset, Oxford, Montague, and young Henry (Earl of Richmond) free Henry from the Tower, and since Warwick made it all possible, he announces that he will be in charge of the government even though Henry shall remain king. Warwick chooses Clarence as Protector and says that he and Clarence will govern jointly so that Henry can, as he wishes, lead a quiet, private life.

Warwick then proclaims that Edward is a traitor, and he ordains that all of Edward's lands and goods must be confiscated. Henry requests that Margaret and their son, Prince Edward, be sent for so that his joy may be complete. Then he notices the young Earl of Richmond, Henry, and says that he is England's hope for the future: "His head by nature [is] fram'd to wear a crown." A messenger suddenly announces that Edward (York) has escaped, and Warwick blames the Archbishop of York for the carelessness. He withdraws to plan strategy with the others while Somerset and Oxford remain with the young Earl of Richmond. They decide that he must be sent to Brittany for safety's sake, "till storms be past of civil enmity."

Edward (York), his brother Gloucester (Richard), and Hastings approach the gates of York with soldiers from Burgundy, only to find the gates locked. The mayor appears on the walls and explains that he and his colleagues are loyal to Henry. Hastings claims that *they* are Henry's friends, and Edward says that he is still Duke of York. Therefore, the mayor (deceived) lets them enter, and Edward "vows" to defend the town.

Sir John Montgomery marches up with soldiers and offers to help Edward regain the crown. Edward tells Gloucester that he will not stake his claim until he is stronger, and the latter replies that he will proclaim Edward as king, which will bring many supporters to the cause. Edward is therefore proclaimed king, and Montgomery throws down his gauntlet as a challenge to anyone who usurps the position.

In London, at the palace, Warwick announces that Edward is march-
ing toward London with many supporters and that troops must be gathered
in order to oppose him. King Henry, meantime, will remain in London.
Later, Henry and Exeter discuss the reasons why people chose Edward
over him and also discuss their chances. Suddenly, Edward, Gloucester,
and soldiers break in and seize Henry and order him to the Tower. Then
they begin their march toward Coventry to meet Warwick.

## ACT V

In Coventry, Warwick receives reports from messengers about the location of his commanders. He hears a flourish, which heralds the arrival
of Edward, Gloucester (Richard), and their men, and, unaware that they
were so close by, Warwick is taken by surprise and has no defense plan
in motion. Within minutes, Oxford, Montague, and Somerset arrive with
reinforcements. Clarence also arrives, but he takes the red rose of Lancaster from his hat and pledges his allegiance to the side of his brother
Edward, who orders Warwick and his troops to prepare for battle. Warwick shouts that he will not defend Coventry but that he will meet Edward
at Barnet, and the latter responds by leading the way.

On a field near Barnet, King Edward (Plantagenet) enters, dragging
a wounded Warwick. He exits to find Montague since he intends to kill
him too. Somerset and Oxford enter to inform Warwick of the queen's
arrival from France with reinforcements. Just before Warwick dies, they
tell him that Montague has also been killed.

King Edward celebrates his victory, but he knows that Margaret must
yet be defeated. Margaret tells Oxford and Somerset that they will replace
Warwick and Montague as the anchors of the quest to get Henry back
on the throne. Edward arrives, and the battle begins.

Shortly afterward, Margaret, Somerset, and Oxford are taken prisoners
by King Edward and Gloucester (Richard). Oxford is sent as a prisoner
to Hames Castle, and Somerset is beheaded. The captured Prince Edward
is brought in, resolute in his demands that King Edward must yield up
the throne. King Edward, Gloucester, and Clarence all stab the young
prince. Margaret faints, and Gloucester tells Clarence that he is off to London "on a serious matter" in the Tower. Margaret is led away to prison.
Edward asks for Gloucester, and Clarence tells him that he has gone "to
make a bloody supper in the Tower." Thus, Edward makes plans to return
to London also.

At the Tower, Gloucester and Henry walk along the walls, talking.
Henry suspects that his death is at hand and, as Gloucester stabs him,
Henry warns him that more slaughter will follow. Evil omens, he says,
were abroad when Richard, the "indigested and deformed lump" was born.
Gloucester stabs him one more time in order to send him to hell, and then,

talking to himself, he plots a scheme to poison Edward's mind against Clarence: "Clarence, beware! Thou keep'st me from the light,/ But I will sort a pitchy day for thee;/ For I will buzz abroad such prophecies/ That Edward shall be fearful of his life,/ And then, to purge his fear, I'll be thy death." Gloucester, of course, hopes to be the future Richard III, and he will stop at nothing to obtain the crown for himself.

In London, Edward recounts a list of men who have died because they desired the throne. Then he calls forth his queen with their son, for whose sake he fought the war. He asks Gloucester (Richard) and Clarence to kiss the child but, as Gloucester does so, he mutters in an aside that his kiss is a "Judas kiss," which will bring harm to the child. Edward then orders that Margaret be sent back to France, desiring that the time now be spent "with stately triumphs, mirthful comic shows,/ Such as befits the pleasure of the court."

When we recall that *Henry VI* was written early in Shakespeare's career, we realize that the drama's shortcomings are often compensated for by the hint of what is to come in future works. In conjunction with *Richard III,* this trilogy constitutes the first series of history plays which Shakespeare wrote, and it is a genre which he will develop considerably as he matures. The three parts of *Henry VI* can be read separately or as parts of a whole, but it must be remembered that the dramas are *not* an accurate presentation of history. Shakespeare contorts and bends historical reality to suit his dramatic purposes, and this often causes confusion if one attempts to follow their plots along strictly historical lines. The historical chroniclers of that era, especially Holinshed and Halle, document an ongoing series of battles and feuds which run through the fifteenth century. Shakespeare, in turn, chooses events which interest him most and uses them as a backbone for his human drama—one of overpowering ambition, courage, and energy.

Henry VI, whose reign spanned the period from 1422 to 1471, was a weak and disastrous king. He was ill-equipped to control the turbulent forces at work in his own country, and he was in no way prepared to lead a defense against the invasion of foreigners. As England sinks deeper and deeper into trouble, Henry's reign unravels as a desperate, insecure tenure. Gloucester represents the old spirit of England, one of faith and courage, of determination and honor. But even Gloucester is unable to stand undaunted by the disintegration of the monarchy, and he is killed in Part 2, the turning point in the trilogy. Without Gloucester, Henry is exposed for what he is: immature, unschooled, and doomed. The chaos of the mob is the most obvious sign of this confusion and represents the low point from which the kingdom must build itself anew. The murder of Gloucester signals the end of an epoch and the beginning of a period which will lead to the relatively more stable reign of the Tudors. Gloucester is one of the few characters for whom we have sympathy and deep feeling; most of the other characters are cold, steel-like caricatures of politically hungry vultures, or else they are one-dimensional, singularly ambitious beings. It causes us no real pain to witness Suffolk's murder. To be sure, it is a tragedy of sorts, but in the overview of the country's situation, this seems like a necessary, inevitable event.

The trilogy presents constant problems of character identification, family lineage, and so on. But when one grasps the notion that there is a handful of central, key figures, one ceases to worry unduly about the occasional minor characters who float in and out of the drama; a list has been included in these *Notes* to aid in this process of identification. Insofar as the characterization is concerned, Shakespeare has obviously done better work. But there are glimmerings of interesting people and of conflicts which stimulate good drama, and the *Henry VI* plays may be considered as essential groundwork for the study of Shakespearean psychology.

It is the pursuit of the crown which primarily intrigues Shakespeare in these dramas and, within this context, his trilogy makes for many gripping moments. The individual characters may suffer at the expense of the general effect, but when one remembers that this was one of Shakespeare's initial attempts at professional drama, it can be seen as a fortunate event in the history of theater.

**1591-92**

# titus
# andronicus

# INTRODUCTION

This play can be classified as a revenge tragedy, one which William Shakespeare wrote during the earliest stages of his career as a playwright. The play was obviously influenced by both Senecan and revenge tragedies, even though it does not fully match all of the common qualifying factors of either classification.

Revenge tragedies were recent developments when Shakespeare was writing. Thomas Kyd's *The Spanish Tragedy* marks the beginning of the tradition. Characteristics of this tradition include and add to those of the older Senecan tradition of a "tragedy of blood." Both types traditionally end with a cartload of bodies and a stage drenched with blood.

Pure Senecan influences which are recognizable in *Titus Andronicus* include the following:

(a) insistent, narrative moralizing
(b) five-act structure
(c) proclivity for sensationalism
(d) action begins near the catastrophe, which limits plot complications
(e) most action, especially violence, occurs off-stage
(f) messengers report the off-stage action
(g) the hero dies

Elizabethans, including Thomas Kyd, tried to shift from Seneca's models of declamation about outer conflict to an inner conflict of emotional and mental passions. Kyd was never good at this; Shakespeare too was poor at the technique until he developed a unique excellence in his mid- to late career. Then, the most elusive quality of inner conflict often proved to be sufficient motivation for revenge. Hamlet, for example, illustrates this concept as he vacillates while seeking some way to internalize his father's (the Ghost's) command to revenge his murder.

Although some divisions between Kyd's and Seneca's conventions seem forced, the components that can be extracted from *The Spanish Tragedy* must be regarded as influential because of that play's enormous popularity with Shakespeare's contemporaries. These characteristics include the following:

(a) a plot structured to build to a climax toward the end, with some use of suspense and counter-action
(b) madness of the hero
(c) inner motivation of the hero and major characters
(d) on-stage dramatization of some sensational action

(e) a villain whose excessive evil dramatizes the contra-Machiavel character, the popular Elizabethan interpretation of Machiavelli's *The Prince*.

Today, tragedy itself has become too large and complicated a genre to reduce to brief unarguable characteristics or definition. Its simplest definition is etymological—that is, *tragos* (goat); *aeidein* (sing). But some of the general conventions of tragedy that Shakespeare inherited are recognizable in *Titus*—conventions such as disguise, deception, intrigue, and a foreign setting (usually Italy).

What Shakespeare did not inherit in this genre was expert development of characterization, character conflict, and other essentials of general dramatic technique which we now regard as essential. Eventually, however, Shakespeare created memorable characters, and he developed and mastered uses of double themes with contrapuntal characters that still fascinate both audiences and critics. Furthermore, he learned to dramatize stories by structuring conflicts from which actions flow. But his dramatic skills, in general, are so poor in *Titus Andronicus*, and the quality of poetry is often so sparse that critics have argued vigorously against his actual authorship of the play.

Nevertheless, enough evidence exists to attribute this play to a very new apprentice stage of Shakespeare's career—probably around 1591–92. Evidence examined to determine authorship includes internal evidence (the play itself), external evidence (documents about the play), quatros (single contemporary copies of plays), and folios (combined plays published after Shakespeare's death). Many critics argue that Shakespeare must, logically, be the playwright, based on combinations of that evidence.

Critics with positive points of view tend to regard *Titus* as an experimental development of the young playwright. Some dramatic experiments in *Titus* appear in later Shakespearean plays as masterful accomplishments, such as the inexorable evil which forces the action to a climax; the pitting of two strong characters against one another in order to set up a complicated conflict (in *Titus*, Shakespeare's dramatic technique is already superior to his contemporaries'); the use of contrasting pairs of characters; the use of contrasting moralities; the creation of Aaron as a prototype of Iago; the dramatic, as well as the poetic, uses of imagery.

Sources for this play have also aroused some critical controversy. Shakespeare usually borrowed his story lines, but he seems to have used rather thin sources for this play. A probable source was a prose *History of Titus Andronicus*, which is believed to have existed at the time. Certainly, he did not rely on a favorite source, Plutarch's *Lives*, nor on any historical source, since no original Titus or Saturninus ever existed. He relied, instead, most heavily on the story of Philomela's rape in Ovid's *Metamorphoses*, Book VI. But he expanded noticeably from Philomela's mutilation (she lost only her tongue), and he added most of the characters and events when he wrote *Titus*.

As is true of all of Shakespeare's plays, *Titus Andronicus* is structured from conventions and traditions and philosophies which were well-known in Shakespeare's time; the play was not created in a vacuum, and although it is vulnerable to negative criticism, it contains some very good dramatic moments.

## A BRIEF SYNOPSIS

A grand procession opens the play. Gathering before the Capitol in Rome are the Tribunes and Senators, along with a crowd of citizens. Significantly, Saturninus and Bassianus, sons of the late Emperor of Rome, enter from opposite sides of the stage with separate groups of followers. Dominating the pomp and circumstance of flourishing trumpets and drums, Saturninus immediately tries to initiate a conflict. Appealing to his credentials as being the first-born son of the previous Emperor, he calls for armed support for his effort to succeed his father. Bassianus challenges him with a call for elections.

Marcus Andronicus enters with the crown and another expositional speech. After chiding the ambitious princes, he announces that his brother, Titus Andronicus, has already been elected as Rome's new Emperor. He then provides the citizens, and the audience, with the information that Titus has just returned from a victorious campaign against the Goths, capping a successful career of battle leadership, during which he sacrificed twenty-one of his twenty-five sons. Apparently persuaded by Marcus' speech, Saturninus and Bassianus dismiss their followers and pledge to end their quests for the crown.

Titus enters with a procession that includes his four remaining sons and a coffin. On display are a number of Goth prisoners, who include Tamora, Queen of the Goths, her three sons, and Aaron the Moor.

Titus inters his dead son or sons (there is one coffin but he refers to "these that I bring . . ."). One of his surviving sons, Lucius, then demands that the proudest of the Goth prisoners should be a just sacrifice for his dead brothers. Titus suggests Alarbus, Tamora's eldest son.

Tamora pleads with Titus to recognize that her son fought nobly for his country and that she loves him as much as he loves the sons whom he lost. She cautions Titus not to dishonor the family tomb with blood, and she directs him to imitate the gods by showing mercy rather than the power to end a life. Titus claims that he is appeasing his gods by severing and burning Alarbus' limbs; Tamora accuses him of cruel impiety. Alarbus never says a word. Demetrius urges his mother to remain strong and begin plotting revenge.

Meanwhile, Titus gives up the emperorship to Saturninus, and Saturninus, spurned by Lavinia (Titus' daughter), chooses Tamora as his bride. Here, Aaron's ambitions soar as he announces to us his intentions to reap the benefits of the high position of his mistress, Tamora. Immediately faced with a potential feud between Tamora's remaining sons, who each want to become Lavinia's lover, Aaron convinces them that they will best please their mother if they team up to rape and kill Lavinia instead of publicly squabbling in the Emperor's court. The boys eagerly join in this plot.

Their chance comes when the Andronicus family reunites with the new Emperor and his court at a hunt. Aaron selects a secluded part of the woods, tells Tamora to start a quarrel with Bassianus, then he leaves to go and fetch Chiron and Demetrius to reinforce her. In the name of revenge, Demetrius stabs Bassianus and throws his body into a previously dug pit. With their mother's fond blessing, Chiron and Demetrius then drag Lavinia off for their long-anticipated pleasure.

Aaron leads a drugged pair of Titus' sons, Martius and Quintus, to the edge of the pit. Martius falls in and Quintus tries to help him out, but he is pulled in just as Saturninus arrives. Before Saturninus can investigate that activity, however, Tamora gives him a letter that describes a plot to murder and bury Bassianus at this very spot. Aaron then produces a damning bag of gold which he had earlier hidden there. Saturninus declares that Martius and Quintus will be subjected to unique torture and execution, denying Titus' plea to allow bond and a trial. As they all leave the murder scene, Tamora falsely promises Titus that she will save his sons.

Chiron and Demetrius enter in high spirits with the raped and mutilated Lavinia. They failed to follow the orders of Aaron and their mother and, indeed, the plea of Lavinia, and murder her. Instead, they cut off her tongue and her hands in order to prevent her from naming her assaulters. The boys leave her there to be discovered by her shocked Uncle Marcus.

Titus, still unaware of Lavinia's desecration, totally debases himself as he pleads with the Tribunes and Senators to spare the lives of Martius and Quintus. He lies down in the path of the parade to the execution site, crying and begging. Lucius finds Titus, informs him that he is all alone, pleading to stones, then explains that he himself has been banished for trying to rescue his brothers. Titus assures his only remaining son that he couldn't be luckier than to live *anywhere* other than Rome.

Then Titus is once again appalled when his brother Marcus arrives to display the mutilated Lavinia. All four of them weep over the horrors which have decimated their family.

Aaron enters to perpetrate a particularly cruel hoax. He claims that Saturninus promised to stop the execution if one of them would send a severed hand to ransom Martius and Quintus. All the men volunteer, but

Titus wins. Aaron helps him cut off his hand, then carries it off while glorifying the pleasure of evil for its own sake.

Titus appears quite mad already when a messenger delivers his hand back to him, along with the heads of his executed sons. Marcus finally rejects reason and succumbs to his own anger, and Titus, beyond tears, now pledges revenge. He orders the exiled Lucius to raise an army of Goths, then he himself organizes a grisly parade, with Marcus bearing one head, himself another in his remaining hand, and Lavinia carrying Titus' hand in her tongueless mouth. Lucius vows revenge as he leaves to raise a Goth army.

Later, at home, Titus vows to learn to understand Lavinia so that she can communicate. His tender mood, however, is shattered when Marcus kills a fly. Yet, Marcus finally convinces Titus that it is all right to murder *anything* which resembles black Aaron. Titus then wanders off to read with Lavinia and his only grandson, young Lucius.

Young Lucius' books provide the first means for the mutilated Lavinia to communicate, but she frightens the boy when she desperately begins plunging at his books. Then, when he drops them, she uses the stumps of her arms to select Ovid's *Metamorphoses*, and she turns to the tale of Philomel. This tale contains the clues of rape, treason, and murder in the woods. Marcus is then inspired to write in the sand by guiding his staff with his feet and mouth, thus inspiring Lavinia to do the same. Lavinia then identifies Chiron and Demetrius as the villains who mutilated her.

This information stirs Marcus to pledge the family to bloody revenge. Titus is ready, and young Lucius quickly catches the spirit. But Titus teaches the boy to avoid combative confrontation and to resort to a subtle plot instead. The boy then delivers a message with a courteous mien while letting the audience know, through asides, that he is seething inside. Only Aaron recognizes that the "message" on the gift of "weapons" implies knowledge of the guilt of Chiron and Demetrius.

Meanwhile, Tamora gives birth to a black son, damning proof of her long affair with Aaron the Moor. Tamora sends the baby to Aaron with the request that he kill it. Chiron and Demetrius are shocked that Aaron has despoiled their mother. Demetrius wants to kill the baby, but Aaron protects his only son and declares that this issue of himself is more important than the mistress-mother. Furthermore, Aaron persuades Tamora's sons that they should protect their half-brother. Aaron enjoys an interlude of killing the three women who witnessed the black child's birth, and he plans now to deliver his son to the Goths for a safe upbringing.

Titus continues to project his reputation as a madman. This gives him the freedom to verbally attack Saturninus. Saturninus is fed up with the spoken and written libels which Titus has distributed throughout Rome. But Tamora dissuades him from killing the old hero long enough so that the cavalry, in the form of the Goth army, arrives in the nick of time and prevents the carrying out of the Emperor's orders to drag in Titus for execution. Saturninus is frightened by Lucius' reappearance not only because of the army but because of Lucius' popularity with the Roman citizens. Tamora soothes her husband by promising to lure Lucius in for slaughter by deceiving old Titus with false promises.

Lucius exhorts the Goth troops to fight Rome because of the citizens' discontent with Saturninus and because of the wrongs dealt out to the Goths. A Goth appears with Aaron and his baby in tow. At first, Lucius wants to cruelly kill the infant while Aaron watches, but he is dissuaded by Aaron's plea for his son's life. Other than this impassioned dedication to his infant son, Aaron displays a complete, self-satisfying commitment to evil.

At this juncture, the plot to lure Lucius to Rome is initiated. Lucius accepts an invitation to attend a parley with Saturninus at Titus' home. Tamora, disguised as Revenge, with her two sons, disguised as Rape and Murder, call on Titus. Confident that Titus is crazy enough not to recognize them, they arrange for the parley to take place during a banquet at Titus' home. Titus persuades Chiron and Demetrius to stay with him, then he kills them and prepares to serve them in a meat pie to their mother during the banquet.

Lucius, Marcus, Saturninus, Tamora, Lavinia, and some assorted Goths and Romans are served by a solicitous Titus. Announcing that he is ending Lavinia's shame and pain, Titus kills her in front of his startled guests. When Saturninus learns that Chiron and Demetrius raped Lavinia, he orders them brought to him for punishment. Titus announces that they were baked in the pie, then he kills Tamora. Saturninus immediately stabs Titus and is, in turn, stabbed by Lucius. Other than the later proclamation that Aaron will starve to death while buried alive, this ends the multitude of dead bodies in this bloody revenge play.

Thus, the Roman Empire is cleansed and can be ruled with justice again under the wise leadership of Lucius. Marcus and young Lucius also demonstrate the reappearance of mercy and wisdom. Marcus orates a general plea for the Romans to understand why Titus sought revenge, he presents Aaron's baby as proof of the dishonorable affair between Tamora and Aaron, and then he offers them a choice of electing Lucius as Emperor or demanding the deaths of the survivors of the Andronicus family. Lucius is elected Emperor by acclamation, and he dispenses a sentence to Aaron, then directs the disposition of the bodies. The innocent baby, it is implied, will live.

# LIST OF CHARACTERS

## Titus Andronicus

A popular Roman general who proves that he is not a wise statesman. Starting from a dramatic high point when he is proclaimed the new Emperor of Rome, he manages to alienate Saturninus, the Emperor whom he selects to replace him, in addition to the high-ranking Goth captives and, at one time or another, his entire family. After feigning madness long enough to gain a reputation for it, he descends to the level of a psychopathic killer. Other than mastering revenge, however, Titus learns nothing; therefore, he cannot be classified as a tragic hero.

## Marcus Andronicus

The brother of Titus Andronicus; a Roman tribune. He represents statesmanship in contrast to his brother's warlike ways. Although he cannot save Titus or most of his nephews and his niece Lavinia, he does manage to help teach Titus' only surviving son, Lucius, and grandson, young Lucius, enough of wisdom and justice to leave the impression that Rome will improve under their leadership.

## Saturninus

Son of the late Emperor of Rome and Titus' personal choice to replace himself as the new Emperor. Like Titus, he displays no ability to learn about statesmanship, wisdom, or justice. Arrogant and demanding in the opening scene, he remains so up to the moment of his death at Titus' bloody revenge banquet.

## Tamora

The captive Queen of the Goths, she is Saturninus' rash choice for a bride only seconds after Lavinia is dragged away from his proposal. Tamora cavorts with Aaron, enjoys the high spirits of her sons when they want to rape Lavinia, and she provides consistently bad advice to her new husband. She dies by Titus' sword.

## Aaron

A Moor attached to the party of captured Goths. Tamora, Queen of the Goths, is his mistress. A black Moor, like Othello, he is also a prototype of Iago. Evil, evil, evil—how he loves it. The mover of bloody action for most of the play, he is ultimately responsible for most of the thirteen dead bodies and for Lavinia's mutilation. Only the black son who is born to Tamora moves him to any recognizably "normal" actions. While fleeing to save the baby's life, he is captured by Lucius, who condemns him to a barbarously cruel death. Aaron regrets only that he has run out of time to enjoy more evil deeds.

## Bassianus

The brother of Saturninus, he is a generally murky character. After a garbled opposition to his brother's plot to win the post of Emperor by force, he drops his own cause to support Titus. Just as quickly, he swings back to Saturninus at Titus' request. When Saturninus wants to marry Lavinia, Bassianus is granted his demand to marry Lavinia. When he briefly reappears as a happy bridegroom, he allows himself to be tricked into quarreling with Tamora. Demetrius, while supposedly defending his mother's honor, kills Bassianus with one quick knife thrust.

## Lavinia

Apparently, Titus' only daughter. After her husband, Bassianus, is killed, she is raped and mutilated by Chiron and Demetrius. Once she is finally able to communicate what happened, however, she initiates the downfall of Saturninus. She is eventually killed by her father in order to free her from her pain and shame.

## Lucius

The only son of Titus Andronicus who survives. At the end of the play, he becomes the new Emperor of Rome.

## Quintus and Martius

Two more sons of Titus Andronicus. They are duped by Aaron and trapped in the pit which holds Bassianus' body. Saturninus orders them executed for that murder.

## Mutius

Another son of Titus Andronicus. He is killed by Titus in the opening scene of the play.

## Young Lucius

The young son of Lucius, grandson of Titus. Like his father, he not only survives, but he learns something during the course of the play.

## Alarbus

The oldest son of Tamora. He is sacrificed to appease the souls of the slain Andronicus brothers.

### Demetrius and Chiron

Two sons of Tamora; they rape and mutilate Lavinia. Titus' revenge is to kill them, bake them in a meat pie, and serve them to their mother. That leaves the black bastard by Aaron as Tamora's only surviving son.

### Publius

The son of Marcus Andronicus. He serves no significant role in the action.

### Sempronius, Caius, and Valentine

Andronicus kinsmen who, like Publius, serve only minor background functions.

### Aemilius

A noble Roman who steps in after the slaughter at the banquet scene to declare that Lucius is to be the new Emperor of Rome.

## SUMMARIES AND COMMENTARIES

### ACT I

### Summary

This act consists of only one scene—the open area near the Capitol in Rome. Gathering to the sounds of drums and trumpets, the Tribunes and the Senators gather on a higher level in preparation for the proclamation of Rome's new Emperor. The conflict for this post is set when Saturninus, the eldest son of the previous Emperor of Rome, gathers his followers on one side of the stage and his brother, Bassianus, enters with his followers on the opposite side.

Saturninus appeals to both the "noble patricians" and his "countrymen" to take up arms and fight for his right to be Emperor. Bassianus calls on the people to fight also, but for the right of election.

Marcus Andronicus, the brother of Titus, enters with the crown in hand. He informs both princes that their ambitions have already been overruled by a special vote which resulted in the unanimous choice of Titus Andronicus as their next Emperor. Enumerating Titus' credentials, Marcus provides a brief history. Titus and his surviving sons have just returned from a ten-year campaign against the militantly strong Goth nation. Today's arrival marks the fifth time that Titus has returned victorious from long and bloody wars, faced with the sad task of burying more of his gallant sons.

Marcus then successfully appeals to the two princes to publicly withdraw their appeals and to dismiss their followers in honor of their government and Titus' heroic reputation. They both call off the proposed civil war and then withdraw to join the Senators and Tribunes.

With the triumphant entry of Titus and his entourage, the remaining major characters are brought into the action. Titus greets the crowd; he pleads for both honor and rewards for his four remaining sons, survivors of twenty-five.

As Titus prepares to inter the coffin in the Andronicus tomb, which is conveniently located within view of the Capitol, Lucius interrupts to demand a Goth prisoner as expiation for his brothers. When Titus selects Alarbus for the sacrifice, Tamora appeals to Titus' understanding of parental love and the nature of war. Titus responds that Tamora must understand that the sacrifice of her son is necessary for his deceased sons' souls to rest in the shadowy world of death. Demetrius advises his mother that she cannot save Alarbus but that she can begin a plan for revenge.

Lavinia arrives to welcome home her father and her remaining brothers and to mourn the dead. Titus expresses pleasure for her virtuous existence.

Marcus then steps forward to welcome them home and to inform Titus that he, Titus, has been elected Emperor of Rome. Titus immediately responds that he is too old, and he says further that in order to save everyone the trouble of electing a successor in a short time, that he would like an honorable retirement instead. Saturninus demands the empty post, and in anger, Bassianus vows to back Titus. Titus, surprisingly however, selects Saturninus. Marcus then leads the acclamation to accept him.

As proof of his gratitude, Saturninus honors the Andronicus family by requesting Lavinia as his bride and empress. But Bassianus demands that *his* betrothal to Lavinia be honored; the Andronicus sons back Bassianus and kidnap Lavinia. Titus kills his son Mutius when he tries to stop his father from preventing Lavinia's escape, and Titus denounces all his children for their treasonous behavior.

Saturninus also denounces the family and chooses Tamora as his bride. Only Titus is not invited to join the wedding party. Fuming at the slight, he confronts his brother and his sons as they return to bury Mutius. Marcus has to convince Titus to allow Mutius in the family tomb.

Saturninus and Bassianus again enter from different doors, this time with their separate wedding parties. Saturninus threatens to punish his brother for the "rape" of Lavinia. Bassianus reiterates his right to marry his betrothed and then pleads Titus' case. Titus retorts that he does not want representation from the very man who caused his family's dishonor.

Tamora publicly entreats Saturninus to forgive Titus, then she privately cautions him against confronting the old soldier when so many of his supporters are gathered. She promises that she will find a way to "massacre them all" without risking insurrection. Tamora vows revenge against those who forced her to beg in vain for the life of Alarbus.

Tamora then fraudulently orchestrates reluctant reconciliation among all of the protesting parties. Saturninus voices forgiveness, invites Lavinia and her wedding party to join his own, and he accepts Titus' invitation to join a hunting party the following day.

## Commentary

Act I presents a series of conflicts without focus. Without a sharp conflict, no plot exists; without focus, no drama exists. This problem, plus some weak characterization and a lot of poor verse, causes many critics to squirm about accepting *Titus Andronicus* as a play written by William Shakespeare.

Although these weaknesses must be acknowledged, they should not obliterate the innate talent of a young playwright who displays some dramatic strengths among the obvious weaknesses.

Conflicts in this act include Saturninus vs. Bassianus, Saturninus vs. Titus Andronicus, Tamora vs. the Andronicus family, honor vs. dishonor, and mercy vs. revenge. Where is the focus? Undoubtedly, during a performance of this play, the focus of the audience would dwell on Titus' stabbing of his son, because the sudden violence and blood would be shocking and memorable. If the actress cast as Tamora plays her part well, she will probably carry the act because she can work with the horror surrounding Alarbus' cruel death, and, in addition, she manipulates everyone into a fake reconciliation at the end of the act. Thus, she can be motivated by hate throughout most of the rest of the act.

In contrast, Saturninus and Titus vacillate throughout this act. They oppose each other, swear loyalty to each other, and then repeat the cycle. Marcus seems to be in a position of focus, but he loses it when he participates in the kidnapping of Lavinia.

Obviously, Titus is supposed to be the protagonist, and he will draw attention because of that. But the audience will see a strong man who cannot define honor, yet a man who storms into action – motivated by quickly changing interpretations of it. We know he fights. We suspect that he does not know what he wants nor does he think deeply. With those handicaps, he cannot initiate action as a good protagonist should.

Saturninus serves as a good example of a character who acts without discernible motivation. At the play's opening, he calls on his followers and the populace to "defend the justice of my cause with arms" rather than "wrong mine age with this indignity." Yet, the cause of persuasion is sufficient to sway him to "commit myself, my person, and the cause." As soon as Titus refuses the offer to become Emperor, Saturninus demands: "Patricians, draw your swords, and sheathe them not/ Till Saturninus be Rome's

Emperor." Within moments after Titus orchestrates his election as Emperor, Saturninus promises to reward the Andronicus family and, for a start, he selects Lavinia as his Empress. When he is thwarted in that effort because his brother claims *his* right to Lavinia, Saturninus turns against Bassianus and the entire Andronicus family. With as much thought as he has given to all of his other actions, Saturninus suddenly chooses Tamora, the captive Queen of the Goths, as his bride and the new Empress of Rome. Although he has not yet even been formally introduced to the woman, he accepts her advice on the proper handling of the Andronicus matter.

Thus, Act I ends on an improbable note. At this stage, we might well conclude that the central conflict will be between Titus and Saturninus, but we would be wrong. We might also believe that a classic revenge tragedy is developing, because so many characters mention *revenge*, but we would again be proven wrong by the actual development of the play.

## ACT II

### Summary

No change of scene or time occurs between the end of Act I and Aaron's soliloquy at the beginning of this act. With the wedding party just begun, Aaron is already reveling in lascivious fantasies about his affair with Tamora and his improved status as the lover of the Empress of Rome.

Tamora's two remaining sons, Chiron and Demetrius, interrupt Aaron's lusty reverie with their own warring lusts. They propose a duel to decide who is to win the right to seduce Lavinia. Aaron chastises them for carrying on this quarrel, especially when the Emperor will certainly hear of it and their mother will be dishonored. He further warns them that Bassianus is a prince who has the power to punish them for their very thoughts.

When asked how he proposes to have Lavinia, Demetrius responds that any woman, no matter the rank of her husband, can be seduced. Aaron takes a moment to smirk about cuckolding someone with the rank of Saturninus. But immediately after this aside, Aaron begins counseling the boys to be reconciled so that they may *both* enjoy Lavinia. He insists that Lavinia is too virtuous to be seduced, but he entices them with the thought of a lustful rape at the reconciliation hunt. Aaron further insists that they involve their mother's talent for treachery in the rape. Chiron and Demetrius, thrilled at the prospect, exit with their new mentor.

Marking the first change of scene, Titus enters to announce "The hunt is up." He cautions his sons to treat the Emperor well, primarily because his, Titus', troubled sleep has left him with a vague foreboding.

The hunting party gathers amidst bawdy jokes about newlyweds and bragging about hunting prowess. Demetrius encapsulates the general tone with a thinly disguised threat to ravish Lavinia.

Setting the scene for the approaching multiple perfidies, Aaron enters to bury a bag of gold and hint at his carefully designed plot. Tamora approaches Aaron with lusty hints about what they could enjoy in this isolated spot. Aaron makes it clear that he wants nothing but revenge this morning.

With the approach of Bassianus and Lavinia, Aaron begins the plot anew with instructions to Tamora to start a quarrel. He exits to fetch her sons for a staged duel of honor. When pricked by Tamora, Bassianus and Lavinia both cast slurs about Tamora's affair with Aaron. When Demetrius enters, Tamora concocts a tale about a threat from Bassianus and Lavinia to tie her up and leave her to die of fright beside the viper-filled pit, embellishing the tale by reporting the truthful slur about her adulterous conduct, then demanding that Demetrius revenge the threat on his mother's life. No duel ensues; Demetrius merely stabs Bassianus, then Chiron finishes him off. When Lavinia challenges them to kill her too, Tamora wants to comply; Demetrius stops her, however, with the thought that revenge should include the loss of Lavinia's virtue. Tamora approves the plan but cautions the boys to kill Lavinia when they're through with their fun.

Lavinia pleads with Tamora to intervene, but Tamora reminds her that no one listened to *her* when she pleaded for Alarbus. Death would be preferable, declares Lavinia, and she asks that Tamora kill her. Tamora refuses to interfere with her sons' fun; the boys then throw Bassianus' body into the prepared pit and drag Lavinia away. Tamora waves them off, reminding them one more time to kill Lavinia when they're through.

Tamora declares satisfaction with Lavinia's plight but vows not to be happy until all the Andronicus family are dead. She wanders off to find Aaron. She misses him, however, because he enters with Quintus and Martius, luring them on with the promise of a panther in the now-familiar pit. Both of Titus' sons complain about their foggy sight and wits, apparently in reference to being drugged. Martius falls into the pit, which is covered over with briars. Quintus notices fresh blood on the briars, so he asks Martius if he has been hurt. Only in the heart, replies Martius, by the sight of Bassianus' body. Aaron slips away, and Quintus is almost paralyzed by a vague fear. Demanding to know how Martius can identify Bassianus in such a dark pit, Quintus is told that Bassianus is wearing a ring that illuminates the hole. Quintus tries to help Martius out of the pit and vows to either accomplish his goal or join Martius. True to his word, Quintus falls in.

Saturninus enters just in time to catch sight of Quintus falling. Mistaking the fall for a leap, he goes over to investigate. At Saturninus' demand for identification, Martius replies that these two unhappy sons of Titus have discovered the body of Bassianus.

At first disbelieving, Saturninus is nudged by the timely entrance of Tamora to read a letter which contains a plot to murder Bassianus. Following the tip in the letter that a reward of gold will be waiting at the elder tree, Saturninus discovers the bag of gold that Aaron had planted there earlier. Tamora implicates Titus by reporting that he handed her the letter. True to form, Saturninus jumps to the conclusion that Quintus and Martius are guilty. He orders that they be tortured and executed without trial. Titus' pleas for bond and a trial go unheeded.

As the Emperor's party leaves with the prisoners, Tamora soothes Titus with the promise that she'll see to the safety of his sons. Titus urges Lucius to leave quietly with him.

Thus, no one is left at the scene when Chiron and Demetrius return with the ravished and mutilated Lavinia. After a few coarse remarks about their independent decision to leave Lavinia alive without hands or tongue to identify them, they leave her. Marcus discovers her and laments the loss of her sweet hands and tongue. He tenderly leads her away.

## Commentary

At the opening of Act II, Aaron swings the focus onto himself and never relinquishes it again. Aaron's plot not only causes him to function as the protagonist; it structures a focus for this entire act. Therefore, at this point, the play tightens up after a meandering, confusing first act.

The conflict here clearly pits Aaron against the Andronicus family. Aaron's allies, Tamora and her sons, take action under her direction. In the only major departure from this turn of events, Chiron and Demetrius commit a fatal error when they ignore their mother's orders to kill Lavinia. (One should note that although Tamora utters the order in this act, Aaron first instructed them to do this in Act I.) In this particular act, you should also note that Saturninus, Titus, Lavinia, Bassianus, Martius, and Quintus act only in response to Aaron's manipulation.

However, characterization is again weak. Aaron and Tamora speak often of a revenge motive, but they certainly do not move in classic fashion. What has Bassianus done to motivate revenge? His murder might be triggered because of his occasional vague mutterings against the Emperor, but this motivation is never strongly developed. Tamora is certainly supplied with a motive for revenge against the Andronicus family because they sacrificed Alarbus, but she has no right to defend her *virtue*. When she falls in with Demetrius' argument against allowing Lavinia to die virtuous, Tamora knows very well that she is guilty of adultery with Aaron and that the slurs by Bassianus and Lavinia do not justify revenge.

Saturninus' character is developing a consistency for rash action, but that hardly translates into an understandable motivation. He is still unaccountably influenced by the Goths in his court and, indeed, he never seems to have a trusted Roman adviser nearby.

Titus is a mere puppet in this act. He never initiates a strong action nor does he seem to have any internal motivation other than subservience to Saturninus.

Motivation for Chiron's and Demetrius' rape of Lavinia is clear and their misdirected "revenge" is understandable. As for the sons of Titus, Martius and Quintus behave like sheep, and Lucius does not contribute a thing.

That leaves Aaron with the only strong motivation, and it is not revenge. He simply loves evil. He loves to plot, to manipulate, to kill or at least cause death. He detests every character thus far introduced and will never change his attitude about any of them. Although Aaron mentions ambition at the opening of this act, he is not really ambitious for anything but the opportunity to indulge in evil. However, his expressed willingness to betray trust is later upheld. This duplicity is evident in his contempt for both Tamora and Saturninus when he declares his intent "to mount aloft with thy imperial mistress,/ And mount her pitch whom thou in triumph long/ Hast prisoner held, fett'red in amourous chains." Aaron is identified as a contra-Machiavel character, which the Elizabethans distilled from Machiavelli's *The Prince*.

Contempt for virtue and honor is upheld as a prevailing theme during this act and will hold as a primary motivation for several characters as the play develops.

# ACT III

## Summary

Before this act is over, all the harm that Rome inflicts on the family of Titus Andronicus will have been done. As the act opens, however, Titus is frantically pleading with the authorities who are leading Martius and Quintus to their execution. Titus, a general who marshaled a grand procession at the beginning of the play, now debases himself by lying prone in the street in a feeble attempt to stop the execution march. Just as Tamora's pleas for Alarbus had been useless, so now are the pleas of Titus for his two doomed sons.

Lucius enters and tells Titus that he is alone, lamenting to the stones that make up the road. He also informs his father that he, Lucius, has been banished because of a vain attempt to rescue his brothers. Titus responds that Rome is "a wilderness of tigers" which is preying on his family, and that Lucius is fortunate to be banished.

At this juncture, Marcus leads Lavinia to Titus and Lucius. Whereas Lucius is speechless before the horror of Lavinia's mutilation, Titus is sturdy and has a lot to say. He expresses a grief that "disdaineth bounds," again curses Rome for what it has done to his family, and in a moment of foreshadowing, offers to cut off both his hands. Titus summarizes the wrongs perpetrated by the Romans that he had fought for: the execution of his two sons, the murder of Bassianus, the mutilation of Lavinia, and now, the banishment of Lucius.

Lavinia is crying; perhaps, Marcus speculates, because she knows that her two brothers are innocent of the murder of her husband. Titus begs to know what they can do to make Lavinia feel better: cut off their hands, bite off their tongues, plot revenge? Lucius tells Titus to stop crying because Lavinia's sorrow increases with his. He then tenderly wipes away his sister's tears.

At this juncture, when horror and grief seem to have peaked for the Andronicus family, Aaron appears with a fiendish plan. He tells Lucius, Titus, and Marcus that if any one of them will sever a hand for him to deliver to Saturninus, then Martius and Quintus will be returned alive. Each of the Andronicus family offers to sacrifice his hand, and they finally concoct a team plan in which Marcus is to fetch the axe, Lucius is to wield it, and Titus is to contribute his hand. When Marcus and Lucius exit, however, Titus quickly convinces Aaron to chop off the hand. Aaron quickly complies, after promising in an aside to deceive Titus within the half hour.

Titus sends his hand with Aaron in a spirit of hopefulness and service. He requests that Saturninus bury the faithful hand and return Titus' two sons. Titus regards the hand as a small price to pay for the lives of Martius and Quintus. Aaron promises Titus that his two sons shall soon be with him, and then he reveals in an aside that he means their *heads*.

Titus and Lavinia pose together, displaying their gore and horrible mutilations, while Titus expresses the immensity of his sorrow. Marcus calls for "reason to govern thy lament." Just as Titus finishes expressing the absence of reason in all that has befallen the Andronicus family, a messenger enters carrying the heads of Martius and Quintus, as well as the hand of Titus.

The messenger, a traditional bearer of bad news, reports that the sacrifice of the hand was mocked and that he feels more sorrow at delivering this message and viewing these events than at the death of his own father.

This sparks the first show of anger in the ever-reasonable Marcus. He urges the unnaturally quiet Titus to now express his overwhelming grief. Titus laughs, saying that all of his tears have been used up, and he declares that sorrow would only interfere with revenge. Urging his remaining family to vow revenge before the severed heads, Titus organizes a grisly parade with the remains of his family. He commands Marcus to carry one head, as he picks up another; he orders Lavinia to pick up his own severed hand with her teeth, and he sends Lucius off to raise an army of Goths. Lucius watches the pathetic parade exit, and then he vows to revenge the woes of the Andronicus family.

The final scene of the act is set at a banquet for those of the Andronicus family who remain in Rome. Here, Lucius' son, young Lucius, is introduced. Titus recites the family's woes for the morose group. Marcus reprimands his brother for suggesting that Lavinia commit suicide if she cannot stop crying. Titus cannot see the harm since she has no hands to enable her to commit such an act. He recites the sadness which he believes his daughter to be feeling, and he vows to learn to understand her so that she can communicate. Young Lucius suggests that his grandfather change the subject and try to amuse Lavinia; then he breaks down and cries.

Suddenly, Marcus violently strikes his plate with a knife. When Titus asks why, Marcus replies that he has killed a fly. Titus, outraged at the murder, commands Marcus to leave. He insists that the fly had a family, was happy and innocent, and deserved to live. But when Marcus compares the black fly to the black Moor, Titus closes the scene by joining in the violence upon the fly and then leading off Lavinia and Lucius for a story hour.

## Commentary

Tension again eases at the opening of this act because Shakespeare presents no clear conflict. Titus and Lucius are reacting against both mute authority and offstage action.

Thus, when Aaron enters with his plot to trick Titus into severing his hand, he again swings the play's focus onto himself. After Aaron exits, this act sinks into meandering melodrama during which the Andronicus family is not even able to identify a definite focus for their planned revenge.

Both Titus and Lucius are vague about their quest for revenge. Titus seems to hear the two heads of his sons speaking, threatening no peace for their father "till all these mischiefs be returned again/ Even in their throats that hath committed them." But Titus names no names and describes no plans. Lucius is more explicit when he vows to "make proud Saturnine and his Empress/ Beg at the gates like Tarquin and his queen," but almost immediately he defuses this specificity by pledging to raise an army of Goths "to be revenged on Rome and Saturnine." Thus, we are left with the impression that the Andronicus family is pitted against all of Rome but that impression, like so many in the vague use of the revenge theme, would be an incorrect one.

Characterization remains weak or nonexistent for most of the characters, unless one supplies undue emphasis for the weeping capacity of the Andronicus family or the capacity for rage in Marcus. Lucius begins displaying leadership strength, but he does not actually do anything with it in this act.

The exception to characterization is, again, Aaron. He succinctly identifies his motivation when he declares: "Let fools do good, and fair men call for grace,/Aaron will have his soul black like his face."

When Titus writhes within the vision of the complete breakdown of nature, he irresistibly invites comparison with Lear's rage at the opening of Act III, Scene 2. But the difference in the quality of language illustrates why so many critics are reluctant to accept the two plays as being written by the same playwright. Lear challenges nature with "Blow, winds, and crack your cheeks. Rage. Blow." In contrast, Titus passively describes his grief in hyperbole: "If the winds rage, doth not the sea wax mad,/ Threat'ning the welkin with his big-swoll'n face?" And whereas Lear parallels the raging storm to "the tempest in my mind," Titus disintegrates to the distasteful: "For why my bowels cannot hide her woes,/ But like a drunkard must I vomit them."

The macabre, melodramatic scenes in Act III have aroused much ridicule. But a comparison to the popularity of modern horror movies should temper that contempt. Is there not something "modern" about displaying gory heads and hands, about severing a limb with a gush of blood, about overdramatizing death and mutilation? Perhaps comparing all this excess with our own bloody box-office movies can tap some understanding for the popularity of this play in its own day.

## ACT IV

### Summary

In a setting not clearly defined in the script, Act IV opens with a frightened young Lucius fleeing from his apparently mad, as well as mutilated, Aunt Lavinia. When the boy appeals to Titus and Marcus for help, they assure him that Lavinia means him no harm and urge him to guess what it is that she wants.

The boy reports that he had thrown down his books in his haste to escape but realizes now that his aunt loves him too much to harm him. Meanwhile, Lavinia is frantically working with Lucius' books, turning them over with the stumps of her arms. All three of them then try to guess why Lavinia is throwing the books into the air, and then, in the first breakthrough of communication, they realize that she is repeatedly throwing Ovid's *Metamorphoses*.

Titus reads the book at the page she has turned to and informs everyone that she has located the tale of Philomel which, he then deduces, identifies rape as the "root of thine annoy." Expanding on this myth, Titus realizes that the rape took place in the woods during that fatal hunt.

Searching now for the name of the rapist, Marcus is inspired to use his staff, guided by his feet and mouth, to write his name in the sand.

He then hands the staff to Lavinia who uses her mouth and stumps to write the word "Stuprum" (rape) and the names of Chiron and Demetrius.

Marcus now joins the other Andronicus members in composing a litany of revenge, requesting Titus and young Lucius to join with him to swear that they will kill the "traitorous Goths," or die in the attempt.

Young Lucius readily learns the stance of revenge, and he cooperates with Titus' plan to carry weapons as gifts to Tamora's sons. Marcus asks the heavens to support this action of Titus and vows to do so himself as a welcome balm for the emotional scars which Titus has suffered.

In Scene 2, young Lucius meets Aaron, Chiron, and Demetrius, again at an unidentified location, to present the gift of weapons. A model of courtesy and deportment during his presentation, young Lucius lets the audience know in asides that he well knows that he is dealing with villains.

Later, Demetrius discovers a message wrapped around the weapons. He recognizes it as a verse from Horace, but only Aaron understands that the Latin inscription translates into a recognition of the boys' guilt. He decides, however, in an aside, not to inform Tamora or the boys yet. During a brief exchange, Tamora's sons gloat over what they believe to be a successful humiliation of the Andronicus family and wish for somewhere between a thousand and twenty thousand Roman women to enjoy as they enjoyed Lavinia. They all agree that Tamora would approve. Then the boys announce that they want to go off to pray for their mother, who is in labor.

At that moment, the Emperor's trumpets sound, announcing the birth of a son. The nurse arrives with the baby who is obviously Aaron's son since it is black. Tamora has sent instructions to have the baby killed. Chiron and Demetrius are shocked and angered at what Aaron has done to their mother. The boys realize that either the baby must die or their mother is ruined. Demetrius volunteers to kill the baby, but Aaron protects his infant son. He warns Tamora's sons that he will kill them if they threaten the baby's life; he instructs the nurse to inform Tamora that he will keep the son and he makes it clear that the child is more precious to him than Tamora is.

Chiron, Demetrius, and the Nurse all berate Aaron for planning to abandon Tamora and her family. Aaron curses them as cowards, making fun of their flushed pale skin while his black son exudes only calmness and smiles. Then Aaron reminds the boys that this baby is their brother.

Believing now that only Aaron can save them, the three frightened people turn to him for advice. As always, Aaron quickly concocts a plot. After learning from the Nurse how many witnesses there were to the birth, he kills her. He explains to the shocked boys that he will leave no witnesses. Aaron instructs them to go and persuade another Moor and his wife, who have a pale newborn, to give up their son in return for their promise that the baby will be raised as the Emperor's son. The boys leave with instructions to bury the Nurse, substitute the other baby, and then send the other witnesses of the birth to Aaron to be killed. Demetrius thanks Aaron for taking such good care of his mother. Aaron delivers his son to the safety of the Goths, who are to raise him as a military leader.

Scene 3 opens with Titus leading a group who bear arrows with messages at their tips. Titus instructs some to shoot the arrows into the air while Publius and Sempronius attempt to dig to the center of the earth in order to leave a message with Pluto. He identifies his motivation as the sorrows inflicted on him by Rome, and he assumes the guilt for aiding Saturninus to the throne.

Marcus and his son Publius cluck their tongues over Titus' madness, for they realize the need to carefully watch him day and night. Marcus also urges his kinsmen to revenge the loss of Titus' mind by joining the Goths in war against Rome.

Titus returns for a progress report on the trip to Hades. Publius reports that Pluto is ready to aid in revenge, but that "Justice" is unavailable. Titus is outraged by the delay and swears to hunt down "Justice" to perform her duty. He then lines up his archers to shoot their messages to all of the gods in a trajectory that will cause all the arrows to fall into the Emperor's court.

A clown enters with a basket and two pigeons. Titus calls for the messages from heaven that the birds will be carrying. The clown protests that he knows nothing of any messages from heaven and is only carrying the pigeons to the Emperor's court in order to settle a dispute. Titus convinces the poor clown to deliver a message to the Emperor.

Scene 4 features Saturninus and Tamora. Saturninus is carrying the arrows which were shot in the previous scene and is raving about the attacks by Titus. The old general's madness serves as no excuse to the enraged Emperor. Saturninus regards the appeals to the gods as libelous against Rome's machinery of justice and vows that if he lives, he'll order Titus executed.

Tamora soothes her husband's distemper but reveals in an aside that she is gloating both for her victory over the Andronicus family and for her escape from condemnation over a black baby's birth.

The hapless clown enters with Titus' letter. After reading the letter, Saturninus orders that the clown be hanged. He then orders that Titus be dragged in for execution, thinking that this will stop a subtle plot for Titus to become Emperor. But Titus is saved when Amelius dashes in with the news that Lucius has arrived with an army of Goths. Saturninus panics because Lucius is even more favored as an Emperor than is Titus. Saturninus is afraid that the citizens will revolt in order to advance Lucius to the throne.

Tamora reassures her husband by promising to enchant Titus in order to lure Lucius to his death. She sends him off to regain his good spirits, and he sends her off to initiate her plot.

## Commentary

Act IV is largely a shambles because it is a repeat of the play's original problem with a lack of focus. Consider the action covered in this act: it includes the first communication by Lavinia; messages from Titus to Tamora's sons and lover which convey their guilts; vows and acts of revenge by Lucius, young Lucius, Marcus, Saturninus, Tamora, and Titus; and, of course, Aaron's plot to save his son. Groups move on and off stage to change the hodgepodge of scenes, always with some spoken reason but with dramatically flimsy motivation.

In spite of all the activity, only three major advances in the action are achieved: Lavinia identifies her attackers, Lucius arrives with the Goth army, and Tamora initiates the arrangements for the final, fatal banquet. Aaron's baby and Titus' madness occupy a lot of time without contributing much to the plot. Most of the characters bemoan what is happening but none of them grow in character nor contribute much to the action.

As usual, character development is difficult to discover. Although Titus is described as incompetent, his conduct will soon surface as a disguise. Young Lucius changes the most, because he learns the fundamentals of revenge. Aaron maintains his evil motivation, especially in his barbaric murder to cover up for the birth of his son.

ACT V

## Summary

Lucius opens Act V with a peroration to the Goth troops, urging them to avenge Rome's recent victory over them. An unnamed Goth wants Tamora's death to be a part of the revenge. Another unnamed Goth enters with Aaron and his son in tow. He narrates the scene of discovery wherein Aaron had been trying to quiet the crying baby. Since Aaron chose to soothe his son with recriminations for being "tawny" instead of "coal-black," everyone realizes that the mother was fair.

Lucius quickly surmises that the mother is Tamora and stirs up the Goths with that news. In a rage because of Aaron's part in the cruel ruin of the Andronicus, Lucius wants to hang the infant where Aaron and the rest can observe its death throes. He orders Aaron to climb a ladder and hang the child.

Aaron suggests, instead, that Lucius save the child and bear it to Tamora in exchange for some vague, wondrous result. As an alternative, he can only conjure a curse. Lucius urges him to develop the plot; Aaron promises to reveal all the villainies if only the child is allowed to live. Aaron demands a vow from Lucius to protect the baby. Lucius asks what he can possibly swear by that Aaron would believe in. Aaron says it does not matter what he believes in because he knows Lucius to be a religious and honorable man.

Having extracted the vow, Aaron reveals that the baby is his and Tamora's, that Tamora's sons killed Bassianus, and that Tamora's sons shared the rape and mutilation of Lavinia.

While Lucius raves at the villains, Aaron rather proudly admits to being their tutor but claims that their potential was inherited from their mother. Aaron presses on with his revelations of his involvement in the various treacheries. He shocks his listeners with the recall of his delight at the incident wherein he tricked Titus into sacrificing his hand in exchange for the heads of his two executed sons, embellishing his story with laughter until his tears run as fast as Titus' tears of sorrow; he recalls also being rewarded by Tamora's "twenty kisses" for such a successful attack on the old man.

When asked if he's sorry for anything that he has done, Aaron replies: "Ay, that I had not done a thousand more." He then recites a list of other cruelties that he has enjoyed in his lifetime and expands his desire to 10,000 other uninflicted cruelties.

Lucius decides that hanging is too easy a death for such a cruel man. When Aaron fantasizes about the pleasurable eternity of being a devil to torment them all in hell, Lucius orders him gagged.

Aemilius then enters to invite Lucius and the Goth princes to a parley at Titus' home. Saturninus offers any hostages which they might demand to feel assured of their safety. Lucius waves away the hostage offer with a request that Saturninus substitute pledges to Titus and Marcus, whereupon they all march off the stage.

That clears the stage for Tamora and her two sons to change the scene to Titus' house. They enter in disguise. Tamora decides that she will identify herself as Revenge when she knocks on Titus' door. At first, Titus refuses entrance to the trio on the grounds that they will interfere with his concentrated melancholy. But when Tamora hints that knowing who she is will change his mind, Titus declares that he is not mad and knows very well that she is Tamora. She declares, however, that she is Revenge, the enemy of Tamora, so she can help torment all those who have been cruel to him. Titus deceives her by pretending to believe the story, and he identifies her sons as Rape and Murder. He challenges her, therefore, to murder them and to bring back the heads of all other murderers so that he can pledge obedience to her. Tamora counters by claiming that her two attendants are actually her *ministers*, called Rape and Murder because they wreak vengeance on those guilty of the two crimes. After marveling at the resemblance of Rape and Murder to Tamora's two sons, Titus pretends to welcome them.

During a brief time when Titus absents himself from the scene, Tamora reveals her plot to her sons. She believes that Titus is both crazy and convinced of her identity as Revenge. This seems to present the possibility that she can invite Lucius and the Goth princes to a banquet so that she can split the alliance.

Titus returns to welcome them, and he makes a few more comments about their resemblance to Tamora and her sons; then he expresses the idle wish that they could also have a black devil Moor to carry out evil schemes. When asked for orders, Titus tells them to go out and find people who look just like themselves, because these people must be murdered for their crimes.

Tamora praises the plan but asks if it wouldn't be better to wait until Lucius attended a banquet, during which she would present the Emperor and his family for revenge. Immediately, Titus calls in Marcus and instructs him to deliver the invitation. Tamora then proposes to leave with her two ministers, but Titus persuades her to leave them if she does not want the invitation to Lucius to be canceled. The deceivers are deceived by their belief in Titus' madness, so they agree to the plan.

Titus then summons Publius, Caius, and Valentine. When Publius identifies Chiron and Demetrius, Titus corrects him by saying they are Rape and Murder and must, therefore, be bound and, if necessary, gagged. Chiron protests, but both are gagged and are unable to plead when Titus returns with a knife. Lavinia appears with a basin. Titus presents Lavinia to her tormentors, summarizes their crimes, and then details what is about to happen to them. He will cut their throats, Lavinia will catch their blood in the basin, then he will cut them up, grind their bones, bake their heads in a meat pie, and serve them to their mother at the banquet. Thus, he cuts their throats, catches the blood, and then they all leave, carrying the boys into the kitchen.

Lucius then enters with Marcus, Aaron and his baby, and the Goths. He tells Marcus that he is content to be there if Titus thinks it's right, but he wants Aaron safely held for testimony against Tamora since he does not trust the Emperor.

Trumpets announce Saturninus' arrival with his attendants. Verbal sparring between Lucius and Saturninus is quieted by Marcus, who calls for them to sit down to a peaceful banquet.

But Titus has other plans. After beginning to serve the banquet, he continues the flow of blood by killing Lavinia—to release her from her suffering, he tells the shocked guests. When Saturninus is informed of the guilt of Chiron and Demetrius, he orders them to be brought to him, but he is informed by Titus that they were served at the dinner and already "daintily fed upon" by their mother. Saturninus then stabs Titus, and Lucius stabs Saturninus.

Marcus immediately initiates arbitration by begging the Romans to listen to the truth that Lucius will share. Lucius then recites the wrongs inflicted upon the Andronicus family. Marcus picks up the story by displaying the son of Aaron and Tamora, then calls upon the Romans to decide whether the remainder of the Andronicus family should kill themselves. Aemilius calls for a vote to designate Lucius as the new Emperor. An acclamation vote accomplishes that.

Marcus summons Aaron to his punishment, then joins Lucius in a reverent farewell to Titus. Young Lucius is also pushed forward to kiss his grandfather a final time. At this juncture, Aaron is presented for judgment. Lucius calls for Aaron to be buried chest-deep and starved to death, portraying an end during which Aaron will be begging for sustenance. Aaron vows that he will not say a word; furthermore, he repents only any good deed that he *might* have performed by *mistake*. Lucius then issues orders for the disposal of the bodies, and the play ends with the mass exit of the survivors.

## Commentary

Act V's bloody climax probably saves the performance. After the restlessness of Acts III and IV, the audience experiences a series of tense, shocking scenes.

The action climaxes in a blood bath in the name of revenge. However, Titus behaves like a pathological killer with his pig-sticking approach to killing Chiron and Demetrius in order to serve them in a cannibalistic pie at the banquet, not to mention summarily murdering his own daughter. The structural weakness of the plot then disintegrates into a morass of verbal maneuvering to put a rightful ruler in place, a situation soothing to Elizabethans but unappreciated today.

The weakness has been present since the beginning of the play; the two opposing forces which must be in conflict in order to create a plot are never clearly identified. In Act V, some of the conflicts are the Andronicus family vs. Saturninus, the Andronicus family vs. Tamora and sons, the Goths vs. Tamora, the Goths vs. the Romans, and Titus vs. Nature (madness).

Aaron is still pitted against the world at large but more as character motivation than plot action. He remains the strongest character to the very end, surely stealing the final scene from Lucius by manipulating his sentence to a horrible death into another show of strength. And, of course, he manages to save his son's life in spite of all the people who were determined to kill the infant.

Shakespeare provides Aaron with a total physical domination during Act V, Scene 1. While Lucius appears to dominate Aaron through capture and the planned executions of father and son, Aaron is perched on a ladder (thus physically dominating the stage) and is provided with shocking, single-action dialogue (thus verbally dominating the scene). One must conclude that Shakespeare favored this character from beginning to end and probably should have written the play about him instead of Titus.

One other point of interest about Act V is the injection of the Morality Interlude. Since the disguise of Tamora and her sons were totally ineffective and the appearance of Revenge had little to do with advancing the plot, the scene is probably there as a result of the playwright's shrewd ability to give everybody in the audience something that they wanted to see. And the important thing to remember after all the negative comments about *Titus Andronicus* is that it was probably a popular play.

1594

# king John

# INTRODUCTION

*King John*, like *Titus Andronicus*, is an early play of Shakespeare's. But unlike *Titus*, the greatest controversy about *John* involves the date of composition, not the authorship. So complicated is the controversy about the date that the only safe assumption we can make is that the play was written about 1594. Strong arguments support dates ranging from 1590 through 1598.

Besides its general classification as being one of Shakespeare's early plays, *King John* is specifically one of his early *history* plays. Because of his production of history plays over a span of fifteen years (1589-1604), Shakespeare is credited with the development of the history play as a separate genre of drama.

All of Shakespeare's history plays were more concerned with arousing patriotic spirit than with adhering to historical accuracy. Sources for *King John* probably did not adhere to historical accuracy either. But there is even more controversy about whether or not any sources were used at all and, if there were any, what they might be. A list of probable source material would include both *The Troublesome Reign of King John,* published in 1591, and Holinshed's *Chronicles,* one of Shakespeare's favorite sources. (Some critics think that the extreme length of *Troublesome Reign,* if Shakespeare did use this, accounts for *John's* gradual weakening at the end; a hardworking, industrious Shakespeare simply grew too weary or too pressed for time to continue the dramatization near the play's end.) A list of possible sources would include John Foxe's *Acts and Monuments* as perhaps providing religious influence. And of possible interest to Shakespeare, one might note the *Wakefield Chronicle,* a Latin manuscript with some details of historical references which appear at times in the play.

But to comprehend *King John* properly, two of the most important views to explore are the Elizabethan concept of the order of the universe and the historical influence of the War of the Roses. Even a slight acquaintance with these views can help with the understanding of some points of view in *King John.*

For a well-structured explanation of the order of the universe, see E. M. W. Tillyard's *The Elizabethan World Picture.* One image used to represent this view of order is the great Chain of Being. In this Chain, each link represents some thing in Creation. All things are linked, beginning with the foot of God's throne and ending with the humblest inanimate object. Together, they form a unity of the universe with an order determined by God. The top three links represent God, the angels, and then man. But high as they are on the Chain, the angels and man are not intended to regulate or alter the order. Instead, the order of the heavens is supposed to be duplicated on earth. Part of this doctrine of noninterference decreed that a king, however poorly he might rule, should not be deposed unless he actually forced the breaking of at least one of God's commandments. This concept is a key to the actions and points of view of the characters in *King John*.

But this ordered structure of the universe has its exceptions. One method of accounting for these exceptions is that God granted the power of free will to angels and men. This free will can be used incorrectly to the detriment of the orderly maintenance of the universe. Another is that fate is conceived of as uncertain and is subject to disorders in the universe. The phenomena of these disorders is often represented by the wheel of fortune and horoscopes and activities of the stars. The turning wheel and the moving stars to some extent rule man's existence, with man frequently a helpless participant. But free will could challenge fortune, if either an angel or a man were willing to risk punishment by exercising it to challenge the universe's operation.

This orderly universe, however, was not the point of view of the Christian Humanists, who did not see morality as a black and white issue. Instead, they measured human behavior against an indistinct gray standard of behavior. Within the context of this humanistic morality, where conduct was measured by the application of conscience, one should pay special attention to the Bastard's evaluation of his mother's illicit relationship with Richard the Lion-hearted. In that scene and in his general point of view, Shakespeare seemed to be more aligned with Christian Humanism than with any other philosophy. Most often, we do not find a total approval or disapproval of any character but, rather, a view that measures humanity against the lessons of conduct which are outlined in the *Elizabethan Homilies*.

While trying to understand the characters in *King John* by using either the idea of a strictly ordered universe or a fluid Christian Humanism, one must remember that, on the whole, Elizabethans showed an optimistic interest in all people, places, and things in contrast with both modern pessimism and medieval grim endurance.

Fears that may be linked to dissatisfaction with a disorderly universe certainly can be linked to the instability of a chaotic government to explain the importance of the Wars of the Roses to the comprehension of *King John*. The Wars of the Roses encompassed about one century, during which England was agonized by a vicious civil war. Although the action of

*King John* takes place prior to the actual war, the events are regarded as an early thirteenth-century indicator of the horrors to come.

The Wars of the Roses involved the heirs and descendants of Edward III, who assumed the throne in 1327. It involved two opposing "houses" which are both traceable to sons of Edward III. The House of Lancaster (represented by a Red Rose) is linked to his third son, John of Gaunt, Duke of Lancaster. The House of York (represented by the White Rose) is traced through his fourth son, Edmund, Duke of York. Counting Richard II, a grandson of Edward III and legitimate heir to the throne, eleven members of the royal family alone were killed or murdered between 1400 and 1483. These ghastly, bloody years of intrigue and kingmaking ended when Henry Tudor, the last of the Lancasters, won a battle at Bosworth Field. Fighting against great odds, Henry defeated the larger, royal York army. Richard III was killed in this battle. Afterwards, Henry VII achieved an alliance with the House of York by marrying Elizabeth of York, thus finally reuniting the warring families.

Henry VII was barely royalty material, for he was the grandson of a commoner, Owen Tudor, who married Katharine of France, the widow of Henry V. But he was sufficiently politically skillful, and so he was able to hold his throne against all opposition. His son, Henry VIII, was the father of Elizabeth I, Queen of England when Shakespeare wrote *King John*. So, Tudor sensitivity to legitimacy to the throne had to be protected, and Shakespeare, politically astute, knew this.

Also important to a conflict in *King John* is Henry VIII's struggle against the Church of Rome during his attempt to divorce Catherine of Aragon. Without accepting a king's sovereignty as superior to the Pope's, Queen Elizabeth would have to be regarded as an illegitimate offspring of Henry VIII.

With this Tudor heritage as part of Shakespeare's society, the contemporary attitude as to whether or not John deserves to lose his monarchy or his life, as well as our attitude toward John's usurpation of the throne, is not as important as his defective title. Thus, the Bastard's decision to remain loyal in order to try to correct the attitude of a wayward king is a correct decision for the time. Shakespeare carefully supports this point of view by rewarding all of English society who remain loyal to King John and loyal also to Prince Henry, John's son.

Historically, this Prince Henry became Henry III, who ruled prior to Edward III. Nevertheless, the point of view of the play clearly refers to the horrors of civil war which were learned during the Wars of the Roses and were part of the lessons learned by the audiences of Shakespeare's time.

Altogether, the play mixes historical accuracy with Elizabethan beliefs and does not pretend to be an accurate documentary of the reign of King John.

## A BRIEF SYNOPSIS

Appealing to the Elizabethan horror of war, this play opens with Chatillon, the ambassador from France, claiming England and all her territories in the name of Arthur, and threatening war as the only option. John stands firm as representative of England's right to remain a separate nation. He honorably orders an escort for Chatillon to carry his answer to Philip, King of France.

Eleanor, King John's mother, hisses that he might have thwarted the worldly ambitions of Constance (Arthur's mother) "with easy arguments of love," and she urges John to maintain the strength of his operative possession of rule—or else risk his relationship with her.

Suddenly a strange controversy occurs between Philip and Robert Faulconbridge. Philip implies that he and his brother Robert may not share the same paternal heritage. (Phillip is referred to throughout the play as the Bastard). Eleanor chides the Bastard for shaming his mother. The Bastard corrects her by stating that is *Robert's* claim, unappealing to him (Philip) because if it's true, he is out of his inheritance.

However, the Bastard points out that his looks are much superior to Robert's, and he is, therefore, thankful that he does not look like old Sir Robert. Eleanor thinks, and John agrees, that the Bastard does indeed resemble her deceased son Richard, Richard the Lion-hearted.

Robert then presents facts which lead them all to conclude that the Bastard was, indeed, fathered by the former king. However, King John rules that old Sir Robert raised Philip as an heir, and that Sir Robert's will was too late in the chain of events to disinherit Philip.

Eleanor then intrigues the Bastard with the choice of remaining the heir of Faulconbridge or claiming his place as a bastard son in the royal family. Philip accepts her offer to become a member of the royal family, and he promises to fight in France. King John then renames Philip Sir Richard, and Philip arises as a spirited Plantagenet. (But he is still referred to as the Bastard throughout the remainder of the play.) Afterward, they all send Robert off to enjoy his inheritance, and Eleanor and King John hastily exit to pack for France.

Philip lingers to explore the social implications of his new identity, and Lady Faulconbridge interrupts him to demand the whereabouts of her son Robert, who has publicly besmirched her honor.

The Bastard frankly confronts his mother with his physical dissimilarity from her husband and requests the identity of his real father. After blustering about her honor and learning of the voluntary disinheritance, Lady Faulconbridge admits that King Richard Coeur-de-Lion was his father. The Bastard graciously supports her inability to resist the king's advances and thanks her for providing him with such a fine father. She then takes him to meet his new royal relatives.

The next scene is set in Angiers, during a conference with King Philip, Lewis the Dauphin, the Duke of Austria, Constance (Arthur's mother), and Arthur. Philip, Lewis, and the Duke of Austria declare their loyalty to the cause of the maturely gracious Arthur. Philip calls for battle in order to deliver Angiers to Arthur, but Constance cautions him to await the response of King John via Chatillon, who, coincidentally, arrives at that moment. The messenger brings bad news: not only did the negotiations fail but, due to winds which delayed him but sped the English ships, the British troops have already landed to fight against Arthur and his allies. Furthermore, these British soldiers are of "uncommon quality."

King Philip seems unsettled by this turn of events, but the Duke of Austria declares that they are ready for battle. King John enters then with a parley group to offer peace if Arthur's cause is retired. King Philip argues that peace can be effected only if the right to rule England is returned to the rightful heir—Arthur, the son of Geoffrey, John's older brother.

Constance and Eleanor enter the verbal battle. Eleanor declares that Arthur is a bastard, *not* Geoffrey's son. Constance retorts that Arthur is the image of Geoffrey, as could be expected of such a faithful wife as she.

The Bastard enters and adds to the blustering while King Philip tries to direct the parleying to a settlement on his terms. King John flatly rejects these terms, but he and Eleanor offer terms to Arthur which are similar to the ones which the Bastard accepted. Constance caustically rejects them, Arthur cries, and the conference disintegrates into a family squabble.

The citizens of Angiers are confronted for a pledge of loyalty from both the King of France, representing Arthur, and the King of England, representing himself. A citizen responds to the dilemma by declaring that they will pledge their loyalty to whoever proves to be *the* king but, until then, they will keep their gates barred. The two kings respond by ordering their armies to battle.

Messengers and then the kings themselves reappear to declare victory for the off-stage battle. The representative citizen of Angiers, unimpressed by the verbiage, keeps them locked out until they can produce a clear-cut victory.

The kings then agree to join forces long enough to destroy the arrogant citizen of Angiers. At this point, the Bastard realizes that he can maneuver the Austrians and the French into directing their fire at each other. Continuing the spirit of cooperation, a citizen of Angiers suggests a compromise—a marriage between Lewis the Dauphin (of France) and Lady Blanch (King John's niece). The union would give Angiers an option to surrender to the united families. All but the Bastard favor this solution.

Constance opens Act III in a fury at the betrayal of her cause. Frightened but proud, she refuses to obey the royal summons to appear before the new allies. They join for a conference on the day of the marriage, but Constance continues to oppose the new alliance, and the Bastard continues to bait the King of Austria.

Pandulph, the Pope's legate, arrives to demand that King John allow the Royal Catholic authority to prevail in England, and King Philip is shocked by England's *absolute denial* of the Pope's authority. Therefore, upon threat of excommunication, he withdraws from the alliance with England. Lewis, meanwhile, urges war in spite of the pleas of Blanch (King John's niece) not to betray his ties to her and her family.

Dramatizing England's initial success in battle, the Bastard displays the head of the Duke of Austria. King John enters to deliver Arthur to the care of Hubert and to deliver instructions to the Bastard to return to England to obtain war funds from Church coffers. In spite of assurances of love and protection to Arthur, King John later commands Hubert to kill the boy.

King Philip, meanwhile, bemoans England's victories. He is assailed by Pandulph's assurances of heavenly rewards and Constance's hysterical grief over the loss of Arthur. After Philip follows Constance to prevent possible suicide, Lewis expresses his own despondency to Pandulph. Pandulph "predicts" that if Lewis is ready at the proper time, the English will revolt when King John kills Arthur; thus Lewis can claim the throne because of his marriage to Blanch.

Reluctantly carrying out his order from King John, Hubert makes the arrangements for blinding and killing Arthur. But Pandulph's prediction and King John's command are displaced by young Arthur's appeals to Hubert, who decides to hide and protect the boy.

Meanwhile, King John perches precariously on his reclaimed throne. Pembroke urges the release of Arthur and expresses his fear that Hubert has killed the boy. When his fears are confirmed by King John, he and Salisbury fear the consequences, and their fears unsettle the king. He is further shocked by the news that a large French army has landed and that his mother is dead. Thus, in a panic, John dispatches the Bastard to lure Bigot and Salisbury back for a chance to regain their loyalty.

King John then castigates Hubert for carrying out the order to kill Arthur. Hubert retorts that he disobeyed the order, and that Arthur is alive. The king apologizes.

Arthur, however, tries to escape and kills himself when he leaps from a tower. The Bastard, Salisbury, Bigot, and Pembroke discover the body, thus shattering King John's hope to reclaim their loyalty. When Hubert shows up to fetch Arthur, he has to defend himself against Salisbury's attack.

Salisbury, Bigot, and Pembroke defect to the Dauphin's invasion force, and the Bastard and Hubert are left to carry Arthur away and to try to resolve the problems he created with his impetuous leap.

The final act opens with King John submitting to the Pope's authority.

Pandulph then promises to end the conflict which he, Pandulph, began. All of John's potential support has joined the Dauphin and, with Arthur dead, John has no choice if he wants to remain King of England.

Lewis flatly refuses Pandulph's order to end the hostilities. He also refuses the Bastard's rhetorical ploys to avoid battle. Just when the English cause looks bleakest, because King John is extremely ill and battles are being lost, news of the sinking of the Dauphin's supply ships injects hope. King John withdraws to recuperate at Swinstead Abbey.

In the next scene, Salisbury, Pembroke, and Bigot share their doubts about a possible victory against the Bastard's effective defense. The dying Count Melun unburdens his soul by struggling to them and informing them that many of the rebellious English nobility have re-pledged their loyalty to England. Motivated by Melun's information and advice, the three rebels exit to provide Melun with a quiet place to die and a place where they can save their own necks.

Bad news prevails in the next few scenes. Lewis, weary from a near-victory in that day's battle, learns about the loss of his supplies and the loss of English allies. Hubert bears the English bad news to the Bastard: King John has been poisoned by a monk.

In the end, England prevails. Lewis is ready to negotiate peace, King John is dying, and the heir-apparent, Prince Henry, gratefully receives pledges of unity and loyalty for the greater good of a united, independent England.

# LIST OF CHARACTERS

### King John

King of England because of his mother's maneuvering after the death of her elder son, Geoffrey. His claim to the throne, and thus England's security, is vulnerable. His two best characteristics in the play are his loyalty to England and his defiance of the Pope.

### Prince Henry

The son of King John; heir-apparent to the throne if his father successfully defends their line of succession. His only role in the play is as a unifying factor at the end.

### Arthur

Duke of Britain, young boy who is the nephew of King John. As the pre-teen son of the previous king, he is the natural successor to the throne. As long as he is alive, he is a tempting rallying cause for civil war.

### The Earl of Pembroke, The Earl of Salisbury, and The Lord Bigot

Three powerful members of English nobility who waver from loyalty to King John, to rebellion after Arthur's death, to loyalty to Prince Henry.

### The Earl of Essex

A member of King John's court.

### Hubert de Burgh

A trusted henchman of King John. He remains loyal to all orders of the king–except for the blinding and killing of Arthur.

### Philip the Bastard

Raised as the elder son of Sir Robert Faulconbridge, he accepts the conclusion that he is actually the illegitimate son of the deceased King Richard Coeur-de-Lion and then assumes an important role as a member of the ruling family.

### Robert Faulconbridge

Apparently, the only son of Sir Robert Faulconbridge.

### James Gurney

A servant to Lady Faulconbridge.

### Peter of Pomfret

A minor character who plays the role of a prophet.

### Philip

The King of France. He first supports Arthur against King John, then interjects religion into the controversy and abandons Arthur's cause.

### Lewis

The Dauphin of France, son of Philip. He marries Blanch, niece of King John, apparently achieving a union between France and England. He becomes the aggressor in a war against England when he is encouraged by Pandulph to take advantage of the weakness caused by King John's errors in judgment in controversies with the Pope and with Arthur.

### Lymoges

The Duke of Austria. When the play begins, he is an ally of France, in support of Arthur's cause. He is defeated and beheaded by the Bastard.

### Cardinal Pandulph

The legate of the Pope. He destroys Arthur's cause by instigating a religious war. Eventually, he helps arbitrate peace between England and France after France's forces are defeated in England.

### Melun

A French lord who helps to convince rebel English lords to save their necks by abandoning their brief alliance with Lewis the Dauphin against King John.

### Chatillon

A French ambassador. He tries to negotiate King John's surrender to Arthur's allies at the opening of the play.

### Queen Eleanor

Mother of King John and the deceased Richard and Geoffrey. She uses her son John to continue her role as the power behind the throne.

### Constance

Arthur's ambitious mother.

### Blanch of Spain

Eleanor's niece. Because of her agreement to marry Lewis the Dauphin, she briefly serves an important role in an alliance between France and England.

### Lady Faulconbridge

Mother of Robert Faulconbridge and Philip the Bastard.

## SUMMARIES AND COMMENTARIES

ACT I

### Summary

Chatillon opens the action by beating diplomatic war drums. Speaking for the King of France, who is acting on behalf of Arthur Plantagenet, he claims England and other specific territories. If John refuses to willingly relinquish his title to Arthur, France is prepared to enforce Arthur's rights through war.

King John listens to the entire presentation, then responds that he is ready for war. He then provides Chatillon with safe passage but warns him that he must hurry to warn King Philip before England's attack.

Eleanor scolds her son for not heeding her warnings about the ambitions of Constance, Arthur's mother. When John blusters that the throne is his because of the power of both possession and right, his mother admits that he possesses it, but that he possesses it by power *only*—he did not rightfully inherit the throne of England.

Essex interrupts their conversation and says that he would like to introduce the Faulconbridge brothers. King John barely has time to decide to levy taxes against the Church (to pay for war expenses) before he patiently agrees to attend to the controversy about the Faulconbridge inheritance.

Philip introduces himself as the eldest son of Sir Robert Faulconbridge, a soldier who was knighted by Coeur-de-Lion. Robert introduces himself as the son and heir of Sir Robert Faulconbridge.

King John questions the authenticity of the mixed claims to the Faulconbridge title. The major question raised by Robert is whether or not his father is also Philip's. Technically, King John rules that Philip is the heir because old Sir Robert raised him as a son, thus legitimatizing Philip; the evidence, however, indicates that Philip is illegitimate. The claim that Robert, on his death bed, dispossessed Philip as illegitimate falls too late in the chain of events, according to John.

However, concerning the evidence that Richard Coeur-de-Lion visited Lady Faulconbridge while old Sir Robert was out of the country on court business and that Philip unquestionably resembles Richard, King John determines that Philip is probably his own illegitimate nephew. Eleanor then offers the Bastard the opportunity to claim his rights as a son of Coeur-de-Lion. When the Bastard declares that that offer is better than his decision to insist that he belong to the inferior Faulconbridge line, Eleanor praises his attitude and urges him to join the English cause against the French campaign.

Philip then renounces his claim to the Faulconbridge fortune and assumes his place as an illegitimate son of Coeur-de-Lion. King John presides at a hasty ceremony for the purpose of re-naming Philip as Sir Richard. The new Sir Richard enthusiastically embraces his identity as a Plantagenet; however, he is referred to throughout the play as the Bastard.

As the Bastard is savoring and adjusting to his new social status, his mother bursts in to demand an explanation for the public shame foisted upon her by her two sons. The Bastard convinces her to name his real father, who is, indeed, Richard Coeur-de-Lion. He assures her that she should not be blamed for succumbing to seduction by a king, and he thanks her for providing so fine a father. He then escorts his mother to meet his new relatives while assuring her that no one could behold his fine physique and declare her act a sin—without risking being killed by the Bastard.

## Commentary

Conflict dominates this play from its opening lines. When Chatillon challenges King John in the name of King Philip, he introduces a number of conflicts: national unity vs. civil war, English sovereignty vs. the Church of Rome, York vs. Lancaster, stability vs. ambition, and world order vs. chaos. Unfortunately, the conflicts are not carefully controlled, and so a central weakness of the play must be identified as Shakespeare's failure to establish a dominant conflict with clever counterpointing of subplots. A component of *all* the conflicts which develop through characterization, however, is honor. Characterizations of honor include esteem and respect, good reputations, integrity, purity, and social courtesy.

For instance, when John's honor as a rightful king is challenged, his next scene involves an honorable resolution of the Faulconbridge dispute. He patiently unravels the legal and moral implications to reach a measured verdict in the dispute that, in itself, involves reputation, integrity, and the purity of Lady Faulconbridge. This scene is followed by the Bastard's soliloquy regarding the social courtesies which are attached to his new station in life. This sequence on honor ends with Lady Faulconbridge's outrage about the attacks on *her* honor.

Before this act ends, King John's character has been established as a patriotic king who is conscientious about his responsibilities. But *his* flaw has also been established: he maintains a willful hold on the crown in spite of the *legitimate* claim of Arthur.

The Bastard is emerging early in the play as a strong individualist. His sense of honor and patriotism are just beginning to manifest themselves as he tests the meaning of his new relationship to the royal family. He does not cling to his Faulconbridge ties when he is given the opportunity to claim his rights as a royal bastard. Nor does he castigate his mother for her illicit liaison with the king, but, instead, he chooses to reinforce her sense of honor.

## ACT II

## Summary

King Philip takes charge of introducing the allies who have gathered just outside the gates of Angiers. He explains to Arthur that the Duke of Austria has volunteered to support Arthur's cause in order to make amends for killing Richard the Lion-hearted, Arthur's late uncle. Since this death allowed King John's usurpation of the English throne, King Philip explains that the Duke of Austria feels obligated to aid the correct realignment of Richard's posterity.

Arthur extends an innocent, loving welcome and graciously declares that God will forgive his uncle's death in return for Austria's defense of the rights of the young Coeur-de-Lion who has been wronged by John. Austria vows that he will not return home until Arthur is established with his rightful powers. Constance joins in the thanks and implies a more substanial reward once Arthur is king. Austria then aligns the cause with heavenly peace and justified war.

King Philip wants to attack Angiers immediately in order to initiate Arthur's territorial claims, but Constance wants to wait for Chatillon in case King John has peacefully relinquished the throne. She wants no unnecessary bloodshed.

Just as Constance finishes her request, Chatillon enters with the advice to forego the siege of Angiers in order to prepare for an attack from England. He explains that adverse winds delayed his passage but those same winds speeded up the English army's advance, so an attack by a strong English army is imminent. Finally, Chatillon describes the royal English party as consisting of King John, the Queen Mother (whom he implies acts as an inciter of vengeance), Lady Blanch of Spain, and the Bastard. When the army's drums portend the arrival of the English army, Chatillon ends his report with the advice to prepare either to parley or to fight.

King Philip seems unprepared for the expedition, and so Austria urges the quick preparation of a defense, for which he thinks they are well-prepared. Before either can act, however, King John enters with his parley party to demand surrender from France—or else do battle with England. He declares his action to be justified by an agent of God.

King Philip responds by bidding peace to England, which he claims he loves and represents in the cause of the rightful King of England—Arthur. He cites the natural succession from John's deceased elder brother, Geoffrey, to Geoffrey's son, Arthur. Thus, King Philip concludes that Arthur's cause fits God's plan, *not* John's *unnatural* succession.

King John questions King Philip's right to usurp authority and declare himself to be Arthur's guardian and champion. Eleanor and Constance then clash. Constance calls John a usurper, and Eleanor calls Arthur a bastard. Constance retorts that Arthur emotionally and physically resembles his father as much as John resembles Eleanor in behavior, and she further implies that *Geoffrey* is more likely to be a bastard, considering the moral inconsistency of Eleanor. After they mutually criticize each other to the hapless Arthur, Austria calls for quiet, and the Bastard concurs. Austria demands identification of the Bastard, who responds by threatening Austria for his wrongs against Richard Coeur-de-Lion. Both Blanch and the Bastard refer to Richard's lion's robe, which Austria is wearing.

King Philip impatiently orders the "women and fools" to keep quiet; then he asks King John if John will peacefully relinquish England, Ireland, Angiers, Touraine, and Maine. King John defies France, declaring that he would rather die. He then attempts to seduce Arthur's loyalty with offers of love and rewards. Eleanor urges the boy to come to his grandmother. After Constance caustically comments that if Arthur gives up his kingdom to his grandmother, he will be rewarded with "a plum, a cherry, and a fig," Arthur cries out that he wishes he were dead instead of in the middle of this "coil." Whereupon, Eleanor and Constance castigate each other for shaming the boy. This time, King John demands quiet. Constance adds that Arthur is being punished for Eleanor's sin, and Eleanor retorts that she can produce a will that bars any rights that Arthur might now claim.

Again, King Philip orders the two women to be quiet, and he quickly calls for a summons to the men of Angiers to choose between Arthur and John. A citizen appears and inquires who has summoned him.

King John quickly responds; he says that England calls its "loving subjects"; King Philip interrupts to call them "Arthur's subjects." King John interrupts Philip to point out that French cannons are aimed at the walls of Angiers, and that the British army is there to protect Angiers; therefore, he requests entrance to the city in order to rest. King Philip follows with the reasonable explanation that he is there on behalf of their rightful ruler, Arthur, and he requests only Angiers's acknowledgment of that fact; otherwise he'll attack.

The citizen of Angiers diplomatically declares that his fellow citizens are loyal subjects of the King of England, but that they have barred their gates until one of the two men proves clear title. Whereupon, the two kings prepare to battle. The Bastard insults Austria, continuing his own personal vendetta.

Heralds of both kings return to Angiers to report bloody battles and claim victory. The citizen of Angiers observes that the battles have been worthy, but that they did not determine who could enter the city. The two kings verbally joust about imminent victory.

The Bastard persuades King John and then King Philip to combine armies against Angiers. His plan is to punish peevish Angiers for defying them, then to battle afterward for the right to rule the conquered city. King John chooses to attack from the West, Austria from the North, and King Philip from the South. The Bastard gleefully realizes that he can manipulate Austria and France into damaging each other by firing artillery into each other's opposite positions.

However, the citizen of Angiers suggests another compromise in order to save his city. Step by step, he leads the kings to consider a match between Lady Blanch of Spain, who is a blood relative of the Coeur-de-Lion, and Lewis, son of the King of France. Blanch's qualities include beauty, virtue, and bloodlines. Each can benefit from the wholeness which marriage provides for them as unfulfilled single people. Furthermore, for the marriage, the gates of Angiers will be unbarred; without it, Angiers will mount a stiff resistance.

The Bastard sullenly mutters that Angiers mounts barrages of words without any force to back their challenge to choose to recognize this proposed marriage or else be prepared to fight a bloody battle. At this point, Eleanor urges King John to grasp this opportunity to prevent King Philip's pursuit of Arthur's cause and thus secure the throne of England.

The citizen of Angiers urges a response from the separately conferring parties. King Philip wants England to speak first because King John had opened the demands for Angiers to choose between them. King John responds by offering a dowry for Lady Blanch "equal with a queen." King Philip then asks Lewis for his reaction. The young prince gazes into Blanch's eyes and declares himself in love.

The Bastard mutters cynicisms about the love match. Lady Blanch promises to do as her uncle wishes and, while stopping short of declarations of love, she does emphasize that she sees nothing in Lewis to hate. After Blanch confirms her willingness to marry, and Lewis confirms his love, King John offers a dowry of the provinces of Volquessen, Touraine, Maine, Poictiers, and Anjou plus "30,000 marks of English coin" to King Philip. The French king accepts the offer and the young couple seals the bethrothal with a kiss.

King Philip tells the citizens of Angiers to open the city gates for the imminent wedding. He then uneasily asks where Constance is, anticipating her disappointment about the arrangements. He asks King John for advice about how to handle the withdrawal. King John thinks that he can assuage Constance with an offer to elevate Arthur's current title to Duke of Bretagne and Earl of Richmond; then the citizens of Angiers will turn their city over to him. Both kings obviously hope to prevent another tirade from Constance.

The Bastard declares his contempt for the "Mad world! mad Kings! mad composition!" Besides recognizing that King John offered an unnecessary compromise by giving Arthur part of John's kingdom and that King Philip betrayed an honorable cause, the Bastard recognizes that he himself has not benefited from the rules of "commodity" which he has just learned. A fast learner, however, he now pledges his loyalty to the personal benefits which will accompany his commitment to dealing in the rules of trade.

## Commentary

Words engulf action in this long, potentially tedious act. Although conflicts seem to abound, the dialogue serves mostly as narrative.

For example, the citizen of Angiers opposes the warring factions and, at one point, he incites the action of battle. However, the battle takes place offstage with its high points narrated for the benefit of the audience; it resolves nothing. That leaves the audience with nothing but the verbal confrontation and, thus, we have little that is dramatic. The Bastard, who agitates for action to settle a conflict, any conflict, aptly summarizes this dialogue between Angiers and the kings when he blurts out: "Here's a large mouth, indeed,/ that spits forth death and mountains, rocks and seas," and he disgustedly summarizes the situation: "Zounds! I was never so be-thumped with words/ Since I first called my brother's father dad."

The war of words between Constance and Eleanor is vicious enough to make a boy (Arthur) cry and unsettle two kings, but it does not move the action forward. This is proven by the fact that when the combined efforts of the kings quiet the two women, nothing has changed. The only place in which it is dramatically effective is in Arthur's case; he is well characterized as a hapless pawn, for he is on-stage and yet separated from all the parleys which will determine his sad fate.

Even the Bastard's conflict with Austria serves only as a belated exposition of the untimely death of Richard the Lion-hearted. This untimely death is verbally structured as the fulcrum of the unbalancing of the Coeur-de-Lion's succession to power and, thus, the cause of the current conflict between King John's and Arthur's supporters.

No single, dominant conflict emerges. Like Act I, this act meanders without a clear focus. Honor, however, appears again as a central factor in characterization. Austria cites his obligation to Arthur, because of his fatal wounding of Richard, albeit in battle, which disrupted the boy's future. Arthur is characterized as innocent and virtuous. Eleanor and Constance scrap over continence and legitimacy. At the opening of the act, Arthur's allies declaim their "just cause" and vow to fight until they win back Arthur's rights by defeating all the forces that John can muster because of his "unnatural succession." However, by the end of the act, the Bastard shares with us the lesson which he has learned.

> Commodity, the bias of the world;
> The world, who of itself is peised well,
> Made to run upon even ground,
> Till this advantage, this vile-drawing bias,
> This sway of motion, this Commodity,
> Makes it take head from all indifferency,
> From all direction, purpose, course, intent.

Honor has been engulfed by greed.

The Bastard admits his envy of the kings' lure by "commodity," while he himself has not had the opportunity to choose. As a "beggar," he condemns the vices of the rich, but he looks forward to the time when he can be rich and condemn the vices of beggars. Impressed by the power of "commodity," he vows to worship "gain." The lure of profit is thus added to his original thrill at the sudden power and possession of a title.

In this act, King John succumbs to his flaw—his willful hold on the crown in spite of the legitimate claim of Arthur. Instead of remaining conscientious about his responsibilities, however, he gives away large portions of English territory, hoping to shore up his crumbling powers.

## ACT III

### Summary

Constance opens the act by summarily rejecting a report of the betrayal of Arthur's cause: "Gone to be married! Gone to swear a peace!/ False blood to false blood joined! Gone to be friends!" She flatly states that she will not accept the hapless messenger's report of the marriage alliance nor the king's gift of provinces since the messenger is a "common man," and she has "a king's oath to the contrary." She threatens the messenger with punishment for alarming her during her vulnerable state. After a series of descriptions of the physical actions of the messenger, who uses body language to support his words, she demands that he speak once more—and then only to confirm the truth of his report.

The messenger, who is Salisbury, does so. Constance, who well understands the implication of the destruction, condemns Salisbury for bringing such a message. Salisbury, trapped by the ill fate that comes to the bearer of bad news, tries to separate his report from his responsibility of the events, but Constance refuses to accept that logic.

Arthur begs his mother to "be content." Constance proclaims that if only he had not been so obviously fit to rule, she would be content, but Arthur is in every way so obviously a potential king. She condemns Fortune for whoring with King John and King Philip, and then orders Salisbury to go berate the two kings and tell them they must come to her. Salisbury protests that he cannot approach them unless she accompanies him, but finally he goes, in spite of his doubts.

The kings appear then, accompanied by others in the wedding party. King Philip proclaims the wedding day to be a "blessed day"; Constance contradicts that it is a "wicked day." King Philip protests that she has no cause to complain because he has pledged his "majesty" to her; Constance counters that his majesty is "counterfeit."

Constance indulges in a general expression of outrages which culminates in an insult to Austria. When Austria brags about what he would do if a *man* said that, the Bastard twice repeats the insult. King John interjects that he disapproves of the Bastard's speaking out of turn.

The entrance of the Pope's legate, Pandulph, interrupts the squabble. He demands to know why King John has interfered with the Pope's appointee as Archbishop of Canterbury. King John responds by denying the power of a mere Pope over the King of England. Speaking for all of

England, the King states that "no Italian priest" can usurp a power over English dominion which is held by heaven alone.

King Philip gasps that this is blasphemy. King John stoutly holds that although all other Christian kings may pay homage to "this meddling priest," *he* opposes the Pope.

Pandulph immediately declares John to be cursed and excommunicated, and he offers blessings to all who revolt against John's rule. He also offers sainthood to anyone who kills John. Constance weaves an alliance with Pandulph, although the Cardinal seems reluctant to admit the similarity of their complaints against King John. Pandulph then orders King Philip to break his alliance with England if John refuses to swear allegiance to Rome. King Philip, for a moment, is unable to act while advice is heaped upon him, with Eleanor, John, and Blanch urging the maintenance of the marital alliance while Austria, Constance, and Lewis urge Philip to forego his pledge to England in order to avoid being cursed as a heretic. King Philip appeals to Pandulph for some gentle compromise to release him from his dilemma, for he is caught between betraying an order of the Pope or betraying the vows of the marriage alliance.

But Pandulph offers no relief. Instead, he demands that King Philip either actively battle England in the name of the Church or expect a curse from the Church. He attacks King Philip's conflict with his conscience by arguing that Philip's vows to the Church take precedence over all other vows. Between Lewis' additional pressure and Pandulph's renewed threat of a curse, Philip succumbs and severs his alliance with England.

After another round of pro and con opinions, France and England prepare to battle. Scene 2 is composed entirely of a brief meeting between King John, Hubert, Arthur, and the Bastard, during which Hubert receives custody of Arthur, and the Bastard assures King John that Eleanor is safe. Scene 3 features a disintegration of the English defenses and of King John's good judgment. King John falsely assures Eleanor that she will be safe if she stays where he is leaving her, and he assures Arthur that *he* will be safe, for he will be under royal protection. King John then dispatches the Bastard to precede them to England, where the Bastard is to amass funds for the war by raiding Church properties. The Bastard declares that "bell, book, and candle" (excommunication) shall not be a defense against his opportunity to amass valuables and money; then he exits to carry out his assignment.

While Eleanor takes Arthur aside to try to calm him, King John woos Hubert's loyalty with praise and vague promises in order to persuade him to kill Arthur. All exit then toward their separate destinies – Eleanor to her guarded sanctuary and spy post, Arthur and Hubert to England, and John with the bulk of the army to Calais.

Scene 4 focuses on King Philip's gloom over France's setbacks. The

French armada has been scattered, Angiers lost, Arthur captured, and the English forces have successfully embarked for England after fortifying all captured territories. The French king cannot tolerate either Constance's remonstrances nor Lewis' assurances that all will eventually go well.

After Constance indulges in grief, Pandulph retorts that she is mad, not grief-stricken. Constance verifies that she *can* distinguish reality, and that it is reality that has driven her to consider suicide rather than to exist with her unrelieved grief. King Philip tries to cajole her, then commands her to bind up the hair she has torn loose. Constance agrees, saying that her hair should not be free while her son is not. She then conjures for Pandulph a scene in which she and Arthur will meet again in heaven, but Arthur will be so disfigured from mistreatment that she will miss the opportunity for reunion because she will not be able to recognize him. Both Pandulph and Philip criticize her fondness for grief. Constance then exits to be alone, and King Philip follows because he fears that she might attempt suicide.

Lewis indulges in melancholy, saying that life is as tedious as a "twice-told tale." Pandulph intrigues him with the prophecy that King John will kill Arthur, which, in turn, will open the way for Lewis and Blanch to claim all that Arthur now holds. Furthermore, they will be supported by all of the English citizens who will rebel because of Arthur's murder. With the additional rebellion which Pandulph predicts will result from the Bastard's ransacking of Church property, Lewis is eager to believe the prophecy that a French invasion of England will be joined by a great army of rebels on English soil. Lewis thus embraces the vision that he will lead this force to a glorious victory and future, and he exits with Pandulph, hoping to convince King Philip to press for the invasion of England.

## Commentary

Unfortunately, the action halts again in the middle of what has already been a predominantly verbal play. Conceivably, Constance's strident speeches hold the focus, thereby countering the forward movement of the action with her ineffective arguments. She moves the other characters—not to action nor to listening—but into the multi-role of a chorus, telling her to keep quiet.

Rhetoric for and against the marriage obscures the marriage's dramatic significance until Pandulph identifies it for Lewis late in the act. Blanch would be next in line if King John were defeated in battle and if Arthur were killed by his uncle. Because of the power of the male (that will be such an anathema to Queen Elizabeth I), Lewis would then rule England as Blanch's husband.

Another conflict, the religious issue, does move action into a new dimension. When King John refuses to acknowledge the Archbishop of

Canterbury, who has been sent by the Pope, King John takes a stand which was popular with Elizabethan Anglican audiences but which was fatal within the historic context of the play. He defies the conditions which Pandulph offers, and thus he destroys the new alliance and, thereby, he structures the play's dramatic resolution. Pandulph breaks up the alliance by threatening excommunication and a curse for all who align themselves with John. Additionally, he sets up John for murder by declaring sainthood for anyone who can accomplish John's murder. By the end of the act, Pandulph convinces Lewis to invade England. But the focus of this act is blurry because King John is not the prime mover of events, as a protagonist should be. Other than defying Pandulph's commands, making some brief strategic decisions for the war, and planting the seeds for Arthur's accidental death, he does not initiate nor focus the action. As a result, the act moves along awkwardly.

Character development is also weak. Pandulph is a stereotyped one-dimensional, ambitious Roman Catholic. Constance rants and raves from motivations which are so obscure that other characters in the play express confusion. King Philip wavers, the Bastard declaims, Lewis emotes, Blanch wheedles, Arthur mews, and Austria vegetates. Hubert alone has some moments of depth as he strives to understand and obey his king.

The only full character development occurs within King John. His character and fortune deteriorate when he persuades Hubert to kill Arthur. His assurances to Arthur turn into lies; he dishonors himself by promising protection to Arthur and then arranging the boy's murder. Thus, the King's flaw—the willful capture of the throne—corrupts the patient and wise leadership qualities that he displayed in Act I.

## ACT IV

### Summary

Hubert orders the executioners, who enter with him, to hide behind the arras until he stamps his foot. Upon hearing the signal, they are to rush out and bind Arthur to a chair. One executioner comments that he hopes Hubert's warrant legitimizes the act. Hubert retorts that the executioner should not voice unacceptable scruples and that he had better obey. The executioners exit then in order to hide.

Arthur enters when Hubert calls him, and he immediately notices that Hubert appears sad. He says that no one but himself should be sad, and he explains further that he could be happy anywhere but in prison, and that he fears his Uncle John's intentions. He observes that it is not *his* fault that he is Geoffrey's son; he would much rather be Hubert's son so that Hubert would love him.

In an aside, Hubert agonizes over the compassion which is aroused by the boy's conversation. He braces himself to carry out his orders quickly, and even as Arthur expresses his love for Hubert, the burly servant thrusts King John's warrant at Arthur, tells him to read it, and complains in another aside about the tears in his eyes.

Arthur asks: "Must you with hot irons burn out both mine eyes?" Hubert declares that he must, and he will. Arthur reminds his torturer of the time when he bound Hubert's aching head with a princess' handerchief without ever asking for its return and lovingly tended him throughout the night. Can Hubert remember that night and still blind the eyes that lovingly gazed upon him? Hubert growls that he must do as he promised the king he would. After another appeal for love and mercy from Arthur, Hubert stamps his foot to summon the executioners. Arthur begs Hubert to save him from "these bloody men," and he says that rather than being bound while the executioners blind him, he would rather have Hubert perform the deed. In return, Arthur promises to sit quietly and to forgive Hubert.

Hubert orders the executioners to leave, and one of them expresses relief for being excused from the order. Arthur realizes that he was mistaken when he ordered the compassionate executioner to leave, so he requests his return. Hubert commands the boy to prepare himself.

Instead of keeping his promise to "sit as quiet as a lamb," Arthur incessantly begs Hubert to spare his eyes. The boy gains precious time when the fire needed to re-heat the cold poker goes out, and he calls upon Hubert to show as much mercy as the fire and the irons have.

Finally, Hubert relents and promises to keep the boy safe. Arthur goes to hide, and Hubert exits to spread false stories about Arthur's death, in spite of the danger to himself for having refused a king's command.

In the following scene, King John and some of his advisers examine the current state of affairs. John hopes that his recent second coronation will prove effective. Pembroke remarks that the first should still be in force, but that it was done when there were no symptoms of revolt. Salisbury adds that this second crowning "is wasteful and ridiculous excess." Pembroke and Salisbury comment further that the second coronation might serve only to awaken suspicion about a fault which would not have been noticed previously. Salisbury then oozes flattery for the king by indicating that although King John ignored their advice, they are always pleased to stand by whatever he wants.

King John responds that he shared some of his reasons prior to the coronation and will offer more when his fears have lessened. In the meantime, he is open to all suggestions for reform. Pembroke asks that Arthur be freed on behalf of all those who value the king's safety. The king grants this wish just as Hubert enters.

Pembroke knows that Hubert had a warrant from King John to blind and execute Arthur, and as he observes Hubert's mannerisms during a private conversation with the king, Pembroke believes that the bloody deed is already done. Salisbury also observes that the king shows signs of emotional distress. King John then announces that his desire to free Arthur cannot be carried out because Arthur has just died.

Both Pembroke and Salisbury mutter their fears that stories of the boy's sickness would end in death. King John asks why they frown at him as if he could control life and death. Salisbury blurts that Arthur's death was apparently the result of foul play, and he criticizes the king for it. He and Pembroke exit to find the poor dead child. They predict trouble. King John expresses his regret: "They burn in indignation. I repent."

A messenger enters to report bad news from France. A huge French army has been quickly assembled and dispatched. King John wonders aloud how such an event could escape his mother's knowledge. The messenger then reports that Eleanor died on April 1st and that, according to rumor, Constance died about three days before that.

King John pleads for time to mourn the loss of his mother, as well as the threat of the gathering French forces, until he can deal with his discontented lords. He is further upset upon learning that Lewis the Dauphin is leading the invasion force.

When the Bastard and Peter of Pomfret enter, the king begs to be spared from more bad news. The Bastard replies that if the king is afraid of "the worst news," then he has none to deliver. King John then composes himself and tells the Bastard to report whatever he wishes to report.

The Bastard says that he was successful in collecting money from Church coffers but, everywhere, he found that people were possessed by unidentifiable fears. He has brought with him the prophet Peter of Pomfret whom he heard predicting that before the next Ascension Day at noon, King John would yield his crown.

King John orders Hubert to imprison the prophet until noon on Ascension Day, when he is to be hanged. Then, Hubert is to return to receive other instructions. After they leave, the king requests any news that the Bastard may have heard about the French army. The Bastard says that everyone is talking about the landing of the army. Furthermore, he himself met with an agitated group led by Bigot and Salisbury, who were searching for Arthur's body.

The king requests that the Bastard find the group and persuade them to come to him so that they can be persuaded to love him again. The Bastard says that he will. King John urges him to hurry because he cannot afford a domestic rebellion when a foreign army is invading. King John then sends the messenger after the Bastard in case messages need to be relayed; afterward, he grieves: "My mother dead!"

Hubert enters to report a natural phenomenon—four fixed moons with a fifth in "wondrous motion." People were awed by the sight and have begun to whisper about Arthur's death. The king is furious at the reminder of the people's fears and Arthur's death. He complains, "Thy hand hath murdered him. I had a mighty cause/ To wish him dead, but thou hadst none to kill him."

Hubert protests that he merely followed orders. King John implies that Hubert *misunderstood* their conversation and acted without authority upon that misunderstanding. While Hubert produces the signed warrant, King John wriggles away from responsibility for the evidence. Instead, he blames Hubert for being there, for looking like a killer, and thus inspiring him to think about the warrant. Hubert, he says, should have employed his conscience and resisted the order instead of turning the king's moment of weakness into a bloody deed. Furthermore, John says that a simple pause at the time he issued the warrant would have been enough resistance to stop him.

Since Hubert made the mistake of carrying out a flawed command, King John dismisses him with the warning to stay out of his sight forever. The king recognizes that his order to kill Arthur has resulted in "civil tumult" just when he needs a kingdom united against the French invasion.

Hubert then assures King John that he can arm the country against the invaders because Arthur is alive. He also complains that the king has misjudged by equating the quality of his conscience with his physical appearance. King John urges Hubert to go and report Arthur's survival to the angry lords, and then he apologizes for his angry criticisms of Hubert's rough looks.

In Scene 3, Arthur counters all efforts to save his life. While poised on the high prison walls, disguised as a ship-boy, Arthur begs the ground below not to hurt him when he jumps. He conjectures that if he does not break any bones, he has many alternatives for his escape; if he dies, he believes that such a fate will be preferable to staying in prison. The jump is fatal.

Arthur dies just as the search party appears. Salisbury, Pembroke, and Bigot decide to accept an invitation to a meeting with Pandulph the next morning. At this point, the Bastard enters to deliver King John's request for an immediate meeting.

Salisbury composes a message for the Bastard to deliver: they will not serve a king with such a stained reputation. The Bastard cautions whatever their thoughts, the lords should use "good words." Salisbury retorts that they are now ruled by grief, not good manners.

Just as the Bastard leads up to the good news that Arthur is alive, they discover the boy's body. Salisbury declares Arthur's murder to be the vilest in history. Pembroke extends this comparison into the future as a murder heinous enough to minimize all murders yet uncommitted. The Bastard agrees it is damnable "if that it be the work of any hand." Salisbury dismisses the "if" and blames King John and Hubert, then vows dedication of his life to revenge. Pembroke and Bigot concur with this view.

Hubert suddenly bursts in to joyously announce that Arthur is alive. Salisbury draws his sword to convince Hubert to get out of their sight. A confused Hubert states that he will defend himself even against a lord of the realm. Bigot and Pembroke join the threats against Hubert; the Bastard urges them to "keep the peace." Salisbury and the Bastard then threaten each other with death. Hubert explains that he loved the boy, left him alive an hour before, and joins them in their mourning.

Salisbury warns his group not to be deceived by Hubert's cunning tears, and he calls for all who abhor such slaughter to leave with him. Bigot and Pembroke announce that they will leave for a meeting with the Dauphin at Bury; King John can find them there.

The Bastard then states how damned Hubert is—if he so much as "agreed" to this vile murder—and he states further that he suspects that Hubert *was* involved. Once again, Hubert cannot utter a convincing word in his own defense. Finally, he declares that if he in any way contributed to the boy's death, hell can inflict its worst tortures, but "I left him well."

As ordered, Hubert picks up Arthur's body to carry it away for burial. The Bastard declares his amazement at "how easy thou dost take all England up!" With a clear vision of the turmoil that now threatens England, the Bastard leaves to join the king.

## Commentary

Action finally moves forward with sudden dramatic focus in Act IV, although the action here, as in the previous acts, is composed of actions which seem complex. All events here center on John's willful hold on the throne.

As an example of improved dramatic focus, the conflict between King John and Arthur is better represented than earlier. Pembroke and Salisbury are more emotionally involved in Arthur's cause than were France and Austria, so they project more emotional tension to the audience. They are also more effective. Furthermore, the threat of civil revolt because of Arthur's death was an emotionally arousing theme for Shakespeare's contemporaries—even more rousing and fearful than a foreign invasion.

Obviously, the conflict between John and Arthur also becomes direct. The king orders the boy to be killed; the boy dissuades the executioners. On the other hand, when King John wants Arthur to live, the boy ironically thwarts the king's wish by his fatal, desperate leap for freedom.

France is still threatening to invade England, as it was when Act I opened, but by being separated from Arthur's cause, France is clearly defined as an enemy. The audience can now focus its sympathies against

France and *for* England. France takes on a hateful image, a ghoul preying on reactions to Arthur's death.

Unfortunately, action is still sometimes heated because of excessive verbiage. For example, the dramatic action of a sword fight between Hubert and Salisbury bogs down in speeches such as Hubert's:

> Stand back, Lord Salisbury, stand back, I say!
> By heaven, I think my sword's as sharp as yours.
> I would not have you, lord, forget yourself,
> Nor tempt the danger of my true defense,
> Lest I, by marking of your rage, forget
> Your worth, your greatness, and nobility.
>
> (IV.iii.80–85)

And all of Arthur's lengthy appeals to spare his sight and life are melodramatically sentimental:

> O heaven, that there were but a mote in your [eyes],
> A grain, a dust, a gnat, a wandering hair.
> Any annoyance in that precious sense.
> Then feeling what small things are boisterous there
> Your vile intent must needs seem horrible.
>
> (IV.iii.92–96)

In addition, two major structural flaws diminish tension and continuity of action. First, the conflict between King John against the Pope, a popular stand for contemporaries of Shakespeare, is not continued from the previous act. Thus, an important link is missing. Second, this act features no human protagonist. Events turn and twist both King John and Arthur—the two featured characters, and although one could argue that England is the protagonist, the argument does not hold up well for the entire play.

If anything, the action in Act IV develops a convoluted philosophy about King John's flaw—his willful hold on the throne. His fearful second coronation arouses suspicions about his right to the throne. Although Shakespeare's contemporaries were aware that the Yorks employed suspicious means to gain and hold the throne of England, they did not believe that mere suspicions or disagreement justified civil rebellion. Rather, measured against a world order in which the kingship was established by God, people believed that no one had the right to overthrow the king unless that king were to issue an order that would demand that the citizens disobey one of God's commandments. Thereby hangs the significance of much of what is said and done in this act. King John's order for Hubert to kill Arthur is judged as heinous murder. Had King John's order been obeyed, the king would have been culpable, and the rebels would have acted correctly. However, since King John is guilty *only of the thought,* and Arthur kills himself by his own foolish, desperate decision, the rebels are wrong. Hubert and the Bastard take actions which are correct for the sake of world order and England.

The Bastard's final line in this act, however, identifies the issue as unresolved: "And heaven itself doth frown upon the land." And subsequent civil war upholds the opinion that England is not operating in a manner which is acceptable to Heaven. The play's historical context represents fearful memories of the thirteenth-century civil war and the subsequent years of instability, which were caused by the conflicts of the Yorks vs. the Lancasters. The Tudor line was regarded as a safeguard against civil war, and Queen Elizabeth I is remembered for her obsession with peace.

> I am amazed, methinks, and lose my way
> Among the thorns and dangers of this world.
>
> *   *   *   *   *   *   *   *   *   *   *   *   *
>
> Now for the bare-picked bone of majesty
> Doth dogged war bristle his angry crest
> And snarleth in the gentle eyes of peace.
> Now powers from home and discontents at home
> Meet in one line, and vast confusion waits,
> As doth a raven on a sick-fallen beast,
> The imminent decay of wrested pomp.
> Now happy he whose cloak and cincture can
> Hold out this tempest.
>
> (IV.iv.139–156)

Hubert successfully fends off all who would stereotype him as a two-dimensional character who looks like and, therefore, is a murderer. His sense of honor emerges in the form of integrity, a quality of which Hubert is proud. In fact, his sense of honor and conscience respond to Arthur's appeals for mercy and creates an inner conflict which eventually overwhelms the order of a king. Thus, Hubert becomes a three-dimensional character during this act.

The Bastard continues to develop. In each previous act, he learned and shared one important lesson. Act IV is no exception. Here, he learns how fearful are disloyalty and disrespect (aspects of honor) that are channeled into civil rebellion. Unlike the bold embracing of new concepts which the Bastard exhibited previously, a cold flailing against an unacceptable lesson emerges when he says, "I am amazed . . . and lose my way." Thus, fear and doubt add another layer to the Bastard's character. With loyalty stretched almost to the breaking point by Arthur's death, the Bastard chooses to support King John for the sake of stability, exhibiting again the quality of honor which, although much shallower before, marked him from his first appearance. The Bastard is now the most fully developed character in the play.

King John does not fare as well. Instead of developing the wise and patient leadership qualities that he exhibited in Act I, he is now deteriorating. His flaw now dominates every action, and it appears to be toppling him from the height of his monarchy. Although still patriotic to the extent that he wants to defend England against foreign invaders, he is no longer conscientious about his responsibilities. He does realize that he has contributed to a disastrous civil tumult. And he refuses to accept responsibility for the death of Arthur. Instead, he blames Hubert, claiming that had Hubert but hesitated, the order would not have been signed. John's moral disintegration has diminished him to a shadow, a character who interacts with no one. His role is reduced to a symbol needed for national security.

## ACT V

### Summary

King John enters into a ceremony of contrition with Pandulph. Having handed over his crown to Pandulph, John receives it again with the blessings of the Pope. In return, Pandulph promises to stop the war that he began. Pandulph marks the day of conversion as Ascension Day. After Pandulph leaves, King John remembers the prophecy and expresses relief that yielding his crown before noon was a voluntary act.

The Bastard brings bad news again: Kent has surrendered; London has welcomed the Dauphin and his troops; most of the English lords have joined the French forces. King John asks why the lords did not return to his service after they had learned that Arthur was alive. The Bastard tells the king of their discovery of Arthur's body. Upon learning that Hubert was mistaken about Arthur's survival, the king is overcome by despair. The Bastard then urges his king to display courage, to challenge his enemies, and to lead his remaining supporters to an attack.

King John announces the agreement which he arranged with the Pope's legate. The Bastard remonstrates his king for this "inglorious" compromise; he disapproves of arranging a truce with the invaders, and he takes special exception to yielding to the arrogant young Dauphin. Again, the Bastard urges a brave defense, if for no other reason, than to act as insurance in case Pandulph cannot deliver the promised peace.

King John assigns the fight to the Bastard's leadership. They leave as the Bastard exhorts his king to meet the odds with courage.

Scene 2 features the Dauphin and his followers. Lewis dictates to Count Melun the oaths sworn by the rebel English lords. Salisbury affirms his allegiance but regrets that he must kill his countrymen. He bewails the sickness within his government that has driven him to heal it by joining forces with invaders of his homeland, then excuses himself to weep.

Lewis praises Salisbury for both his decision and the war of conscience that he is fighting. The Dauphin declares that even he himself is moved by Salisbury's manly tears. He urges Salisbury to compose himself, to fight, and to look forward to the rewards. Seeing Pandulph, Lewis anticipates a blessing on their enterprise.

Instead, Pandulph announces King John's reconciliation with the Pope as a cause for withdrawing the French attack. Lewis responds that he is too proud and "high-born" to be controlled by the commands of a second-ary power. He says that Pandulph's voice kindled the war but that Pandulph is too weak to blow out the resulting flames. Lewis claims that John's peace with Rome has nothing to do with peace with France. Furthermore, the Dauphin claims England because of his marriage to Blanch. He wants to press the battles that have nearly guaranteed the prize. He denies that Rome has any jurisdiction over this campaign. Pandulph says that Lewis is considering only externals in this issue. Lewis declares that he will not return until he wins this war.

At this unfavorable moment, the Bastard arrives to inquire about the progress of the negotiations. Pandulph reports on the Dauphin's refusal to stop the war. The Bastard hurls brave challenges at both the Dauphin and the English rebels, painting a portrait of a brave King John who stands ready to lead his loyal countrymen in a successful defense.

Lewis dismisses both the Bastard and Pandulph, refusing to listen any more. He announces that war will win his arguments. The Bastard warns the Dauphin that his drums announce the beginning of the battle that will defeat the invaders.

Scene 3 consists of bad news for the British. Hubert informs King John that their forces are faring badly in the day's battle. King John tells Hubert that he feels ill. A messenger informs the king that the Bastard wants him to leave the battlefield. King John informs everyone that he is withdraw-ing to go to the abbey at Swinstead; he complains the fact that fever prevents him from celebrating the news that the French supply armada was wrecked at sea, and he orders a litter to carry him away.

In Scene 4, the rebel English lords worry about their setbacks. Salisbury expresses surprise at the number of supporters of King John, Pembroke urges vigorous support for the French or they themselves will lose, and Bigot blames the Bastard for the astonishing defense.

A mortally wounded Count Melun manages to reach the group and urges them to join other English lords who have abandoned their cause in order to re-pledge loyalty to King John because Lewis has pledged to behead any rebels upon the moment of his victory. When the lords express doubt, Count Melun assures them that he tells the truth because he is dying and because his grandfather was English. In return, Melun requests help to assist him to a quiet place to die. The English lords agree both to help Melun and to rush back to King John.

In Scene 5, Lewis must cope with bad news about Count Melun's death, the English lords' defection, and the armada's destruction.

In the next scene, through a series of codes which lead one to believe that they cannot see each other in the black night, Hubert and the Bastard meet. Their exchange of news is also bleak. Hubert reports that the king has been poisoned, apparently by a monk, but has a slight chance of recovering. The good news is that all of the English lords have returned and been pardoned at Prince Henry's request. The Bastard, in turn, reports that half his fighting forces have been lost to a sudden, devastating turn in the battle. Having barely escaped on his fast horse, he asks Hubert to lead him to the king.

In the seventh and final scene, Prince Henry appears and takes charge. He reports that King John is dying. Pembroke adds that the king believes that he can recover if he is brought into the fresh air; he is more patient now and has been singing. When Prince Henry mourns death's deterioration of his father's body and mind, Salisbury assures him that Henry is well suited to fit the vacant throne.

King John is carried in. He praises the comfort of the open air for his fever and pain. He tells Prince Henry that he, John, has been poisoned, and he blames all around him for not supplying cold air to help him. Prince Henry offers his tears, but they are rejected as too hot and salty.

The king clings to a thread of life until the Bastard can deliver his news. This news is that the Dauphin is advancing against defense forces that were devastated by the unexpected turn in the battle. King John dies.

Salisbury urges Prince Henry to take over the monarchy. The prince is unnerved by his father's "demonstration of mortality." The Bastard appeals to Heaven to aid him in avenging the king's death, after which he pledges continued servitude after death.

Salisbury says that Pandulph awaits within for acceptance of a tolerable offer of peace. The Bastard urges a strong defense first. But Salisbury convinces the Bastard that nothing else is necessary because the Dauphin has already prepared for the ceremony.

## Commentary

Unfortunately, Act V does not maintain Act IV's improved focus. There is, however, a focal point—King John's deterioration and death occupy our thoughts. But that focus is not dramatic because it is not the center of conflict and tension. John, leader of England, is no longer opposing the rebellion. Instead, he assigns England's defense to the Bastard and withdraws eventually to Swinstead Abbey. After Salisbury's vascillation, all of the rebels return to the fold and await the death of the man whom they swore to destroy. But they do not act on King John's initiative, and so this entire conflict recedes in dramatic impact.

When word of France's peace offer arrives, no one even verifies the terms; they just grab what they can get. And this peace offer leaves a question: why did the Dauphin give up the fight? After jeopardizing his immortal soul in a confrontation with Pandulph, Lewis reappears in one brief scene to hear some bad news. The next thing we know, he has given up—even though the Bastard dropped his defense.

In addition, the role of Pandulph deteriorates. We are left wondering whether or not he actually convinced Lewis to negotiate the peace (which would answer the question as to why Lewis gave up), or whether he has been reduced to the role of an emissary. Either way, Shakespeare fails to justify Pandulph's actions; Shakespeare thus withholds a potentially important dramatic change from the audience.

That failure, plus the failure to resolve the end of the rebellion through dramatic conflict, are key weaknesses in this play. It is doubtful that anyone deeply cares when John, who is intended to be the central character in this play, faces failure and dies. His deterioration and death, the reuniting of England under Prince Henry, and the withdrawal of the French forces are merely catalogued in a series of narrative speeches. John's death serves the playwright's need to resolve all of the issues and set up Prince Henry as a reconciliation figure in order to end this play.

Because Shakespeare wrote a weak, forced conclusion which does not grow naturally out of events which preceded it, he could do little more than provide his characters with declamatory speeches.

Characterization fares little better than plot in Act V. As mentioned in the preceding summary, characters do not interact in order to develop conflict; they declaim. Prince Henry arouses curiosity, but he is a wooden figure without personality. Identified as the son of King John and as the only hope for England's unity, he nevertheless remains a dull character when he should be rousing hope and inspiring cheers.

Even the Bastard departs from the pattern of learning one important lesson per act. Here, he serves only to lead an unsuccessful defense and to deliver bad news. He is devastated when he is told to accept the peace.

One interpretation of this ending which can structure unity is that in the end, everyone must capitulate to political reality—the merciless, unyielding "policy" which overrules humanistic, passionate objections. Constance rebels against the system but hers is a hopeless, uncompromising protest which results in a frenzied death. In contrast, once the Bastard accepts the fact, he gains power. Once he comes to terms with political realities, he accepts without protest the French terms of peace, King John's death, and the need to prepare Prince Henry to take over the government. The spirited protester at Angiers is as dead as the illegitimate king.

That interpretation notwithstanding, plot and characterization, both of which displayed intermittent promise during the development of the play, diminish toward the conclusion of *King John.* Perhaps it was enough for Elizabethan audiences to witness the reuniting of England and the defeat of the French, but those events are not, in themselves, sufficient to stir modern audiences to cheers or catharsis at the climax of the play.

## King John Genealogy

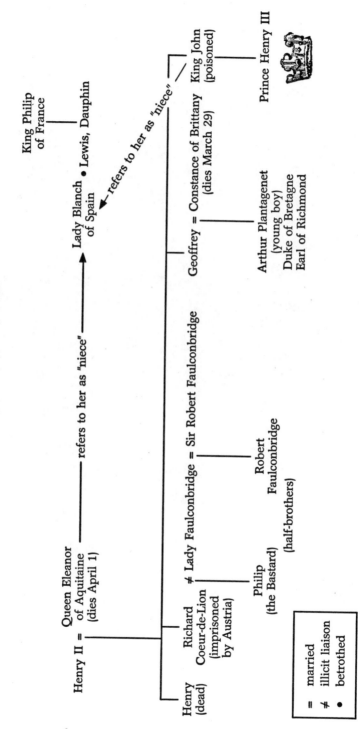

- = married
- ≠ illicit liaison
- • betrothed

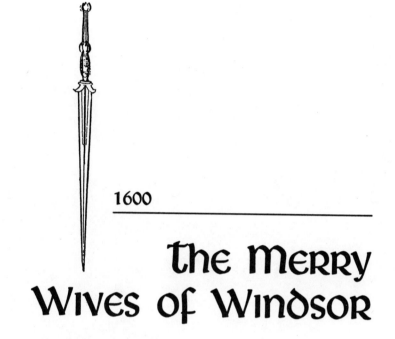

1600

# the Merry
# Wives of Windsor

# INTRODUCTION

There are three early texts of *Merry Wives;* the first two (printed in the First Quarto and the Second Quarto) are garbled and are only half as long as the version printed in what we have come to believe is the authoritative version – that is, the version in the First Folio. Seemingly, however, even the First Folio edition is incomplete, for there are non sequiturs in the play, referring to a horse-stealing episode and a deer-poaching episode which are not developed. Furthermore, it is believed that the First Folio version was taken from a script that belonged to the man playing the Host of the Garter Inn. Only his lines are fully developed. The rest of the play is largely filled with paraphrases and mangled lines.

Critics also tend to believe an eighteenth-century writer who refers to this play as having been commissioned by Queen Elizabeth herself. "It [*Merry Wives*] had pleased one of the greatest Queens that ever was in the World," he writes, adding that "this Comedy was written at her Command . . . and she commanded it to be finished in fourteen days." Another eighteenth-century scholar mentions that Elizabeth was "so well pleas'd with that admirable Character of *Falstaff*, in the two parts of *Henry the Fourth,* that she commanded him to continue it for one Play more, and to shew him in Love." This deadline, of course, could explain the sloppy attention to plot and subplot lines.

Scholars have also said that the verse in *Merry Wives* is so poor that the comedy *sounds* un-Shakespearean. But they laud the creation yet again of the Falstaff character. He is a glorious figure of fun. And the "wives" are indeed "merry," and even the jealous Ford is changed into a man of merriment when the play finally ends.

# A BRIEF SYNOPSIS

*The Merry Wives of Windsor* is the most purely farcical of all of Shakespeare's plays. It depends on lightning-quick timing between the actors and the carefully choreographed actions. The "meaning" cannot be separated from the "performance."

The incidents themselves are as follows: There is a main plot in which Sir John Falstaff conspires to seduce Mrs. Page and Mrs. Ford, the wives of two prominent Windsor citizens. The women play along with him in order to expose him as a preposterous lecher. Then, to complicate matters, the insanely jealous Mr. Ford disguises himself as one "Mr. Brook" and hires Falstaff to procure Mrs. Ford for him in order to (so he plans) reveal her suspected infidelity. But Mrs. Ford and Mrs. Page dupe both Falstaff *and* Mr. Ford. On one occasion, Falstaff is tricked into hiding in a basket of dirty clothes, then dropped into the river ("I have a kind of alacrity in sinking," he says); on another occasion, he must disguise himself as a fat old woman, a "witch" much hated by Mr. Ford, who summarily pummels "her"/him. Finally, both husbands join their "merry wives" in an elaborate masque-like entertainment, the high point of which is the humiliation of Falstaff, who has this time disguised himself as the ghostly "Herne the Hunter," complete with a massive set of horns on his head.

The secondary plot concerns the comical antics of a pair of would-be suitors for the hand of the lovely Anne Page. Doctor Caius, a quick-tempered French doctor, and Slender, the stupid nephew of Justice Shallow, vie for Anne's favor, while she finds both of them abhorrent. Sir Hugh Evans, a friend to Shallow and a supporter of Slender's cause, comes into conflict with Doctor Caius, and because the *Welshman* Evans and the *Frenchman* Caius persistently garble the English language, their meetings and arguments give special pleasure to all present.

In the end, Anne Page marries her true love, a poor young gentleman named Fenton. Mr. Ford promises to desist from being jealous of his wife, Falstaff is made a laughingstock, and then he is reconciled to the group. The spirit of the comedy is best summed up in Mrs. Page's last lines:

> Master Fenton
> Heaven give you many, many merry days!
> Good husband, let us every one go home,
> And laugh this sport o'er by a country fire;
> Sir John and all.

> (253–57)

## LIST OF CHARACTERS

### Sir John Falstaff

Consistent with the image of the ne'er-do-well companion of Prince Hal (later to be Henry V) in several of Shakespeare's history plays, the Falstaff of *The Merry Wives of Windsor* is self-consciously pompous and eloquent, self-pitying when the occasion arises, and always ready to exploit anyone—man or woman—to achieve his desired ends. His appetites and his humor are as large as his enormous belly, and it is fitting that when he makes a fool of himself, as he does no less than three times in this play, his folly looms larger than that of the rest of the company combined. In order to secure his financial position and also to indulge his sexual fancy, he makes romantic overtures to the "merry wives" of Windsor, Mrs. Page and Mrs. Ford. They dupe him again and again: first, they stuff him into a "buck-basket" full of ill-smelling linens and then have him dumped into the Thames River; then, they disguise him as the fat "witch of Brainford," who is hated by Mr. Ford, who beats him black and blue; and finally, they trick him into playing the part of "Herne the Hunter," a ghost who haunts Windsor Park with great ragged horns on his head. In the last disguise, Falstaff is surprised by the entire company and is made the butt of their jokes. He admits to being "made an ass" in the very last scene and is welcomed to join the group to "laugh this sport o'er by a country fire."

### Fenton, a Young Gentleman

Master Fenton is the well-born but impecunious rightful lover in this romantic farce. He successfully pursues young Anne Page over the objections of both her mother and her father. The play ends fittingly just after he announces their secret wedding. His bride has married him in defiance of her parents, he says, "to shun/ A thousand irreligious cursed hours/ Which forced marriage would have brought upon her."

### Shallow, a Country Justice

Shallow's main part in the action, aside from swearing to be revenged on Falstaff, is to propose and encourage the courtship of Anne Page by his nephew, Slender.

### Slender, Nephew to Shallow

Slender's name describes his wit. He is one of Anne Page's unlikely suitors, a man possessing "a little wee face, with a little yellow beard," who prefers talking sport (dogs, bears, and "jests with geese") to courting women. At his uncle's insistence, he makes several romantic overtures to Anne, deluding even himself into thinking that he's in love with her, before the whole enterprise founders.

### Ford, a Citizen of Windsor ("Brook," in disguise)

Ford is a man of property who can be "mad as a mad dog" when jealousy overtakes him. Disguised as Brook, he pays Falstaff handsomely to compromise "Ford's" wife, but on both occasions, Mrs. Ford has the laugh on both Falstaff and on her husband. In the end, Ford admits his folly ("Pardon me, wife") and joins her in humiliating Falstaff in the final Herne-the-Hunter episode.

### Page, a Citizen of Windsor

Page is more reasonable than his friend Ford in every respect but one. Though he can see through his friend's jealousy, he cannot see the folly in his own choice of a husband for his daughter Anne. Refusing to consider Fenton as a possibility because Fenton has no property or money, Page favors Slender. His values are stolidly middle class; but for Shakespeare, who came from the same middle class himself, Page's good sense finally prevails over his property instincts, and he consents (after the fact) to the wedding of Anne and Fenton.

### William Page, the young son of Page

William appears in two scenes: first, he is doing his Latin lessons before Hugh Evans and Mistress Quickly; and second, he acts as one of the forest creatures in the elaborate ritual to unmask Falstaff in Windsor Park.

### Sir Hugh Evans, a Welsh Parson

Falstaff aptly hits on the most interesting feature of this character when he says that Evans "makes fritters of English." This remark is in response to Sir Hugh's line, typically in dialect: "Seese is not goot to give putter. Your pelly is all putter.": (Cheese is not good to give butter; your belly is all butter.)

### Doctor Caius, a French Physician

Another practitioner of fractured English (*e.g.,* "If dere be one, or two, I shall make a de turd" ["third"]), Doctor Caius is Hugh Evans' chief antagonist. A revenger's subplot ensues when Caius learns that Hugh Evans is aiding Slender and Shallow in pursuit of Anne Page, a woman whom Caius himself fancies. Engineered by the Host of the Garter, a duel between these two is set to take place—in *different* locations. The Host, and the audience, would rather hear them argue than see them fight anyway. As retribution, Evans and Caius plan to seek joint revenge on the Host for this trick, and vague reference is made in the play to horses which they *may* have arranged to have stolen from the Host.

### The Host of the Garter Inn

The Host's chief motivation seems to be to enjoy himself. He babbles endlessly to all around him while engineering such schemes as the abortive duel between Doctor Caius and Sir Hugh Evans. This trickster, however, finds himself also tricked by the end of the play.

### Bardolph, Pistol, and Nym; followers of Falstaff

This crew of motley thieves, familiar from the other "Falstaff plays," has only a small part in the action here. They form a rogues' context for Falstaff. Their attitudes toward one another seem to be ones of mutual contempt, for they betray each other at every turn. Nym seems to utter the word "humour" in every sentence which he speaks; Bardolph becomes quickly familiar to us because of his references to his bulbous nose and his scarlet complexion; and Pistol stands out as the most venomous of Falstaff's inner circle of "friends."

### Simple, Servant to Slender

Even more stupid than his master, Simple is usually the yo-yo of other people's witticisms.

### Mistress Ford

Reasonably cautious at first, Mrs. Ford soon decides not only to teach Falstaff a lesson for his outrageous presumption in trying to seduce her, but also to irritate her jealous husband and to expose his foolishness. At the end of the play, this "merry wife" reaffirms her marriage on the basis of trust, thereby creating a second reason for celebrating Fenton and Anne Page's nuptials.

### Mistress Page

Mrs. Page has the luxury of material comfort, a trusting husband, and lovely children. Hers is the advantage of the Elizabethan middle class. Her sense of morality is outraged by fat John Falstaff's proposals, and she sets out with her partner, Mrs. Ford, to expose Falstaff as a lecher and a fraud. This done, her (and her class') morality is reaffirmed. Yet Mrs. Page has a blind spot: she prefers the advantages which highly placed social connections can give her and believes that her daughter, Anne Page, should marry Doctor Caius. Anne's opinion of the Frenchman is clear: "I had rather be set quick i' th' earth,/ And bowled to death with turnips." The audience, of course, concurs and is happy that Mrs. Page can finally see the rightness of her daughter's marriage to Fenton.

### Anne Page

Anne is the model of "pretty virginity," the conventional beautiful maiden at the core of a romantic comedy. She adds her mother's pluck and forthrightness to her physical attributes, resists her parents' choice of suitors, and finally has her way with her male counterpart, Fenton.

### Mistress Quickly

Mistress Quickly, the talkative and meddlesome servant of Doctor Caius, uses her intimate friendship with Anne Page to turn a profit. She promotes all comers who think they have a hope of successfully wooing Anne Page.

Quickly is as apt to misuse the English language as the Frenchman or Welshman are in the play, and she also provides some comedy in her penchant for obscene puns. It is especially amusing that she should play the part of the delicate Fairy Queen in the climactic "masque scene."

# SUMMARIES AND COMMENTARIES

## ACT I–SCENE 1

### Summary

The "Country Justice" Shallow complains to Sir Hugh Evans, a Welsh parson, about a wrong which has been done to him by Sir John Falstaff: "I will make a Star-Chamber matter of it. If he were twenty Sir John Falstaffs, he shall not abuse Robert Shallow, Esquire." Sir Hugh momentarily calms the angry waters by suggesting a profitable scheme involving Shallow's nephew, Slender, who is also present. He suggests a "marriage between Master Abraham [Slender] and Mistress Anne Page," the beautiful and soon-to-be-wealthy daughter of a prominent "citizen of Windsor." Slender, the would-be wooer, thinks that he knows her: "She has brown hair and speaks small like a woman?"

The three then make plans to go to Page's house, where Falstaff is said to be. After exchanging greetings with Page, Shallow faces the wrongdoer himself:

> *Falstaff:* Now, Master Shallow, you'll complain of me to the King?
> *Shallow:* Knight, you have beaten my man, killed my deer, and broke open my lodge.
> *Falstaff:* But not kissed your keeper's daughter?
> *Shallow:* Tut, a pin [a trifle]! This shall be answered.
> *Falstaff:* I will answer it straight. I have done all this. That is now answered.
>
> (112–18)

Slender adds his complaint against Falstaff's "cony-catching" rascal-friends, Bardolph, Nym, and Pistol. "They carried me to the tavern and made me drunk, and afterward picked my pocket." Egged on by their ringleader, Falstaff, the three "rascals" make elaborate denials of any questionable behavior.

Mistress Ford, Mistress Page, and Anne Page enter and, together with the rest of the company, are bid by Miss Page to come to "have a hot venison pasty to dinner." Sir Hugh and Shallow prevail upon Slender to pursue Anne Page. "I will marry her, sir, at your request; but if there be no great love in the beginning, yet heaven may decrease it upon better acquaintance when we are married and have more occasion to know one another. I hope, upon familiarity will grow more content." The scene ends with a conversation between Anne and Slender about "why" he cannot join them in dinner. Eventually, however, Page persuades him to do so.

## Commentary

The first words of the play introduce its main figure by name—Sir John Falstaff. Though Justice Shallow's complaint against Falstaff (deer trapping) is completely forgotten once the main action gets underway, Shakespeare's choice to open the play in this way is dramatically effective. For Shakespeare's contemporary audience—and for anyone today who is familiar with his *Henry IV* plays—a mere reference to the comical misdeeds of the "huge hill of flesh," as Prince Hal (in *Henry IV*) refers to Falstaff, would whet the appetite. The buzz of anger which consumes Shallow conjures up memories of Falstaff's past chicanery and the irritation it has caused, especially to "right-thinking" citizens in other plays. Falstaff's first appearance in *Merry Wives*, pompous and full of disdain for others, is eminently enjoyable. In response to Shallow's bluster of accusation, Falstaff chooses to be tight-lipped: "I will answer it straight. . . . That is now answered." In other words, "I did it. So what?"

From the start, this comedy is different from Shakespeare's other comedies. It is his only completely "English" comedy, set in Windsor, and dealing with distinctly contemporary types. The language has the highest percentage of prose of all of Shakespeare's plays, indicating an attention to the "everyday" aspect and a focus on comic situations rather than style.

The comic types in the first scene are broadly sketched. Sir Hugh Evans, the Welshman, is fond of displaying his learning, and he speaks in dialect, much to Falstaff's (and the audience's) amusement:

> Evans: *Pauca verba* [few words], Sir John; goot worts
> [good words].
> *Falstaff:* Good worts [cabbage]! Good cabbage.
> Slender, I broke your head.

> (123–25)

Shallow is eager to match his rather slow-witted nephew to Anne Page because there is money to be made in the deal ("seven hundred pounds and possibilities"). The issues of money, morality, and marriage, then, are at the core of this farce. Slender, only vaguely aware of the money issue, is a monument of foolishness. His real joy is talking about dogs (to Page) and bears (to Anne), which makes him a comical suitor for the hand of the beautiful and gracious Mistress Page. Their scenes together offer some of the funniest moments in the play.

## ACT I – SCENES 2 & 3

### Summary

Evans sends Slender's servant, Simple, with a message to Mistress Quickly "to desire and require her to solicit your master's desires to Mistress Anne Page."

Falstaff, meanwhile, conspires with his men at the Garter Inn to "make love to Ford's wife" because "the report goes she has all the rule of her husband's purse." He sends Nym and Pistol with love letters to Mistress Page *and* to Mistress Ford, then exits. With Falstaff out of the room, his confederates prepare to betray him:

> *Nym:* I will discuss the humour of his love to Page
> [Mistress Page's husband].
> *Pistol:* And I to Ford shall eke unfold
> How Falstaff, varlet vile,
> His dove will prove, his gold will hold,
> And his soft couch defile.
>
> (104–08)

### Commentary

Falstaff is a knight "almost out at heels," and therefore, he sees as his natural prey the well-off middle class. Since he fancies himself a lover – "Page's wife . . . gave me good eyes too" – it is this talent which he will exploit to make money. The language which he uses to describe the woman whom he plans to woo is replete with references to the great age of the English merchant-adventurers:

> She bears the purse too. She is a region in Guiana, all
> gold and bounty. I will be cheaters [both financial
> Warder and "cheat," in the modern sense] to them both,
> and they shall be exchequers to me. They shall be my
> East and West Indies, and I will trade to them both.
>
> (75–79)

To see this "cheater" cheated – that is, Falstaff – will be one of the chief pleasures in the play, and Pistol and Nym's quick decision to betray their captain anticipates the fun.

## ACT I – SCENE 4

### Summary

Simple describes his master to Mistress Quickly, to whom he has gone at Hugh Evans' bidding:

He hath but a little wee face, with a little yellow beard –
a Cain-coloured [red] beard.

(22-23)

Quickly agrees to help Shallow in his plans to woo Anne Page, but before
she can elaborate, her own master, the "French physician" Doctor Caius,
returns home. Simple is shuffled into a "closet," or a small side room, just
seconds before Caius enters. The doctor plans to go to the "court," taking
his servant John Rugby with him. He discovers Simple and is outraged
to learn that the latter is on an errand to curry favor with Anne Page
through the agency of Mistress Quickly. Since Caius wants the young lady
for himself, he immediately writes a letter of challenge to Sir Hugh and
sends it with Simple. The last of the suitors then arrives, a "young
gentleman" by the name of Fenton. Quickly assures him that he too will
continue his courtship of Anne Page.

> *Quickly:* Have not your worship a wart above your eye?
> *Fenton:* Yes, marry, have I. What of that?
> *Quickly:* Well, thereby hangs a tale. Good faith, it is
>             such another Nan [girl]; but, I detest, an honest
>             maid as ever broke bread. We had an hour's talk of
>             that wart.

(156-60)

Fenton gives her money for her efforts and exits, whereupon she admits
(to the audience) that "Anne loves him not."

## Commentary

Shakespeare expands his gallery of odd characters in this scene – Rugby,
whose "worst fault is that he is given to prayer"; Quickly, who is ready
to please anyone as a go-between if the price is right, and who fractures
the English language every time she opens her mouth ("but, I detest, an
honest maid," etc.); and finally, the irascible French doctor and would-be
lover, Caius. One of the few more or less "normal" characters in the play,
Fenton has a "wart above his eye."

The pacing of this play must be *very* fast or the farce will not be effective. In the first moments of this short scene, there is a concealment and
a near-discovery (Caius first sends Quickly to fetch his "green box" from
the "closet" where Simple is hiding), which makes the discovery which
follows all the more comical. The joke is compounded by Doctor Caius'
unintentional pun when he returns to the "closet" himself:

> Dere is some simples in my closset dat I vill not
> Vor de varld I shall leave behind.

(65-66)

Caius means "medicines" by the word "simples," but Quickly and Rugby (along with the audience) know of the other "Simple" who is hiding in the closet. Added to the complications of rival lovers in this scene is a new subplot, in which an irate Frenchman vows to revenge himself on the cagey Welsh parson. The very thought of these two making "fritters of the English language" (as Falstaff will later say of Hugh) as they battle it out is sure to please an audience.

## ACT II–SCENE 1

### Summary

Mrs. Page, then Mrs. Ford enters with the news that they have received identical letters from Falstaff, pledging his love to each. Needless to say, they are both outraged. *Mrs. Page:* "One that is well-nigh worn to pieces with age to show himself a young gallant"; *Mrs. Ford:* "I shall think the worse of fat men as long as I have an eye to make difference of men's liking" [tell the difference between men]. They determine to "be revenged on him" and set off with Mistress Quickly to lay the plot.

Their husbands arrive onstage, discussing what "a yoke of his [Falstaff's] discarded men," Pistol and Nym, have told them concerning Falstaff's amorous plans for their "merry wives." Ford plans to pass himself off as a man named "Brook" to Falstaff in order to get further information.

As the scene ends, the subplot moves forward. Shallow reports that "there is a fray to be fought between Sir Hugh the Welsh parson and Caius the French doctor" and that they have been "appointed contrary [different] places" to meet for the duel. Page says that he would "rather hear them scold [argue] than fight."

### Commentary

Shakespeare differentiates between the two husbands–Page and Ford–and, to a lesser extent, between the two wives in this scene. Mrs. Page is openly contemptuous of Falstaff's scheme right from the start, while Mrs. Ford worries about its consequences and seems fearful at first even to tell her friend about Falstaff's letter. When Mrs. Ford does speak, however, her scathing comments about Falstaff are quite colorful:

> What tempest, I trow, threw this whale, with so many
> tuns of oil in his belly, ashore at Windsor? How shall I
> be revenged on him? I think the best way were to enter-
> tain him with hope, till the wicked fire of lust have
> melted him in his own grease.
>
> (64–68)

Perhaps Mrs. Ford's initial apprehension was justifiable, given the kind of person Ford turns out to be. His jealousy and his tendency to believe that his wife is a willing partner of Falstaff, contrasts sharply with Page's reaction to Falstaff:

> *Page:* If he should intend his voyage toward my wife, I
> would turn her loose to him; and what he gets more
> of her than sharp words, let it lie on my head.
> *Ford:* I do not misdoubt my wife, but I would be loath
> to turn them together. A man may be too confident.
>
> (188–92)

Ford's idea to disguise himself as another person — Brook — adds a final wrinkle to the plot's complications, whose working out will be the business of the rest of the play.

## ACT II – SCENE 2

### Summary

Pistol begs a loan from Falstaff; after all, it is *he* who usually takes the risks in their petty crimes. Falstaff reminds the lesser partner that it is only through his — Falstaff's — greater influence and connections that Pistol avoids failure. In typically pompous fashion, Falstaff asks, "Think'st thou I'll endanger my soul gratis?" His rationalization for his crooked ways echoes the Falstaff of *Henry IV, Part 1:* "Ay, I myself sometimes, leaving the fear of God on the left hand and hiding mine honor in necessity, am fain to shuffle, to hedge, and to lurch . . ."

Mistress Quickly interrupts with the happy news that *both* Mrs. Page and Mrs. Ford are infatuated with the scholar knight, "The best courtier of them all, when the court lay at Windsor, could never have brought her [Mrs. Ford] to such a canary." Falstaff's ego swells at the idea of a successful conquest (or two!). As he addresses himself affectionately, now alone on stage, one imagines the comic effect that could be had if a large full-length mirror were present for him to peer into:

> Will they yet look after thee?
> Wilt thou, after the expense of so much money,
> Be now a gainer? Good body, I thank thee.
> Let them say 'tis grossly [a pun on "fat"] done;
> So it be fairly done, no matter.
>
> (145–49)

Disguised as "Mr. Brook," Ford solicits the aid of Falstaff in seducing Mrs. Ford (for the purpose of justifying his unfounded jealousy). The "bag of money" which he swings before Falstaff's nose is enough to convince this "gentleman of excellent breeding" to accept the project. "You shall, if you will, enjoy Ford's wife," Falstaff assures "Brook." Falstaff then hurls several gratuitous insults at Ford before the scene ends: "Hang him, mechanical salt-butter [vulgar, smelly] rogue!"

## Commentary

The multiple references to money give this scene its special edge. It opens with Falstaff haggling over money with someone he undoubtedly exploits with regularity. Virtually every character in the play has his part determined by his wealth (or lack of it). This is common enough in a farce of this kind, yet it reaches grotesque proportions in this scene. Ford (Brook) knows the great lure of hard cash to a nobleman fallen on hard times. Note the way he entices Falstaff:

> There is money. Spend it, spend it;
> Spend more; spend all I have.
>
> (240–41)

Undoubtedly Ford waves real coins in front of Falstaff at this moment. One can imagine the impecunious knight's pleasure in fingering the silver. The final joke here, though, is on Ford himself, whose obsession with "property," one imagines, extends to his wife. His jealousy has actually distorted his vision of things to the point where he will risk actually having his wife dishonor herself in order to prove his (unfounded) jealousy. His language is almost that of a madman:

> Page is an ass, a secure ass. He will trust his wife; he
> will not be jealous. I will rather trust a Fleming with my
> butter, Parson Hugh the Welshman with my cheese, an
> Irishman with my aqua-vitae [whiskey] bottle, or a thief
> to walk my ambling gelding, than my wife with herself.
> Then she plots, then she ruminates, then she devises.
> And what they think in their hearts they may effect; they
> will break their hearts but they will effect. God be praised
> for my jealousy!
>
> (316–24)

His next action is to catch his wife "in the act" at "eleven o'clock the hour," as Falstaff has promised.

## ACT II—SCENE 3

### Summary

In a field near Windsor, Doctor Caius and his servant, John Rugby, have already waited beyond the appointed hour for Sir Hugh Evans. When Shallow arrives with several others, he muses that it is for the best that no duel has taken place, since it would "go against the hair of your profession"; that is, for a healer of bodies and a healer of souls to fight to the death would be wrong. Shallow, the Host of the Garter, Slender, Page, and Doctor Caius set off for the village of Frogmore, where Sir Hugh Evans is awaiting them.

## Commentary

Besides advancing the subplot, this scene offers the comic spectacle of John Rugby fending off his master Doctor Caius who, it seems, is a bit over-eager for a scrap:

> *Caius:* Take your rapier, Jack, I vill tell you how I vill
> kill him.
> *Rugby:* Alas, sir, I cannot fence.
> *Caius:* Villainy, take your rapier.

The Host of the Garter, who has arranged this absurd duel in the first place, seizes every opportunity to mock Doctor Caius' poor grasp of the English language. He mischievously substitutes "adversary" for "advocate."

> *Caius:* By gar, me dank you vor dat . . .
> *Host:* For the which I will be thy adversary toward
> Anne Page. Said I well?
> *Caius:* By gar, 'tis good; vell said.

> (94–97)

### ACT III–SCENES 1 & 2

## Summary

The scene shifts to Frogmore, where Hugh Evans vows to "knog [Caius'] urinals about his knave's costard [head]." When he notices Page, Slender, and Shallow on their way toward him, he quickly puts on his gown and reads from his holy book. They notice the sword, and Shallow asks, "What, the sword and the word [bible]! Do you study them both, Master Parson?" Then Caius arrives, ripe for battle, and Hugh Evans tries his best to pull him aside and postpone the duel: "Pray you, let us not be laughingstocks to other men's humours." The Host takes great pleasure in their embarrassment, commenting, "Peace, I say, Gallia [Wales] and Gaul [France], French and Welsh, soul-curer and body curer!" And then he admits that the whole ruse was his private brainchild: "I have deceived you both: I have directed you to wrong places." Left alone with his adversary, Hugh Evans proposes to Caius a new revenge plot: ". . . let us knog or prains together to be revenge on this same scall [scurvy fellow], scurvy, cogging [conniving] companion, the Host of the Garter."

In Scene 2, Ford comes across Mrs. Page in the company of Falstaff's emissary, the young page Robin. This spurs his jealousy on, and he tests her:

> *Ford:* I think if your husbands were dead, you two
> [Robin and Mrs. Page] would marry.
> *Mrs. Page:* Be sure of that—two other husbands.
>
> (14–15)

The company of duelists and witnesses arrives from Frogmore, and the debate continues as to which of Anne Page's various suitors is most fitting to have her hand. Page explains that he favors Master Slender, while his wife prefers Doctor Caius. When the Host of the Garter mentions the gentleman Master Fenton, Page adamantly refuses to hear of such a thing:

> The gentleman is of no having [has no property]. . . .
> The wealth I have waits on my consent, and my consent
> goes not that way.
>
> (72; 78–79)

## Commentary

The flow of these two scenes gives us an idea just how much this play belongs to the stage. In reading it, there is nothing remarkable or new, and the literary value of the writing is slim. On stage, however, the mounting confusion and visual high jinks would more than compensate. There is a virtual dance between Caius and Evans, the one eager to fight at all costs, and the other embarrassed by his predicament, first trying to hide behind his holy "cloth" and bible, then trying to explain to the French doctor (in a series of frantic asides) that it would be best to call the whole thing off. Then there is Slender. He has very little to say here, and he hardly needs to be present to advance the plot. His presence, however, as Shakespeare outlines it, is potentially highly comical. Apparently, his two encounters with Anne Page have utterly transformed him from a young (and slow-witted) sport, fit only to discuss such things as the finer qualities of local greyhounds, into a moonstruck lover. Earlier in the play, he was the picture of vagueness when he bowed to Shallow's proposal that he try to win Anne Page's hand; in the present scenes, Shakespeare has him totally enraptured by the very thought of the same woman. "Ah, sweet Anne Page!" is all he can say, which he does repeatedly, in perfect oblivion of the goings-on around him. The fact that Slender is an ass is indisputable; and that Mister Page is convinced that this is the man for his daughter is therefore all the more amazing.

Ford's peculiar madness is stressed in these scenes as well. He is positively gleeful at the thought of surprising his wife and Falstaff together:

Good plots! They are laid, and our revolted wives share
damnation together. Well, I will take him [Falstaff], then
torture my wife, pluck the borrowed veil of modesty from
the so-seeming Mistress Page, divulge Page himself for a
secure and willful Acteon [cuckold]; and to these violent
proceedings all my neighbours shall cry aim [hurrah!].

(39–45)

## ACT III–SCENE 3

### Summary

Falstaff steps into the trap set for him by Mrs. Page and Mrs. Ford.
"Have I caught thee, my heavenly jewel?" the fat knight croons to Mrs.
Ford upon arrival, only to find himself a few minutes later demeaningly
transported out of her house in a "buck-basket" (a dirty linen hamper) to
avoid discovery by her husband. Ford is fooled as well, since he fully
expected to find the fat knight compromising his wife's "honesty." For Mrs.
Ford's part, the pleasure is a double one: "I know not which pleases me
better—that my husband is deceived, or Sir John." The two women immediately plan a further adventure in order to offer Falstaff "another hope,
to betray him to another punishment."

Disappointed and embarrassed, Ford invites Page, Caius, and Evans
to a dinner which he has promised them. At the end of the scene, Caius
and Evans reaffirm their plan to be revenged on the Host.

### Commentary

Falstaff enters the scene; now he is "sweet Sir John," the over-age,
would-be courtly lover, spouting poetry and eager for a sexual conquest.
He exits this scene as a whale with so many "tuns of oil in his belly,"
crammed into a basket which no doubt sags precariously between its unfortunate bearers. Imagine the sight of Falstaff trying to save his skin by
squeezing into the basket:

> *Mrs. Ford:* He's too big to go in there. What shall I do?
> *Falstaff:* Let me see it, let me see it. O let me see it! I'll
>    in, I'll in! Follow your friend's counsel. I'll in!

(142–44)

Shakespeare compounds the insult by strongly contrasting the language
of Falstaff to the reality of his situation. References made to smelling "like
Bucklersbury in simple-time" (the street in London where herbs were sold)
are especially comical when one considers the stench of dirty linen under
which Falstaff will soon find himself. Mrs. Ford extends the idea, no doubt
hardly able to stifle her laughter, when she explains to Mrs. Page that

Falstaff's extreme fear may cause him to loose his bowels, so that he'll be in a *real* need of ducking in ditch water, which they have instructed the servants to give him:

> *Mrs. Page:* What a taking [fright] was he in when your
>    husband asked who was in the basket!
> *Mrs. Ford:* I am half afraid he will have need of wash-
>    ing; so throwing him into the water will do him a
>    benefit.
>
> (191–95)

Just as Falstaff is being lugged off-stage, Ford hesitates before the basket, but he does not inspect anything. The tension is exquisitely comic, and it intensifies when Ford hears the buzz-word "buck" (cuckold) uttered by his wife, albeit with a different meaning. One wonders if she puts stress on the word, however, in order to raise his hackles.

> *Mrs. Ford:* Why, what have you to do whither they bear
>    it [the basket]? You were best meddle with
>    buck-washing!
> *Ford:* Buck? I would I could wash myself of the buck
>    [horned animal—*i.e.,* cuckold]! Buck, buck buck! Ay,
>    buck; I warrant you, buck—and of the season too, it
>    shall appear.
>
> (163–69)

Ford's extreme reaction and Falstaff's extreme debasement highlight the scene.

## ACT III – SCENES 4 & 5

### Summary

Fenton assures Anne Page that he truly loves her, although he admits her "father's wealth/ Was the first motive that I wooed thee." Their conversation ends abruptly when Slender arrives. Anne despairingly speaks her thoughts on the matter in an aside:

> This is my father's choice. O what a world of vile,
> ill-favoured faults looks handsome in three hundred
> pounds a year.
>
> (31–33)

Slender attempts to engage Anne in small talk for a few moments, but Mrs. Page and Mistress Quickly suddenly join them. Anne's mother's choice of a suitor is equally distasteful, and when Quickly refers to her "Master Doctor" as a possible husband, Anne unequivocally refuses:

Alas, I had rather be set quick i' th' earth
And bowled to death with turnips.

(90–91)

Scene 4 ends with Mistress Quickly on stage, determined to "do what I can for them all three"—that is, whatever she can do for the potential husbands, for a *price!* (She has just taken a ring and a bribe to deliver the ring to Anne from Fenton.)

In Scene 5, Falstaff guzzles wine to counter the effect of his dousing in the river, both the wet and the horror of it. As he explains,

And you may know by my size that I have a kind of alacrity in sinking. If the bottom were as deep as hell, I should down. . . . I should have been a mountain of mummy [dead flesh].

(11–13; 18)

The sight of Master Brook (Ford in disguise) cheers Falstaff into considering another try with Mrs. Ford: "I like his money well." The scene ends as Ford, fuming with anger at having been tricked with the buck-basket (as Falstaff just explained), determines to catch the "lecher" the next time.

## Commentary

Fenton and Anne Page are the normative characters in the comedy. Although ruled at first by the same motivations as the rest of the world, Fenton honestly explains that he would now love Anne—even if he didn't need her money. The audience, conventionally, accepts this as a fact and therefore turns its keener attention to the idiocies of the alternate lovers. The scene between Anne Page and Slender is a classic piece of comedy. From previous scenes, we know that Slender is taken with the idea of marrying Anne Page, yet once he is with her, he freezes and becomes a tongue-tied adolescent. Shallow encourages the small talk between them, but Slender can barely function:

*Shallow:* She's coming; to her, coz. O boy, thou hadst a
father!
*Slender:* I had a father, Mistress Anne [here, one
imagines a pause, then an exasperated pitch for
help]; my uncle can tell you good jests of him. Pray
you, uncle, tell Mistress Anne the jest how my father
stole two geese out of a pen, good uncle.
*Shallow:* Mistress Anne, my cousin loves you.
*Slender:* Ay, that I do. . . .
*Anne:* Good Master Shallow, let him woo for himself.

(36–43; 51)

To top this comic turn, Slender reverts to his old self (or at least his old words) when he tells Anne that the whole idea was hatched by his uncle and her father in the first place. Anything, it seems, is preferable to poor Slender than having to come face-to-face with such a young, energetic woman!

Falstaff's description of his misadventure ranks among the richest displays of language in the play. He has just consumed immense quantities of wine in a short period, and he now unloads his woeful tale on Master Brook/Ford. Of course, Ford has very mixed emotions here. Undoubtedly he loves the idea of Falstaff's smelly demise; on the other hand, he is furious at having been duped himself. He is also worried that Falstaff won't be willing to give it another try. One must read the following speech in the spirit of pompous (and theatrical) injured dignity which only a Falstaff can muster:

> I suffered the pangs of three several deaths: first, an
> intolerable fright to be detected with [by] a jealous rotten
> bell-wether [cuckold]; next, to be compassed like a good
> bilbo [flexed sword] in the circumference of a peck, hilt
> to point, heel to head; and then, to be stopp'd in, like a
> strong distillation, with stinking clothes that fretted in
> their own grease. Think of that, a man of my kidney
> [temperament]—think of that—that am as subject to heat
> as butter; a man of continued dissolution and thaw. It
> was a miracle to 'scape suffocation. And in the height of
> this bath, when I was more than half stewed in grease,
> like a Dutch dish, to be thrown into the Thames, and
> cooled, glowing hot, in that surge, like a horseshoe.
> Think of that—hissing hot—think of that, Master Brook!
>
> (109–23)

Remember that Falstaff is also putting on a performance here for a fee. He wants Brook to know the full extent of the suffering he has endured "to bring this woman to evil for your good." Each of them is eager beyond all previous measure to see the plot succeed next time—one out of greed, the other because of jealousy.

## ACT IV—SCENE 1

### Summary

Mrs. Page asks Sir Hugh Evans to test her son William in his Latin grammatical inflections. While Sir Hugh does so, Mistress Quickly repeatedly interrupts with absurd comments and off-color remarks, deriving from unintentional puns on the Latin words which William recites.

## Commentary

This scene has absolutely nothing to do with the plot of the play, and various commentators have suggested that Shakespeare added it as an amusement for an educated audience at a special performance, since only they would understand the Latin puns. That is debatable, however, since even the middle class would have had enough schooling (as had William in the play) to catch most of the references. The scene serves at least the technical function of allowing bridging action between Falstaff's resolve to try his luck again with Mrs. Ford, and his arrival at her house. Furthermore, what transpires is amusing in itself (or was, for an audience that understood Latin), as we witness a poor schoolboy caught between a pedant and a daffy woman while he tries to do his lessons. When William hears "focative case" (vocative, in Welsh dialect), he answers "O–vocativo, O"–in all innocence! But Quickly and a sophisticated audience know that "case" also means "pudenda," making the "O" an unintentional, obscene pun.

## ACT IV–SCENES 2-4

### Summary

The wives engineer a second narrow escape for Falstaff from the furious Ford, this time as "the witch of Brainford," Mrs. Ford's maid's fat aunt, the mere sight of whom sends Ford into a rage. Falstaff submits to disguising himself as a woman so that he can evade Ford and the crowd which accompanies him. To escape, however, he must first endure a cudgeling:

> Ford: I'll 'prat' [best] her. Out of my door, you witch,
> you hag, you baggage, you polecat, you ronyon!
> Out, out!

(194–95)

Still asserting that his "jealousy is reasonable," Ford searches for evidence of his wife's unfaithfulness–again in vain.

Scene 3 is an interlude in which Bardolph tells the host of the Garter Inn about the arrival of a German duke. Three of his compatriots need to hire horses to go meet him. The Host emphasizes that he will "make them pay; I'll sauce them."

The "merry wives" determine to carry on their harrassment of John Falstaff, if their husbands so wish. In Scene 4, Ford begs pardon of his wife for his being such a fool–"I rather will suspect the sun with cold/ Than thee with wantonness"–and the group decides to have one last sport at Falstaff's expense. A local folk tale has it that "Herne the Hunter," many years ago a gamekeeper in Windsor Forest, haunts the area in wintertime, blighting the trees and bewitching the cattle. He walks around an old oak tree, wearing "great ragg'd horns," and shaking a chain "in a most hideous and dreadful manner." The plan is to induce Falstaff to meet both women at Herne's oak, wearing horns on his head and disguised as the ancient gamekeeper. The rest of the company will surprise him and "mock him home to Windsor." Before the scene ends, both Page and Mrs. Page separately reveal (in asides) that they will help their daughter sneak off to marry each one's favorite suitor, respectively Slender and Doctor Caius.

## Commentary

The merry pace of the farce continues here, showing an absurd disguising of Falstaff as a fat witch and promising yet another, Falstaff horned like a beast, as "Herne the Hunter." There is a gleeful sense of mischief in Mrs. Page and Mrs. Ford's actions, which dictates the tone of the scenes. As Mrs. Page puts it, "We'll leave a proof by that which we will do/ Wives may be merry, and yet honest too." In order to keep the wives' high spirits on this side of sadism and to break the monotony, Shakespeare draws the husbands into the final plot to unmask Falstaff. Indeed, there is something almost festive about the two families' plans for the midnight plot.

> *Mrs. Page:* Nan Page, my daughter, and my little son,
>     and three or four more of their growth, we'll dress
>     like urchins, ouphes [elves], and fairies, green and
>     white, with rounds of waxen tapers on their heads,
>     and rattles in their hands. Upon a sudden, as
>     Falstaff, she, and I are newly met. . . . Let them all
>     encircle him about. And, fairy-like, to pinch the
>     unclean knight.
>
> (47–52; 56–57)

Even Mrs. Page and her benevolent husband have blind spots when it comes to the marriage of their daughter Anne. The mother's desire for social connections ("friends potent at court") spurs her on to propose a secret wedding with Doctor Caius; and, as before, Mr. Page is intent on having the financially sound "Master Slender steal my Nan away." Folly is not the sole property of Falstaff in this play.

## ACT IV–SCENES 5 & 6

### Summary

Slender has sent his man Simple to seek the advice of the "Witch of Brainford" on two matters: (1) a chain which he suspects Nym to have stolen and (2) the prospects of his marrying Anne Page. Falstaff explains that the fat woman has just left, but not before they discussed these very things. Stupidly satisfied that his master will be pleased to hear that Anne Page "might or might not" accept Slender, Simple leaves. Next, we learn of the Host's ill-fortune. His horses have been stolen by "three cozen-Germans." Falstaff, in a depressed state himself, welcomes the news of anyone else's misery: "I would all the world might be cozened, for I have been cozened [cheated] and beaten too." Quickly lures Falstaff to his chamber with a letter which promises a means of bringing him together with "two parties." He follows her.

Fenton solicits the aid of the Host in procuring Anne Page as his wife. He explains her mother's and father's separate plans to marry her to men of *their* choice.

> *Host:* Which means she to deceive, father or mother?
> *Fenton:* Both, my good Host, to go along with me.
>
> (46–47)

The Host agrees to help by hiring a priest and be waiting in an appointed spot.

### Commentary

Falstaff is the largest figure in *The Merry Wives of Windsor* in every imaginable way. What a colossal ego it must take to find oneself thwarted twice in secret assignations with a woman—only to be seduced by the idea of having one's way with two women at a time! The fun is amplified by the hypocrisy of the perpetrator. Falstaff is loved because he is incorrigible: "Well, if my wind were but long enough to say my prayers, I would repent." References to the petty idiocies of characters such as Slender and to the more ordinary machinations of Evans (who, with Caius, probably stole the Host's horses) make Falstaff seem even a greater (while lesser) character.

The Fenton episode is purely traditional in inspiration: in romantic comedy, true love must find its way to fruition.

### ACT V—SCENES 1–5

### Summary

Falstaff promises Master Brook some "wonders" at midnight by Herne's oak; Page reminds Slender that his daughter will be waiting; and Mrs. Page reassures Caius that Anne Page is ready to be swept away "to the deanery" (to be married); Hugh Evans, disguised as a satyr, calls "Trib, trib [trip], fairies" and leads a troop of revelers to their rendezvous in Windsor Park. So much for the first four scenes of the final act of *The Merry Wives of Windsor*.

Scene 5 is the climax of the play. Horns on his head, Falstaff calls on "the hot-blooded gods" to assist him. He is virtually licking his lips in anticipation when the two women appear. He "magnanimously" proposes to both of them: "Divide me like a bribed [filched] buck, each a haunch." Immediately the general hubbub of the assembled "fairies" is heard, and the two women run off, leaving Falstaff believing that hell itself has had a hand in preventing his sexual mischief these three times: "I think the devil will not have me damned, lest the oil that's in me should set hell on fire. He would never else cross me thus."

Falstaff throws himself down but is discovered (hardly surprising!) by the satyr (Evans) and the Fairy Queen (Quickly). They put him to the test of chastity: touching his "finger end" with fire. When he cries out in pain, the lecher is denounced:

> Corrupt, corrupt, and tainted in desire!
> About him, fairies, sing a scornful rhyme;
> And, as you trip, still pinch him to your time.
>
> (94–96)

When all decide to end the jest, Falstaff confesses, "I do begin to perceive that I am made an ass." Both Slender and Doctor Caius arrive before long and announce that they have been tricked into running off with *boys,* whom they mistook for Anne Page. To end the play, the newly married couple, Master Fenton and Anne Page, explain themselves:

> The truth is, she and I, long since contracted, are now so
> Sure [wedded] that nothing can dissolve us.
>
> (234–35)

All present cheer the outcome and follow Mrs. Page:

> Heaven give you [Anne and Fenton] many, many
>     merry days!
> Good husband, let us every one go home,
> And laugh this sport o'er by a country fire;
> Sir John and all.
>
> (254–57)

## Commentary

A change in style marks the very last scene of the play. The verse, the elaborate costumes, and the ceremonial nature of the events involving the "fairy kingdom" in the harrassment and final exposure of Falstaff resemble a courtly masque in form. The masque was a courtly entertainment that stressed allegorical figures, splendid costuming, and dancing, in which audience members were encouraged to participate. It highlighted special occasions at court. Many scholars associate *The Merry Wives of Windsor* (certainly this part of it) with the installation of new members into the honored Order of the Garter by Queen Elizabeth in May, 1597.

(Indeed, George Carey, the second Lord Hunsdon and a favorite of the Queen, was installed on that occasion.) He was also the patron of Shakespeare's company of actors at the time. When Mistress Quickly, incongruously decked out as the Fairy Queen, instructs the fairy troupe to search the area for any creatures unfit to be present, she makes direct references to Windsor and to the chapel of St. George, where the Knights of the Garter had their stalls.

> *Quickly:* About, about.
> Search Windsor Castle, elves, within and out.
> Strew good luck, ouphes, on every sacred room,
> That it may stand till the perpetual doom,
> In state as wholesome as in state 'tis fit,
> Worthy the owner, and the owner it.
> The several chairs of order [of the Garter] look
>     you scour
> With juice of balm and every precious flower.
>
> (59–66)

Regardless of these historical details, the final scene offers a splendid and fantastical ending to the comedy. Major characters are transformed and amazed, one after the other. Falstaff has become a horned beast, then an "ass," by his own admittance. His physical torment is real when they "put tapers to his fingers," but one imagines the humiliation which he endures goes beyond that pain: "Have I lived to stand at the taunt of one that makes fritters of English [that is, of Hugh Evans, the Welshman]?"

In the spirit of this good-natured farce, no resistance is offered to the final piece of trickery which results in a perfect matrimonial match between Fenton and Anne Page. General applause and a "country fire" round out the play, which includes *all* of the characters in its final celebration.

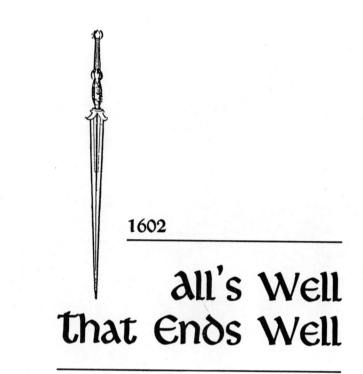

1602

# All's Well That Ends Well

# INTRODUCTION

It is difficult to assign a date to the composition of *All's Well*. There are no definite allusions or associations with contemporary slang or happenings. There are a good number of rimed couplets, suggesting that this play might be an early work of Shakespeare's. But because these couplets are such fine examples, they suggest a mastery of the couplet tradition instead of immaturity. Most scholars who note errors in characterization, as well as entrance and exit notations, seem to think that this First Folio edition is probably a recast, rewritten version of the play, lacking Shakespeare's final editing. And because of one of its key lines, they think that it may be a "lost play" of Shakespeare's—*Love's Labour's Won.*

Shakespeare's plot of a beautiful woman who is turned down by the man whom she loves—after she has cured a king of a critical illness—is clearly taken from William Painter's *Palace of Pleasure* (1566), a situation that had already been explored by Boccaccio in his *Decameron;* both stories also contain the ingenious "bed trick." At that time, Helena's cleverness in getting a child from Bertram would have been applauded. The baby would have been proof of her deep love and courage. It was sterling—if ironic—proof of her vow of fidelity. Then, as well as today, Bertram would have had few redeeming qualities. He lacks all sense of honor; he is a cad. Thus, the comedy is ultimately flawed. We cannot totally rejoice at Helena's "success" in regaining her husband. The play simply has a rapid "happy ending," which was required. Ultimately, we feel that Helena is such a remarkable woman that her absolute infatuation with a fraud makes her character suspect. The meaning of *All's Well* is, therefore, ambiguous and seemingly ironic.

# A BRIEF SYNOPSIS

The central action of *All's Well That Ends Well* concerns Helena, a beautiful woman, and her pursuit of a man of higher social position than herself in the French court of Rousillon. Helena is the daughter of a recently deceased court physician; the man whom she pursues is Bertram, a young man of the nobility, who is in mourning for his late father, the Count.

Helena follows Bertram to Paris where, as a reward for "miraculously" curing the king of an apparently terminal illness, she is granted the husband of her choice. She chooses Bertram. Bertram at first refuses to have her, but then he submits to the angry king's command—but only outwardly.

Together with his dubious "follower" Parolles, Bertram flees France to fight in the Italian wars, where he plans to achieve the necessary "honor" suitable to his rank. Furthermore, he vows never to consummate his marriage with Helena unless she can perform two "impossible" tasks: (1) "get the ring upon [which is on] my finger," and (2) "show me a child begotten of thy body that I am father to." Helena does just that, with the help of a widow (whom she pays handsomely) and the widow's virgin daughter, Diana. During the well-known "bed trick," Bertram is fooled into believing that he has made love to Diana, whereas, in reality, Helena has smuggled herself into the bed. An exchange of rings also takes place. Diana and Helena continue the ruse until the last minutes of the play, when they surprise the entire Parisian court (who think that Helena is dead), and they then embarrass Bertram deeply when they reveal what has transpired. But Helena finally has her man, and "all" has apparently ended "well."

In a comical subplot, another "trick" is used, this time to reveal Parolles' dishonesty in the presence of Bertram; Parolles is taken captive, blindfolded, and outrageous denunciations are extracted from him about Bertram and others. But even Parolles is grudgingly accepted back into the company at the end of the play. Again, "all's well that ends well"—apparently.

# LIST OF CHARACTERS

### Helena

The daughter of a very famous, recently deceased court physician, Helena has the physical and mental attributes which could command the attention of virtually any eligible bachelor, but unfortunately, she does not have the correct social pedigree to entice the man whom she loves, Bertram, a Count's son. Through the use of her native wit and the body of knowledge which she inherits from her father, as well as because of her sheer strength of will, she overcomes all obstacles and wins Bertram. To some commentators on this play, Helena's tactics seem questionable, although no one underestimates her strength of character.

### Bertram

For several reasons, Bertram seems significantly inferior to Helena. He is under the influence of the patently superficial Parolles, and he lies outright on more than one occasion. Furthermore, he blatantly disregards the king's wishes. To a twentieth-century audience, he might seem to have every right to refuse a forced marriage, but to the world which the play inhabits, that is not the case. Besides, Helena is clearly (in everyone else's opinion) a splendid person. The play ends, however, in such an abrupt manner that Shakespeare leaves us wondering just how "well" all has "ended" for Bertram and his "rightful" bride.

## King of France

In his prime, the king was a valiant warrior and a staunch friend of Bertram's father. He is utterly charmed by Helena, and he is grateful for the cure which she administers to him. All of this makes his outrage even greater when Bertram refuses to accept Helena as a bride. He exerts his royal authority to force the marriage, and in Shakespeare's scheme of things in the play, he seems to be right in doing so.

## Countess of Rousillon

Bertram's mother fully sympathizes with Helena in her state of love-lorn agony, and she goes so far as to say that she will disown her son as a result of his rejection of her adopted "daughter." She does what she can to make things "end well."

## Lafeu

Lafeu is an elderly friend of the Countess and her family. His role is that of adviser and mollifier. He is the first to see through Parolles' schemes, and it is his daughter whose planned marriage to Bertram (before Helena is "resurrected" at the end of the play) will signal a return to good order.

## Parolles

Lafeu sums up the character of Parolles when he says: "The soul of this man is his clothes." Parolles is the tempter of Bertram as a "prodigal son," and in the end, Parolles is seen as such and rejected.

## Clown (Lavache)

The Countess' servant offers comic reflections about several characters in the play, most pointedly about Parolles. His mouth is lewd, and his manner is absurd.

## A Widow of Florence

For a fee, the widow helps Helena arrange and execute the old "bed trick"; here, Bertram is trapped into sleeping with his own wife in the belief that she is another woman.

## Diana

Diana is the widow's daughter and Helena's ally in her pursuit of Bertram. She is the bait used to trap Bertram. Diana displays a good deal of wit and a composed bearing under the pressure of the courtly observers during the final "revelation scene."

## Mariana

A neighbor of the widow.

## Two French Lords, the Brothers Dumain

The two noblemen who mastermind the plot to expose Parolles. They are friends to Bertram.

# SUMMARIES AND COMMENTARIES

## ACT I—SCENE 1

### Summary

At the opening of this play, the main figures of the plot are weighed down with thoughts of two recent deaths. "Young Bertram," the Count of Rousillon (in France), has lost his father, as has Helena, the beautiful daughter of a famed physician, Gerard de Narbon, "whose skill was almost as great as his honesty." Bertram's mother is further distressed that she must say farewell to her son, now a ward of the ailing king of France. Opening the play, she exclaims: "In delivering my son from me [to the king's court], I bury a second husband." As an older lord and a close family friend, Lafeu assures the Countess that in the king she shall find someone as good as a second husband for herself and a second father for Bertram.

Once mother and son have said their goodbyes and he has departed, Helena delivers a soliloquy in which she reveals a double reason for her sadness. "I am undone; there is no living, none, if Bertram be away . . ." A "follower" of Bertram, named Parolles, interrupts her and engages her in an extended dialogue on the subject of virginity. He pledges that he will "return [a] perfect courtier" from Paris, where he is about to go with Bertram. A second soliloquy, this time by Helena, reveals her to be resolute in her pledge to pursue her unlikely attempt at capturing Bertram's heart: ". . . my project may deceive me, but my intents are fixed, and will not leave me."

### Commentary

A gloomy mood at the opening of the play is often customary for a Shakespearean comedy. But amidst the general lamentation over departures and deaths, there is some emotional ambiguity which sets a tone for this "problem play," as *All's Well* has been called by some critics. Lafeu remarks on Helena's tears at the Countess' praise, whereupon the older woman kindly says that Helena must *not* cry lest people think that she is "affecting" or putting on her sad demeanor. Helena's answer—"I do affect a sorrow indeed, but I have it too"—seems puzzling, until we learn in her soliloquy that she is crying for the sake of her unacknowledged lover, and not (or not entirely) for her deceased father. Helena keeps to herself much of the time, partly because she may be embarrassed at the feelings she has for a person beyond her station, socially. In the first moments of the play, she is uneasy, aware that Bertram is "so far above me."

One wonders what Bertram's feelings in this first scene may be. Though some editors have disputed the placement of Lafeu's second line in the following exchange, it seems possible that the wise, older gentleman is reacting to Bertram's abruptness in cutting off his mother's speech.

> *Lafeu:* Moderate lamentation is the right of the dead,
>    Excessive grief the enemy to the living.
> *Countess:* If the living be enemy to the grief,
>    The excess makes it soon mortal.
> *Bertram:* Madam, I desire your holy wishes.
> *Lafeu:* How understand we that?

(64–69)

There is something of a gentle handslap in the tone of Lafeu's last line. Bertram may be speaking rudely, overstepping the quite normal impatience of a young man about to leave home (and to leave off mourning) for a more adventuresome life in Paris. Consider for yourself if this line—"How understand we that?"—makes sense here, or if it might better fit in just before the words "moderate lamentation," where some editors place it.

There is an abrupt shift in tone at Parolles' entrance. Helena confides that he is a "notorious liar" whom she tolerates only because of his association with Bertram. The conversation between the two, saturated in polite obscenity, gives the audience a clear view of the play's heroine as someone who is not so romantic and frail that she cannot survive in the gritty world of court sexuality. Parolles argues conventionally that virginity is nonsensical since it goes against nature and since it condemns, as it were, its own mother, and furthermore, he says that it loses its value proportionately with age. Helena can bandy easily enough with this affected man of the world and can ask in her own private interest, "How might one do, sir, to lose it [one's virginity] to her own liking?" But her mind is fixed on Bertram, for he will soon appear at court in Paris. Notice the way that her lines are broken to indicate breathlessness and distraction as she imagines Bertram there amidst pretty mistresses:

> . . . with a world of pretty, fond, adoptious christendoms
> [young women with adopted names] that blinking Cupid

> gossips [*i.e.*, that the god of love godfathers]. Now shall
> he—I know not what he shall. God send him well! The
> court's a learning place, and he is one—
>
> (187–92)

Helena insults Parolles, calling him a coward and an overdressed fool, and
he beats a hasty retreat. Her feistiness is evident.

Helena's second soliloquy differs from the first in its view of fate. Now
the focus is on individual determination.

> Our remedies oft in ourselves do lie,
> Which we ascribe to heaven. The fated sky
>     [influence of the stars]
> Gives us free scope; only doth backward pull
> Our slow designs when we ourselves are dull.
>
> (231–34)

The exchange between Helena and Parolles seems to have had the effect
of bolstering her courage.

## ACT I–SCENE 2

### Summary

Bertram presents himself at court in Paris just as the king is bidding
his soldiers to fight in the Italian wars. The sight of Bertram, Lafeu, and
Parolles spurs memories of former days:

> I would I had that corporal soundness now,
> As when thy father and myself in friendship
> First tried our soldiership!
>
> (24–26)

At the end of this short scene, the king asks how long it has been since
the court physician at Rousillon died; if he were still alive—perhaps he
could cure the king's illness.

### Commentary

Shakespeare broadly contrasts youth and age here, with Bertram
greeting the feeble king while preparations are made for a war in which
the young gentlemen of France can prove themselves. Note that the war
is described as being more a training ground than anything else: ". . . freely
have they leave/ To stand on either part" means they can fight for either
Siena or Florence, as far as the king is concerned. In this play, "honor"
has a number of different connotations, one of which is the prestige a young
man like Bertram can achieve in battle.

One remark which the king makes in describing Bertram's father has a bearing on the previous scene. The king says:

> Who were below him he used as creatures of another place,
> And bowed his eminent top to their low ranks,
> Making them proud of his humility,
> In their poor praise he humbled.

(42–45)

The gist of the comment is that Bertram's father was *not* a social snob. Ironically, a motivating factor in Bertram's behavior toward Helena (whom we know to be sensitive to the issue) is just such snobbery.

### ACT I – SCENE 3

**Summary**

The clown Lavache begs the Countess for permission to marry Isbel for the simple reason that he is "driven on by the flesh." The Countess listens to his facetious and cynical logic concerning marriage, and then playfully (though this will change), she remonstrates with him: "Wilt thou ever be a foul-mouthed and calumnious knave?"

In the second part of the scene, the Countess' steward informs her that he has overheard Helena, who thought she was alone, saying that "she loved your son." "Keep it to yourself," is the Countess' advice, adding, "Many likelihoods informed me of this before. . . ." Helena enters and when confronted with the fact—"You love my son"—she begs pardon. But, to her surprise, she receives Bertram's mother's blessing in her endeavor—"Thou shalt have my leave and love"—and so Helena makes plans to go to Paris with a remedy "to cure the desperate languishings whereof/ The King is rendered lost." Of course, her plan is also to pursue the man she loves.

**Commentary**

In the encounter with the clown, the Countess engages in explicit sexual talk, just as Helena did with Parolles. Shakespeare's clowns, of course, had license to say things which smack of the other side of respectability, but these two scenes which depict refined women at ease with the language of obscene puns and innuendoes give a strong impression of the very real sexual matter at the heart of *All's Well That Ends Well.*

The steward's description of Helena, who expressed herself "in the most bitter touch of sorrow that e'er I heard virgin exclaim in," moves the Countess to reflect on her own past romantic involvements:

> Even so it was with me, when I was young;

> If ever we are nature's, these [pains] are ours; this thorn
> Doth to our rose of youth rightly belong;
> Our blood [passion] to us, this to our blood is born.
>
> (134–37)

This observation, and the affection it implies for Helena, parallels the scene between Bertram and the King of France, where age views youth with compassion and understanding. Helena's tortured evasiveness (she doesn't want to be considered the Countess' daughter and therefore merely Bertram's "sister") is matched by her pluck. She describes herself as coming from "poor but honest" stock and will not "have him [Bertram] till I do deserve him," for—as yet—she hasn't singlemindedly made an effort to pursue him. However, the idea of going to Paris with a secret remedy of her father's to cure the king was surely prompted by her desire to follow Bertram. She impresses the Countess enormously by the end of the scene. Some critics have been less sympathetic to Helena, viewing her as merely a clever fortune-hunter who lays her plans in these early scenes. Is there any justification for that view?

## ACT II – SCENE 1

### Summary

In Paris, the king wishes his young warriors well as they leave for the Italian wars: ". . . be you the sons/ Of worthy Frenchmen . . . see that you come/ Not to woo honor, but to wed it." He adds a sly note to "beware the Italian women!" Bertram, who is unhappy that he must linger behind— and be told that he is "too young" and that he must wait until "the next year"—succumbs to Parolles' and the other lords' urging to steal away on his own, for "there's honour in the theft."

Lafeu and the king now exchange formal greetings, and the elder statesman politely urges the king to shake off despair:

> . . . O, will you eat no grapes, my royal fox?
> Yes, but you will my noble grapes . . . if my royal fox
> Could reach them. I have seen a medicine
> That's able to breathe life into a stone.
>
> (72–75)

Soon, Lafeu introduces Helena, "Doctor She," who explains her presence and describes her deceased father's special cure:

> And, hearing your high majesty is touched
> With that malignant cause wherein the honour
> Of my dear father's gift stands chief in power,

I come to tender it and my appliance
With all bound humbleness.

(113-17)

After a short debate between himself and Helena, the king decides to give her a chance to cure him. She offers her life as the penalty should she fail; and as the reward for success:

Then shalt thou give me with thy kingly hand
What husband in thy power I will command.

(198-99)

(Out of modesty, she of course excludes the royal bloodline of France.) The sickly king, amazed by this bold young woman, agrees, and then he asks to be helped from the stage:

Unquestioned, welcome and undoubted blest.
Give me some help here, ho! If thou proceed
As high as word, my deed shall match thy deed.

(211-13)

## Commentary

The framework of this scene provides insights into the two central characters, although Bertram and Helena are not seen together. There is something puppyish about Bertram; his feelings are hurt deeply because the rest of the young noblemen are riding off to battle while he must remain behind. Shakespeare paints a picture of youthful petulance and malleability in this part of the scene, as Parolles acts as a tempter and as a bad influence to Bertram. His advice is to ignore the king's command and, furthermore, to study the ways of the courtly gentlemen and soldiers in order to become a perfectly fashionable man of the world—presumably like Parolles himself. Of course, the audience (and virtually everyone else on stage besides Bertram) can see right through Parolles' bombast. One imagines the other noblemen urging Bertram and Parolles into their company with their tongues tucked firmly into their cheeks. Parolles typically stresses fashion (one wonders how outlandishly he is dressed) when talking to his companion: "Be more expressive to them, for they wear themselves in the cap of time; there do muster true gait, eat, speak, and move under the influence of the most received [up-to-date] star; and though the devil lead the measure, such are to be followed. After them, and take a more dilated [extended] farewell." The reference here to "devil" is Shakespeare's way of underlining a similarity in this situation to the "prodigal son" stories in the Bible and other traditional sources.

Consider Helena's behavior in the latter section of the scene. As a woman, she is conventionally conceived of as being frail; the thought of her being a professional (a doctor) is absurd; and the notion that she – a mere woman – could cure a *king* would normally be beyond imagining. Nevertheless, she overcomes the king's doubts, which are, given his time, reasonable enough. He fears that people will think that he's downright dotty if it were known that a "maiden" is attending him as a physician:

> I say we must not so stain our judgment or corrupt our hope,
> To prostitute our past-cure malady to empirics [quacks],
> Or to dissever so our great self and our credit,
> To esteem a senseless help, when help past sense we deem.
>
> (122-25)

Using her skill of rhetoric, larded with aphoristic remarks like,

> Oft expectation fails, and most oft there
> Where most it promises, and oft it hits
> Where hope is coldest and despair most fits.
>
> (145-47)

Helena finally sways the king to give her a chance. Perhaps she nudges him over the edge by hinting that she is a divine emissary:

> But most it is presumption in us when
> The help of Heaven we count the act of men.
>
> (154-55)

Some critics have observed a trace of the fairy tale formula in this section of the play, in which the young virgin "magically" cures an ailing king. This may be so, but one cannot fail to be impressed by the sheer doggedness of Shakespeare's heroine. Her effort of will commands the end of the scene, contrasting with Bertram's jellyfish compliance at its opening.

## ACT II – SCENE 2

### Summary

The Countess and her clown/servant, Lavache, discourse on the subject of the "court," where he is shortly to be sent on an errand.

### Commentary

This comical interlude has a threefold function: (1) as a bridge, (2) as an emotional and thematic gloss on the scenes either side of it, and (3) as a simple entertainment in itself. Remember, Shakespeare's comic actors were given room for improvisation, and hence a scene like this one, obliquely satirizing courtly manners, could be largely visual in the person of the clown preparing himself to make an appearance before a group of courtiers. While practicing the art of foppishly affected speech – the inanely repeated "universal answer" to every question is "O Lord, sir!" – the clown is no doubt also training himself physically, in highly artificial, dance-like movements. *This,* Shakespeare seems to be saying, is the world to which Bertram wants to attach himself.

## ACT II – SCENE 3

### Summary

At first, Parolles, Bertram, and Lafeu are alone on stage, responding in awe to the healing of the king. Lafeu reads a report: "A showing of a heavenly effect in an earthly actor."

The king is quick to fulfill his promise, as he commands his noblemen to assemble before the triumphant healer, Helena:

> Thy frank election [choice] make;
> Thou hast power to choose, and they none to forsake . . .
> Who shuns thy love shuns all his love in me.

(61–62/79)

Helena tells all present that she has already made up her mind which man she'll have, but she nonetheless playfully approaches, and rejects, four others before coming to Bertram and saying,

> I dare not say I take you, but I give
> Me and my service, ever whilst I live,
> Into your guiding power. This is the man.

(109–11)

Bertram's shock at her choice prompts not only a feeling of rejection within Helena, but what amounts to an insult – "A poor physician's daughter my wife! Disdain/ Rather corrupt me ever!" The king will have none of this, and he immediately lectures Bertram on the foolishness of social snobbery; then he exerts his power to command, forcing Bertram to take Helena's hand. Bertram submits, and the company disperses.

Parolles denies his master to Lafeu,

> *Parolles:* Recantation! My lord! My master!
> *Lafeu:* Ay; is it not a language I speak?
> *Parolles:* A most harsh one, and not to be understood
>    without bloody succeeding. My master!

(196–99)

And Lafeu, who admits having been impressed by the hanger-on, says,

> I did think thee, for two ordinaries [meals],
> To be a pretty wise fellow,

(211–12)

and then bids him good riddance:

> *Parolles:* My lord, you give me most egregious indignity.
> *Lafeu:* Ay, with all my heart, and thou art worthy of it.
> > (228–29)

At Lafeu's exit, Bertram returns to Parolles with the words

> O my Parolles, they have married me!
> I'll to the Tuscan wars and never bed her.
> > (289–90)

Only too eager to escape a further confrontation with Lafeu and possible exposure as a false friend to Bertram, Parolles urges the younger man on "to other regions!"

## Commentary

The exposure of Parolles and the disgrace of Bertram accentuate this scene, one which otherwise would have depicted Helena's triumph. There is something unsettling in the atmosphere from the start, and even the curing of the king leaves little room overall for celebration, ending as it does in an outburst of anger by the healed party.

Shakespeare's dramaturgy works by continuously using contrasting scenes. Parolles' inane stuttering in Scene 3 – "So I say, so I say, So would I have said" – echoes the clown's mockery of "court" speech in Scene 2.

Contrast Helena's eloquence and wit in dealing with the assembled noblemen after, as she puts it, "Heaven hath through me restored the King to health." She typically snubs the First Lord with a quick rhyme: suit/mute.

> *Helena:* Now, Dian, from thy altar do I fly,
> > And to Imperial love, that god most high,
> > Do my sighs stream. [To First Lord:]
> > Sir, will you hear my suit?
> *First Lord:* And grant it.
> *Helena:* Thanks, sir, all the rest is mute.
> > (80–85)

Since Bertram has himself been mute through most of this scene, one wonders if it gradually dawns on him that Helena is preparing to choose him as her husband. In an earlier scene, she did say that "'Twas pretty, though a plague,/ To see him every hour, to sit and draw/ His arched brows, his hawking eye, his curls,/ In our heart's table." (I.1. 103–04). She apparently has spent hours watching him, perhaps not unnoticed. Still, there is a shock when the "sentence," as it seems to him, is pronounced:

> *King:* Why then, young Bertram, take her; she's thy wife.
> *Bertram:* My wife, my liege! I shall beseech your Highness,
> > In such business give me leave to use
> > The help of mine own eyes.

> *King:* Know'st thou not, Bertram,
>     What she has done for me?
> *Bertram:* Yes, my good lord;
>     But never hope to know why I should marry her.
>
> (112-19)

Note that the king and the people in attendance on him were, according to the conventional pattern of social behavior in Shakespeare's day, undoubtedly shocked, and correctly so, at Bertram's refusal. Marriage was *not* considered primarily a romantic matter, though that of course played a part. The idea was that one could easily enough learn to love one's partner, and as the king clearly states, Helena's wealth and social station can be adjusted by his edict:

> If thou canst like this creature as a maid,
> I can create the rest. Virtue and she
> Is her own dower; honour and wealth from me.
>
> (149-51)

Bertram's outburst is, to say the least, not very tactful in the presence of an old king and the lady who has restored the old king's life. Helena is embarrassed into saying, "Let the rest go [forget it]," when Bertram persists. There is a tremendous emotional awkwardness when the angry king insists on the marriage, saying that he "must produce [his] power" to secure his honor. Bertram's quick turnabout (a lie) and his exit with his "bride to be" must leave both the stage audience and the one in the theater feeling uneasy:

> I find that she, which late
> Was in my nobler thoughts most base, is now
> The praised of the King; who, so ennobled,
> Is as 'twere born so.
>
> (177-80)

This is especially so since Bertram and the doubly disgraced Parolles (who denied his master, then acted the coward toward old Lafeu) soon conspire to leave France and their obligations there for the wars in Italy, where, ironically, Bertram expects to attain his "honour." As a final, sordid touch, Shakespeare has Bertram plan to send Helena back to Rousillon in possession of a sealed envelope addressed to the Countess, which will "acquaint my mother with my hate to her [Helena]."

## ACT II—SCENES 4 & 5

**Summary**

Parolles interrupts Helena and the clown with a message from Bertram: Helena is to beg leave of the king, "strength'ned with what apology you think/ May make it probable need," and then to report back to Bertram. She "wait[s] upon his will."

In Scene 5, Lafeu tries to disillusion Bertram with regard to his false friend Parolles, but to little avail. Bertram: "I do assure you, my lord, he is very great in knowledge and accordingly valiant." Lafeu then openly insults Parolles to expose him: "There can be no kernel in this light nut; the soul of this man is his clothes." After Helena dutifully takes the letter which Bertram had planned to write in Scene 3 and is ready to go as commanded back to Rousillon, Bertram brushes her off, refusing to give her even a polite kiss in parting.

## Commentary

Even the clown mocks Parolles in this part of the play—"much fool may you find in you"—and Shakespeare makes it abundantly clear that either Bertram lacks all good judgment or else he is willfully behaving against the better advice of those around him in continuing his association with Parolles. Lafeu's departing words to Parolles, and Bertram's comment, perhaps indicate a slight second thought on the young man's part:

> *Lafeu:* Farewell, monsieur! I have spoken better of you
>   Than you have or will to deserve at my hand,
>   But we must do good against evil. *[Exit]*
> *Parolles:* An idle [stupid] lord, I swear.
> *Bertram:* I think so.
> *Parolles:* Why, do you not know him?
> *Bertram:* Yes, I do know him well, and common speech
>   Gives him a worthy pass [reputation].
>
> (50–57)

Helena's arrival prevents this line of talk from going any further, however. Imagine the circumstances: Bertram, forced to take Helena's hand in marriage in full view of the assembled courtiers whose respect he craves, must now pretend at least a passing courtesy toward his "wife," even when in relative privacy. We know that he holds her in some contempt, and that the letter which he commands her to deliver viciously denounces her. She seems pathetic here, begging for Bertram's attention.

> *Bertram:* What would you have?
> *Helena:* Something, and scarce so much: nothing, indeed.
>   I would not tell you what I would, my lord.
>   Faith, yes!
>   Strangers and foes do sunder and not kiss.
> *Bertram:* I pray you, stay not, but in haste to horse.
>
> (87–92)

Shakespeare doesn't say what Bertram does when Helena asks for a departing kiss, and one wonders what would be most effective: a half-hearted kiss, equivalent to a pat on the head, or a silence of two beats and an abruptly turned back?

## ACT III – SCENES 1 & 2

**Summary**

In twenty-three lines, Shakespeare introduces the city of Florence, Italy, to the play while that city's Duke puzzles aloud to a French nobleman about the king of France's neutrality in the Italian wars. The French lord concurs: "Holy seems the quarrel/ Upon your Grace's part; black and fearful/ On the opposer."

In Scene 2, the clown has returned to Rousillon, where he delivers a letter from Bertram to his mother advising her that he has run away from his marriage; in the letter, he says: "If there be breadth enough in the world, I will hold a long distance." This upsets the Countess: "This is not well, rash and unbridled boy,/ To fly the favours of so good a King. . . ." Helena's distress, when she reads Bertram's letter to her, compounds the feeling. She labels his note a "passport"—that is, a license to beg on the open road—and says that it is a "dreadful sentence."

> When thou canst get the ring upon my finger,
> Which never shall come off, and show me a child
> Begotten of thy body that I am father to, then call
> Me husband; but in such a "then" I write a "Never."
>
> (59–62)

The Countess disavows Bertram as her son and then asks whether or not he is still traveling in the company of Parolles, the "very tainted fellow, and full of wickedness." The scene ends with a monologue by Helena, who vows to leave France to clear the way for Bertram to return home from the dangerous wars:

> No; come thou home, Rousillon,
> Whence honour but of danger wins a scar,
> As oft it loses all. I will be gone, –
> My being here it is that holds thee hence.
> Shall I stay here to do it? No, no.
>
> (123–27)

**Commentary**

No doubt the clown has altered his appearance, somewhat, to be like the fashionable set that he mingled with in Paris. His attitude toward "mere provincials" has taken a radical turn too. Isbel was the wench whom he begged permission to marry in Act I, but now,

> I have no mind to Isbel since I was at court.
> Our old lings [salt cod, slang for lechers] and our
> Isbels o' th' country are nothing like your
> Old lings, and your Isbels o' th' court.
>
> (13–16)

The Countess, for her part, responds to her "altered" son, young Bertram. Note the number of times that he is referred to by her and others as a "boy," implying immaturity. She cannot understand his disobedience to the king in refusing to honor Helena, especially since Helena is such a fine person. The Countess' words are meant to assuage poor Helena's grief, but they seem harsh to her son:

> I prithee, lady, have a better cheer.
> If thou engrossest [take] all the griefs are thine,
> Thou robb'st me of a moiety [share]. He was my son,
> But I do wash his name out of my blood
> And thou art all my child.
>
> (67–71)

The "dreadful sentence" which Helena reads conjures up further associations with fairy tales and stories of legend. Here, one should remember the reference to the archetypal "curing of the king" story earlier in the play. Shakespeare uses a tradition in which a beleaguered bride must accomplish several "impossible" tasks, or overcome a number of severe trials in order to prove herself, and (usually) win the love of the man whom she loves. The plot elements in the rest of the play hinge on this "sentence," as Helena sets out to solve the riddle and overcome the obstacles which Bertram has set. She must get the ring from his finger (symbolic of family tradition and honor) and she must also become pregnant—despite Bertram's avowed dislike of her.

In a play which has far fewer passages of sheer poetic beauty than we have come to expect from Shakespeare, Helena's soliloquy here, expressing her torment, stands out even if it does use fairly commonplace metaphors:

> And is it I that drive thee from the sportive court,
> Where thou wast shot at with fair eyes,
> To be the mark of smoky muskets?
> O you leaden messengers,
> That ride upon the violent speed of fire,

Fly with false aim, move the still-peering [self-repairing] air
That sings with piercing; do not touch my lord!

(111–17)

## ACT III – SCENES 3 & 4

### Summary

With the Duke's blessing, Bertram enters battle on behalf of the city state of Florence: "A lover of thy [Mars, god of War] drum, hater of love." In Rousillon, the Countess learns that Helena has left France, where she was a religious pilgrim; thus, she sends a letter via her steward to lure Bertram back:

Write, write, Rinaldo, to this unworthy husband of his wife;
Let every word lay heavy of her worth that he does
     weigh too light.
My greatest grief, though little he do feel it, set
     down sharply.
Dispatch the most convenient messenger.
When haply he shall hear that she is gone,
He will return.

(29–34)

### Commentary

Helena's dismay and Bertram's eagerness to be an honorable soldier contrast sharply in these short scenes. Note that as the play moves along, more and more people are becoming embroiled in deceptive schemes. Now the Countess hopes to lure her son back with the news that Helena is out of the country. She is sure that Helena will then come back, "led hither by pure love."

## ACT III – SCENE 5

### Summary

The "old Widow of Florence," her daughter Diana, and a girl named Mariana, a "neighbor to the Widow," talk about the brave exploits of the "French Count" (Bertram), and about his wooing of Diana (through his intermediary, the "filthy officer" Parolles). Mariana warns Diana of Bertram's and Parolles' trickery ("engines of lust"), and at that moment, Helena arrives, "disguised as a [religious] pilgrim." After exchanging pleasantries and establishing that Helena will stay overnight in the widow's house, the women turn their attention to the triumphantly returning Count Bertram. Diana says,

> He stole from France, as 'tis reported,
> For the King had married him against his liking.
>
> (55–56)

Helena further learns that the Count's follower Parolles "reports coarsely" of Bertram's wife, and with irony, she sadly says of the "wife" (herself): "She is too mean [common] to have her name repeated." The Count arrives, and he briefly luxuriates in his glorious return, and then the women go to the widow's, where Helena has invited all of them to dinner at her expense.

## Commentary

Shakespeare was no geographer. He has Helena on her way to a shrine in Santiago de Compostela, Spain, by way of Florence, although Helena started out in southern France. But no matter. The dramatic point is that Helena, who has humbled herself for the sake of her love, further associates herself with "heaven" by adopting the guise of a pilgrim, and is now about to reach a low point in her personal anguish before reversing the order of things. She stresses her own unworthiness while learning of the Count's lascivious pursuit of other women. When she asks about Bertram's interest in Diana, one wonders whether a plan to ensnare him is hatching itself in her brain:

> Widow: This young maid might do her a shrewd turn
>     [help her out].
> Helena: How do you mean? Maybe the amorous Count
>     Solicits her in the unlawful purpose.
> Widow: He does indeed, and brokes [deals]
>     With all that can in such a suit
>     Corrupt the tender honour of a maid.
>
> (69–74)

When Bertram actually appears with "drum and colors," Helena pretends not to know who he is. "Which is the Frenchman?" she asks. Perhaps she wants to give Diana the opportunity to betray any secret romantic longing which she might have for him. Diana's tone of voice, if not her words, would be sure to give her away. Apparently, Helena is satisfied that no such attraction exists, for she soon solicits Diana's aid in trapping Bertram.

## ACT III – SCENES 6 & 7

### Summary

Several French lords prevail upon Bertram to let them prove that Parolles is a scoundrel unworthy of his company. They will set Parolles up to recapture a drum which he lost in battle (a military disgrace), then they will capture and blindfold him, and in Bertram's presence, they will get him to "betray you [Bertram] and deliver all the intelligence in his power against you." Bertram agrees to the plot. Parolles enters and takes the bait:

> *Parolles:* I know not what the success will be,
>     My lord, but the attempt I vow.
> *Bertram:* I know, thou'rt valiant; and to the
>     Possibility of thy soldiership will subscribe
>     For thee. Farewell.
> *Parolles:* I love not many words. *[Exit]*
> *First Lord:* No more than fish loves water.
>     Is not this a strange fellow, my lord,
>     That so confidently seems to undertake this
>     Business, which he knows is not to be done,
>     Damns himself to do, and dares better be
>     Damned than to do it?
>
> (86–97)

Bertram ends Scene 6 asking a lord to intercede for him to "the lass I spoke of" (Diana).

Helena, for her part, bribes the Widow of Florence to help her convince Diana to allow herself to be used as a decoy in trapping Bertram. Helena wants Diana to, first, get the Count's ring in exchange for the promise of future favors, and then to set up an "encounter" with him.

> In fine, delivers me to fill the time,
> Herself most chastely absent. After,
> To marry her [pay her dowry] I'll add three thousand
>     crowns
> To what is past already.
>
> (33–36)

## Commentary

A "noble" Count (Bertram) agrees to entrap a friend, and a "chaste" maiden (Helena) offers large sums of money to a mother to get her daughter to arrange to have sexual intercourse with a legally married man. The plot now grows murky in this unusual "comedy." As Parolles is himself dishonest, however, there is a kind of justice in ensnaring him: the trickster will himself be tricked. Yet Bertram himself (like Parolles) seems disloyal. A similar parallel exists in Shakespeare's *Henry IV, Part 1,* in which Hal's delightful scoundrel-companion, fat Jack Falstaff, is exposed publicly as a coward for the good of young Prince Hal. The difference, of course, is that Hal has known all along what mettle Falstaff is made of, and Hal himself is of enormously greater stature than Bertram. Bertram is petty by comparison, as is this scheme to expose and tease the loathsome Parolles.

Helena's plan also has a darker element, for she does have the matter of "right" on her side:

> *Helena:* Why then tonight let us essay our plot,
>     Which, if it speed, is wicked meaning [Bertram's]
>     In a lawful deed, and lawful meaning
>     In a lawful act [Helena's]
>     Where both not sin, and yet a sinful fact.
>     But let's about it.
>
> (43-48)

Helena undertakes the adventure with relish, and she paves the way with purses of gold to the Widow of Florence and her virgin daughter, Diana. The quoted passage captures all the ambiguity of the plot — Bertram will be making love to Helena, his rightful wife, though he thinks that she is Diana, an attractive virgin whom he fancies. His *intention* will be sinful, although the *act* will be lawful. "Ethics be damned!" seems to be Helena's attitude, so long as "all ends well" and is just.

## ACT IV–SCENE 1

### Summary

One of the French lords and a band of soldiers set a trap for Parolles as previously planned. They capture and blindfold him and speak in a hilarious nonsense language which he takes to be Russian — that is, *"Throca movousus, cargo, cargo, cargo."* To save his life, Parolles, as predicted, immediately volunteers to betray anyone and anything:

> Oh, let me live!
> And all the secrets of our camp I'll show,
> Their force, their purposes; nay, I'll speak that
> Which you will wonder at.
>
> (92-95)

### Commentary

For Parolles, the Falstaffian mock-motto, "Discretion is the better part of valor," seems to apply. There is no real surprise in his behavior, although his captors marvel at his self-knowledge:

> *Parolles:* What shall I say I have done? It must be a very
>     Plausive [plausible] invention that carries it.
>     They begin to smoke me [find me out], and disgraces
>     Have of late knocked too often at my door. I find
>     My tongue is too foolhardy.

*First Lord [aside]:* This is the first truth that e'er thine own
    Tongue was guilty of.
*Second Lord:* Is it possible he should know what he is, and
    Be that he is?

(28-36)

There is a sly joke embedded in this scene, in which the "man of words" (which is what Parolles' *name* literally means) is tricked by a plot which makes use of some assorted syllables of a gobbledygook language that Parolles thinks is Russian.

## ACT IV–SCENE 2

### Summary

Bertram woos the widow's daughter, Diana, with success, or so he thinks, and therefore, he gives her his family ring as a token of their arranged meeting:

*Bertram:* It is an honour, 'longing to our house,
    Bequeathed down from many ancestors,
    Which were the greatest obloquy i' th' world
    In me to lose.
*Diana:* Mine honour's such a ring;
    My chastity's the jewel of our house,
    Bequeathed down from many ancestors,
    Which were the greatest obloquy i' th' world
    In me to lose.

(42-50)

Diana agrees to let Bertram into her chamber at midnight on condition that he remain absolutely silent during their encounter and that they stay together for one hour only. At that time, she will place another ring on his finger, "that what [which] in time proceeds/ May token to the future our past deeds."

### Commentary

The language in this scene is bland – Bertram utters cliches, calculated to capture the fancy of a girl with whom he wants to have sex, and she knows it:

My mother told me just how he would woo,
As if she sat in 's heart. She says all men
Have the like oaths.

(67-69)

Diana is, of course, acting for a price, yet notice the delight she takes in teasing Bertram along the way. He tells her, Parolles-like, that her cold manner is inappropriate, that she should be "as your mother was/ When your sweet self was got." Diana's reply is calculated to irritate:

> *Diana:* No. My mother did but duty;
>     Such my lord, as you owe to your wife.
> *Bertram:* No more o' that!
>
> (12–14)

Shakespeare drives the point home that Bertram is very irresponsible when he relinquishes his family ring; Diana mockingly repeats, word for word, his "bequeathed down from many ancestors" speech.

## ACT IV–SCENE 3

### Summary

Two French lords, the brothers Dumain, discuss Bertram's situation briefly before he enters to witness their exposure of Parolles. They are aware of Bertram's improprieties, including the deception of Helena (whom they presume to be dead, as rumor has it) and the "perversion" of Diana, "a young gentlewoman here in Florence, of a most chaste renown." They are certain that his current glory will do no good when he returns to France: "The great dignity that his valour hath here acquired for him shall at home be encount'red with a shame as ample."

Bertram swaggers before his countrymen as he enters: "I have congied with [taken leave of] the Duke, done my adieu with his nearest, buried a wife, mourned for her, writ to my lady mother I am returning, entertained my convoy, and between these main parcels of dispatch effected many nicer needs; the last was the greatest, but that I have not ended yet."

The bulk of the scene is taken up with Parolles' exposure and disgrace. Brought in blindfolded and pricked on with the merest hint of physical torture, he reveals military secrets (probably made-up), slanders Bertram and the brothers Dumain, and shows himself to be an utterly craven liar and a cheat. Bertram had thought of him as a confidant, yet the letter which Parolles planned to give Diana reads:

> Men are to mell with, boys are not to kiss:
> For count of this, the Count's a fool, I know it,
> Who pays before, but not when he does owe it.
>
> (257–59)

When his life seems threatened, Parolles' hypocrisy is at its greatest:

> My life, sir, in any case! Not that I
> Am afraid to die, but that my offenses

Being many I would repent out the remainder of nature.
Let me live, sir, in a dungeon, i' th' stocks,
Or anywhere, so I may live.

(270–74)

Bertram and the others squeeze as much villainy from him as they can before removing his hood, whereupon, speechless he must face them. When they leave, he shrugs a remark to one of the soldiers, "Who cannot be crushed with a plot?"

## Commentary

Parolles is what he is! Small consolation when the subject is so mean-spirited, yet Shakespeare in this scene almost seems to place the "gallant knave" in positive contrast against his master, Bertram. Dumain marvels at the extent of Parolles' corruption. It is clear to the French lord that this man is embroidering falsehoods in order to save his skin, and it becomes enjoyable to witness.

> *Parolles* [of the French Lord]: I have but little more to say,
>    Sir, of his honesty—he has everything that an
>    Honest man should not have; what an honest man
>    Should have, he has nothing.
> *First Lord* [aside]: I begin to love him for this.
> *Bertram* [aside]: For this description of thine honesty?
>    A pox upon him for me, he's more and more a cat.

(287–93)

The First Lord, enjoying the exposure of Parolles, seems to confirm the feeling that the culprit expresses at the very end of the scene: "There's place and means for every man alive."

### ACT IV–SCENES 4 & 5

## Summary

Helena assures the widow and Diana that their help will be rewarded: ". . . Heaven/ Hath brought me up to be your daughter's dower." In other words, they will simply have to endure a bit longer until the plot reaches its end.

In Rousillon, Lafeu comforts the Countess, who believes that Helena has died, "the most virtuous gentlewoman that ever Nature had praise for creating." They discuss the return of Bertram and the anticipated arrival of the King of France, who "comes post [haste] from Marseilles, of as able body as when he numbered thirty [was thirty years old]." A match is proposed between Lafeu's daughter and Bertram. Also present is the clown Lavache, whose wordplay and sexual jokes grow tedious to Lafeu.

## Commentary

Things grow worse before they get better, although "all's well that ends well," as Helena assures Diana. The scene at Rousillon is out of joint, and even the clown "has no face, but runs where he will." The "death" of Helena weighs on their minds, and the clown's off-color foolery seems grating and very much out of place, even to the point where Lafeu "grows aweary" of him. The clown remarks on a scar which Bertram is covering with "a patch of velvet." Such a scar might be the result of an honorable encounter in battle, yet to Lavache it seems more likely to be the mark of a lanced ulcer, of the sort which appears on syphilitics. This ugly note closes the scene.

## ACT V—SCENES 1 & 2

### Summary

Helena, the widow and Diana are in pursuit of the king, whom they know to have traveled to Marseilles. Once there, they learn from a gentleman that the king has left in haste for Rousillon. Helena asks him to speed ahead with a message for the king.

In Rousillon, Parolles is begging the clown to deliver a letter of his own to Lafeu, when that gentleman appears. After teasing Parolles about his fallen status, Lafeu shows pity and bids Parolles to follow him to the count's palace (where the king has arrived), saying, "Though you are a fool and a knave, you shall eat."

### Commentary

Noteworthy here is the clown's relish in teasing Parolles with numerous scatological references to the "stench" he finds himself in with Fortune and society—"Fortune's close-stool" [toilet] and "a purr [dung] of Fortune"—and Lafeu's contrasting good-humored forgiveness of the knavish fellow.

## ACT V—SCENE 3

### Summary

The Countess begs the king to forgive her son, which he does at once, and he also confirms a match between Lafeu's daughter (Maudlin) and Bertram. Bertram is quick to accept the king's suggestion of a bride *this* time:

> *King:* You remember the daughter of this lord?

*Bertram:* Admiringly, my liege. At first
   I stuck my choice upon her, ere my heart
   Durst make too bold a herald of my tongue.

                (43–46)

He gives Lafeu a ring as token of his pledge, and the old gentleman recognizes it immediately:

   Helen, that's dead, was a sweet creature;
   Such a ring as this,
   The last that e'er I took her leave at court,
   I saw upon her finger.

                (74–77)

To make matters worse for Bertram, the king now recognizes the ring as the one which he gave to Helena as a "token" by which she could summon help if she ever needed it. Furthermore, the king says,

   She [Helena] called the saints to surety
   That she would never put it from her finger,
   Unless she gave it to yourself in bed.

               (108–10)

Bertram is taken away. Helena's messenger then enters with a letter claiming to be from Diana, which sues for her right to be Bertram's wife: "Otherwise a seducer flourishes and a poor maid is undone."

Diana confronts Bertram, then Parolles is brought in to testify as to the details of Bertram's behavior. The king nearly reaches the point of exasperation with Diana's cryptic half-explanations of what actually went on: "She does abuse our ears. To prison with her!" Then Helena reveals herself, at which sight the king says:

   Is there no exorcist
   Beguiles the truer office of mine eyes?
   Is't real that I see?

               (305–07)

The play quickly resolves itself, with Helena and Bertram together and Diana promised a dowry. "All yet seems well, and if it end so meet," says the king, "The bitter past, more welcome is the sweet."

### Commentary

So much transpires so quickly in this scene that it threatens to "run away with the play," turning it into a romp and a farce. Consider the hero, who has apparently returned home as a respected (penitent) nobleman, fresh from the Florentine wars. The king forgives him, as does his mother, for his disobedience and his disgraceful behavior toward Helena, whom they describe in hushed tones fitting for a saint. Ready to accept the king's second offer of a bride (Lafeu's daughter) and thus secure his position in Rousillon, the world suddenly turns upside down for him. The king recognizes his ring, and all accuse Bertram of foul play in Helena's demise: "I am wrapped in dismal thinkings," comments the king. Furthermore, Diana appears, demanding her rights as Bertram's "lawful bride." Before Helena appears to clarify the situation, Bertram undergoes a painful series of embarrassments, all the more troubling to him because he had opened the scene in full command of his new life. Now, he is forced into a situation in which his lies are openly revealed, even before the weasel Parolles— his "equivocal companion."

In the language of riddles, Diana prepares the way for the sudden re-reversal:

> He knows himself my bed he hath defiled,
> And at that time, he got his wife with child.
> Dead though she be, she feels her young one kick.
> So, there's my riddle: one that's dead is quick
> > [both alive *and* pregnant].
> > (301–04)

When Helena walks onstage, resurrected from the "dead" and pregnant with a new "life," the king (and presumably everyone else present except Diana) stands aghast. Thus it is that he calls for an exorcist. The comedy has run its course from opening gloom to "miraculous" joy. Between here and the end of the play, barely thirty-five lines transpire, hardly time for reflection. There is also something tentative (and comical) in this love-pledge by Count Bertram of Rousillon:

> If she, my liege, can make me know this clearly [that is,
> > all that has transpired],
> I'll love her dearly, ever, ever dearly.
> > (316–17)

Ironically, one wonders, finally, just how "well" all this has really ended.

1602

# Troilus
# and Cressida

# INTRODUCTION TO THE PLAY

Although some dissenting opinions place *Troilus and Cressida* much earlier, the year 1602 is generally held to be the date of composition. On February 7, 1602/3, the play was entered in the Stationers' Register in the name of James Roberts. Moreover, the Prologue provides additional reason for assigning this play to the year 1602:

> and hither am I come
> A prologue arm'd, but not in confidence
> Of author's pen or actor's voice, but suited
> In like condition as our argument . . .

> (22-25)

The "prologue arm'd" is surely a reference to the armed Prologue in Ben Jonson's *Poetaster* (1601). Roberts' entry in the Stationers' Register was apparently a "holding" one—that is, an entry made to prevent pirating of the play. *Troilus and Cressida* was not printed until 1609, when Richard Bonian and Henry Walley, to whom Roberts had assigned the rights, brought out two Quarto editions, the title pages of which differ, although the texts are identical. The play was included in the First Folio (1623) under rather curious conditions which will be discussed below. This text differs in several ways from that of the Quarto, but Sir Edmund K. Chambers, who argues that Quarto and Folio represent substantially the same text, is correct in concluding that the verbal differences here and there are relatively unimportant. (*William Shakespeare*, I (1930), 439.)

Whether or not *Troilus and Cressida* was produced on the stage prior to publication has been a matter of dispute. The title page of the first issue of the Quarto reads: "The Historie of Troylus and Cresseida. As it was acted by the Kings Maiesties seruants at the Globe." But the second issue not only omits any references to a stage performance but includes a most interesting Epistle to the Reader, in which it is stated that "you have here a new play, never staled with the stage, never clapper-clawed with the palms of the vulgar . . ." It has been argued that a production of the play had failed to win popularity and had been withdrawn, and that Bonian and Walley, seeking to win approval for the published edition, did so by boasting that *Troilus and Cressida* was caviar to the general public—an intellectual treat which only the cultured, sophisticated reader could appreciate. Conjecture has not stopped here. Still other critics are convinced that the play was especially written for performance at one of the Inns of Court, where the audience possessed the necessary sophistication to appreciate the lacerating satire which characterizes *Troilus and Cressida*. One may reasonably conclude that, at the Globe or elsewhere, the play was produced but failed to hold the boards for any length of time. Lines written by one I. C. in his *Saint Marie Magdalens Conversion* (1603) indicate that the play was known to many:

> Of Helens rape and Troyes beseiged Towne,
> Of Troylus faith and Cressids falsitie,
> Of Richards stratagems for the English crowne,
> Of Tarquins lust, and Lucrece chastitie,
> Of these, of none of these my muse now treates.

As Sir Edmund K. Chambers states (op. cit., 443), "Here both the *Troilus and Cressida* themes are linked with two others, both Shakespearean."

Structurally, the play divides into two parts: the love scenes, in which the titular hero and heroine and Paris dominate, and the camp scenes, in which the Greek leaders and warriors hold the stage. Shakespeare did not write two plays in one, however, even though the division has posed many problems which have troubled the critics. Since the Troilus–Cressida story was widely popular throughout the sixteenth century, Shakespeare could have found material in many sources, including Robert Henryson's *Testament of Cressid* (1593), but his main source was Chaucer's remarkable psychological novel in verse, *Troilus and Cressyde*. If Shakespeare made Cressida into a complete wanton, he did no more than accept the widely current estimate of her character. Typical of the references to her is Pistol's speaking of Doll Tearsheet as a "lazar kite of Cressid's kind" in *Henry V*, II.i.80.

For the camp scenes, the poet made use of Caxton's *Recuyell of the Historyes of Troye* and more especially of Homer's *Iliad* in George Chapman's translation of Books I, II, VII, X, XII, and XVIII (1598). In Chapman he found the story of Achilles, Ajax, and Hector, as well as the basic character of the malcontent and railer Thersites. As usual, he transmuted the story elements and characterization into a play which is essentially original in plot, most characterizations, speeches, and situations—a play which has been described as the most intellectual in the Shakespearean canon.

If indeed *Troilus and Cressida* is notably intellectual, it remains to many the most puzzling and disturbing play written by the poet, a play that has provided field days for those addicted to subjective interpretation. As H. N. Hildebrand, editor of the Variorum edition (1953) points out, "It has been called the least Shakespearean of plays and the one in which the poet seems to be writing most for himself. It has been called a marvel of genius and bad piece of bungling." Certainly one does not find lyrical love but rather lust, which the romantically inclined understandably find distasteful.

Many critics are disturbed by the absurd Epilogue addressed to the

"hold-door trade" and assigned to Pandar, whose appearance on the battlefield is unaccounted for. And since the level of writing in Act V, Scenes
iv–x is quite uneven, a few have denied that they are Shakespeare's. With
reference to the Epilogue, discussion must be postponed until we come
to the play itself. Sir Edmund K. Chambers has the proper answer for those
who would deny that Shakespeare wrote the entire play. Conceding that
there are "huddled scenes, with some poor work in them," he points out
that "Shakespeare did sometimes scamp his work, especially at the end
of a play" (op. cit., 447). In this connection, one may recall Ben Jonson's
criticism of his great contemporary. The players boasted of Shakespeare
that he never blotted a line. "Would he had blotted a thousand," wrote
Jonson with pardonable exaggeration.

Exactly how to classify the play has been another problem. The Quarto
refers to it as a comedy, whereas the Folio editors call it a tragedy. Since
those editors put the play between the histories and the tragedies, it has
been suggested that they themselves were uncertain how the play should
be classified. But other critics argue that, in all probability, the original
editors had some trouble getting permission to print the play and were
successful only at the last minute.

*Troilus and Cressida* does contain important elements of tragedy, set
as the action is within the framework of the Trojan War. Often the speeches
of both Greeks and Trojans are marked by the tragic manner, particularly
Ulysses' doctrinally important speech on order and degree (I.iii.75ff.) and
Hector's eloquent and telling reply to Troilus and Paris (II.ii.163ff.). Certainly the tragic death of Hector, which takes place on stage, does not belong
to comedy, bitterly satirical or otherwise. Further, it may be argued that
the entire action, motivated as it is by human passions, moves to an
unhappy end, and even sympathetic characters like Hector and Cassandra suffer greatly. The difficulty, however, is that the ending has not the
finality one expects in either a tragedy or a comedy, and in the course
of the play all important characters except Ulysses and Hector become
targets of ridicule.

No serious student of the play can afford to ignore Professor O. J.
Campbell's *Comicall Satyre and Shakespeare's* Troilus and Cressida (1938).
He states that Shakespeare did not intend to write either a comedy or a
tragedy, but rather a "comicall satyre," the new genre popularized by Ben
Jonson's *Everyman Out of His Humour* (1600). Such a play combines the
wit of comedy and the ferocity of Juvenalian satire and tragedy. Looseness
of structure characterizes a play of this type. It is the mocking criticism
of one or more commentators whose function is to point up the significance
of the action, which provides a kind of unity. One such commentator, like
Carlo Buffone in Jonson's play, is a railing buffoon, whose coarse vituperation is intended to call forth derisive laughter and to teach as well. This,

of course, is the role of Thersites in *Troilus and Cressida*. In comical satire, the objects of satire are either made to see their folly and are purged of it, or (like Malvolio in *Twelfth Night*, the most Jonsonian of Shakespeare's plays) are scornfully laughed off the stage. In such a play one does not look for a resolution which has finality; the ending points up the theme of futility. Professor Campbell further states that lust and inconstancy, dominant themes in *Troilus and Cressida*, were favorite subjects of Elizabethan satirists. Admittedly all this does not explain away the tragic elements in the play. And there are those critics who vehemently deny that either Cressida or Troilus is intended to be satirized for lust and treachery. Cressida, to be sure, has not fared as well as her Trojan lover, but Professor Tucker Brooke, for example, found "daintiness" and "wistful sincerity" in her and saw her as an innocent girl caught up in a sordid environment ("Shakespeare's Study in Culture and Anarchy," *Yale Review*, XVII [1928], 573). Professor E. M. W. Tillyard speaks of Troilus' "noble devotion" (*Shakespeare's Problem Plays* [1945], 51). We must postpone an attempt to resolve these conflicting views until we have completed the summary of the action and turn to the commentary.

# LIST OF MAIN CHARACTERS

### Troilus

In a sense, there are two Troiluses in this play. The young Trojan prince is a heroic figure—except where Cressida is concerned. One recalls the high praise for him voiced by Ulysses and other Greek commanders, who see him as a second Hector. Hector himself, although earlier he described his brother as being too immature to endure the dangers of battle, has the highest praise for Troilus. But there are two qualifications to be made in this estimate of his martial character. First, unlike Hector, he is impelled to return to the battlefield not by a sense of duty but as a means of obtaining vengeance for the loss of Cressida. Second, his ruthlessness, refusing as he does to spare the life of a fallen adversary, reveals him as one who lacks the high sense of chivalry and the nobility of Hector.

Troilus the lover is the victim of infatuation. There are some commentators, to be sure, who see him as a tragic figure whose very idealism and trust lead him astray. True, it is not he who proves to be faithless, and he has difficulty in believing the testimony of his ears and eyes concerning Cressida's perfidy. All this, however, is the measure of his infatuation. He suffers from a distemper comparable to that of Achilles, which was correctly diagnosed by Ulysses in his long speech on order and degree. When Cassandra first makes her dire prophecy that Troy will fall if the fight to keep Helen continues, Hector addresses his brother in these words:

Now, youthful Troilus, do not these high strains
Of divination in our sister work
Some touches of remorse? Or is your blood
So madly hot that no discourse of reason,
Nor fear of bad success in a bad cause,
Can qualify [moderate] the same?

(II.ii.115 ff.)

Troilus does suffer what Hector calls "hot passion of distempered blood" to the extent that he rejects reason. Shakespeare here makes use of technical terms from Elizabethan faculty psychology to make clear the fact that the prince has permitted will to dominate reason and thus has become passion's slave.

### Cressida

Daughter to the traitor Calchas and niece to the prurient Pandarus, Cressida is described as a beauty second only to Helen of Troy. Her soliloquy at the end of Act I, Scene ii, reveals her as a sophisticated young lady precocious in the art of dalliance and expert at whetting the sexual appetites of her lovers. Her protestations of eternal love made to Troilus in the parting scene are rendered ridiculous in view of her behavior when she is escorted to the Greek camp by Diomedes, who has no trouble winning her favors. Despite occasional lyrical flights as she expresses her love for Troilus and her insistence that she will remain faithful, there is abundant evidence that love to her is no more than the physical. One cannot call her merely a weak vessel who cannot control her emotions. She is in control at all times—aware of her uncle's intentions from the first, aware of just how far to go in the love game, first with Troilus and then with Diomedes. One hardly needs the coarse comments of a Thersites or the enlightened observations of a Ulysses to recognize her for what she is—a highly sexed, fickle woman who is in love only with herself.

### Pandarus

Cressida's uncle is an old, retired voluptuary, living on the memories of a sensual life and now helping others to enjoy such a life. He has been called the "walking chronicle of court and city," a self-appointed arbiter of social elegance, and "a Polonius of the boudoir and the salon." He is indeed as vain and as affected in his speech as King Claudius' Lord Chamberlain; like him, he is given to platitudes. But, to give credit where some kind of credit is due, he is masterful enough in his chosen profession, that of one who arranges assignations. Nor is he lacking in sardonic wit, off-color though it usually is, as is evidenced by his greeting of Cressida after she spends the night with Troilus. He becomes the completely comic character when he learns that no longer will he be able to continue his management of the affair between Troilus and Cressida. Especially in his final soliloquy addressed to all bawds does he invite derisive laughter.

### Thersites

Coleridge called this railing malcontent "the Caliban of demagogic life"; other critics describe him as "a Goliath of abuse" and as one akin to Swift's Yahoo, described in Gulliver's final voyage. All agree that he is a finely realized comic character. Thersites actually is the most vicious type of political malcontent—the cynical type that can find no good in anyone, not even such admirable characters as Ulysses and Nestor. He is the unrivaled master of vituperation. Add to this that, as he himself admits, he is a coward. But offensive and exaggerated as his discourse is, this misshapen fellow voices fundamental truth when he insists that "all is war and lechery." As Professor O. J. Campbell has pointed out, he is the buffoonish commentator of characters and events in this play.

### Ulysses

This Greek commander has been called the real hero of the play, and it may be argued that he speaks for Shakespeare himself. Certainly he is the most sagacious character, for he accurately diagnoses the source of infection in the Greek camp and nearly succeeds in removing the infection. His perspicuity is shown further by the fact that he is prompt to see Cressida for what she is. The traditionally wise Nestor bows, in a sense, to Ulysses' superior wisdom. His courtliness and chivalry are revealed in his exchange with Hector and his high praise of Troilus as a warrior. In directing Troilus to follow Diomedes and in accompanying him to Calchas' tent, he further shows goodwill toward an enemy warrior during the truce.

### Ajax

The most effective description of this loutish warrior is found in Alexander's speech to Cressida (I.ii.24 ff.). Shakespeare followed earlier conceptions of him found in Ovid, Apuleius, Chapman, Gossin, and Harrington. His Ajax is a comic, ridiculous figure—vain, stupid, surly. At times he comes close to rivaling Thersites as a railer. In him are combined senseless vanity and great physical strength. One may add that he is sufficiently credulous, for he is easily convinced that Ulysses and others believe him to be Achilles' superior as a warrior.

### Achilles

This famous Greek warrior is depicted as an inordinately proud and arrogant individual who has permitted his will to rule his reason. Like

Troilus, he is too hot-blooded. While his fellow commanders and princes take the field, he keeps to his tent, pampering himself and finding amusement in the outbursts of Thersites and the antics of Patroclus. Not only has he fallen in love with one of King Priam's daughters (the ostensible reason for his refusal to continue fighting), but his relationship with Patroclus seems to be more than platonic. The cowardly attack upon the unarmed Hector and the treatment of the dead prince's corpse reveal the Achilles of this play to be a contemptible figure. He is indeed the "architect of chaos" in the Greek camp.

## Helen

Helen of Troy appears in only one scene, the first in Act III. At one point she says to Pandarus: "Let thy song be love: this love will undo us all. O Cupid, Cupid, Cupid!" Love to her is a weak, almost absurd obsession with sex, although a few commentators do insist that she is the "worthy object of Trojan idealism," apparently convinced by the eloquence of Paris and Troilus in Act II, Scene ii. Helen stands in relation to Paris as does Cressida in relation to Troilus, although Cressida is not a faithless wife. "Brother, she is not worth what she doth cost the holding," says Hector. And the evidence in the play supports his view. In prurient wit, Helen almost rivals Pandarus.

## Hector

Among the Trojans, this prince is as admirable as is Ulysses among the Greeks. When we first meet him in Act II, Scene ii, he is revealed not only as the premier warrior but as a clear-sighted counselor. He does not hesitate to tell Paris the true nature of the affair with Helen, which has proved to be so costly to the Trojans so far. Yet if he sees the morally superior side of the question, he chooses the inferior one, a decision which would seem to reflect on his character. But Troilus insisted that the course of action the Trojans must take was already determined and that they could not change that course any more than a man could cast off a wife whom he no longer loved. To Hector, it is a logical necessity that he agree.

Hector's martial prowess is recognized by Trojan and Greek alike. Agamemnon, Ulysses, and Achilles all pay high tribute to him. Add to this his great sense of honor and chivalry and he indeed emerges as the one character who comes closest to being the tragic hero in this play, one who seems to occupy the middle ground between comedy and tragedy.

# SUMMARIES AND COMMENTARIES

## THE PROLOGUE

The Prologue, "armed" in imitation of the armed Prologues introduced by Ben Jonson (*Poetaster*, 1601) and John Marston (*Antonio and Mellida*, 1602), speaks thirty-one lines which provide exposition as to time, place, and much of the action in the camp scenes of the play. No mention is made of either Troilus or Cressida. The drama, we are told, is concerned with events which took place during the Trojan War. The mention of "princes orgillous" (that is, filled with pride), the catalogue of polysyllabic proper names, the Latinized vocabulary—all suggest that here indeed is a play which could turn out to be a tragedy, involving as it does great public issues, as well as the fates of Troy and Greece.

## ACT I–SCENE 1

### Summary

As the play opens, Troilus and Pandarus enter, the former avowing his uncontrollable passion for Cressida. Since he endures the rage of battle within his heart, why, he asks, should he concern himself with the war between the Greeks and the Trojans? Clearly his yearning for Pandarus' niece threatens to unman him, a prince and leader among the embattled Trojans who should never ignore public duty. Stating that the Greeks are "strong and skillful," he indicts himself as one who is "tamer than sleep," less valiant than "the virgin in the night." Pandarus, speaking in brittle prose as a practical man of the world whets Troilus' sensual appetite in lines packed with food imagery. "He that will have the cake must tarry the grinding," he counsels, and the food image is sustained throughout the subsequent dialogue. As Pandarus slyly emphasizes Cressida's physical beauty while insisting that, since she is his kinswoman, it is not for him to praise her, the young Trojan prince has difficulty in restraining himself. "I tell thee I am mad/In Cressid's love," he exclaims, and declares that the references to "her eyes, her hair, her cheek, her gait" pour into the "open ulcer" of his heart. Pandarus, enjoying his role as go-between, complains that his labors have not been appreciated. From his lines we learn that her father, Calchas, deserted to the Greeks and, in Pandarus' opinion, she is "a fool to stay behind her father." He concludes that he is through with meddling, despite Troilus' fervant pleas.

Pandarus leaves the stage as the sound of an alarum (battle trumpet) is heard. In soliloquy, Troilus protests the sound, which reminds him of his public duty to his father and the state. He declares that the war is being waged for an unworthy cause: Helen's desertion of Menelaus in favor of

Paris. Troilus "cannot fight upon this argument." He then bewails his own lot. He cannot reach Cressida except through Pandarus, who now proves difficult. Ironically, he appeals to Apollo to be informed "what Cressid is, what Pandar, and what we."

Again the alarum sounds. Aeneas enters and hails Troilus—asking why he is not in the field. Troilus gives a "woman's answer"—he is not there because he is not there. He then admits that it is womanish of him to absent himself. Aeneas informs him that his brother Paris has returned home after being injured by Menelaus, betrayed husband of Helen. "Let Paris bleed," says Troilus. "'Tis but a scar to scorn./Paris is gored with Menelaus' horn." The metaphor points up the fact that Menelaus is a cuckold.

## Commentary

Troilus is the love-sick warrior son of Priam, King of Troy, brother to Hector, Paris, Deiphobus, Helenus, and Cassandra, who appear later. He is presented from the start as a young sensualist who is beside himself in his infatuation for Cressida. Admittedly he does sound almost lyrical in his passionate outbursts, as when he speaks of Cressida's hand as one

> In whose comparison all whites are ink
> Writing their own reproach, to whose soft seizure
> The cygnet's down is harsh and spirit of sense
> Hard as the palm of a ploughman.
>
> (56–59)

But this is not idealistic, lyrical love like that of Romeo for Juliet. His words throughout constitute a self-indictment. That he should depend upon the like of Pandarus to serve him as intermediary underscores the fact that he is slave to an unworthy passion. He is capable of self-criticism, although he refuses to act on it. It is he who recognizes himself as one who is sacrificing manliness and ignoring filial and public duty.

Pandarus is the elderly uncle of the beauteous Cressida; he is a conceited, prurient man who sees himself as a worldly wise man. Witness the Polonius-like platitudes which he mouths from time to time, as when he says: "He that will have a cake out of the wheat must needs tarry the grinding" (14–16). It is apparent that he gets a vicarious thrill out of stimulating Troilus' sexual appetite and placing the youth in a position where he must beg for aid in order to win Cressida.

The purpose of this scene is (1) to provide the inciting incident which starts the action rising in the love plot, (2) to develop the basic characters of Troilus and of Pandarus, (3) to prepare the audience for the appearance of Cressida, and (4) to provide necessary exposition relating to the Trojan War and the state of affairs in the Trojan camp.

Troilus has no right to let private matters interfere with public ones because Renaissance theory stressed the importance of "vocation" and the "speciality of rule." Troilus' vocation is that of a warrior; in time of war nothing should prevent his single-minded devotion to his duty. Elsewhere in Shakespeare, notably in *Much Ado About Nothing* and in *Henry V*, this principle is emphasized. Paris is also a prince of the blood and "speciality of rule" applies to him also: public duty should always take precedence over private desire.

The most telling argument in defense of Troilus' conduct is the fact that the war is being fought for an unworthy cause. The Greeks seek the return of the adulterous Helen; the Trojans fight to keep her as Paris' paramour. There is much truth in Troilus' exclamation: "Fools on both sides!"

The theme of treachery is introduced when Cressida is identified as the daughter of Calchas, a man who deserted the Trojans and went to the Greek camp. This looks forward to Cressida's ultimate desertion of Troilus.

The appearance of Aeneas and the reference to Hector are especially significant because these two serve to provide tacit commentary on the love-sick Troilus, who asked, "Why should I war without [outside] the walls of Troy?" Hector especially is the famous warrior who follows vocation.

The images that support the themes of lust and infection are a cluster of images focusing on food, lines 13–26, with the emphasis on the sensitive appetite. In Shakespeare's *Antony and Cleopatra,* Enobarbus calls the Egyptian queen "a dainty morsel for an emperor." This same idea, with the stress on the physical, is conveyed through the food image here and elsewhere in the play. Infection or disease is suggested when Troilus refers to the "open ulcer" of his heart (53).

## ACT I–SCENE 2

### Summary

Cressida enters accompanied by Alexander, her serving man. In response to her question, Alexander tells her that Queen Hecuba and Helen just passed on their way to the eastern tower, where they can view the battle taking place outside the walls of Troy. He adds that the angered Hector had been especially anxious to return to battle. According to one report, Ajax, who is scurrilously described as a ridiculous, oafish warrior, had struck down Hector the day before.

Pandarus enters just as Cressida praises Hector as a gallant man. He is filled with questions. When was Cressida at Ilium, the citadel and royal palace of Troy? Was Hector already armed and on the battlefield? Was Helen up? Yes, he is told, Hector was gone; but Helen has not yet risen. Pandarus then states that he knows the cause of Hector's anger and that the Trojan prince will surely "lay about him today"—all of which finally provides him the opportunity to introduce Troilus' name. Troilus, he assures his niece, will not be far behind Hector: "Let them take heed of Troilus, I can tell them that too."

There follows an amusing colloquy in which Pandarus heaps praise upon Troilus, and Cressida provides a witty rebuttal in lines packed with puns. He assures his niece that Helen herself has only high praise for Troilus and concludes that she loves him better than she does Paris. Laconically, Cressida answers that Helen indeed is a merry Greek (a frivolous person) if such be the case.

Pandarus is not to be stopped. Troilus, he insists, is becomingly young, yet as manful as his illustrious brother; he has attractive dimples and a winning smile. But it is not Helen to whom he is attracted. Troilus has a fine wit. Recall his reply to Helen, who remarked, "Here's but two and fifty hairs on your chin, and one of them is white." The white hair, said the young Trojan, is my father; the rest are his sons. Pandarus assures Cressida that all present had been vastly amused, especially when Troilus told Helen that the forked hair among the dark ones was Paris and that it should be plucked out and given to him—another reference to cuckoldry, which reminds us of the theme of illicit sex. Pandarus reminds her that he "told her a thing yesterday" and urges her to think on it, an obvious reference to his importuning her on behalf of Troilus.

A retreat is sounded, signaling the return of the Trojan warriors, and Cressida agrees to remain with her uncle to see them pass toward Ilium. Especially she must note Troilus, says Pandarus. In succession Aeneas, Antenor, Hector, Paris, and Helenus pass. Pandarus has some words of praise for Antenor and Hector, in particular, and comments on all, but with each remark he brings up Troilus' name: "Would I could see Troilus now! You shall see Troilus anon." His preoccupation is shown by his reply to Cressida's question about Helenus, who, he says, can fight "indifferent well" and then adds that Helenus is a priest.

Cressida, who all along has been wittily baiting her uncle, then asks: "What sneaking fellow comes yonder?" It is Troilus, of course. Pandarus now almost outdoes himself in praising the man whom he is trying to bring together with Cressida. "Mark him, note him. O, brave Troilus! The prince of chivalry!" Common soldiers pass by, but to Pandarus they are "Asses, fools, dolts," and he vows that he "could live and die in the eyes of Troilus." His niece must know that Troilus possesses the "birth, beauty, good shape, discourse, manhood, learning, gentleness, virtue, youth, liberality, and such like the spice and salt that season a man."

"Aye, a minced man./ And then to be baked with no date in the pie, for then the man's date is out," Cressida replies, thus sustaining the food-cooking pattern of images as she puns on the word *minced,* which also means "mincing or affected," and the word *date.* The last clause may be paraphrased to read "for the man's time is up." As her next speech indicates

(284–289), Cressida is, in Pandarus' words, "indeed such a woman!" The verbal exercise in punning continues.

Troilus' boy-servant enters with the news that Troilus, now unarming himself at Pandarus' house, wishes to see him. Pandarus bids goodbye to his niece and promises to return soon with a token from Troilus. "By that same token, you are a bawd," she says, indicating that she recognizes her kinsman as a procurer.

In soliloquy, Cressida gives us an insight into the psychology of women who play the love game—at least her type of woman. She did not need her uncle's testimony to recognize the attractions of Troilus, but she held off because "Things won are done, joy's soul lies in the doing" and "Men prize the thing ungained more than it is." Her final maxim is that "Achievement is command; ungained beseech." In other words, the man rules once the woman is won, but he is the one ruled during the pursuit.

## Commentary

Cressida is the daughter of the traitor Calchas and niece to Pandarus. She is attractive enough to bear comparison with Helen of Troy. In this scene she emerges as light-hearted, uninhibited, and sophisticated—indeed as a "merry" Trojan. She is mistress of witty repartee, often risque—as lines 283–289 illustrate. It is clear that she enjoys the love game she is playing and is fully aware of Pandarus' role in it.

Pandarus' character as the prurient go-between is advanced in this scene as he seeks to convince his niece that she should accept Troilus as her lover. Amusingly enough, often inadvertently so, he is hardly a match for Cressida in the combat of wits. But he is never at a loss for words, for he remains as loquacious here as in the earlier scene. Hector is pre-eminent among the Trojan warriors. His valor and dedication are emphasized by his impatience to get back into battle after having been felled by Ajax.

Troilus is mad for the love of Cressida and can hardly wait to get Pandarus' report about how his suit fares. In the course of his argument, Pandarus insists that Troilus is better than the great Hector.

The purpose of this scene is (1) to introduce Cressida and develop her character, (2) to advance the love plot, (3) to depict Pandarus at his calling as he importunes his niece on Troilus' behalf, and (4) to present the first view of other Trojan warriors and give us further insight into the affairs within the Trojans' walled city.

In the dialogue, lines 76 ff., Pandarus insists that Troilus is not himself, and Cressida argues that he is indeed himself. In reply to her, Pandarus says: "Condition, I had gone barefoot to India." This passage is best explained by the fact that Pandarus is trying to convince his niece that Troilus is madly in love with her and thus is "not himself." In his reply to her, the uncle is saying that he wishes Troilus were himself – even if he (Pandarus) had to walk barefoot all the way to India.

The themes of lust and treachery are sustained in the scene in several passages. For example, the reference to the forked hair supposedly growing on Troilus' chin, a symbol of infidelity (178 ff.); Pandarus' insistence that Helen, the unfaithful, actually loves Troilus better than she does Paris (116 ff.); Cressida's reply to Pandarus' conclusion, "One knows not at what ward [position of defense] you lie" (284 ff.).

Note the three examples of functional food and cookery images which Shakespeare introduced earlier to support the theme of sensuality. Pandarus provides two: (1) his description of the common soldiers as being "chaff and bran, chaff and bran! Porridge after meat!" – all this in comparison to Troilus who had just passed by (262–263) and (2) his insistence that Troilus has all the "spice and salt that season a man" (278). Cressida's reply immediately following these provides the third example.

Pandarus' role in this play can be summed up in the first two lines spoken by Cressida in soliloquy at the end of the scene (308–309):

> Words, vows, gifts, tears, and love's full sacrifice,
> He offers in another's enterprise.

### ACT I – SCENE 3

**Summary**

The action now shifts to the Greek camp and takes place before Agamemnon's tent. Addressing Nestor, Ulysses, and Menelaus, the Greek general asks why all look so crestfallen. He points out that often "checks and disaster" meet those who undertake great actions. From the subsequent lines we learn that the Greeks have been waging war for seven long years, yet the walls of Troy still stand. In his desire to encourage his fellow Greeks, Agamemnon declares that great Jove is testing their patience and ability to persist in the effort to subdue the enemy.

Nestor next speaks, augmenting the words of Agamemnon. He agrees that men prove their worth when they defy fortune. Shifting to metaphor, he adds that when the seas are smooth, the frailest crafts sail upon its surface, but when the north wind blows and the sea rages, only the strong-ribbed ship dares to brave the storm; "Even so/ Doth valor's show and valor's worth divide/ In storms of Fortune."

Ulysses applauds the encouraging words of Agamemnon and Nestor and then asks permission to speak. The Greek general graciously states that, unlike the ranting of Thersites, Ulysses' words will be filled with harmony and sense. Ulysses now delivers a long speech in which he analyzes the troubles in the Greek camp and identifies their cause. This is his great speech on order and degree. The fundamental idea advanced is that organized societies flourish only if every member observes the "degree and vocation" which are peculiar to his status; thus one concerns himself not with private desires but with the welfare of the society in general. Whatever his rank may be in the community, he must fulfill the obligations of that rank. Only if this hierarchy of vocations is preserved and authority recognized and obeyed can there be a healthy society: "Degree being vizarded,/ The unworthiest shows as fairly in the mask" (83–84). This is a universal principle which, Ulysses points out, operates throughout the universe:

> The heavens themselves, the planets, and this centre
> Observes degree, priority, and place,
> Insisture, course, proportion, season, form,
> Office, and custom, in all line of order . . .
>
> (85–88)

And so on the human plane, for how else could communities, degrees in schools, urban brotherhoods, peaceful commerce, the principle of primogeniture, the "Prerogative of age, crowns, sceptres, laurels" survive? Once this order is violated, chaos is come again. Disorder in the heavens would lead to plagues, frightening portents, tempests, earthquakes which would "deracinate/ The unity and married calm of states/ Quite from their fixture" (99–101). Once degree, which makes for harmony, is taken away, mere brute strength would rule. If the principle of order and degree are ignored, justice, tranquility, and virtue will no longer flourish in the human social organization: men will become bestial and will ultimately destroy themselves. By implication, Ulysses argues, when the laws of order are not observed, they must inevitably fail and bring destruction.

Having provided the philosophical groundwork, Ulysses moves to his main point. In all human social organizations, there must be those whose vocation is to rule, to govern the whole society or body. Among the Greeks, it is Agamemnon who is the "head and general." Well up in the hierarchy is Achilles, "whom opinion crowns/ The sinew and forehand of our host . . ." And it is he who is guilty of violating the basic principles of order and degree by refusing to fight, ignoring the orders of his natural superior, scoffing at Agamemnon. As a result, the entire army is infected with inaction and disobedience:

> The speciality of rule has been neglected.
> And look how many Grecian tents do stand
> Hollow upon this plain, so many hollow factions.
> When that the general is not like the hive
> To whom the foragers shall all repair
> What honey is expected?
>
> (78–83)

Later, Ulysses tells how Achilles' behavior has seriously disrupted the Greek camp. His neglect makes the Greeks retreat when they intend to advance. Successively those in lower ranks disdain the general. Nestor agrees that Ulysses has discovered "the fever whereof all our power is sick."

"What is the remedy?" asks Agamemnon, and again the wise Ulysses holds forth at length. Achilles, most famous of warriors, now languishes in his tent with Patroclus, both mocking the high designs of Agamemnon and other leaders. Patroclus clownishly imitates them and wins Achilles' applause. Nestor adds that many others have become so infected, and he cites, as an example, Ajax, who has grown self-willed, keeps to his tent, and "rails on our state in war . . ." All this, Nestor says, sets Thersites to mouthing scurrilous insults directed against the leaders in an attempt to discredit them. Ulysses elaborates. These malcontents criticize the policy adopted in a council of war, condemn forethought, and take notice only of the immediate present. They scorn what they call "bed work" (armchair strategy) and "mappery" (futile making of maps).

A Trojan trumpet is heard, announcing the arrival of Aeneas. After a courteous exchange between him and Agamemnon, who bids the Trojan speak "frankly as the wind," Aeneas announces that Hector challenges any Greek warrior who counts himself valorous and truly in love with his lady; the fight will take place in plain view of both Trojans and Greeks, midway between the Greek camp and the walls of Troy. If there is no one to accept this challenge, Hector will say that the Greek dames are "sunburnt" (that is, country wenches and, therefore, not worth fighting for). Agamemnon replies that Hector will not lack an opponent even if Agamemnon himself should have to accept the challenge. Nestor, conceding that he is far advanced in age, also vows to fight if no Greek warrior volunteers. Agamemnon then assures Aeneas that Achilles "shall have word of this intent."

Alone with Nestor, Ulysses reveals a plan which he has just formulated. He knows that Hector's challenge was really made to Achilles, most famous of the Greek warriors. Nestor agrees: who else could hope to defeat Hector in single combat? He adds that there is much at stake, for the loser will adversely influence all of his fellow soldiers. The champion on each side will be thought to have been chosen by the general and his staff: defeat will reflect upon them. Ulysses then states:

> Let us, like merchants, show our foulest wares,
> And think perchance they'll sell. If not,
> The lustre of the better yet to show
> Shall sell the better.

(359–362)

In other words, do not select Achilles as their champion, for he is filled with overweening pride and insolence. If victorious he would become worse. Ulysses then nominates the loutish Ajax, urging that he be told that he is the better man. This choice, Ulysses hopes, will serve as a goad to Achilles, rousing him from his state of torpor and irascibility and subduing his excessive pride, which is a serious threat to the entire Greek camp. Nestor concurs, and both leave to find Agamemnon.

## Commentary

Agamemnon is the Greek general who, in legend, was King of Mycenae and, in Homer's *Iliad*, the ruler over all Argos. He is the brother to Menelaus. In this scene he is depicted as a dignified leader, soliciting counsel in order to solve the difficulties which have led to a stalemate in the siege of Troy.

Nestor is a Greek commander who, in legend, was King of Pylos. He was recognized as the most experienced and wisest of the chieftains who went to the siege of Troy. In this scene he typically amplifies the views of Agamemnon and endorses those of Ulysses.

Ulysses is the Roman name of the Greek Odysseus, hero of Homer's *Odyssey* and a prominent figure in the *Iliad*. Although the name of Nestor is frequently applied as an epithet to the wisest man in a group, it is Ulysses who emerges here as the most perspicacious, what with his profound speech on order and degree and his plan to revive in Achilles a willingness to follow vocation and recognize the speciality of rule. Ulysses was King of Ithaca.

Aeneas is one of the Trojan commanders who here serves as an emissary bringing Hector's challenge to Agamemnon. Like Agamemnon, he strictly observes the code of chivalry in addressing his adversaries.

The purpose of this scene is (1) to provide essential exposition relating to the state of affairs in the Greek camp, (2) to set forth fully a sound diagnosis of the source of difficulties which have made it impossible for the Greeks to advance their cause, (3) to start the rising action in the camp scenes by making clear what initial steps are to be taken to restore order, and (4) to develop character, particularly that of Ulysses.

Shakespeare relates this scene to the earlier ones in which the action takes place among the Trojans when he reveals that violation of order, the failure to follow vocation, is the source of infection among both Greeks and Trojans.

According to Ulysses, there is a significant relationship between the macrocosm and the body politic. Note, for example, the close correspondence between the order in both macrocosm and state, and any violation of that order is monstrous. As critic E. M. W. Tillyard has pointed out (*The Elizabethan World Picture*, (1950), 82), this was a commonplace in Renaissance England. It is set forth, for example, in the official *Homily on Obedience* (1547), which all Englishmen were required to hear in their churches at least three times a year in Shakespeare's day. The most relevant passage reads:

> In the earth God hath assigned kings and princes with other governors under them, all in good and necessary order. The water above is kept and raineth down in due time and season. The sun, moon, stars, rainbow, thunder, lightning, clouds, and all birds of the air do keep their order.

Ulysses uses a convincing analogy in developing his argument on order and degree when he compares the community to a colony of bees:

> When that the general is not like the hive
> To whom the foragers shall all repair,
> What honey is expected?

(81–83)

This analogy, developed at length in the literature on order and degree, goes back at least to the *Summa Theologica* of St. Thomas Aquinas. It is important to note in this scene that Ulysses selects *Ajax* rather than some other warrior to supplant Achilles as the one to meet Hector in single combat. Ulysses himself first says that it would be wise to select a warrior second to the renowned Achilles and thus hold in reserve the premier warrior in case of a Greek defeat. But it will be recalled that Ajax felled Hector not long ago, thus arousing the ire of the Trojan. There is a chance that the powerful Ajax may win, for he surely is *not* a straw man.

One might best describe the exchange between Aeneas and Agamemnon by observing that it is conducted in a manner consistent with the medieval code of chivalry, each participant carefully observing the amenities. Relevant also is the fact that Hector's challenge calls for an opponent who will fight in the name of his lady love. It is as if Trojan and Greek combatants were principals in a medieval romance.

## ACT II – SCENE 1

### Summary

After references to Ajax and Thersites in the first act, we now meet these two malcontents as they vie with each other in an exchange of the coarsest scurrility. Ignoring Ajax, who calls to him, Thersites rails against Agamemnon on the grounds that the general is completely ineffective. If Agamemnon were covered with boils which did erupt, "were not that a botchy core?" His point is that he sees no "matter," or sense, in the general now. In anger at having been ignored, Ajax upbraids Thersites and strikes him. The two insult each other, Ajax calling Thersites a "bitch wolf's son" and Thersites describing his adversary as "a mongrel beef-witted lord." And so it goes: Ajax threatens to strike again, and Thersites boasts that he will give Ajax continued tongue lashings. Ajax finally is able to say that he wanted to learn about the new proclamation, but Thersites refuses to give him any information. Instead he charges him with being envious of Achilles, at whom he rails. For this Thersites earns for himself another good beating but is not silenced. As he denounces Ajax as the fool of the god of war ("Mars his idiot"), Achilles and Patroclus enter.

When Achilles inquires as to the cause of the altercation, Thersites gives him a typically scurrilous answer: Ajax is a fool who does not know himself. "Therefore I beat thee," says Ajax, and Achilles intercedes as the giant warrior starts to strike the railer again. Finally Achilles learns the cause of the altercation. Thersites complains that he is not Ajax's servant to do as bid and that as a volunteer in the Greek camp, he is not subject to orders from others. He then charges that a great deal of Achilles' wit lies in his sinews and adds that Hector will have "a great catch" if he bests this witless brute. Not content with this, he adds the names of Ulysses and Nestor to those who are deficient in wit, as is proven by the fact that they induce Achilles to fight. Patroclus does not escape vituperation when he endeavors to quiet Thersites, and the latter departs, vowing that he will "leave the faction of fools."

From Achilles, Ajax at last learns about the proclamation: early in the morning Hector will appear midway between the Greek camp and the walls of Troy, and the sound of a trumpet will be the signal for one of the Greek warriors to come forth and meet him in single combat. All this news Achilles describes as "trash." When Ajax learns that Hector has not asked for a particular opponent, he is determined to learn more about the matter. The three leave the stage.

## Commentary

As we observe and listen to Ajax in this scene, he emerges as a warrior who is all brawn and no brain. Although he rivals Thersites in scurrility at times, he depends largely on his brute strength in an argument. In the words of Alexander, Cressida's serving man, he appears "churlish as a bear" and as one whose "valor is crushed with folly," as is evidenced by his envy of Achilles.

Thersites appears in this scene as a scurrilous volunteer officer in the Greek camp, notorious as a railing malcontent whose lacerating commentary is directed toward all the leaders, as well as the chief warriors among the Greeks. He serves as a kind of satiric chorus as he gives his views on the state of affairs.

Here again we see Shakespeare emphasizing that Achilles is the premier warrior among the Greeks, just as Hector is among the Trojans. Achilles' excessive pride is indicated by his conviction that Hector "knew his man"—that is, if the greatest warrior was to be challenged, he would inevitably be Achilles. That he fails to follow vocation is indicated by his contemptuous dismissal of the proclamation as "trash."

The purpose of this scene is (1) to develop the characters of Thersites and Ajax, (2) to illustrate the extent of infection in the Greek camp, and (3) to advance the plot in the camp scenes by preparing the way for Ajax's election as the warrior to face Hector.

Thersites makes great use of the disease image in his discourse because it is one way in which Shakespeare can carry forward the theme of infection in the Greek camp, which is so well illustrated in this short scene. In addition to his constant use of abusive language, Thersites shows his irascibility. He is adamant in his refusal to tell Ajax about the proclamation and even ignores him at first. Among the many insulting terms Thersites uses are "mongrel beef-witted lord," "assinego," and "clotpoles." You should have some knowledge of the meaning of these terms. The first means someone of mixed breed whose wit has been impaired as a result of having eaten too much meat (in accordance with the then current theory regarding the effect of meat upon the brain). The second means "little ass," and the third "blockheads."

## ACT II—SCENE 2

### Summary

Priam and four of his sons enter a room in the palace. Priam reports that Nestor has once more sent word that Helen must be sent back if war is to cease, and he solicits Hector's opinion. Disavowing any fear of the Greeks, Hector states that it behooves the Trojans not to be overly confident but to exercise "modest doubt" as to the outcome of the conflict. He flatly states that Helen should be returned, reminding his father and brother of the many who have died because of her presence among the Trojans—and she "a thing not ours, or worth to us." How, he concludes, can anyone reasonably argue that she is worth keeping? Troilus promptly objects, arguing that the honor of their royal father is at stake. They cannot capitulate to the Greeks under any circumstances—"Fie, for godly shame!"

It is now Helenus' turn to speak, and he reproves Troilus for offering counsel devoid of reason and suggesting that Priam should not seek for reasons in determining the issue. Replying that his priestly brother is interested only in "dreams and slumbers" and voices only cowardly words, Troilus gives what he insists is the gist of Helenus' argument. Afraid of the armed enemy, the priest panics and sound reason deserts him. "Nay," he continues, "if we talk of reason./ Let's shut our gates and sleep," for all manhood and honor will be lost.

Hector tells Troilus that Helen is not worth the cost and adds that "'Tis mad idolatry to make the service greater than the god." But his brother does not concur. He argues that if he were to take to wife a woman of his own choosing, his desire (lust) kindled by his eyes and ears, he could not reject her even if he no longer desired her, for his honor would be involved. Moreover, he continues, Hector himself had agreed that Paris should "do some vengeance on the Greeks." He reminds his brother of the circumstances relating to the taking of Helen: the Greeks still held an old aunt, and therefore Paris had taken Helen. And, peerless beauty that Helen is, she is worth keeping and fighting for. If Hector now changes his mind, he shows himself to be more fickle than Fortune. Troilus concludes by insisting that all were enthusiastic when Paris brought Helen back to Troy, but now apparently they cravenly argue that she is not worth keeping.

The disputation is interrupted by the dramatic appearance of Cassandra with her hair disarrayed, exclaiming: "Cry, Trojans, Cry." Hector unsuccessfully tries to quiet her. Her direful prophecy is that their "firebrand brother burns us all . . . Troy burns, or else let Helen go." When she leaves, Hector asks Troilus if these "high strains of divination" make him feel remorseful. The latter dismisses Cassandra's prophecy as "brainsick raptures." Paris, to be sure, sides with Troilus: if Helen is returned to the Greeks, the earlier Trojan counsels and undertakings will be considered frivolous and the Trojans themselves reputed to be cowards.

Priam reproves Paris, stating that his son speaks "Like one besotten on [his] sweet delights." But Paris insists that Helen's beauty is a source of pleasure to all Trojans and that it would be dishonorable to return her to the Greeks "on terms of base compulsion." Now Hector answers him and Troilus in a long, doctrinally important speech (163–193). He concedes that both have been eloquent enough but actually have ignored the basic issue. They have advanced arguments inspired by hot passion, not pure reason. By the law of nature, a man desires and should have possession of his wife; it is lust of another which leads to the abrogation of this law. Helen is the wife of Menelaus, Sparta's king; thus the moral law of nature and of nations informs against the Trojans. But despite his orthodox views, Hector states that he will incline to his brother's wishes to keep Helen because the cause for which they fight depends upon their "joint and several dignities." Troilus applauds this decision, saying that Hector has come to the very heart of the matter; glory, not rancor, is the motivation for continuing the fight against the Greeks. He praises Helen as "a theme of honour and renown" and as "a spur to valiant and magnanimous deeds." He says that he knows Hector would not miss such an opportunity to win glory for himself. "I am yours," replies Hector, and he tells his brothers about the challenge which he has sent to the Greeks.

## Commentary

Priam, King of the Trojans, has little to say in this scene. His rebuke of Paris reveals his astuteness, for he correctly analyzes Paris' motive for continuing the war. Unfortunately, he, like Hector, chooses to continue the fight rather than have dissension within his royal family.

In this scene, Hector has the most important speech from the standpoint of doctrine. He elaborates the point of view taken by Priam. He emphasizes the injustice and immorality of Paris' relationship with Helen and argues correctly that, however physically beautiful she may be, she is not worth the cost of Trojan lives. All of this points to the theme of futility which runs through this play. Yet, true to his vocation as a warrior and anxious to avoid dissension, Hector agrees to remain loyal to the cause for which they have been fighting.

In Troilus' championing the position taken by Paris and eloquent praise of Helen, he remains the voluptuary that he has been established to be in Act I. Here, it is passion, not reason, that interests him; it is enough that a fair lady is involved. The general welfare of Troy does not enter into his thinking.

Like his father, Priam, Helenus voices words of wisdom, but since he is a priest, not primarily a warrior, his words carry no weight, and he is easily quieted by the voluble Troilus.

Cassandra, the prophetess daughter to Priam and Hecuba, is fated never to be believed. Thus when she prophesies that Troy will fall unless Helen is returned to the Greeks, Troilus scoffs that all this is no more than "brainsick raptures."

The purpose of this scene is (1) to make clear the issues from the Trojan point of view and thus identify the elements of the conflict among the Trojans, (2) to show the source and extent of infection among the Trojans in a scene which balances Act I, Scene ii, wherein the same thing was shown in the Greek camp, and (3) to develop the characters of Hector, Paris, and Troilus in particular.

There is specific evidence here that Troilus, already established as a votary of sensual love, champions Paris' cause, and it is Troilus who rejects reason. In his defense, particularly in lines 61–70, he uses imagery notable for its emphasis on the sensual. For example, he speaks of *will* opposed to *judgment,* the first word being used in the sense of "lust" or "desire." One should recall also the words of the clear-sighted Hector, who states that Helen "is not worth what she does cost the holding" (51–52). Troilus asks, "What's aught but as 'tis valued?" Hector replies: "But value dwells not in particular will"—that is, in individual desire.

A noteworthy line from the work of another poet-dramatist is echoed in this scene. In his praise of Helen, Troilus exclaims:

> Why, she is a pearl
> Whose price hath launched above a thousand ships . . .
>
> (81–82)

This is a deliberate echo of a line—"Was this the face that launched a thousand ships?"—spoken by Dr. Faustus when the image of Helen of Troy appears before him in Christopher Marlowe's well-known tragedy.

Troilus' passionate insistence that the Trojans fight to the bitter end is particularly ironic because in Act I, Scene i, Troilus declared that he would "unarm again"—that he would let others fight. He exclaimed to Pandarus:

> Fools on both sides! Helen needs be fair
> When with your blood you daily paint her thus
> I cannot fight on this argument.
>
> (92–94)

Now he wants to continue the fight exactly on that argument. Shakespeare is not, however, to be charged with inconsistency in character portrayal. Troilus' shift in point of view is quite consistent, since he is a devotee of voluptuous love, one who declares that reason and a consideration of consequences only make one a coward.

## ACT II—SCENE 3

### Summary

The action takes place before the tent of Achilles in the Greek camp. Thersites enters alone and voices his anger that "the elephant Ajax" has beaten him, while he could only rail. He heaps more spiteful execrations, as he correctly calls them, on Ajax and on Achilles. He offers mock prayers to the devil Envy, asking that he be able to avenge himself on them and the entire camp, since the Greeks have gone to war because of a wench, the faithless Helen of Troy.

Patroclus enters, recognizes Thersites, and invites him to "come in and rail." But Thersites does not have to enter the tent to engage in his favorite exercise. He expresses regret that he had forgotten to include Patroclus along with Ajax and Achilles in his most recent outburst and he now makes up for his lapse of memory, concluding with an "amen," which brings a taunt from Patroclus. Achilles enters at this point, and a colloquy follows. Calling Thersites "a privileged man"—that is, a licensed fool like a court jester—Achilles permits him to castigate all present. In Thersites' words:

> Agamemnon is a fool to offer to command Achilles,
> Achilles is a fool to be commanded of Agamemnon,
> Thersites is a fool to serve such a fool, and
> Patroclus is a fool positive.
>
> (67–70)

As Agamemnon, Ulysses, Nestor, Diomedes, and Ajax approach, Achilles tells Patroclus that he will see no one and he then retires to his tent. As Thersites leaves, he rails against what he calls the pretense and knavery in the Greek camp and the unworthy cause for which the Greeks fight: "Now the dry serpigo [eruptions of the skin] on the subject [everyone], and war and lechery confound all!"

Agamemnon asks Patroclus to tell him where Achilles is and is informed that the warrior is indisposed. The general then orders Patroclus to tell Achilles that he and his lieutenants must see him at once. As Patroclus leaves, Ulysses remarks that they saw Achilles sleeping in his tent and that he was not sick. Ajax says that the warrior is indeed sick—"sick of proud heart," and why, he does not know. He begs a private word with Agamemnon.

Ulysses then explains to Nestor that Ajax barks at Achilles because the latter took his "fool," Thersites, from him. It is Nestor's opinion that the quarrel will work to the advantage of both Ulysses and himself in their plan to school Achilles.

Patroclus reenters and reports that Achilles expresses the hope that Agamemnon and his group come only for sport and pleasure; that is, he is not concerned with serious matters. The general sternly replies that he does not miss the scornful tone of Achilles and his messenger, acknowledges the fact that Achilles has proved his martial superiority, but adds that the warrior's reputation is now becoming dim because of inactivity. He orders Patroclus to return to Achilles and tell him that the general and his entourage must see him, adding that Patroclus can also state that all deem Achilles to be "overproud and underhonest." Tell him this, Agamemnon concludes, and warn him that if he continues to "overhold his price so much," they will forsake him: "A stirring dwarf we do allowance give/ Before a sleeping giant." Patroclus leaves, and at Agamemnon's command Ulysses follows him into the tent.

Ajax, showing his envy, asks Agamemnon if he thinks Achilles is the better man. Humoring the warrior, the general assures him that he is "as strong, as valiant, as wise, no less noble, much more gentle, and altogether more tractable." He concedes that Achilles is excessively proud and adds: "He that is proud eats up himself." Ajax declares that he detests a proud man, and, in an aside, Nestor remarks: "Yet he loves himself. Is't not strange?"

Ulysses returns to report that Achilles absolutely refuses to go to the battlefield the next day and offers no reason for his refusal. He describes the insubordinate warrior as completely self-centered and "plaguey proud." Agamemnon suggests that Ajax be sent to Achilles, who it is believed, esteems the loutish warrior. But Ulysses, holding fast to his plan, urges Agamemnon not to take such an action. He then praises Ajax extravagantly, calling him "this thrice worthy and right valiant lord" and arguing that Ajax should not be asked to debase himself by appealing to the arrogant Achilles, who would become even prouder. Ajax's avowal that if he did go he would "pash him o'er the face" tells us that Ajax is easily gulled. The huge warrior, now puffed up with pride, boasts of how he will beat Achilles, whom he descibes in insulting terms. All this bluster gives Ulysses, abetted by Nestor and Diomedes, the opportunity to nominate Ajax as Hector's opponent. Responding once more to Ulysses' praise of him as one "thrice-famed beyond, beyond all erudition" and responding to the urgings of Nestor and Diomedes, Ajax is easily won over.

Ulysses states that there is no time to be wasted and urges Agamemnon to call together his chief commanders for "fresh kings are come to Troy." Ajax, he concludes, will cope with the best.

## Commentary

Thersites, the railing political malcontent, a volunteer warrior in the Greek camp, remains completely in character here as he excoriates one and all. It is especially clear that he is intended to be the buffoonish commentator who, despite the vileness of his language and his gross exaggerations, is an important commentator on the events of the war and the reason for which it is being fought.

Achilles, the most famous Greek warrior, now beset with pride, refuses to fight. The words of Agamemnon and others testify to the fact that he has indeed earned the accolade of premier warrior but because of arrogance and overweening pride, he now chooses to languish in his tent and to concern himself only with sport and pleasure.

Agamemnon, the Greek general, vainly tries to arouse Achilles from insubordination and sloth and wisely observes that, however great Achilles reputation has been, it will not survive unless the warrior continues to justify it.

In this scene as elsewhere, Ulysses, the wisest of Agamemnon's counselors, succeeds in advancing the plan which he authored in an effort to bring Achilles to his senses and restore order in the Greek camp. Nestor's courage and loyalty are shown by his declaring that he will meet Hector in combat if no younger man volunteers. Here we find him helping Ulysses maneuver matters so that Ajax will be chosen as the Greek champion. Meanwhile, Ajax, the giant-sized, brainless Greek warrior, one-time friend of Achilles vies with Achilles in his excessive pride. Typical of him are his boasts that he will thrash his adversary and his naive response to extravagant praise.

The purpose of this scene is (1) to advance the plot in the camp scenes by showing how Ulysses, with help principally from Nestor, capitalizes on the enmity between Ajax and Achilles and prepares the way for the selection of the former as Hector's opponent, (2) to emphasize the fact that Achilles is truly the "chief architect of chaos" in the Greek camp, and (3) to provide Thersites further opportunities to fulfill his function as the bitterly satiric commentator on the action.

Suspense is sustained in this scene by the extent to which Agamemnon goes in an effort to convince Achilles that he must reform and again take his place as premier warrior. It will be recalled that the general sends the wise Ulysses to confer with Achilles, and there is no reason to believe that this wise emissary did not perform his duty to the best of his ability. The scene is more than half over before Ulysses returns with the final report: "Achilles will not to the field tomorrow."

The most important functional images in the play are found in the food-cooking cluster of images first introduced in the love scenes. There are several examples: (1) Achilles says to Thersites: "Why, my cheese, my digestion, why has thou not served thyself in to my table so many meals" (43–45); (2) Ulysses refers to Achilles as "the proud lard/ That bastes his arrogance with his own seam" (194–195); (3) Ajax boasts that he will *knead* Achilles (231).

Achilles puts up with the foul-mouthed Thersites because he himself states that the malcontent amuses him and that he is therefore "a privileged man," one licensed to speak his mind so long as he is amusing. In view of this attitude Achilles now takes toward the leaders and the war, his tolerance is quite understandable; he welcomes indictments of the others.

## ACT III–SCENE 1

### Summary

The action takes place in Priam's palace. Pandarus and a servant enter. The former asks if the latter serves Paris. The servant impudently chooses to interpret Pandarus' words literally throughout the exchange, and Pandarus finally says: "Friend, we understand not one another. I am too courtly, and thou art too cunning" (29–30). But at last he does learn that this is Paris' servant and that the musicians present have come at the request of Paris, who is now with the "mortal Venus," Helen. Pandarus states that he comes at Prince Troilus' request to speak with Paris about urgent business.

Paris and Helen enter with attendants and are greeted by Pandarus. The verbal exchange that follows is filled with puns relating to music. Pandarus endeavors to have a private talk with Paris, but Helen, now in high spirits, will not permit it. So Pandarus delivers Troilus' request: the young lover asks that Paris make an excuse for him if the king calls him to supper. Both Paris and Helen are filled with curiosity as to the reason for this request, and Paris expresses the belief that his brother sups with Cressida. Pandarus is quick to deny that such is the case. Paris then agrees to make the excuse, but neither he nor Helen lets the subject drop. Helen, in particular, jests at Pandarus' expense, her words often being off-colored. At one point she says to him: "Let thy song be love. This love will undo us all. O Cupid, Cupid, Cupid!" (119–120) And Pandarus does sing a love song, one notably risque and ending with a "Heigh-ho!" Paris provides the appropriate comment: Pandarus "eats nothing but doves . . . and that breeds hot blood, and hot blood begets hot thoughts and hot thoughts beget hot deeds, and hot deeds is love" (140–143).

Pandarus changes the subject, asking who is afield today. Paris tells him and adds that he would have armed himself and joined the other warriors but Helen insisted that he stay with her. He then asks why Troilus did not go, but Pandarus evades the question and again makes reference to Troilus' request that Paris provide an excuse for his absence from Priam's table. Pandarus then leaves.

The sound of a retreat is heard. Paris asks Helen to join him at Priam's hall to greet the returned warriors. Helen, he says, must help unarm Hector with her "white enchanted fingers." She shall then have excelled all others, for she will have disarmed the great Hector. She agrees to help unarm the hero, and Paris expresses his deep love for her.

## Commentary

Pandarus zealously continues to exert himself on Troilus' behalf. In the exchange with the servant he emerges as a kind of primitive character not unlike Polonius in *Hamlet* – one quite confident with himself but easily made to look rather foolish. Throughout this scene his pruriency is evident, as in his song with its erotic pun on the word *die*. Paris' serving man finds it amusing to appear quite literal-minded and thus have fun at Pandarus' expense.

Here, for the first time, we find Paris in the company of Helen. It is significant that he is as enthusiastic as any of the others in joking about illicit sex. Interestingly, Helen contributes to the off-color dialogue.

The purpose of this scene is (1) to advance the love plot by showing how Pandarus, in accordance with instructions, helps make it possible for Troilus and Cressida to come together, (2) to illustrate the extent of infection among the Trojans in a play in which, to use Thersites' words, "all is war and lechery." It is the latter which prevails in this scene, and (3) to develop character, particularly that of Paris, Helen, and Pandarus.

It is especially significant that Shakespeare refers to the returning warriors, particularly Hector, because he provides a commentary on both Paris and Troilus, passion's slaves who remain in Troy while others fight the Greeks.

Note the irony in the following lines spoken by Paris to Helen:

> You shall do more than all
> the island kings – disarm great Hector.

(166–167)

At the literal level, of course, Helen will help to unarm, not disarm, Hector. But the war is being fought because of her, and ultimately Hector will be disarmed; indeed he will be slain. In this scene Helen may be said to have disarmed him.

Likewise, there is a double meaning in these lines:

> Pan.   I come to speak with Paris from Prince Troilus. I
>       will make a complimental assault upon him, for
>       my business seethes.
> Serv.   Sodden business! There's a stewed phrase indeed.

At the literal level Pandarus is saying that he will attack Paris with compliments because his business is most urgent. But *seethes* also means "boils," which makes it possible for the servant to call it *sodden* business, and *sodden* also means "stupid." When he makes reference to "a stewed phrase," he tactily refers to lechery, since "stews" was a common term used to refer to brothels. It would seem that he knows Pandarus for what he is, a *panderer*!

### ACT III – SCENE 2

**Summary**

Pandarus and Troilus' serving boy meet in an orchard at the former's house. Pandarus learns that Troilus waits for him as escort to his house. At this point, the young prince himself arrives and the boy is dismissed. Troilus then tells Pandarus that he has not seen Cressida, although he stalked "about her door like a strange soul upon the Stygian banks, staying for waftage." He implores Pandarus to be his Charon

> And give me swift transportation to those fields
> Where I may wallow in the lily beds
> Proposed for the deserver!

(12–14)

Pandarus assures him that he will bring Cressida promptly. In soliloquy the warrior describes himself as being giddy with expectation, and, in extravagant language, he vows that once the "watery palates taste indeed Love's thrice-repured [reputed] nectar," he doubts he will survive. Pandarus returns to announce that Cressida is preparing herself for the encounter, describing her as being in a state of embarrassment and excitement. "She fetches her breath as short as a new-ta'en sparrow" (35). Again alone, Troilus declares that he is no less passionate in expectancy.

Pandarus re-enters with Cressida, urging her not to blush: "Shame's a baby." Now, he continues, the prince must swear the oaths to her that he swore in her absence. Using metaphors derived from bowling, in which the ball was rolled toward another smaller ball called the "mistress," Pandarus urges the two to show their love for each other: "So, so, rub on, and kiss the mistress . . . go to, go to" (51 ff.). When Troilus tells Cressida that he is speechless, Pandarus declares that Troilus must give her deeds, for "words pay no debts." He then leaves the two alone together.

With sufficient eloquence, Troilus declares his great love for Cressida, who plays to perfection her role of one who is shy and fearful. He assures her that there are no dregs in the fountain of their love, except that "the will is infinite and the execution confined, that the desire is boundless and the act a slave to limit" (88–90). Let him prove to her, he urges, that he is not one who has "the voice of lions and the act of hares" (95–96). He vows that he will be faithful to her. Just as Pandarus re-appears, Cressida invites Troilus to enter the house.

To Pandarus, Cressida dedicates any folly which she may be guilty of. He thanks her: "If my lord gets a boy of you, you'll give him me" (111–112). Troilus then states that she has two hostages, her uncle's words and his own firm faith. Pandarus assures the young lover that his niece will be the soul of fidelity. And Cressida promptly declares her love for Troilus. Indeed she adds that she has loved him from the start—and then expresses regret that she has admitted as much. In response, Troilus speaks passionately of "a winnowed purity in love" and says that he is "as true as truth's simplicity." Cressida matches him in fervor as she swears complete faithfulness to him. "Go to, a bargain made. Seal it, seal it," says Pandarus, and adds that he will witness the ceremony. As he takes their hands, he reminds them that it was he who brought them together: if their love does not endure, "let all constant men be Troiluses, all false women Cressids, and all brokers-between Pandars!" (209–211). To this, all say "Amen," and Pandarus conducts the two to a bedchamber.

### Commentary

In this scene, Troilus can hardly contain himself as he approaches the conquest of the lady and anticipates the consummation of their love. Cressida, meanwhile, in keeping with what she said in soliloquy at the end of Act I, Scene ii, has played the perfect coquette. In this scene, she is depicted as one who is in control of matters, and she succeeds in stimulating in Troilus an even greater passion. As for Pandarus, he now succeeds in his mission of bringing Troilus and Cressida together and in arranging for them to be safely alone together. Typical of him is his admoni-

tion to Cressida: "Come, come, what need you blush? Shame's a baby."
It is he who provides chamber and bed for the lovers.

The purpose of this scene is (1) to provide the climax in the love plot
of the play and (2) to develop the character of Troilus as a young sensualist,
that of Cressida as a mistress of the love game, and that of Pandarus as
one who views love as only animal passion.

Some first-time readers of this play equate Troilus' feelings with romantic lyricism, but there is a clear indication here that Troilus' passion is anything *but* lyrical and idealistic. For example, the imagery and word choice
in general in his first, longer speeches (9–16 and 21–30) indicate that he
is an impatient young sensualist. Thus he yearns to "wallow in the lily
beds/ Proposed for the deserver." Further, the food imagery (19–23), with
its emphasis on the sensitive appetite, points up his sensuality. Significant
in this connection are also his words: "This is the monstrosity in love, lady,
that the will is infinite and the execution confined, that the desire is
boundless and the act a slave to limit" (87–90).

Note that Cressida shows herself here to be a superior performer in
the love game. Having decided that she must not wait too long before giving herself to Troilus, she then admits that she had only seemed hard to
win. With assumed naivete she bewails the fact that women cannot keep
their counsel in such matters, and she urges Troilus to stop her mouth —
an obvious invitation for him to kiss her. Next she is at pains to convince
him that she had no intention of begging for a kiss. All this only whets
the appetite of the increasingly anxious and impatient Troilus.

An interesting example of dramatic irony presages this scene. Note
Cressida's speech beginning "If I be false or swerve a hair from truth" and
ending "Yea, let them say, to stick the heart of falsehood,/ 'As false as
Cressid'." (191 ff.). Note also Pandarus' speech immediately following; it
also includes dramatic irony and dramatic presaging. Just as Cressida will
prove false and become the exemplar of infidelity, so Pandarus will lend
his name to the "goers-between" who arrange assignations.

### ACT III – SCENE 3

**Summary**

Agamemnon, Ulysses, Diomedes, Nestor, Ajax, Menelaus, and Calchas
enter as this scene in the Greek camp opens. Calchas, Trojan priest and
father of Cressida, is first to speak. He reminds the others that he abandoned Troy, incurring the name of traitor and endangering his own person in order to serve the Greeks. In return, he was promised many rewards;
he now requests that one be given to him. When Agamemnon tells him
to make his request, Calchas reminds the group that the prisoner in the
Greek camp is the Trojan commander Antenor, for whose return the

Trojans would pay almost any price. Let him, urges Calchas, be exchanged for Cressida, and then any debt the Greeks owed Calchas would be paid. Agamemnon promptly agrees to this scheme and orders Diomedes to arrange for the exchange. At the same time, Diomedes is told to find out if Hector is willing to fight the Greek champion the next day. Ajax, the general concludes, stands ready to meet the Trojan prince. Diomedes and Calchas depart just as Achilles and Patroclus appear before their tent.

Ulysses proposes that the princes walk past Achilles but look upon him only with disapproval, for this action will give Ulysses the chance to give the warrior salutary advice which may cure him of excessive pride and arrogance. Agreeing to the plan, Agamemnon leads the way. Each plays his part to perfection. Achilles is sure that the general has come once more to beg him to fight. But Agamemnon, snubbing the warrior, leaves it to Nestor to say that they have no interest in him. Next, Menelaus and Ajax file past, and again Achilles is snubbed. Referring to Menelaus, the thoroughly puzzled warrior asks: "What, does the cuckold scorn me?" Ajax does no more than voice a perfunctory "Good morrow," and adds "Aye, and good next day too," and follows Menelaus. Both Achilles and Patroclus are confused. As the latter says, "They were used to bend./ To send their smiles before them to Achilles . . ." (71–72). Achilles wonders why he has become "poor of late." He knows that men lose "place, riches, favor," that they no longer attract admirers. But he is sure that he is no such man because Fortune has not deserted him.

When Ulysses appears, Achilles hails him and asks what he is reading, thus affording Ulysses the opportunity to try to school "great Thetis' son." The writer, says Ulysses, claims that, however well endowed a man may be, he cannot claim to have real virtues unless his attributes are made known to others. In their approving faces he sees the reflection of his superiority. Achilles replies that the writer is correct: one may be beautiful of face, but that beauty "commends itself to others' eyes," and the eye cannot see itself. Ulysses states that the argument is familiar enough and that he does not question it. But he still finds it strange that no man can be lord of anything, however superior he may be, until "he communicates his parts to others" and "behold them formed in the applause"—that is, in the commendation of others. Now all this, he adds, is applicable to Ajax:

> Heavens, what a man is here! A very horse,
> That has he knows not what.

(126–127)

He finds it strange that invaluable things are sometimes despised, and useless things prized. Tomorrow Ajax will have his chance to win renown: "O heavens, what some men do/ While some men leave to do!" (134–135). Now the Greek lords are lauding Ajax as if he had already defeated the great Hector.

In view of his most recent experience with those lords, Achilles does not question this statement, but he asks why his deeds have been forgotten. Then Ulysses lectures him at length. Good deeds are soon forgotten, only perseverance keeps honor bright.

> to have done is to hang
> Quite out of fashion, like a rusty mail
> In monumental mockery.

(151–153)

One must continue, therefore, along the direct path of fame, not lag behind to be overrun and trampled on. Present deeds, though they may be less distinguished than past ones, seem great; virtue should not see "remuneration for the thing it was . . ." And since the "present eye praises the present object," Achilles should not marvel that all the Greeks now begin to worship Ajax. But if Achilles would no longer entomb himself in his tent, he could retrieve his once-great reputation.

Achilles says that he has good reason for keeping to his tent, but Ulysses replies that there are "more potent and heroical" reasons for him to rouse himself. He adds that it is known that Achilles is in love with Polyxena, Hector's sister. When the warrior expresses surprise, he is told that such things inevitably become known. Ulysses asks if it would not be better for him to triumph over Hector than to win Polyxena's favor. And to emphasize his point, he states that Pyrrhus, Achilles' son, will be filled with shame if Greek maids are heard to sing

> "Great Hector's sister did Achilles win,
> But our great Ajax bravely beat him down."

(212–213)

Having made his case, Ulysses leaves.

Patroclus reminds Achilles that he too urged the warrior to don armor again and states that he, himself a warrior, has been charged with effeminacy because he also remains idle. Moreover, he continues, the other Greeks believe that it is really Achilles' obsessive love for Patroclus that explains his absence from the battlefield. When Patroclus confirms the fact that Ajax has been chosen to fight Hector, Achilles admits that his reputation has suffered greatly. Patroclus then warns his friend to beware, for the wounds men give themselves do not heal easily.

Achilles instructs Patroclus to bring Thersites to him. He plans to have the railer ask Ajax to invite the Trojan lords to see him after the combat. He says that he longs to see Hector and talk with him. At this very moment Thersites enters.

Thersites describes Ajax as being preposterously vain and boastful since he was selected to meet Hector on the next day: "Why he stalks up and down like a peacock—a stride and a stand" (251–252). The malcontent predicts that if Hector does not break Ajax's neck in the combat, the giant warrior will break it himself in vainglory. Achilles tells Thersites that he must serve as his ambassador to Ajax and is told that Ajax, in his pride, will speak to no one. Thersites adds that he in turn will now imitate Ajax and keep silent: let Patroclus attempt to communicate with Ajax. At Achilles' request, Patroclus addresses the railer as if he were Ajax, but receives in answer little more than "Hum!" and "Ha!" When Patroclus finally demands an answer, Thersites replies, "Fare you well, with all my heart." Achilles then asks him to bear a letter to Ajax, but is told that it would be better to address a letter to the warrior's horse, which is the more intelligent. Speaking of his troubled mind, Achilles leaves with Patroclus. Alone, Thersites rails against Achilles, referring to his "valiant ignorance," as the scene ends.

## Commentary

The fact that the Greek lords promised Calchas, Cressida's father, many rewards may indicate that his desertion did not involve any moral conviction on his part but a selfish desire for gain.

In this scene, we see Agamemnon, general of the Greek forces, still willing to be guided by the counsel of Ulysses.

Ulysses, King of Ithaca and one of the Greek commanders, has meanwhile assumed the position as the wisest of the general's advisers. If Achilles is the "architect of chaos" in his Greek camp, it is Ulysses who strives to be the architect of order. His discourse with Achilles, replete with wisdom, enhances his position as a valuable counselor.

Achilles, the famous warrior, has been shirking his duty in order to indulge his private desire. Here, he has to endure being snubbed by the Greek lords, with the exception of Ulysses. Because of his arrogance and pride, he is greatly puzzled by the fact that he no longer is treated with admiration and respect. Obviously he badly needs to master the lesson which Ulysses attempts to teach him. And we should not overlook Patroclus, the volunteer Greek warrior who has joined Achilles in idleness. It is of interest to learn that he urged the great warrior to return to the battlefield, arguing that both their reputations are at stake.

The purpose of this scene is (1) to provide a turning point in the action of the camp scenes by having Ulysses make an effort to school Achilles, (2) to introduce a motive for Achilles' inactivity and thus to complicate the action, (3) to provide an important link between the love scenes and the camp scenes by having Agamemnon agree to exchange Antenor for Cressida, and (4) to develop further the characters of Ajax and Ulysses.

Note Ulysses' words as he says that "unplausive eyes are bent on" Achilles (48). He is saying that others look with disapproval upon the now-inactive warrior. Likewise, note Ulysses calling Achilles "great Thetis' son."

Thetis was the queen of the Nereids, the sea nymphs of Greek mythology. By Peleus, King of the Myrmidons, she was the mother of Achilles. Thus Ulysses tacitly reminds Achilles of his famous lineage and implies that rank has its obligations.

These facts being known, one can more easily interpret the following lines spoken by Ulysses to Achilles:

> To have done is to hang
> Quite out of fashion, like a rusty mail
> In monumental mockery.

(151–153)

That is, to have accomplished deeds in the past and then to remain idle is to become like an unused suit of armor, which is no more than a derisive reminder of the warrior who once wore it.

### ACT IV–SCENE 1

**Summary**

The action now shifts to a street in Troy. It is night. At one side, Aeneas enters with a servant bearing a torch; at the other side, Paris, Deiphobus, Antenor, and Diomedes approach, also bearing torches. Once he is identified by his fellow Trojans, Aeneas expresses apparent surprise that Paris is still absenting himself from the felicity of fair Helen's company. Had he a Helen, says the warrior, nothing but "heaven's business" would make him act in such a way. Diomedes cynically agrees. Aeneas then greets Diomedes courteously in keeping with the amenities pertaining to a truce, but adds that he will meet him in warlike manner on the battlefield. The Greek replies in the same vein. Having listened to this exchange, now amiable, now threatening, Paris wittily remarks:

> This is the most despiteful gentle greeting,
> The noblest hateful love, that e'er I heard of.

(32–33)

He then asks Aeneas what is the reason for his appearance in the street and learns that Aeneas comes at the king's bidding. Paris informs him that his orders are to conduct Diomedes to Calchas' house and, in exchange for Antenor, give Cressida into the custody of the Greek. He further instructs Aeneas to precede them in order to rouse Troilus and explain matters to him, for Troilus will surely protest vigorously. Aeneas fully agrees:

> Troilus had rather Troy were borne to Greece
> Than Cressid borne from Troy.

(46–47)

He leaves with his servant.

Paris next asks Diomedes who, in his opinion, "merits fair Helen most," Paris himself or Menelaus. Both alike, frankly replies the Greek. He emphasizes her dishonorable conduct and refers to Menelaus as a "puling cuckold," mourning for a worthless woman, and to Paris as a lecher content to take his pleasure with a woman who has been enjoyed by another man. When Paris states that Diomedes is unduly bitter to a native of his own country, the Greek replies that it is she who is bitter toward her country:

> For every false drop in her bawdy veins
> A Grecian life hath sunk; for every scruple
> Of her contaminated carrion weight,
> A Trojan hath been slain.
>
> (69–72)

Paris has the last word. He accuses Diomedes of acting as do haggling traders who speak disparagingly of the thing they really want to buy.

## Commentary

In Paris' exchange with Diomedes, he is again revealed as one obsessed with the beauty of Menelaus' wife, one willing to have the slaughter continue rather than deprive himself of her charms. Diomedes, an outspoken Greek commander, is now carrying out his mission to the Trojans. Although he is not a railing malcontent, to some degree he takes over the function of Thersites in this scene as he minces no words in expressing his scorn for Helen, Menelaus, and Paris.

Antenor is a Trojan commander who was taken captive by the Greeks. He is valued sufficiently as a warrior so that the Trojans willingly ransom him.

The purpose of this scene is two-fold: (1) to develop the rising action as it approaches the climax, arrangements being completed for sending Cressida to her father and (2) to emphasize again the unworthy cause for which the costly war is being fought and thus to underscore the theme of futility.

In this short scene, it is made apparent (in the words of Thersites) that all is war and lechery. This rather cynical first speech of Aeneas, with its tacit reference to the charms of Helen, immediately introduces the theme of infidelity and lechery. Diomedes' exchange with Paris at the end of the scene (51 ff.) develops the theme at some length. The epic boasts of Diomedes and Aeneas, and the former's reference to slaughter of both Greeks and Trojans links war with lechery.

In this scene, elements of irony are threaded throughout. In view of the fact that the war is being fought for the possession of a faithless woman, it is particularly ironic to hear the noble Aeneas swear by Jove that he will prove his prowess in combat and then to hear Diomedes vie with him in his avowals. Indeed, what Paris calls this "noblest hateful love"–the exchange between Diomedes and Aeneas (10-30)–is packed with irony. Most ironic of all, however, is the fact that the Trojans willingly give up Cressida, paramour of Prince Troilus, for the return of one warrior, but they will *not* give up Helen, paramour of Prince Paris, although such an action would end the slaughter.

## ACT IV–SCENE 2

### Summary

Troilus and Cressida enter the court of Pandarus' house after spending the night together. The young prince entreats Cressida not to accompany him to the gate nor to trouble her uncle to do so since it is quite cold. When he urges her to return to bed, she complains that he must be weary of her already. Troilus assures her that, had not the "busy day . . . roused the ribald crows" and were it not for the fact that the night will no longer hide the lovers' joys, he would not leave her. Both complain that the night has been far too brief, and Cressida again begs him not to leave her. When the two hear Pandarus' voice, Cressida says she is sure her uncle will mock her. He uncle appears, and in lines characterized by obscenity, he does exactly that. "Did I not tell you?" says Cressida to her lover. "Would he were knocked i' the head."

At the sound of knocking at the door, the lovers depart. Pandarus opens the door and is greeted by Aeneas, who has come with an important message for Troilus. Pandarus does his best to convince Aeneas that the prince is not there: "What should he do here?" But the Trojan commander warns him that he is doing Troilus no favor.

At this point in the action, the prince himself enters. He is told that the immediate business is so urgent that time cannot be wasted. Further, he learns that Paris and Deiphobus, Antenor, and Diomedes await and that Cressida must be given to the Greek commander. "Is it so concluded?" asks Troilus. He is told that it is the decision of Priam and of the general assembly. Exclaiming against his bad luck, Troilus agrees to meet with them, but asks Aeneas not to say that he was found at Pandarus' house. Aeneas agrees to say nothing and the two leave.

"Is it possible? No sooner got but lost?" asks the bewildered Pandarus. His niece returns and asks what is the matter. She has to listen to her uncle's exclamations against Antenor and expressions of sympathy for Troilus before she gets an answer. When she learns that she must go to her father, she vows that she will *not* do so, insisting that Troilus is dearer to her than is any blood relation:

> O you gods divine!
> Make Cressid's name the very crown of falsehood
> If ever she leave Troilus.
>
> (105–107)

She leaves in tears, still protesting vehemently.

## Commentary

Here we meet young Prince Troilus on the morning after his conquest of Cressida. There is a note of petulance in his first exchange with her, and his concern for secrecy hardly points to a lyrical, idealized love – thus the reference to the "ribald crows" (9) and his concern that Aeneas not give away the fact that he was found in Pandarus' house.

As is true of Troilus' discourse, the tone of Cressida's lines is one of impatient irritation, not that of a person who has experienced "thrice repured" love, but of one who is consciously seductive. This conclusion is supported by her replies to her lascivious uncle. Nevertheless the intensity of her passion, however unworthy, seems to be underscored by her lament when she learns that she and Troilus must part. Later action will measure her sincerity.

Pandarus, the go-between, is meanwhile enjoying himself in his peculiar way of mocking his niece as he meets her on the morning after the night of love-making, which he arranged. So much has he been entertained by the liaison that he is as extravagant in his protests as Cressida when he learns that she is to be exchanged for Antenor.

The purpose of this scene is (1) to provide the climax of the conflict in the love plot (the questions now posed are (a) Will Cressida be able to remain in Troy? and (b) Will she indeed remain faithful to Troilus?) and (2) to make clear the sensual nature of the love between Troilus and Cressida, especially by showing Pandarus enjoying himself at his niece's expense.

Be aware in this scene that key lines provide a hint of Cressida's later perfidy. For example, Cressida reproves Troilus for not tarrying, saying that men never do tarry and that she was foolish not to have held him off longer (15–18). Thus, we have an indication that she is hardly one who believes in absolute fidelity and trust between lovers.

Troilus seems anxious that his royal father and the assembly remain ignorant of the fact that he has spent the night at Pandarus' house, but it is not so much that he may be embarrassed to have them find evidence of his sensuality; it is primarily that his father and the members of the assembly will know that he has permitted private desire to take precedence over public duty.

Other than Pandarus' indecent baiting of Cressida, there are other comic elements in this scene. Note Pandarus' exaggerated protests when he learns that the lovers are to be separated, "Why sigh you so profoundly?" asks his niece, to which he replies, "Would I were as deep under the earth as I am above!" The entire passage (81–92) is good, broad comedy.

## ACT IV–SCENE 3

### Summary

In this twelve-line scene, Paris, Troilus, Aeneas, Deiphobus, Antenor, and Diomedes appear on the street in front of Pandarus' house. Paris instructs his brother Troilus to tell Cressida what she must do immediately—that is, surrender herself to the custody of Diomedes, who will conduct her to the Greek camp. Sorrowfully, Troilus agrees, describing himself as a priest about to make an offering on a sacred alter. Paris offers him sympathy: "I know what 'tis to love . . ."

### Commentary

Paris, as lover of Helen, can properly understand Troilus' passion and grief. Troilus must now make what seems to him the supreme sacrifice—giving up Cressida.

The purpose of this scene is (1) to provide the transition preparatory to the actual surrender of Cressida and (2) to emphasize the depth of Troilus' sorrow at the loss of Cressida.

It is particularly appropriate that Paris should be the active member of the group arranging the surrender of Cressida. The motivating raison d'etre in this play, his love for the unfaithful Helen, parallels that of Troilus for Cressida. It will be recalled that Troilus was voluble in his insistence that Helen should not be returned to Menelaus and that the fighting should continue. Both brothers are sensual victims of infatuation. Troilus' speech, wherein he sees himself as a priest about to make a sacrifice, is highly ironic, for earlier scenes have made it abundantly clear that his is not a "holy" love, but one based on self-indulgence.

## ACT IV–SCENE 4

### Summary

At home, Pandarus endeavors to calm the distraught Cressida, but she appears to be inconsolable:

> My love admits no qualifying dross;
> No more my grief, in such a precious loss.
>
> (9–10)

When Troilus enters, she passionately embraces him, for this is the touching farewell of the two lovers. Troilus knows that the separation is inevitable. The two vie with each other in protestations of love and fidelity. Pandarus is no less concerned, since he was responsible for bringing them together. Aeneas is on hand to see that there is no delay: "My lord, is the lady ready?" Words uttered by Troilus become a refrain as he warns Cressida against the merry Greeks, so well endowed: "Be thou true to me." For her part, Cressida is vehement in her promise never to forsake the young prince. But, although the two exchange love tokens, there is a notable lack of wholehearted trust between the two lovers. "O heavens! you love me not," exclaims Cressida at one point in the action; in reply, Troilus can do little more than warn her to avoid temptation.

Both Aeneas and Paris call to Troilus. The two enter with Antenor, Deiphobus, and Diomedes. Once more Troilus assures Cressida that he will be true to her, and, as he hands her over to Diomedes, he tells him that the lady is "as far high-soaring o'er [his] praises as [he] unworthy to be called her servant." Further, the Trojan prince tells the Greek that if the two meet on the battlefield, the mere mention of Cressida's name will save Diomedes from harm. Diomedes promises Troilus that Cressida will be prized "to her own worth" and that he will respect and honor her accordingly. Troilus then takes Cressida's hand, and the two lovers leave with the Greek emissary.

The sound of Hector's trumpet is heard, and Aeneas reproves himself for not riding ahead of the famous warrior in the field. "'Tis Troilus' fault," says Paris, and the two leave with Deiphobus for the battlefield.

## Commentary

Here, Troilus is a sad but resigned young lover, eloquent in his avowals of everlasting love for Cressida, but obviously still worried that she will not continue to love him. It is such a scene as this which has led some critics to refer to Troilus' "noble passion." Students must judge for themselves, but it is important to note the tacit reference to infidelity so prominent in this scene. Already Troilus' love has been established as one hardly marked by spirituality but, rather, characterized by sensuality.

Cressida matches Troilus in her protestations of love and fidelity and her expression of grief. As in Act III, Scene ii, however, there appears a note of petulance in her discourse. "O heavens 'be true' again," she exclaims, and a bit later, "O heavens, you love me not."

Meanwhile, Pandarus functions as a kind of chorus commenting on the sad spectacle of two lovers about to be separated.

The purpose of this scene is (1) to start the action falling toward the resolution in the love plot and (2) to emphasize the related themes of true love and fidelity and their opposites.

It is especially appropriate that Paris should be the one of several brothers who is prominent in this scene of the lovers' parting because, like Troilus, he is infatuated with a lady, one who has already proved her infidelity. Paris' presence is quite appropriate.

Note that Shakespeare stresses the fact that, however moving this scene may be to the romantic, Troilus is at fault. Near the end of the scene, the sound of Hector's trumpet is heard. When Aeneas says that the great warrior will think him "tardy and remiss," Paris immediately says, "Tis Troilus' fault." For indeed the great business of the Trojan state has been and is being neglected while the young prince has been "wallowing in the lily bed" of his infatuation.

## ACT IV–SCENE 5

### Summary

In the Greek camp, the fully armed Ajax enters, accompanied by Agamemnon, Achilles, Patroclus, Menelaus, Ulysses, Nestor, and others. Praising Ajax for his courage and readiness, Agamemnon bids him sound the trumpet call of challenge to call forth the "great combatant," Hector. The warrior addresses his trumpet in ranting terms, bidding it stretch its chest and let its eyes spout blood, for it blows for Hector. When no trumpet sound in return is heard, Achilles reminds the group that it is still early in the morning. Then Diomedes enters with Cressida, who is courteously greeted. Agamemnon, appropriately, first addresses her. "Our general doth salute you with a kiss," says Nestor, and Ulysses sardonically adds,

> Yet is the kindness but particular.
> 'Twere better she were kiss'd in general.
>
> (19-20)

This is hardly a tribute to the lady's moral character. First Nestor and then Achilles kisses her. When Menelaus says that he once had good reason to kiss a lady, Patroclus reminds him that he has no such reason now, for the bold Paris deprived him of it. "O deadly gall," exclaims Ulysses, "and theme of all our scorns! For which we lose our heads to gild his horns!" Poor Menelaus continues to be the target for jests about his being a cuckold, Patroclus remarking that he and Paris now kiss for Helen's aggrieved husband. Cressida, who in the previous scene appeared inconsolable, has made a remarkable recovery. Now she is in sufficiently high spirits as she joins willingly in the exchange on the subject of kissing and cuckoldry. It remains for Ulysses ironically to ask Cressida to kiss him "for Venus' sake" and then to add that he will receive the kiss only when "Helen is a maid again"—in other words, never. When Cressida leaves with Diomedes, Nestor describes her as "a woman of quick sense," but Ulysses scorns her as a loose woman who yields to every occasion:

> There's language in her eye, her cheek, her lip,
> Nay, her foot speaks; her wanton spirits look out
> At every joint and motive [limb] of her body.
>
> (55–57)

"Enter all Troy"—the fully armed Hector, Paris, Aeneas, Helenus, Troilus, and other Trojans, with attendants. Aeneas exclaims, "Hail all you state of Greece!" and then announces that Hector wishes to know what rules of combat are to be observed by both contestants: are they free to pursue each other "to the edge of all extremity" or are they to be restricted by "any voice or order of the field?" Hector, according to Aeneas, does not care what the choice may be. Achilles states that Hector is behaving rather proudly and that he is underestimating his opponent. Learning that it is Achilles addressing him, Aeneas declares that "valour and pride excel themselves in Hector," and that Ajax, half Greek, half Trojan, will face a man who chooses to be only half himself. "A maiden battle, then?" taunts Achilles. "O, I perceive you." Agamemnon, with the assistance of Aeneas and Diomedes, arranges matters, and the two great adversaries face each other.

Agamemnon sees Troilus and asks who he is. Ulysses tells him that Troilus is a "true knight, not yet mature" and adds words of high praise for the young prince; unlike his great brother Hector, Troilus is not merciful to the weak but is "more vindictive than jealous love." Aeneas, says Ulysses, sees Troilus as a second Hector.

The encounter between Hector and Ajax that follows is indeed a kind of "maiden battle." Troilus cries out to Hector to fight more vigorously, while Agamemnon praises Ajax for his well-disposed blows. "You must no more," shouts Diomedes, and the trumpets become silent. Aeneas then calls a halt to the fight. Ajax is anxious to resume, but Diomedes informs him that the decision to continue fighting must be Hector's. The Trojan hero flatly states: "Why, then will I no more." He explains that Ajax is his father's sister's son, and this his cousin; it is not proper that blood relations should fight each other:

> Let me embrace thee, Ajax.
> By him that thunders, thou hast lusty arms.
> Hector would have them fall upon him thus.
> Cousin, all honour to thee.
>
> (135–138)

Ajax thanks him, but states that he came to win fame by killing Hector. Aeneas interrupts to say that both Trojans and Greeks wish to know what the two warriors plan to do, and Hector tells him that neither he nor his cousin Ajax will continue the fight. Ajax then invites Hector to the Greek tents, and Diomedes states that such is the wish of Agamemnon and

Achilles. Next, Hector asks Aeneas to call his brother to him and to inform the other Trojans what will transpire.

When Agamemnon and his attendants arrive, there is an exchange of compliments between them and Hector. Both Agamemnon and Menelaus welcome Troilus, the "well-fam'd lord of Troy," in the same chivalrous manner. Learning that Menelaus addresses him, Hector states that the Greek's "quondam wife" still swears by Venus' glove, and that she is well but does not send her greetings. "Name her not now, sir," replies Menelaus, "she's a deadly theme." Hector apologizes. Now it is Nestor's turn to greet Hector warmly and to receive the Trojan's gracious reply, both contending with each other in courtesy. To Hector, Ulysses says:

> I wonder now how yonder city stands
> When we have here her base and pillar by us.
>
> (211–212)

Hector is reminded of his earlier meeting with the Greek commander when the latter came to Ilium with Diomedes as an emissary from Agamemnon. Ulysses repeats the prophecy he made at that time: Troy will fall. To this, Hector replies that the "fall of every Phrygian stone will cost a drop of Grecian blood" and that Time will be the arbitrator of the prolonged battle. Again Ulysses welcomes Hector graciously, describing him as "most gentle and most valiant."

It is now Achilles' turn to address Hector. The two champions of their espective forces view each other, and it is apparent that each sees the other as his prime adversary. Still excessively proud and arrogant, Achilles vows that he will slay Hector. Hector is no less confident that he will best Achilles, but adds,

> You wisest Grecians, pardon me this brag.
> His insolence draws folly from my lips . . .
>
> (257–258)

Achilles declares that he will meet Hector on the morrow; at present the amenities will be observed. "Thy hand upon that match," replies the Trojan prince. Agamemnon then dismisses the assembly, although Troilus and Ulysses remain on stage.

Troilus asks where he may find Calchas, and is told that Cressida's father is at Menelaus' tent; he is further told that Diomedes now has eyes for the fair Cressida. Ulysses agrees to conduct Troilus to the tent.

## Commentary

In this scene, Agamemnon, the Greek general, is conducting himself as a generous and chivalrous leader, while Ulysses, Agamemnon's counselor, once more demonstrates his sagacity by immediately recognizing

Cressida for what she is—a wanton. He demonstrates his foresight by again prophesying the fall of Troy.

Troilus, hailed as a valiant warrior, second only to Hector among the Trojans, understandably remains concerned about being reunited with Cressida. Like that of the other Trojans, his conduct is impeccable in this scene.

Nestor, the veteran commander in the camp, voices his regrets that his advanced age prevents him from meeting Hector on the battlefield. It will be noted that, famed for his wisdom as he was in Greek story, he does not recognize the true character of Cressida.

The purpose of this scene is (1) to bring to a climax the action in the camp scenes (Hector and Ajax finally meet—and there is no conflict between the two; in a sense, then, the climax turns out to be an anticlimax, underscoring the theme of futility), (2) to prepare the way for a resolution of the action in the camp scenes as the way is prepared for the later meeting of Achilles and Hector, and (3) to advance the love plot by having Troilus learn that Diomedes has become infatuated with Cressida.

## ACT V—SCENE 1

### Summary

Achilles and Patroclus appear in front of Achilles' tent. The great warrior states that he will heat Hector's blood with Greek wine this night and then will cool the wine with his scimitar on the next day. Before Patroclus can reply to this boast, Thersites enters. Achilles addresses him as a "core of envy" (core meaning the center of a boil) and as a "crusty batch" (an overbaked loaf of bread). In return, Thersites calls Achilles an "idol of idiot-worshippers" and then hands him a letter from Troy. An exchange of insults continues, now between the railer and Patroclus, who is denounced as "Achilles' male varlet" and as his "masculine whore." The disease image is especially prominent in Thersites' speech. Patroclus does his best to return in kind, but is hardly a match for the foul-mouthed malcontent.

Achilles interrupts to tell Patroclus what he has learned from reading the letter, which was written by Hecuba. The Trojan queen and her daughter Polyxena insist that he keep the promise he made to them; therefore, he cannot fight Hector:

> Fall Greeks; fail fame; honor or go or stay;
> My major vow lies here, this I'll obey.

(48–49)

Achilles then asks Patroclus to help him prepare for the banquet in honor of Hector, and the two leave the stage.

In soliloquy, Thersites again employs invective to denounce the two, as well as Agamemnon and Menelaus. He has great contempt for that "memorial of cuckolds," Menelaus, and states that he would rather be anything than the King of Sparta. The malcontent is surprised to see lights approaching. Almost immediately Hector, Troilus, Ajax, Agamemnon, Ulysses, Menelaus, and Diomedes enter bearing torches. It is clear that they are not sure that they have taken the right direction to reach their destination. Hector insists that he has put the group to a great deal of trouble, but Ajax courteously says that such is not the case.

Achilles returns and welcomes Hector and the others. The Trojan warrior offers his thanks and says good night to Agamemnon and to Menelaus, who return the courtesy and leave. Achilles then asks Nestor and Diomedes to keep Hector company for an hour or two, but Diomedes explains that he cannot do so because he has important business which demands his immediate attention. In an aside, Ulysses says to Troilus: "Follow his torch, he goes to Calchas' tent." Ulysses himself accompanies the young prince.

Once more alone on the stage, Thersites provides biting, satiric comments on events. He denounces Diomedes as "a false-hearted rogue" and says that he will "dog" him, for it is reported that he keeps "a Trojan drab" and uses Calchas' tent.

### Commentary

At the beginning of this scene, Achilles seems to have benefited by the wise counsel of Ulysses, for he is determined to fight Hector, but the letter from Queen Hecuba promptly makes him change his mind, so he still violates the principle of order and degree. After listening to his epic boast, we see him exchange insults with Thersites, and then courteously welcome Hector and others.

Thersites, the scurrilous malcontent, is as foul-mouthed as ever as he insults Achilles and then Patroclus. And again Agamemnon and especially Menelaus are excoriated by him. Typical of this type of malcontent, he sees himself as an honest critic motivated by righteousness; thus he says that he will be a "curer of madmen."

Agamemnon once again demonstrates his chivalry as he leads Hector to Achilles' tent, where the Trojan warrior is to dine.

Ulysses, the wise counselor and Greek commander, is a third member of the general's party, but his role is not a passive one, for it is he who advises Troilus to follow Diomedes to Calchas' tent, where he will find Cressida.

The purpose of this scene is (1) to prepare for the resolution of the love plot by having Troilus follow Diomedes to Calchas' tent, where Cressida is, (2) to show that Ulysses' plan to rouse Achilles is not yet working successfully, and (3) to provide Thersites with yet another opportunity to emphasize, in his own peculiar manner, the themes of lust and futility.

The key images that are prominent in this scene are those of food-cookery and of disease. They occur notably in the soliloquies of Thersites and in his lines addressed to Achilles and Patroclus. Both point to moral corruption.

Note the following lines:

> *Patr.* Who keeps the tent now?
> *Ther.* The surgeon's box, or the patient's wound.

Patroclus, asking a rhetorical question, is saying that the news of a letter from Troy brought Achilles promptly from his tent. Thersites pretends to have understood the word *tent* in the sense of "lint," used for cleaning wounds.

## ACT V–SCENE 2

### Summary

Diomedes appears before Calchas' tent and calls out. Calchas answers, telling him that Cressida will come to him. Troilus and Ulysses enter, followed at some distance by Thersites. The three remain far enough back so that their presence will not be known to the others on stage. Cressida appears and returns Diomedes' greeting, calling him her "sweet guardian." The Greek warrior reminds her of a promise she made to him, but Cressida, in keeping with her way of playing the love game (which she herself described in soliloquy at the end of Act I, Scene ii) prefers to appear coy. "Sweet honey Greek, tempt me no more to folly," she says (18), and, a bit later, after Diomedes pleads and threatens that he will no longer permit himself to be made a fool by her:

> I prithee, do not hold me to mine oath.
> Bid me do anything but that, sweet Greek.
>
> (26–27)

But when it seems that Diomedes will leave her, she is quick to win him back as she strokes his cheek and renews the promise she made: "In faith, I will, la; never trust me else" (59). As a surety, she gives him a sleeve, the love token Troilus gave to her at the time of their passionate farewell in Troy. Moreover, she kisses him. Diomedes wants to know from whom she received the sleeve, but Cressida will not tell him. Again she becomes coy, saying that she will not keep her promise. And, once more, Diomedes says that he has no intention of being mocked. But there is another shift in mood: she will welcome him, she says as he leaves. In soliloquy, Cressida says her farewell to Troilus:

> one eye yet looks on thee,
> But with my heart the other eye doth see.
>
> (107-108)

All this while Troilus has been in torment, although he repeatedly assures Ulysses that he will be patient. "O plague and madness!" he exclaims as he listens to the first part of the conversation between Cressida and his rival. "O beauty! where is thy faith?" he asks as he sees Cressida offer the sleeve to Diomedes. And when the latter promises to wear it on his helmet the next day and "grieve his spirit that does not challenge it," the disconsolate prince vows:

> Wert thou the Devil, and wor'st it on thy horn
> It should be challenged.
>
> (94-95)

It is with difficulty that Ulysses is able to restrain him.

In the background, Thersites remains to comment caustically upon the meeting of Cressida and Diomedes. Typically he exclaims as he sees her stroke the Greek's cheek:

> How the devil Luxury, with his fat rump and
> potato finger, tickles these two together!
> Fry, lechery, fry!
>
> (55-57)

Ulysses asks Troilus why, since all is over, they remain outside Calchas' tent. The young prince replies that he stays to make a rememberance of what he has heard and seen. To him, Cressida's perfidy seems so incredible that he wonders if she was indeed present. Ulysses assures him that the two they saw were flesh and blood—not spirits. Troilus argues that if it was indeed Cressida then she has brought dishonor on all members of her sex, for all will be judged in terms of her behavior. In a long speech, the distraught prince presents an argument ("This is, and is not, Cressid!") that is wildly inconsistent, the essence of it being that it is both reasonable and insane to believe or disbelieve what he has seen. He then vows to slay Diomedes and concludes:

> O Cressid! O false Cressid! False, false, false!
> Let all untruths stand by thy stained name,
> And they'll seem glorious.
>
> (178-180)

Aeneas enters and announces that Hector is already back in Troy arming himself and that Ajax will conduct Troilus back to the city. When all three have left the stage, Thersites remains, still functioning as the scurrilous chorus:

> Lechery, lechery! still wars and lechery!
> Nothing else holds fashion.
> A burning devil take them!
>
> (196–197)

## Commentary

Diomedes has obviously importuned Cressida and comes to hold her to the promise she made to him. This was the urgent business of which he spoke in the preceding scene. Whatever else may be said of him, he is sufficiently independent and manly. He makes it clear that he does not intend to have a woman mock him or make a fool of him. Furthermore, he has no intention of absenting himself from the battlefield on the next day.

Meanwhile, Cressida, still adept in amorous exchange, plays her role as coquette with obvious enjoyment. She knows exactly how far to go in protestations and when to acquiesce. If anything can be said to her credit, aside from her skill in the love game, it is that she is honest enough to recognize her own perfidy, although she does rationalize about it.

Troilus is anguished as he gets visible proof of Cressida's infidelity. The Trojan prince, however, restrains himself – but only with great difficulty. If one is tempted to accept all that he says as evidence of a "noble passion," it would be well to recall the earlier love scenes, particularly the assignation one, when the two lovers were together in Troy, and to consider the import of Thersites' cynical remark in this scene: "He'll tickle it for his concupy" (77) – that is, Troilus will be tickled for his lust. *Tickle* as an adjective meant "fickle"; used here as a verb, it obviously relates to the fact that Troilus has lost Cressida.

The purpose of this scene is (1) to present in action evidence of Cressida's unfaithfulness and (2) to start the resolution of the action in the love plot.

The "sleeve" which figures so prominently in this scene is the love token which Troilus gave to Cressida. The "sleeve" was often richly embroidered and was worn separately from the main garment.

When Cressida swears by "all Diana's waiting women," the allusion is to Diana, goddess of the moon; therefore, all the "waiting women" are the stars. The allusion is somewhat ironic, since Diana was the chaste goddess in classical mythology.

The following lines are of key importance in this scene:

> *Ulyss.* She will sing any man at first sight.
> *Ther.*  And any man may sing her, if he can take her
> cliff. She's noted.
>
> (9–11)

Ulysses is implying that Cressida is a fickle woman ready to offer herself to any man. In his cunning reply, Thersites is saying that any man can win her favors. *Cliff* means "clef," a key in music, *noted* means "observed," with a pun on musical notes.

## ACT V–SCENE 3

**Summary**

Appearing before Priam's palace, Andromache urges Hector not to fight on this day because she has had ominous dreams. Her husband is adamant: "By the everlasting gods, I'll go!" Cassandra enters, looking for Hector, and Andromache urges her to help her dissuade her brother from fighting. When she learns of the wife's terrifying dreams of "shapes and forms of slaughter," the prophetess implores Hector not to go to the battlefield; but he dismisses her as curtly as he did his wife. Both women renew their pleas. In reply, Hector argues that his honor is at stake:

> Life every man holds dear, but the brave man
> Holds honor far more precious-dear than life.
>
> (27–28)

As Troilus enters, Cassandra leaves to see if she can convince her royal father to intervene. Seeing that his brother is fully armed, Hector now urges him to disarm, insisting that he is still too young to experience the bruises of combat: "I'll stand today for thee and me and Troy." Troilus reproves Hector for what he calls "a vice of mercy," explaining that his brother invariably permits a fallen foe to rise and live. When Hector says that it is a matter of fair play, Troilus insists that, rather, it is fool's play, and he urges his brother to be ruthless. In reply, Hector calls his brother a savage. He then returns to the subject of Troilus' fighting, but the younger prince is as determined in his course of action as is Hector in his.

At this point, Cassandra returns with King Priam, calling on him to lay hold of Hector and hold him fast because Priam and all Troy depend upon its peerless warrior. Reminding his son of Andromache's dreams, Queen Hecuba's visions, and Cassandra's prophecies, the king describes the day as ominous and commands his son to remain in Troy. Hector argues that Aeneas is already in the field and that faith must not be broken. Both women again entreat him to stay, but the annoyed Hector merely orders his wife to go into the palace. She does so.

Troilus scorns his sister Cassandra's gloomy prophecies, but in a formal, highly rhetorical eight-line speech she repeats them: all will cry "Hector! Hector's dead! O Hector!" Troilus orders her to leave; she does leave, but not before addressing Hector: "Thou dost thyself and all our Troy deceive." Hector asks his father to "go in and cheer the town," and the king, aware that he cannot make his valiant son change his mind, gives him his blessings and departs. Hector leaves in another direction.

Now alone, Troilus renews his vow to meet Diomedes, saying that he will either lose his arm or win his sleeve. Pandarus enters with a letter from Cressida, which Troilus asks to read. As he reads it, Pandarus complains that he is miserable because of a bad cough and concern for his niece. When asked what was written, Troilus replies: "Words, words, mere words, no matter from the heart." He tears the letter into pieces and throws them to the wind:

> Go, wind, to wind, there turn and change together.
> My love with words and errors still she feeds,
> But edifies another with her deeds.

(110–112)

## Commentary

Hector, described by Cassandra as the crutch, the stay of Troy, is indeed the Trojans' chief source of strength and valor. He is so firmly convinced that honor means more than life that neither father, sister, nor wife can make him remain in Troy rather than join Aeneas on the battlefield. His chivalry is shown by the fact that he never takes advantage of a fallen enemy.

Andromache, Hector's wife, is stirred by frightening dreams, and she pleads with her husband to remain at home. Meanwhile Cassandra, Hector's sister, the prophetess, also tries her best to convince her brother that he should not tempt fate. Similarly, Priam, King of Troy and father to Hector, Troilus, and Cassandra, says to his son "Aye, but thou shalt not go," but even he fails to prevent Hector from leaving for battle. The implication is that there is weakness in Priam's character; Hector's status as premier warrior must be taken into consideration.

The purpose of this scene is (1) to increase the sense of conflict by emphasizing the hazards both Hector and Troilus face on the battlefield this day: one will defy omens and prophecy; the other will fight despite what Hector calls his physical immaturity, (2) to centralize the action of the love plot by setting Troilus against Diomedes, (3) to provide the transition for the shift of the action to the battlefield, where it will continue to the end of the play, and (4) to enhance the character of Hector, who comes closest to being a tragic hero in this play.

In this scene, note the difference between Hector's motive for fighting and that of Troilus. Hector is dedicated to honor; he feels that not to fight is to be proved faithless. He is true to his chivalric code. On the other hand, neither public issues, service, nor chivalry motivates Troilus. He seeks revenge on the man who has replaced him in the affections of Cressida; he fights for a love token.

In a similar vein, note in what other way the two brothers differ, aside from age and physical prowess. The soul of chivalry, Hector spares the lives of fallen foes. Troilus sees all this as foolishness. As we learned from Ulysses' speech in Act IV, Scene v, 96 ff., the younger prince "in heat of action/ Is more vindicative than jealous love"–a most appropriate simile.

## ACT V–SCENE 4

### Summary

A fight is in progress on the field between Troy and the Greek camp. Thersites enters and soliloquizes in his usual vulgar style. Now that the warriors are scratching and clawing each other, he says, he will watch the action. Particularly he wants to see the meeting of Troilus and Diomedes, who is wearing the sleeve on his helmet. Thersites uses coarse, indecent names for both adversaries, and he refers to Cressida as "the dissembling luxurious [lecherous] drab." He then excoriates Ulysses and the other Greek leaders. According to this railer, their policy has "not proved worth a blackberry" because Ajax, having been chosen in place of Achilles, has become prouder than the latter and has refused to arm himself on this day. Thersites concludes that the Greeks now prefer ignorance to cleverness. His discourse is interrupted: "Soft! Here comes sleeve and the other"–and Diomedes and Troilus enter.

Troilus accuses his opponent of flying from him and declares that he would swim after Diomedes if the Greek warrior did "take the river Styx." The Greek denies that he has fled from Troilus, saying that he sought only to free himself from the multitude. As the two begin fighting and move off the stage, Thersites coarsely calls out to them.

Hector enters and asks if Thersites is a Greek and a match for him. The malcontent frankly describes himself as a rascal and as "a scurvy railing knave, a very filthy rogue." "I do believe thee. Live," replies Hector, and he departs. Expressing his relief, Thersites then leaves to find the "wenching rogues," Troilus and Diomedes.

### Commentary

Here again we see that Thersites is still the railer, foully estimating the character and actions of others. Like Shakespeare's villains in other plays, he can and does speak honestly of himself; thus his reply to Hector.

Troilus, a determined young prince is now face-to-face with his chief adversary and rival, determined to win back the love token, although he has lost the woman to whom he gave it.

Diomedes, the no-less-determined Greek commander denies that he fears Troilus and readily exchanges blows with him.

Hector, Troy's great warrior, once more manifests his chivalry by disdaining to attack Thersites.

The purpose of this scene is (1) to bring Troilus and Diomedes together on the battlefield, (2) to provide Thersites another opportunity to complain that all is "war and lechery," and (3) to show Hector on the battlefield, valiant and chivalrous as ever.

## ACT V–SCENE 5

### Summary

The action takes place on another part of the field. Diomedes instructs his servant to take Troilus' horse as a present to "my Lady Cressid" and after telling her that Diomedes is dedicated to her service, announces that he has won the honor of being her knight by chastising Troilus. The servant leaves.

Agamemnon enters, calling upon Diomedes to renew the fight because the Greeks are in great danger. Among other reversals, Polyxenes is slain and Patroclus has either been taken prisoner or killed. "To reinforcement, or we perish all." Nestor enters and gives orders to his followers. They are to carry Patroclus' body to Achilles and to "bid the snail-paced Achilles arm for shame." To Nestor, it seems that there are a thousand Hectors on the field, so well has the great adversary of the Greeks fought.

Next, Ulysses enters and urges the Greek princes to have courage. He brings the welcome news that both Ajax and Achilles, enraged by the fate of Patroclus, are arming themselves. Ajax, described as foaming at the mouth, is roaring for Troilus, who, according to Ulysses, has distinquished himself in battle:

> With such a careless force and forceless care
> As if that luck, in spite of cunning
> Bade him win all.

(40–42)

Now Ajax enters and indeed roars for Troilus as he crosses the stage and leaves. Finally the armed Achilles enters, asking the whereabouts of Hector, whom he calls a "boy-queller." He will have none but Hector.

### Commentary

Diomedes now appears to have bested Troilus, in view of his instructions to his servant, and to have secured the right to Cressida's love. Agamemnon worriedly reports the progress of the battle on this day, revealing that the Greeks are in great difficulty and urging Diomedes to lose no time in getting back into the fight before all is lost. Nestor supplements the information given by Agamemnon in words especially important for what they let us know of Hector's prowess. Ulysses, meanwhile, never violates the principles of the philosophy he enunciates. He brings additional news, this time encouraging to his fellow Greeks. It is he who pays tribute to the valor and prowess of Troilus. Achilles, called "snail-paced," is now roused by the news of his friend's death and seeks his chosen adversary, Hector.

The purpose of this scene is (1) to provide the motivation for the rousing of Achilles at long last and for the re-arming of Ajax, the one to seek out Hector, the other to seek out Troilus, and (2) to add to the resolution of the love plot by having Diomedes declare himself the victor over Troilus.

The "dreadful sagittary" that terrifies the Greeks, according to Agamemnon (14), was a mythological centaur, half-man, half-horse, who fought on the side of the Trojans.

Achilles calls Hector a "boy-queller" because he killed Patroclus, who is usually portrayed as a youth rather than a mature man.

The suspense in this scene is created by the question of Troilus' actual fate; the crisis among the Greeks, who have not fared well in this day's conflict, and the fact that apparently both Trojan princes, Troilus and Hector, will face dangerous adversaries.

## ACT V–SCENE 6

### Summary

Ajax appears on another part of the field, still calling for Troilus. Immediately Diomedes enters and voices the same call. The privilege of fighting the Trojan belongs to Ajax, the giant warrior tells him. Then Troilus appears and denounces Diomedes as a traitor. He adds that the Greek will pay with his life. Both Diomedes and Ajax argue about which one will fight the Trojan prince. Impatient, Troilus challenges both of them, and the three move off the stage fighting.

Hector enters and speaks words of praise for his brother: "Oh, well fought, my youngest brother." Achilles enters and challenges Hector. But the Trojan asks for a respite until he has rested himself after strenuous fighting. Achilles vows that Hector will hear from him again and departs.

Troilus returns to report that Ajax has captured Aeneas. He declares that he will rescue the Trojan commander or become a captive too:

Fate, hear me what I say!
I reck not though thou end my life to-day.

(25–26)

When he leaves, an unnamed Greek warrior appears and is challenged by Hector. The Greek flees, and Hector vows to hunt him "for his hide."

## Commentary

Ajax, still roaring his challenge, now meets Troilus. Achilles confronts Hector on the field, but grants his foe a respite, with the excuse that he himself is out of practice in the use of weapons. Diomedes joins the powerful Ajax in attacking Troilus, the youthful Trojan prince. Hector, seeking rest after such vigorous fighting, invokes the code of chivalry to postpone a fight with the great Achilles. But he is not too exhausted to challenge an ordinary Greek warrior.

The purpose of this scene is (1) to report on and to depict in part the progress of the day's fighting, with special emphasis on the daring and courage of Troilus, and (2) to bring the Trojan princes face to face with their opponents.

Since both Trojan princes fight bravely, one might rightly wonder: can we assume that one of them is as admirable as the other? It may be argued reasonably that Hector alone is the admirable, heroic figure, for he is motivated solely by his high sense of honor. In contrast, Troilus has been motivated by Cressida's perfidy, a fact which hardly marks him as a heroic figure, however well he may fight.

## ACT V–SCENE 7

## Summary

Achilles enters with his Myrmidons. He instructs them to follow him but not to engage in fighting until he has "the bloody Hector found." Then they are to encircle the Trojan prince with their weapons and in the fullest manner execute their aims: "It is decreed Hector the great must die." The group then leave the stage.

Menelaus and Paris enter, exchanging sword blows. Promptly Thersites makes his appearance, gleefully exclaiming: "The cuckold and the cuckold-maker are at it." As the two combatants move off stage, Margarelon, who identifies himself as an illegitimate son of Priam, enters and challenges Thersites. But the malcontent has no intention of fighting; that is not his function. He declares that he also is illegitimate, and since the two have something in common, they should not fight. When he leaves hastily, Margarelon denounces him as a coward and then also departs.

## Commentary

Achilles is so determined to slay Hector that he has brought along his Myrmidons to insure the Greek's death, an action in marked contrast to the chivalrous Hector. Thersites spews his venom on Menelaus and Paris as he carries forward his favorite theme of war and lechery. Personally a coward, he again does not hesitate to debase himself in order to avoid fighting.

The purpose of this scene is (1) to provide the transition to the final meeting between Achilles and Hector, and (2) to emphasize once more the important theme of disorder and futility by having cuckold fight cuckold-maker and the illegitimate Margarelon hear Thersites identify himself as one who also is illegitimate.

## ACT V–SCENE 8

### Summary

Hector appears on another part of the battlefield. He has just slain a Greek and declares that his day's work is done. He takes off his helmet and hangs his shield behind him. Achilles and his band of Myrmidons enter. The Greek warrior tells Hector that just as the day is near its end so is the Trojan's life. The prince replies: "I am unarmed, forgo this vantage, Greek." But Achilles commands his followers to strike Hector, who falls to the ground a slain man. Achilles is elated, and he commands his men to spread the news: "Achilles hath the mighty Hector slain." Trumpets sound the retreat of both Greek and Trojan forces. As he sheathes his sword, Achilles addresses his warriors:

> Come, tie his body to my horse's tail.
> Along the field I will the Trojan trail.

> (21–22)

### Commentary

Hector, rightly called the heart, sinews, and bone of Troy, meets his death at the hands of Achilles and his Myrmidons, having no chance to defend himself.

The purpose of this scene is (1) to show how Cassandra's dire prophecy came true in a scene which embodies the final major action of the battle scene and (2) to point up the contrasting characters of Hector and Achilles.

In this scene, Achilles emerges as a contemptible figure in marked contrast to the noble Hector. He is utterly devoid of chivalry, and his personal courage is cast in doubt in view of the fact that he will not permit his adversary to arm himself and that he depends upon his followers to attack the Trojan prince. It will be noted that Achilles is not motivated by a sense of public duty but by a desire for personal vengeance. Having his brave adversary's body dragged across the field is as shameful an act as can be imagined.

## ACT V—SCENE 9

### Summary

In this ten-line scene, Agamemnon, Ajax, Menelaus, Nestor, Diomedes, and other Greeks march across the field and then stop to rest. Shouts are heard and Nestor silences the drums. All hear the news: "Achilles! Achilles! Hector's slain! Achilles!" Ajax, with apparent magnanimity, says that if the report be true none should boast about it, for Hector was as good a man as Achilles. Agamemnon gives the order for the march to be resumed and for someone to bid Achilles see him in his tent. If Hector is indeed slain, he adds, "Great Troy is ours, and our sharp wars are ended."

### Commentary

The purpose of this scene is (1) to bring to a conclusion the war scenes as far as the Greeks are concerned (it has been argued that this is the real ending of the play) and (2) to show that the news of Achilles' deed has reached the ears of Agamemnon and his chief commanders.

## ACT V—SCENE 10

### Summary

Aeneas, Paris, Antenor, and Deiphobus appear on another part of the field. Aeneas calls a halt, saying that they are masters of the field and will spend the night here. Troilus enters and announces that Hector has been slain. "The gods forbid!" all exclaim. The young prince then fills in the details, telling how Hector's body was "in beastly sort dragged through the shameful field" and calling for divine vengeance. He then vows that nothing will prevent him from meeting Achilles in combat:

> I'll haunt thee like a wicked conscience still,
> That mouldeth goblins swift as frenzy's thought.
>
> (28–29)

At his word, the group continue the march to Troy, sustained by the hope of revenge. Troilus remains behind.

As Aeneas and his group leave, Pandarus enters and begs Troilus to listen to him. But the prince has only contempt for his man, whom he calls "broker lackey." He expresses the hope that ignominy and shame will follow Pandarus throughout the rest of his life. Alone, Pandarus voices his complaint against an ungrateful world which sets traitors and bawds to work and then ill requites them: "Why should our endeavor be so loved and the performance so loathed?" Addressing all "traders in flesh," he declares that their painted clothes (imitation tapestry, usually painted with allegorical or scriptual scenes) should bear this message: all who are like Pandar should grieve at his downfall, or at least groan—if not for him at least for their aching bones.

He announces to these "brethren and sisters of the hold-door trade" that he will make his will within two months and adds that it would be made now but that he fears some irate prostitute would hiss. In the meantime he will try to find comfort; later he will bequeath them his diseases.

## Commentary

The purpose of this scene is (1) to provide the resolution, inconclusive as it seems to many, to the action of the play and (2) to give the audience its last view of the titular hero and to show by his dismissal of Pandarus that he is over his infatuation for the faithless Cressida.

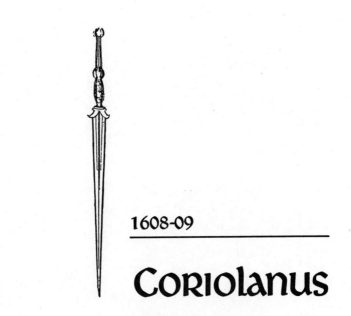

1608-09

# Coriolanus

# A BRIEF SYNOPSIS

Mobs of hungry, enraged citizens, armed with weapons, have gathered on a street in Rome. They are starving, and they demand that they should be able to buy corn at a fair price. The man who is most responsible for this critical situation, according to them, is Caius Marcius (later called Coriolanus). Their anger toward him is so fierce that they vow to kill him. When Coriolanus enters, he spurns these "commoners" and their "demands," and we have immediate proof of his pride and arrogance. He has absolute contempt for the "masses."

Moments later, news of an imminent attack from the Volscians, the Romans' archenemies, is announced. The Roman senators choose Coriolanus as one of the key commanders of the city's defense, and Coriolanus accepts the offer. He curses the angry populace, then turns and exits. Afterward, two tribunes, representatives of the people, comment on Coriolanus' excessive pride and elitist prejudice toward the common people of Rome.

Coriolanus' mother, Volumnia, is immensely proud that her son has been chosen as one of the three men responsible for Rome's safety. She tries to comfort her distraught daugher-in-law, Virgilia, but is unsuccessful. Virgilia is terribly afraid that Coriolanus may be killed, and Volumnia cannot understand such simpleminded histrionics. According to Volumnia, a man's code of military honor should comprise the entirety of his character; she would rather have eleven sons die bravely in battle than have one son remain alive, devoting his life to idle pleasures.

Coriolanus arrives at the city of Corioli and rallies the Roman troops forward after he discovers that they have been forced to make a quick retreat. Coriolanus is so caught up in the fervor of battle, however, that he follows the Volscians inside the city gates, the gates are locked, and, for a short time, his fellow soldiers are convinced that he is probably dead. Finally, though, Coriolanus emerges, covered with blood; he gives courage to his troops, then departs to aid the forces of Cominius, another of the Roman commanders. When he arrives on the battlefront, he is ecstatic; once again, he is able to engage in one of his lifelong desires – a hand-to-hand combat with Aufidius, the Volscians' best warrior. He defeats Aufidius, but the Volscian is able to escape before Coriolanus can kill him. Nevertheless, the Romans are so pleased with their military victory that they formally honor Caius Marcius with the new name of "Coriolanus" (because of his part in capturing the Volscian capital of Corioli). Aufidius,

235

meanwhile, grieves over the defeat of his forces and the taking of Corioli; he vows eventual vengeance on Coriolanus.

When Coriolanus returns to Rome, he is uncomfortable in his role as a Roman "hero." He is singled out by the Senate as their choice for consul, but he is reluctant to accept the position. He feels that he is a warrior—not a consul; in addition, he detests the fraudulent show of humility which he would have to assume, if he were to seek the position of consul. The tribunes (the representatives of the common people) know how proud Coriolanus is; they know how painful it would be for him to don the "gown of humility" and "beg," as it were, consent from the masses to be their consul.

Heavily pressured, however, Coriolanus does decide to ask for the consulship, but it is soon evident that he is incapable of "begging" the masses to accept him. To him, the masses are ignorant and they are fickle; they lack all sense of character and principle. He parades before them in the unwanted gown of humility and scorns them for their faults, stating that if they do indeed want him as their consul, they should consider his angry but uncompromisingly honest behavior, not his heroics.

The tribunes could not be happier as they witness Coriolanus' fierce rage; his unleashed fury and bigoted haughtiness are more than they had hoped for. They are confident that later they can manipulate the masses and convince them that Coriolanus is their enemy and that he deserves a sentence of death for his hatred of the Roman people.

The tribunes are successful in swaying public opinion, and before long, a riot erupts, against not only Coriolanus, but also the entire patrician class itself. All of the nobles are fearful for their lives. Volumnia tries to convince Coriolanus to retract his statements but, taunted by the cunning tribunes, Coriolanus cannot condescend to the masses. Thus they banish him. But Coriolanus' feelings toward the mob are so intense that he refuses to accept *their* banishment. "*I*," he says, "banish you."

Frustrated and angered by the behavior of the Romans, Coriolanus disguises himself and seeks out his archenemy, Aufidius. He tells him his story and offers his services to revenge himself upon Rome. Aufidius considers the offer, then accepts it. Then two things happen in swift succession: chaos reigns in Rome when it is discovered that Coriolanus, their great commander, has joined the enemy; shortly thereafter, Aufidius grows progressively more angry and envious of the popularity and the power which the Volscians offer Coriolanus.

An attack on Rome is prepared for by the Volscians, but at the last moment, Coriolanus' mother, wife, and young son come to him to ask him to spare Rome. Coriolanus cannot refuse his mother. Everything he is, he owes to her; yet he is torn that his young son witnesses this "flaw," this iron allegiance to Volumnia.

Volumnia and Virgilia are honored when they return to Rome, but

Coriolanus' fate is not a happy one. Because Aufidius' envy has become so excessive, he orders Coriolanus killed. Thus the play ends as Coriolanus' dead body is borne out, and Aufidius repents for what he ordered in anger. His rage now gone, he vows that Coriolanus shall "have a noble memory."

# LIST OF CHARACTERS

### Caius Marcius (Coriolanus)

He receives the honorary name of "Coriolanus" following his exploits in the battle at Corioli. His pride and his supremely conservative political views in support of patrician rule are products of his early training by a military-oriented and class-conscious mother. He has little control over his behavior if he is angered, and he cannot compromise on matters concerning politics or honor. After Coriolanus leads the Roman army to victory over the Volscians, the plebeians enthusiastically support his bid to become consul, but after the tribunes use their "brain-washing" tactics, the plebeians reverse their initial endorsement of Coriolanus and banish him. As a result, Coriolanus joins the Volscian army and marches on Rome, but he ultimately yields to the pleas of his mother and calls off the attack. Driven by envy and jealousy, the Volscians' chief commander, Aufidius, has Coriolanus murdered.

### Cominius

A senator and the chief general of the Roman army that opposes the Volscians. After the battle at Corioli, he rewards Marcius with the appellation "Coriolanus" and later supports him for consul; significantly, Cominius is more willing than Coriolanus to compromise with the plebeians and their representatives. Later in the play, even he fails to persuade Coriolanus to call off his attack on Rome.

### Titus Lartius

Along with Cominius and Coriolanus, he is a general in charge of the Roman army fighting the Volscians. He is junior in rank to Cominius, and although he is a constant admirer of Coriolanus' bravery and nobility during the early battle scenes, he ceases to be a factor in the climactic action of the play.

### Menenius Agrippa

A conservative senator of Rome who serves as a patrician ambassador to the plebeians. The plebeians like him and, to a degree, they trust him, and he is willing to offer compromises to calm the rioting citizens. However, he is firmly convinced that the patrician class *alone* should possess political power. He is unsuccessful in his early attempts to have Coriolanus moderate his antiplebeian expression and also in his later efforts to convince Coriolanus to spare Rome. Throughout the play, however, Menenius remains a devoted friend and admirer of Coriolanus.

### Sicinius Velutus and Junius Brutus

Two newly elected tribunes responsible for protecting the rights of the plebeian class. They oppose Coriolanus because they think that he is the epitome of elitist, patrician social bigotry. They are convinced that Coriolanus genuinely hates the lower-class citizens of Rome. These two tribunes are, ironically, strongly politically ambitious themselves and, moreover, are cleverly manipulative; in a sense, they are able to turn the people against Coriolanus almost too easily. Later, of course, they regret their role in banishing Coriolanus when he joins Aufidius. When Coriolanus threatens to besiege Rome with the Volscian army, the citizens hold the tribunes responsible, and they turn on Brutus and threaten to torture him to death.

### Young Marcius

The son of Coriolanus and Virgilia. He has only a small role in the drama, but Valeria's (a family friend) description of his tearing a butterfly to pieces with his teeth indicates that Marcius is very much like his father; this is evidence that Volumnia, his grandmother, has had more influence on his upbringing than Virgilia, and here, in miniature, we have a sense of what Coriolanus' own childhood may have been like.

### Tullus Aufidius

The military leader of the Volscians and also the opponent whom Coriolanus respects most of all those whom he has met in battle. Defeated by Coriolanus several times in combat, Aufidius likewise respects Coriolanus as a noble enemy in the first portion of the play; not really unsurprisingly, he welcomes the exiled Coriolanus as an ally. Nevertheless, his envy becomes compounded with jealousy when Coriolanus easily wins the broad admiration of the Volscian army. As a consequence, Aufidius has Coriolanus murdered after the armistice with Rome.

### Volumnia

The mother of Coriolanus. She is responsible for her son's military-oriented upbringing and for instilling in him his concepts of honor, nobility, and class superiority. When she asks Coriolanus to compromise his political and social principles in order to appease the plebeians—while seeking election as consul—Coriolanus becomes frustrated; his mother's early training taught him that victory alone is honorable and that compromise is ignoble. Volumnia finally convinces her son to spare Rome, but it is a decision that leads directly to his death at the hands of the Volscians.

### Virgilia

The devoted wife of Coriolanus. She does not share Volumnia's love of honor, nobility, and valor. Instead, she fears for Coriolanus' safety whenever he is involved in battle, and she would prefer a life with him that is family-oriented, rather than one that focuses on his duty to the state. Virgilia is characterized primarily by her silent presence.

### Valeria

A friend of Volumnia and Virgilia; she admires Coriolanus for his achievements and for his ideals. She attempts to prompt Virgilia to take more satisfaction in her husband's accomplishments and to suffer less in fearing for his well-being. She accompanies Volumnia, Virgilia, and young Marcius to the Volscian camp outside Rome when Volumnia finally convinces Coriolanus to call off his proposed attack against Rome.

### Nicanor

A Roman who spies for the Volscians. He meets Adrian and reports the plebeian uprising, Coriolanus' banishment, and the susceptibility of Rome to an attack by Aufidius.

### Adrian

A Volscian agent who is sent to contact Nicanor.

## SUMMARIES AND COMMENTARIES

### ACT I

**Summary**

The first scene opens in Rome, where a hungry, unruly mob has gathered to protest the Senate's injustice. Armed with clubs and spears, the citizens demand that action must finally be taken: they are starving, and the corn which is due them will not be released at a fair price from the city's warehouses. The First Citizen names the man who is most responsible for their problems: a patrician, Caius Marcius (later known as Coriolanus). The First Citizen says that the mob must unite and kill Coriolanus, even though they may die in the attempt. Death, he says, is not to be feared;

he himself would rather "die than famish." The mob is ready to rush to the Capitol when Menenius Agrippa, a patrician, enters.

As one of the city's elders, he asks the meaning of this riot, and the Second Citizen tells him that the unrest among the citizens is not new. On the contrary, the discontent among the populace is common knowledge to the Senate. Furthermore, Coriolanus is determined not to be dissuaded from acting on their common resolve now that the moment is climactic. He is convinced that the patrician class cares only for itself and that it makes rules that profit only itself and Rome's usurers. Menenius urges the Citizen to reconsider his plan; he tells him that revolt against the Roman state is futile.

At this point, the object of the mob's fury, Caius Marcius—Coriolanus— enters. His tone is haughty as he addresses the mob. Asking for the meaning of these "dissentious rogues," he arrogantly asserts that by "rubbing the poor itch of [their] opinion," they make themselves no more than "scabs." He calls them all "curs," and sardonically he declares that while some of the mob may fancy themselves as "lions," in reality they are merely "hares"; moreover, they are ignorant and fickle, changing their loyalties in a moment. He reminds them that they defy "the noble Senate," and thus they defy "the gods [who] keep [them] in awe" lest they devour one another. When he is told that they demand "corn at their own rates," his fury increases. "Hang 'em!" he cries; if he had *his* way, he would "make a quarry/ With thousands of these quartered slaves as high/ As I could pick my lance." He tells Menenius that revolt has already erupted in the city, with the citizens demanding the same thing—corn at a fair price. He says that he quelled that dissension by granting the "dogs" five tribunes to defend their "vulgar wisdoms." This action, however, was done against his better judgment; were he in absolute command of the situation, "the rabble" could have "unroofed the city," and he would not have yielded; he would have resisted unto the death. He says that no good can come from placating such mobs; they will ultimately only demand more, and eventually they will become even more rebellious. Turning to the crowd of citizens, he orders them to go home: "Go . . . you fragments!"

A messenger suddenly rushes onstage with news: the Volscians have gathered arms and now threaten Rome. Coriolanus is jubilant: now that there is a threat to Rome from without, this rabble can be dispersed, and more important matters can be attended to. Moments later, a deputation of senators arrives and confirms the news of the Volscians' preparations for war. Coriolanus comments on the enemy's leader, Tullus Aufidius. He says that he envies the man's "nobility": ". . . were I anything but what I am,/ I would wish me only he." He compares his opponent to a lion, one whom he is "proud to hunt." The prospect of battle pleases him, especially a battle against an enemy who is so daring and courageous.

The First Senator then asks a favor from Coriolanus: Titus Lartius is not well and cannot fully assist Cominius during battle; would Coriolanus aid or replace him? Coriolanus is grateful for the chance to do so. The Volscians, he says, have much corn; "take these rats [the mob] thither/ To gnaw their garners." He exits with the senators, and the mob disperses.

The two tribunes, Sicinius and Brutus, are left onstage, and Sicinius asks his comrade if there was ever a man as proud as Coriolanus. Brutus answers that he knows of no one to match Coriolanus. In Sicinius' opinion, Coriolanus is filled with such excessive pride that he was surprised that Coriolanus agreed "to be commanded/ Under Cominius." To this, Brutus answers that Coriolanus' actions are only further proof of his proud craftiness: if the battle miscarries, the fault will be Cominius'—not Coriolanus'; if "things go well," Coriolanus will see that he himself reaps many honors "though indeed . . . he merit not." To this, Sicinius says that it is time that they should leave and learn what Coriolanus is doing—how "he goes/ Upon this present action."

Scene 2 opens a few days later in the Senate-house of the Volscians. Tullus Aufidius, the man singled out by Coriolanus as an enviable "lion" is speaking with several Volscian senators. He acknowledges that the Romans already know of the Volscian preparations for war and, despite the fact that the Roman citizens are mutinous, they have begun to march forward toward Corioli, the Volscian capital, led by Cominius, Titus Lartius, and Coriolanus, Aufidius' "old enemy." Aufidius is angered at being foiled in his military strategy, and he accuses the First Senator of indiscretion in keeping their "great pretences veiled"; Aufidius had hoped to subdue the towns between their own capital and Rome. Then he could have conquered Rome before she could mount a defense. Such a maneuver is now impossible. The Second Senator speaks up and asks Aufidius if he, the senator himself, and the First Senator might guard Corioli; meanwhile, Aufidius could make war where he might choose to. If the Romans attacked Corioli, the Volscian army could surprise them and surround them. "I think," he says reassuringly, "you'll find/ They've not prepared for us." Aufidius knows better; the Romans are wise in matters of warfare. He leaves, announcing that if he and Coriolanus meet in battle, they have sworn to fight "till one can do no more," and his followers wish him well: "The gods assist you!"

The setting for Scene 3 is Coriolanus' house, where Volumnia (Coriolanus' mother) and Virgilia (Coriolanus' wife) are sewing and talking. Volumnia chides her daughter-in-law for her low spirits. If *she* were married to Coriolanus, she would rejoice in his exploits on the battlefield, rather than mourn for his absence in their empty marriage bed. To her, military honor excels love. She recalls when Coriolanus was a boy; she loved him so dearly that not even "kings' entreaties" could have taken him from her. She has wanted only one thing for her beloved son: honor and glory. Therefore, she decided long ago "to let him seek danger where he was like to find fame"—that is, in warfare. She remembers when Coriolanus returned from his first battle; he wore the oak wreath of a hero around his brow. She saw him being honored as a *man*, and she was more overjoyed than when she first heard the news that she had given birth to a "man-child."

Virgilia is unimpressed. She asks her mother-in-law how she would have felt if Coriolanus had been killed in battle. Volumnia's answer is quick: if she had twelve sons, she would rather see eleven of them die bravely in battle than be mother to a son who preferred a life of idle, sensual pleasure.

Valeria, one of Virgilia's friends is announced, and Virgilia asks permission to leave; she is depressed and wants to be alone. Volumnia refuses her daughter-in-law's request; she tells Virgilia that perhaps Valeria brings news from the battlefield. She envisions her son's "bloody brow" and his armored hand, mowing down his enemies in a harvest of destruction. The image sickens Virgilia: "O Jupiter, no blood!"

Volumnia loses her patience; angrily, she tells the servant to bring Valeria to them. Blood, she tells her daughter-in-law, becomes a real man; not even Hecuba's breasts, as Hector suckled them, were as beautiful as Hector's forehead "when it spit forth blood." She vows that Coriolanus will "beat Aufidius' head below his knee/ And tread upon his neck."

Valeria enters, compliments the ladies on their superb housekeeping, and asks about Virgilia's young son, Marcius. Volumnia answers that her grandson is splendid: "He had rather see the swords and hear a drum than look upon his schoolmaster." Valeria is delighted at the news. "The father's son," she comments, adding that she recently saw the young boy running after a "gilded butterfly." He teased it so unmercifully, she says, that he finally fell upon it and tore it to pieces with his teeth. Valeria recalls the scene with awe; the boy is truly "a noble child," she declares. Then she tries to coax Virgilia to go with her to see an ailing neighbor, but Virgilia declines; she will not go "over the threshold till [her] lord return from the wars." Valeria scoffs at her friend's melodramatics; she tells Virgilia that she is another silly Penelope who accomplished nothing—except that she filled "Ithaca full of moths."

Valeria pleads again with Virgilia to accompany her, but Virgilia is resolute. Thus, Valeria teases her with news of Coriolanus; according to one of the senators, she says, Cominius is soon to meet Aufidius in battle, and Coriolanus and Titus Lartius are besieging the city of Corioli. Virgilia repeats her decision: she will *not* leave the house. Volumnia is exasperated with her son's wife; she puts her sewing aside and tells Valeria that they will leave: "As [Virgilia] is now, she will but disease our better mirth." Valeria asks Virgilia one final time if Virgilia will go with them, but Virgilia says she cannot leave; she is too troubled to indulge in gaiety and gossip.

Scene 4 is set outside the city of Corioli; Coriolanus sees a messenger approaching, and because he is anxious for good news, he turns to Lartius and bets his prized horse against Lartius' horse that they will soon learn that Cominius has already engaged the enemy in battle. The messenger arrives and says, however, that Cominius has sighted the enemy, but that he has not yet attacked them. Lartius is overjoyed: "The good horse is mine," he cries. Coriolanus is not anxious to loose his steed: "I'll buy him of you," he says, but Lartius refuses. He will lend his friend the horse, but he will neither return Coriolanus' horse nor will he resell it to him. Then he changes the subject to matters of warfare. "Summon the town," he says, for he wants to parley with those still remaining inside the besieged city.

Two Senators, along with others, appear on the walls, and Coriolanus asks them if Aufidius is still inside the city. The answer is curt: Aufidius is not in the city, nor is there "a man [within] that fears you less than he."

From far off, the sounds of a battle can be heard. The citizens of Corioli rally; they believe that their men have been victorious. Lartius thinks otherwise; the noise, he says, is his "instructions," and he calls for ladders to be placed against the city walls. At that moment however, the Volscian army rushes through the city gates and forces the Romans to retreat to their trenches.

Coriolanus re-enters a moment later, cursing his cowardly comrades—"boils and plagues/ Plaster you o'er." He despairs at the lack of courage in his men, and he tells them that they have the "souls of geese." Then he orders them forward and says that if they refuse to advance on the Volscians, he will "leave the foe/ And make [his] wars on [his own men]." Another alarum is heard, and the Volscians flee into the city. Coriolanus follows behind them, and the city gates close.

Lartius enters and asks for Coriolanus. One of the soldiers tells him that Coriolanus is doubtlessly slain "following the fliers at the very heels. . . . He is himself alone,/ To answer all the city." Lartius wails aloud: "O noble fellow," he cries, recounting his comrade's daring. Yet hardly has he finished his oration than Coriolanus enters, bleeding and wounded. The Roman forces cheer: their leader lives. Within moments, they mass together and besiege the city in one last victorious battle. When they are finished, Corioli is theirs.

In Scene 5, the Romans are exulting over the victory and relishing in the spoils when Coriolanus enters. He reprimands his men for their vulgar greediness, and then, hearing the sounds of battle in the distance, he orders them to pack up. Corioli may be taken, but Aufidius is still alive and "piercing our Romans." He means to finally destroy "the man of my soul's hate." He tells Lartius to take the necessary men whom he needs to hold the city, and he himself will take the rest and relieve Cominius. Lartius reminds his friend of his wounds, but Coriolanus is unconcerned; not even this last battle has "yet . . . warmed [him]"; the blood that he loses is only "physical"—that is, his spirit has not been injured nor is it sated: "To Aufidius . . . I will appear, and fight." He exits and Lartius wishes him well.

In Scene 6, Cominius enters camp and speaks with his men. They are in retreat, but he assures them all that they have fought well. They have fought like Romans—"neither foolish . . . nor cowardly." He expects the enemy to attack again, but he is not afraid; he has heard the sounds of Coriolanus doing battle against the soldiers defending Corioli, and he expects reinforcements from his comrade to arrive shortly. A messenger enters, but his news is not good. He says that Coriolanus was forced to retreat. This is so; initially, Coriolanus' forces *were* driven back, but later they were able to regroup and were successful in claiming the city. When Coriolanus' men fell back, the messenger says, he himself fled, with a number of Volscian soldiers behind him.

Unexpectedly, Coriolanus enters. Cominius is aghast. His comrade is so bloody that he scarcely recognizes him. Coriolanus, however, is absolutely unconcerned with his wounds. His only concern is whether or not he has arrived too late: "Where is the enemy? Are you lords o' the field?"

Cominius tells him that they have retreated, momentarily, but that he believes Aufidius to be among the vanguard that may presently attack. This is good news to Coriolanus. He begs Cominius "by the blood we have shed together [and] by the vows/ We have made . . . to set [him] against Aufidius." Cominius would prefer to see Coriolanus bathed and bandaged, but he cannot deny this request. Thus he offers his comrade whatever men are necessary to quell the next attack. Coriolanus states that he will choose only those soldiers who "love this painting [his blood]/ Wherein you see me smeared"; he wants only those soldiers who value their country more than their lives. The soldiers shout, wave their swords, and hoist Coriolanus on their shoulders, and he acknowledges that he alone is fit to be the "sword" that will be used against the Volscians. He also recognizes that only a small number of these soldiers are bold and daring enough to accompany him. He will take those men and leave the rest to fight wherever Cominius thinks best. Cominius orders his men to do as Coriolanus commands; all spoils will be equally divided later.

Scene 7 is set outside the gates of Corioli; Lartius has assigned guards and is now ready to leave and join Cominius and Coriolanus. He speaks briefly with one of his lieutenants and reminds him to guard the city well. It is possible that Lartius and his fellow commanders may need more soldiers; if so, the lieutenant is to send reinforcements as soon as possible.

Scene 8 opens on the battlefield. Coriolanus and Aufidius meet one another at last. They restate their fierce hatred for one another and vow to fight until one of them is dead. Coriolanus taunts Aufidius that the blood which covers his body is not his own; it is Volscian blood, shed only three hours earlier during the conquest of Corioli. Then swords are drawn and the battle begins. Several Volscians rush to Aufidius' side, but Coriolanus finally manages to drive back Aufidius until the latter flees, crying out in shame as he realizes that Coriolanus has "shamed [him in what he hoped would be Coriolanus' last] condemned seconds."

As Scene 9 opens, an alarum is sounded in one of the Roman camps, and Cominius enters. Speaking with Coriolanus, he praises his comrade's exploits and says that the Roman senators will soon hear of Coriolanus' deeds. Cominius himself will tell them, and Romans everywhere will praise Coriolanus and will "thank the gods [that] Rome hath such a soldier." Lartius enters then and also begins to praise Coriolanus, but Coriolanus interrupts him. He says that he acted only as any Roman soldier would; he did only what was necessary; thus, he will hear no more praise. It is excessive and it is unhealthy; it reminds him of his mother's too often excessive praise for his military deeds. He asks to be excused so that he can attend to his wounds, but Cominius insists that Coriolanus stay and help divide the spoils. Coriolanus refuses, calling the booty "bribe."

At that moment, there is a loud flourish of trumpets, and all the soldiers hail their hero. When the camp is quiet again, Coriolanus reiterates his earlier statement. His deeds were only those of a Roman soldier, and a Roman soldier should not be seduced by the flattery of drums and trumpets. Cominius chides his friend for such modesty and offers him all glory of the battle—"this war's garland." From now on, he says, his comrade will no longer be known as Caius Marcius; he will now bear a new name: Coriolanus, named in honor of his conquest of Corioli. Trumpets and drums again sound a tribute, and Cominius issues orders to be sent to Rome, announcing this day's military success. Coriolanus then asks one favor: there is a man who is still imprisoned in Corioli, one who helped him and whom he could not rescue because of his vow to defeat Aufidius; he asks Cominius to ensure this man's safety. Cominius agrees to see that Coriolanus' wish is granted, and the two men exit to attend to Coriolanus' wounds.

Back in camp, in Scene 10, Aufidius discusses the capture of Corioli with one of his soldiers. He cannot fathom the soldier's naive concern about whether or not the city is in "good condition" following its defeat. To him, the defeat of Corioli has been a devastating blow. He knows the Roman mind; they will exercise no mercy to their enemies. Coriolanus has already defeated him five times in battle; there is sure to be another encounter, and once more, they will battle until one of them is dead—or until Aufidius has fled. He vows anew to kill his enemy, once and for all, whether it be by "true sword to sword" or by "wrath or craft." Then he turns to one of his soldiers and instructs him to find out how many hostages have been taken to Rome and what the terms of surrender are. Then he will decide how he must "spur on my journey"—that is, what he must do next to regain his pride and his nation.

## Commentary

*Coriolanus* is a play which deals with class warfare in Rome. In the first act, Shakespeare dramatizes this social conflict by focusing on the confrontation between the plebeian-citizen faction and an elitist patrician, Caius Marcius (later honored with the name "Coriolanus"). Coriolanus is the symbol of the mob's fury and wrath; they believe that his death will solve the problem of high grain prices. Significantly, Coriolanus' first words reveal his attitude toward the people. He shows utter contempt for them; he calls them "dissentious rogues" and tells them: "With every minute you do change a mind"; to him, the mob's chief trait is fickleness, both in war and peace, and he welcomes the news of impending war as a means of ridding Rome of this surplus plebeian "rabble," for whom he has no compassion. Coriolanus believes that patricians alone should rule because of the plebeians' inferior powers of reason. He is convinced that civic order can be maintained only by a strong Senate which will control the people. He passionately disapproves of the concessions now being made by the Senate because they will lead only to other demands which will cause further insurrection if not met and will lead to political chaos if the decision-making process is extended any further to the irrational lower class. At the end of the first scene, two tribunes, Brutus and Sicinius, acknowledge that they are also aware of the plebeians' "giddy censure" and fickle opinion. In contrast to this attitude throughout the play is the steadfastness of Coriolanus' ethics. The common citizens are depicted as being men of very little character, while Coriolanus, although certainly not a model hero, remains remarkably consistent to his views.

On the surface, the old and sage patrician Menenius seems like a good man; the citizens respect him and listen to his reasoned fable, but they do not genuinely comprehend the true opinions of this man whom they consider to be their greatest friend within the ruling class. Actually, however, Menenius believes that the patricians are so superior to the plebeians that the possibility of a successful citizen revolt does not exist. He tells them, "You may as well/Strike at the heaven with your staves as lift them/ Against the Roman state." Nevertheless, he does realize that the plebeians have the power to create chaos, and he urges Coriolanus not to provoke them further.

Many of Coriolanus' values are due to the influence of his mother, Volumnia. She educated him to commit his life to a set of heroic and noble principles, and she sent him to war as a teenager so that he would learn to value the honor and fame that would result from valiant combat; she deeply wanted him to always seek danger and glory in war. As a result, Coriolanus developed a sense of honor based more on egoism and social station than on patriotism. Consequently, later in the play, he will see no treason in his joining Aufidius because righting a personal wrong will mean more to him than abstract loyalty to a country from which he is estranged. In addition, Volumnia has succeeded so well in training her son that he believes absolutely in adhering to her concepts of honor. Honor is more valuable to him, ultimately, than life. For that reason, Coriolanus will later feel that his mother has betrayed him when she asks him to compromise and appease the plebeians.

During the battle scenes in Act I, note how Coriolanus acts when the Volscian army proves momentarily to be braver and more eager to fight than the Romans. Coriolanus reacts in a rage, cursing his soldiers with an even greater intensity than he had cursed the plebeians who were rioting in Rome. However, it is Coriolanus' *anger* which is one of his greatest martial assets, causing him to attack the enemy with a ferocity that even his own men and Lartius consider foolhardy but which ultimately inspires the Romans to victory. He refuses to consider the possibility that his brave soldiers can be beaten, and his immediate response is a counterattack, spurring his men onward not only with exhortations of honor and patriotism but with deadly threats. He seems obsessed, and so by devoutly following the principles which he has learned from Volumnia and his previous experiences in war, this is the moment of glory which he has lived for. His lack of control in moments of high passion characterize him; they make him the exemplary warrior he is; but, ironically, it is this quality which will destroy him eventually in the political arena into which his victories will thrust him.

Unlike Coriolanus, who can accept nothing less than immediate and total victory, Cominius commends his soldiers for having fought honorably—even if they have retreated. When Coriolanus enters, however, his first words are, "Come I too late?" He assumes command of the Roman offensive, and the Roman soldiers are inspired to new boldness by this consummate man of action who is eager for battle. Characteristically, Coriolanus shuns recounting his own bravery and success, desiring, instead, to be apprised of the present situation and to lead the attack against Aufidius' strongest position. His enthusiasm infects the entire army, causing all of them to volunteer to follow him into the most dangerous part of the battlefield.

After the battle is over, and Cominius suggests that Coriolanus' feats may go unrecognized unless public acknowledgment is made of them, Coriolanus confesses that he finds praise uncomfortable. He does not like to receive public acclaims. He has satisfied his and his mother's desires by simply living up to the standards which they revere. He even commends his soldiers for having surpassed him in bravery. Of particular significance here is Coriolanus' consistency of character in his rejection of his share of the spoils of Corioli. To accept them would make him a mercenary, and war is far too important to him to be equated in any way with financial gain.

As the act ends, Aufidius laments having been beaten by Coriolanus for the fifth time in single combat. Defeat and shame have altered him. He is no longer proud to be a Volscian; he admits to Coriolanus' superiority as a soldier, but he is determined to destroy the man who has humiliated him. Ironically, he wishes he were a Roman, just as Coriolanus will soon desire to become a Volscian. Aufidius thoroughly understands Coriolanus, whom he assesses as being "bolder, though not so subtle" as the devil. And of equal importance here is Aufidius' realization that "craft" may be the most promising approach to use against a man who lacks the cunning to use deceit either to gain his own ends or to detect it when it is used against him.

## ACT II

### Summary

In Rome, Menenius and the tribunes Sicinius and Brutus argue about the excessive pride of Coriolanus. Menenius says that the tribunes themselves are ambitious and foolishly proud; he admits that he himself is intemperate in drink, argument, and the free expression of his opinion, but he criticizes them for being excessively ambitious and exceptionally poor magistrates who fail to recognize their own pride while attacking Coriolanus for his pride.

Volumnia, Virgilia, and Valeria enter, and Volumnia greatly pleases Menenius with the news that Coriolanus has written letters to him, to her, to Virgilia, and to the state informing them that he will presently return, acclaimed as a hero. Volumnia and Menenius discuss Coriolanus' wounds, his bravery, his fight with Aufidius, and Volumnia is sure that his fresh wounds, combined with his earlier battle scars, will be advantageous when he shows them to the populace and asks to be a candidate for consul. Cominius, Lartius, and their army enter, then, escorting Coriolanus, who wears the oaken garland of victory. A herald announces Coriolanus' single fight within the gates of Corioli and the honorable addition to his name. Coriolanus asks for the adulation to cease; he kneels before his mother, then leaves for the Capitol to visit the Senate. Volumnia confesses her long desire for him to finally become consul, but Coriolanus expresses reluctance to enter politics.

Left alone, Brutus and Sicinius note that all classes of Romans are equally enthusiastic over Coriolanus, and they fear that they and the other tribunes will lose power if a worshipful populace accepts Coriolanus as consul. They agree, however, that it shouldn't be too difficult to remind everyone of Coriolanus' excessive pride; thus, it should be equally easy to provoke him into revealing his true contempt for the lower classes. A messenger enters and tells them that the Senate awaits them and that the people will likely choose Coriolanus to be consul. The tribunes leave, agreeing that they will pretend to honor Coriolanus while, in fact, they will be trying to conjure up some means whereby Coriolanus' temper and pride will destroy him.

At the Capitol, a group of officials and senators enter, and Menenius asks Cominius to delineate the deeds of Coriolanus. A senator implores him to be thorough and asks the tribunes to listen carefully and to inform the people. The tribunes agree, but ask for Coriolanus to change his behavior.

Coriolanus leaves, not wishing to hear his heroism proclaimed, and Menenius reminds the tribunes that Coriolanus' modesty will also prevent his flattering the people. Cominius then speaks of Coriolanus' valor, his many battles, his bravery at Corioli, his responsibility for the recent victory, and his lack of greed while the spoils of Corioli were being meted out. The Senate calls Coriolanus back, and Menenius tells him that the Senate has chosen him as a candidate for consul. Coriolanus promises always to follow the will of the Senate, but he asks if he might waive the custom of wearing the coarse garment of humility; likewise, he does not want to display his wounds and plead, as it were, for plebeian votes. Menenius urges him to follow tradition, and finally Coriolanus agrees. The tribunes, confident that Coriolanus cannot but help conceal his true contempt for the people, leave to inform the populace.

At the Forum, a group of citizens who await Coriolanus discuss his ingratitude, as well as the patricians' contempt for the plebeian class. Then, accompanied by Menenius, and cursing the common people, Coriolanus enters, wearing the traditional gown of humility. Menenius urges his friend to moderate his speech, then exits. Three citizens approach Coriolanus and ask why he is in the Forum, and he answers that he is there because he deserves to be, not because he desires to "beg" for their votes. Two more citizens approach and accuse him of abusing them; he maintains that his honest elitism is a virtue, but he says that he will act as he is supposed to act and that he will "plead" for their votes. They consent—even though he refuses to show them his wounds.

Coriolanus is deeply troubled; he laments having to humble himself for an office which he has already earned and which the Senate has already granted him. However, he decides to forbear since his ordeal is half over. Three more citizens approach, and he "begs" for their votes. They give them to him, then exit as Menenius returns with the news that the tribunes have verified the election.

After Menenius and Coriolanus have left so that Coriolanus can change out of his gown of humility and have his election made official, Brutus and Sicinius comment on the proud bearing of Coriolanus; similarly, several citizens recount his mocking behavior and his refusal to show them his wounds. The tribunes secretly rejoice and chide the citizens for approving Coriolanus too willingly. The citizens proclaim that they can still reverse the unofficial election, and the tribunes urge them to do so and to act swiftly. Craftily, the tribunes take care to hide their instigation of the people from the Senate; they want to make it appear that they have argued *for* Coriolanus. Brutus contends that a preventative mutiny now will forestall a greater rebellion later, and the tribunes thus make plans to take advantage of Coriolanus' reaction to the news of his rejection.

## Commentary

Before word of the Roman victory has had time to reach Rome, it is clear that peace will bring about an even greater polarization between the plebeian and the patrician classes. The tribunes have become the chief spokesmen for the plebeian faction, and Coriolanus has become both representative for and emblem of the extreme, conservative element within the patrician ranks. However, with Coriolanus absent, Menenius has taken over the role of protector of patrician interests.

The tribunes Sicinius and Brutus are the first popularly elected officials of the young Roman democracy, and in Menenius' estimation the new system has already produced representatives who are inefficient and incompetent; to him, they attempt to compensate for their inabilities and to protect their positions by using demagoguery. Although the tribunes' suspicion of Coriolanus' class arrogance has been shown to be well-founded because of his many slurs against the plebeians, the private conversation between the tribunes at the end of the first scene of this act reveals Menenius' assessment to be at least partially correct. Sicinius and Brutus resent the adoration which the people are giving to Coriolanus, and they clearly reveal to us their plan to take advantage of their newly gained power. They plan to deceive the Senate by feigning support for Coriolanus, while scheming to publicly provoke Coriolanus' haughtiness. Significantly, the patricians grossly underestimate the capacity of the tribunes to undermine their authority. Menenius, for example, looks on the tribunes and their function as subjects of ridicule. He dismisses them as "herdsmen of the beastly plebeians."

Coriolanus has returned to Rome at the zenith of his exceptional military career. He has achieved all that a soldier could imagine: the Roman nobility and populace have given him sole credit for having inspired and led a resounding victory. But he is not the only one to have succeeded to the utmost; Coriolanus' mother, Volumnia, has fulfilled her mission to mold her son into the ideal warrior, and Coriolanus acknowledges her contribution by kneeling respectfully before her even before he greets his wife and son. Note here that Volumnia welcomes her son *not* with warmth and relief that he has returned home safely but, rather, she welcomes him with pride and satisfaction that he has returned from war for the third time wearing the garland of victory and bearing the title of his nation's hero. Likewise, Menenius, Cominius, and Lartius worship and respect Coriolanus for embodying abstract qualities honored by Roman soldiers and patricians, but they do not relate to him as a mutual friend. Only Coriolanus' wife, Virgilia, loves him in purely human and emotional terms, but in his presence she remains always in the background; she is never assertive and she seldom speaks.

Volumnia's role in Coriolanus' life and in this drama is a key factor. She trained Coriolanus to adhere to a strict code of conduct applicable only to the military and to patrician society, and Coriolanus has consistently followed the principles of the code devoutly; those principles have dictated his attitudes and his reactions, and, consequently, he has not had to develop an ability to apply reason to circumstances and situations. He has always relied on his mother's code for concepts and on his mother for guidance. Therefore, when Volumnia decides that the next step in her son's career should be his election as consul, she thrusts him into a situation where the assets that have made his success possible will quickly become detriments which will doom him to utter failure. Initially, Coriolanus rejects her suggestions about role-playing in order to please the masses, but he has grown too used to following her principles to deny her now.

Although the government of Rome has convened specifically to honor Coriolanus for his latest military deeds and to nominate him to run for consul, the tribunes have already initiated their plan to destroy Coriolanus. They begin with Brutus' sarcastic suggestion that it is *not* modesty that compels Coriolanus to leave the highly formalized ceremony; Brutus implies that Coriolanus is incapable of following tradition and humbly pleading for votes. Menenius quickly comes to Coriolanus' defense, and he tells the tribunes that Coriolanus "loves your people,/ But tie him not to be their bedfellow," contending that Coriolanus can serve the interest of the people without attempting to meet them as social equals. The debate continues, but by the end of Scene 2, we see that the tribunes are satisfied that their plan to provoke Coriolanus will work. They have cunningly enfolded themselves in the mantle of righteousness by arguing that *custom* must be upheld—for the rights of the people—while in actuality they are using subterfuge to establish a condition in which they will be able to take advantage of Coriolanus' "flaw"—that is, his dislike of "begging" for approval and, also, publicly showing his wounds to the masses.

When the citizens have gathered in the Forum, they agree that Coriolanus' military accomplishments have indeed qualified him to be a worthy candidate for consul. *If* he follows the prescribed practices of displaying his wounds, proclaiming his services to the people, and requesting their votes, they in turn will be bound by the dictates of the "law of gratitude" to approve him. The citizens also resolve to ignore Coriolanus' earlier attitude towards them.

Suspense is keen at this point—approval seems certain—because the populace is caught up in the emotion of the victory celebration and seems willing to approve Coriolanus as consul. Yet we see in the final scene of Act II that Coriolanus' pride and the code of conduct which he learned from Volumnia will prevent him from playing the role of humble suppli-cant. In fact, nowhere in the play, thus far, is Coriolanus' pride more evi-dent than here. He disregards Menenius' entreaties to moderate his speech, and he proceeds to ridicule the ritual which he is trying to follow. With biting sarcasm and mockery, he scorns the people as being cowards and simple-minded creatures worthy only of hanging. He believes that he should already be consul because of his record in war, his position within the patrician class and his selection by the Senate. He does not think that the people should have the power to approve *or* reject the Senate's selec-tion, and he remains firm in his conviction that the Senate made a grave mistake by conceding such power to the people. He considers himself to be an innovator who should be exempt from all traditional rules. In his opinion, it is men such as he who correct existing wrongs, and the cur-rent wrong which he would immediately correct is the growing power of the common people.

He refuses to display his wounds, and he sheds his traditional gown of humility as quickly as possible. He says that he should be honored by the people and respected for expressing his attitudes honestly and for not offending the populace by condescending to flatter them with unfelt affec-tion. He sarcastically proclaims that, if he must, he *will* become a false-speaking flatterer, but what Coriolanus does not comprehend at this point is that he *must*, at this moment, choose either to abandon his candidacy or become, in actuality, a demagogue and pretend to speak to the people as an equal. As a consequence of his conduct in the Forum, he will become easy prey for the tribunes when they set about attempting to reverse the decision of the people. It will be then that the masses will quickly recall Coriolanus' proud behavior. Moreover, the tribunes will easily use the citi-zens' inconstancy, a trait which Shakespeare has emphasized several times already. Thus, they can manipulate them into changing their minds and rejecting Coriolanus.

The tribunes' plan succeeds, of course. The citizens not only remember Coriolanus' behavior, but they remember it in detail; therefore, we see that the tribunes are easily appealing to the people's fickle natures and manipulating them into nullifying the election. Clearly, the "villains" of this play are the tribunes.

Coriolanus, without doubt, hates the common people and objects to sharing power with the plebeian class, and the tribunes are fulfilling their duty to protect the rights of the people when they oppose him. However, the tribunes have also become demagogues obsessed with protecting and extending their own power, and they have no reluctance to gain their ends by taking advantage of both Coriolanus' proud nature and the people's fickleness. They have instructed the people to follow a procedure during the election designed to provoke Coriolanus into offensive acts of pride and contempt. The citizens approach him in groups of two or three, rather than *en masse* in order to prolong his ordeal and to try his patience. Nevertheless, they fail to follow the tribunes' explicit instructions to shower the candidate with provocative questions which will force him either to commit himself to enforcing plebeian rights or to expose himself as an enemy of the people—an enemy not deserving to be consul. However, note that the tribunes refuse to concede defeat and that they patiently instruct the people again. They are determined to revoke the people's initial vote by inflaming them against Coriolanus with accounts of his behavior in the Forum and by insisting to the Senate that they were too blinded by their admiration of Coriolanus' service to detect his true nature. The tribunes justify their devious maneuverings to themselves with the argument that a provoked rebellion by the populace now will prevent greater bloodshed in the future. At the center of their plan is Coriolanus, who cannot lie nor flatter; he is locked in combat for which he is poorly prepared with men who have no scruples against using any weapons which promise expediency.

## ACT III

### Summary

Coriolanus, along with several members of the Roman Senate and a number of patricians, is on his way to the marketplace to receive confirmation of his election. Lartius reports that Aufidius has raised a new army, and Coriolanus says that he is eager to fight him again. A few moments later, the patricians meet the tribunes Sicinius and Brutus, who command them to halt. They announce the revocation of the election and predict that the people will riot if the procession continues to the marketplace. Coriolanus angrily accuses the tribunes of plotting to usurp political power, and, of course, Brutus denies instigating any such plot; he lays all blame on Coriolanus. As the debate grows more heated, Sicinius warns Coriolanus to moderate his speech if he hopes to become consul. Cominius, like Coriolanus, agrees that the people have been deliberately deceived.

Menenius and a senator try to restore calm, and, at this point, Coriolanus curses the common people and advises against sharing power with them. Brutus accuses Coriolanus of speaking like a wrathful god, and Sicinius tells him that his mind is like a poison which "shall remain" out of government. Coriolanus takes issue with the word "shall," with its connotation that the tribunes have the authority to command him; he warns them that the word "shall" is indicative of a political movement which, if not halted, will lead to absolute plebeian rule. Cominius suggests that they continue on their way.

Menenius attempts to restrain Coriolanus, but Coriolanus continues to scorn the common people: they are undeserving cowards whose claim to authority is based solely on their numbers, and they do not have the ability to rule responsibly. He suggests that the Senate suppress the plebeians before they gain the power to destroy both themselves and the state. The tribunes label Coriolanus as a traitor, and he answers that they should be removed from office. Incensed, they cry out for the aediles (officers attached to the Tribune) and instruct them to arrest Coriolanus. The gentry try to defend Coriolanus, more aediles enter, and a "rabble of citizens" enters. Chaos ensues, and while Menenius again asks for calm, Sicinius warns the people that Coriolanus deserves to die. They tell the aediles to apprehend him and to execute him. Menenius pleads with Brutus, but Brutus answers that violence is the only way to curb Coriolanus. Another scuffle ensues, and after the gentry finally prevail, they urge Coriolanus to go home. Coriolanus calls the plebeians "barbarians" and says that he could beat forty of them, but Cominius notes the odds and again urges him to leave. Most of the gentry leave, but Menenius and two patricians remain behind.

Menenius says that Coriolanus is "too noble for the world," that Coriolanus is a man who will not flatter, one who always speaks his mind. The tribunes, however, insist that Coriolanus must be executed. Menenius reminds the tribunes and the people of Coriolanus' service to Rome, and he begs them to follow due process of law; otherwise, Rome will become divided and destroyed by civil strife. He reminds them that Coriolanus is a warrior who is unversed in polite speech, and he promises to bring him before a court of law in order to answer all their charges. The tribunes accept Menenius' offer, while maintaining that they retain the authority to proceed as they please against Coriolanus if Menenius should fail.

Attended by a group of patricians at his home, Coriolanus insists that he will continue to act according to his principles, in defiance of the tribunes; then he questions why his mother has not been more supportive of his stand. Volumnia enters and reproaches him for not being more reserved until his appointment as consul has been actually confirmed. Menenius and some senators enter, and he and Volumnia agree that Coriolanus *must* make some concessions in order to maintain civic order. Volumnia argues that since deceit is an honorable strategy in war, it can now be considered an honorable policy to maintain the stability of the government.

Coriolanus asks his mother why she is being so persistent. Admitting that her suggestions are indeed repugnant, she advises her son to feign a role and to speak kindly to the people in order to safeguard the fortunes of Rome, as well as his own. She contends that the people are more emotional than reasonable, and she urges him to kneel before them, to apologize to them, and to promise them that he will change. Cominius enters and he also advises Coriolanus to calm the mob with conciliatory words; Volumnia continues to plead, and, finally, Coriolanus yields. Momentarily, he changes his mind. Then Volumnia tells him to do as he likes, noting that it is as dishonorable for her to plead with him as it is for him to humble himself before the plebeians. He tells her to have patience; he will act a false role and return home as consul. Cominius warns him against further provocation by the tribunes, and the two men leave for the marketplace.

At the Forum, Brutus tells Sicinius to provoke Coriolanus with accusations of tyrannical ambition and, if that fails, to charge him with harboring malice toward the people and hoarding the spoils of war. An aedile then brings news that Coriolanus is on his way, and Sicinius orders the aedile to assemble the people and to instruct them to shout either "Fine" or "Death" for Coriolanus when they hear the tribune say "It shall be so/ I' the right and strength o' the commons." Coriolanus and his party arrive, and he assures Menenius that he will remain calm. The aedile returns with a group of citizens, and Coriolanus asks if any further charges will be brought against him. Sicinius answers Coriolanus by asking him if he will submit to questioning by the people and their representatives. Coriolanus agrees and asks why he has been deprived of the consulship. Sicinius charges him with tyrannical ambition and with being a traitor. Coriolanus heatedly calls Sicinius a liar. Sicinius asks the people to note Coriolanus' service to Rome. Rashly, Coriolanus objects to Brutus' mentioning his service, and Menenius quickly reminds him of his promise to his mother; Coriolanus, however, says he *cannot* beg. Sicinius then decrees that Coriolanus must be banished from Rome forever; if he returns, he will be executed. Sicinius then signals to the aedile and the people. On cue, the citizens shout for banishment. Cominius attempts to defend Coriolanus, but Brutus says that the sentence is final. Coriolanus predicts that after he is exiled, Rome will become an easy target for invaders, and he leaves stating, "There is a world elsewhere." The citizens shout in triumphant joy, and Sicinius goads them to follow and torment Coriolanus as he leaves the gates of the city.

## Commentary

Coriolanus' attitude toward the state, the people, and the tribunes does not change with his election. Even before he learns that the people have reversed their vote, he scorns the tribunes when he sees them because he is offended by their acting like figures of authority. The revocation of his position by the people only reinforces his belief that they are too irresponsible to be trusted with political power, and he warns the patricians again that anarchy will result if the people are not curbed immediately, because once the masses have been given power, they will never again submit to patrician rule. He acknowledges that granting the people's demand to select tribunes may have been good policy as a means of halting a rebellion, but he fervently believes that the nobles must resume their traditional power and must remove the tribunes from office now that order has been restored.

Coriolanus sees no loss of honor by the patricians' reversing their promises to the plebeians, for the plebeians are not a class which deserves fair treatment. For Coriolanus, the only acceptable government for Rome is a benevolent patrician dictatorship, and thus he refers to the Senate's gift of grain as an instance when the patricians demonstrated their *care* for the working class. In reality, however, Coriolanus views the distribution of food as a courtesy to a populace that had to be conscripted to defend their homeland when the Volscians threatened invasion; in contrast, the people and the tribunes view it as a concession to their demands, a concession which has encouraged them to seek more freedom and more authority. Coriolanus is a wary man; he warns the nobles what might happen if they continue to submit to the people, and he points to Sicinius' use of the imperative "shall," with its connotation that a tribune has authority to command a noble; this is also an example of what the future holds if the tribunes are not removed. Coriolanus' theory is that when two factions contend for political power, one will inevitably dominate the other, and the people have numbers on their side. Only a commitment to compromise by both parties can reconcile their differences, and neither is willing to compromise. Indeed, Coriolanus cannot.

In their class struggle, the two parties have decidedly different concepts of what constitutes "Rome." The patricians define Rome in terms of its established social order and its buildings, both of which they desire to preserve. Coriolanus, as the most extreme conservative among the patricians, thinks of Rome as consisting pre-eminently of its *nobility*, and all else is worth risking to protect noble rule. The tribunes and the plebeians, on the other hand, consider the people as the essence of "Rome." Thus, Act III dramatically embodies class warfare; here, Shakespeare focuses on the clash between the tribunes (supported by the citizens) and Coriolanus (supported by the patricians).

In his efforts to restore calm, Menenius appeals to the tribunes to act as good citizens, but he fails to see that a wide difference of opinion exists between what he considers to be good citizenship and what the tribunes consider to be good citizenship. Menenius wants patrician-dominated order restored; the tribunes believe that they are acting as good citizens by inciting the people as a means of eliminating Coriolanus from the government while simultaneously increasing their own power. They believe that Coriolanus considers himself to be above the law, and it is essential to their success to show that he is *subject* to the law and that they have the authority to apply the law in his case.

In their political battle against Coriolanus and the patricians, the tribunes consistently display a superior ability to understand their opponents, to plan thoroughly, and to rally the people to their support. After they succeed in stopping the patricians from continuing to the Forum, the tribunes know that they can provoke Coriolanus into a rage by referring to his demand for their removal from office as being "manifest treason"; as a result, they can label him a traitor, a rebel, and an enemy to Rome. When Coriolanus does return to the Forum to face questions, he immediately reveals his incapacity to be a political leader in a democracy. He turns to the people whom he promised to placate and accuses them of being dishonorable in reversing their votes. Sicinius seizes on this flare of temper and calls Coriolanus a "traitor to the people." He knows that the word "traitor" will outrage Coriolanus; and, as expected, Coriolanus damns the tribunes *and* the people, fulfilling the tribunes' hope that he would offend the people and force them into even further support of their "representatives."

By manipulating Coriolanus' public behavior, the tribunes have established their right to try him—where it counts—in the minds of the plebeians. The tribunes are equally effective with the patricians. Because the patricians are uncertain about the outcome of a widespread plebeian revolt, the tribunes take every advantage of this fear of political chaos in order to drive a wedge between the nobles and Coriolanus. Throughout the entirety of Act III, we see them focusing wholly on the short-term goals of getting rid of their most formidable opponent and of solidifying their recent accumulation of power.

At the end of Act III, the tribunes clearly represent a dangerous challenge to the existing order. Following the armed clash, when the patricians offer to go surety for Coriolanus, and Menenius pleads for due process of law, the patricians, in effect, recognize the tribunes as being the de facto authority of Rome. Volumnia, second only to Coriolanus in her hatred of the plebeians and their representatives, upbraids her son for voicing his anti-plebeian opinions prior to his confirmation. Coriolanus agrees; the tribunes *are* legal officials and they do have the right to question him; but now they have charged him with treason and have sentenced him to banishment; these two acts establish beyond all doubt that they are now the men who will determine the fate of Rome. However, they do not carry their new stature flawlessly, for they reveal weaknesses in themselves which they have condemned in Coriolanus. They exhibited their excessive pride when they interrupted Cominius in midsentence without regard for his social standing in Rome, and they added unnecessary insult to Coriolanus when they ordered the plebeians to hound him to the gates of the city. Caught up in the excitement of the moment, they clearly intend to humiliate their victim.

At the end of Act III, the citizens hail them with "The gods preserve our noble tribunes!" but the phrase is potent with foreshadowing. The tribunes have, in fact, replaced the nobles in real power, and they have succeeded in preventing Coriolanus' confirmation as consul; but they have acted ignobly in using deceit to defeat him, and they have set up a condition in Rome that will jeopardize *all* classes of citizens.

## ACT IV

### Summary

Coriolanus bids farewell to his family, his friends, and several young nobles at the gates of Rome. He consoles his mother and his wife, and he declines an offer by Cominius to accompany him for a month. He promises that they will hear good reports of him, and he leaves. Following his departure, the tribunes disperse the people to avoid further confrontations with the patricians. Along with Menenius and Virgilia, Volumnia approaches and curses the tribunes for banishing her son, who she hopes will revenge himself upon them. Declaring Volumnia to be mad, the tribunes exit. Volumnia grows even more furious as she leaves, escorting Virgilia.

On a highway between Rome and Antium, Nicanor, a Roman spying for the Volscians meets the Volscian Adrian, who is on his way to Rome to search for Nicanor. Nicanor describes the recent insurrection and the banishment of Coriolanus, and he suggests that Aufidius attack while civil strife is still rampant in Rome. Adrian predicts that Aufidius will probably do so, since his army is prepared to move on an hour's notice.

Disguised as a poor man in Antium, Coriolanus learns from a passerby that he is standing in front of Aufidius' house. Considering whether he should use this chance to make enemies of friends and friends of enemies, he enters the house, knowing that he will either be slain by his former enemy or else he will be invited to join him. A servingman asks Coriolanus to leave, and then more servingmen enter and join in an exchange of mild insults with Coriolanus.

A servant leaves and returns with Aufidius, who asks Coriolanus to identify himself, but Aufidius fails to recognize Coriolanus until Coriolanus mentions their battles and blames his banishment on the cowardice of the nobles of Rome. He states his desire to join the Volscians so that both of them can take revenge on Rome. He advises Aufidius either to accept his offer or to kill him, since those are the only options Aufidius has of freeing himself of the shame of defeat. Aufidius welcomes him with an embrace and a promise of friendship. He professes to love Coriolanus more than he loved his wife on their wedding night, and he informs Coriolanus that the Volscian army is waiting in readiness to fight. He invites Coriolanus to speak to several senators who are making preparations to invade Roman territory, he gives him command over half of the Volscian army, and he invites him to decide whether or not they should first attack outlying territory or whether they should attack Rome itself. Coriolanus and Aufidius exit, and two servants consider which man is the more formidable, carefully and comically avoiding absolute statements. Another servant enters with a description of the senators' treatment of Coriolanus and with news that the army will move within hours. The servants talk of the advantages which war has over peace; they clearly welcome the upcoming engagement.

In Rome, Sicinius compliments himself and Brutus for the peace that has followed the banishment of Coriolanus. Menenius enters and argues that matters would be even better if Coriolanus had compromised. Several citizens pass by and pay their regards to the tribunes. An aedile enters to tell them of a "slave's" claim that the Volscians have successfully invaded Roman territory with two armies. Menenius comments that Coriolanus' absence has given Aufidius courage. A messenger reports that the slave's rumor is true, but that the Senate is planning a defense, and that Coriolanus is in command of one of the invading armies. The tribunes insist it can only be a rumor, and Menenius agrees that a reconciliation between Coriolanus and Aufidius is highly unlikely. Another messenger brings news of Volscian victories and of the Senate's desire for the presence of the tribunes.

Cominius enters, blaming the tribunes for all these troubles, and he reports that Coriolanus has indeed joined with Aufidius and that citizens in the invaded regions have either joined the Volscians or have been defeated by them. Menenius hopes that Coriolanus will be merciful, but Cominius does not expect mercy from one who has been treated so inconsiderately. A group of citizens enters, and Menenius curses them for bringing the wrath of Coriolanus upon Rome; they, of course, deny ever really wanting to banish him. Cominius and Menenius leave for the Capitol, followed by the tribunes, after they have tried to calm the confused, frightened citizens.

In a camp near Rome, a lieutenant tells Aufidius that the Volscian soldiers have grown to worship Coriolanus. Aufidius is aware that Coriolanus has behaved proudly, but at this point, Aufidius does not wish to harm the Volscian cause by trying to restrain his new comrade. He admits that Coriolanus has managed his unit of the army well and that he has fought ferociously, but he insinuates "yet he hath left undone" something that will endanger one or the other of them. Aufidius foresees little resistance from Rome, but he is aware that some defect in character has caused Coriolanus' banishment, and he plans to deal with his old enemy—once Rome has been captured.

## Commentary

After the people have derided Coriolanus on his way to the gates of the city as a way of demonstrating their complete victory over him, the tribunes are astute enough to try to heal political wounds by avoiding any further provocation of the patricians. Brutus suggests, "Let us seem humbler after it is done/ Than when it was a-doing." The tribunes smugly believe that they have brought about tranquility and that they have proven the patricians wrong who had feared that chaos would be the result of any further plebeian gains. Sicinius gleefully notes that they now receive even kinder treatment from Menenius, who admits that Coriolanus should have been more temperate.

The people credit the tribunes for bringing peace, but it is not long before they become fickle and blame the tribunes (while absolving themselves) for provoking Coriolanus and the Volscians to lay siege to the city. Sicinius tries to make the best of a bad situation by telling the people that the resulting turmoil pleases the patricians, but his efforts are futile. People in the outlying areas revolt, and it is not long before Cominius and Menenius defend Coriolanus for seeking revenge for wrongs done him by the tribunes, the people, and the nobles who betrayed him. The tribunes panic: at first, they proclaim the news to be a rumor spread by the patricians to frighten the citizens into accepting Coriolanus' return, and they order the aediles to whip the bearer of bad news. Significantly, they willingly relinquish policy making to the Senate.

Volumnia has been devastated by her son's banishment. She accuses the tribunes of inciting the people, and she prays that the working class will be utterly destroyed. When she confronts the tribunes, she commands that they "shall" stay to hear her scorn, and this command echoes Sicinius' earlier "shall," which was directed to Coriolanus. Of course, Volumnia no longer has any actual authority to command them, and her curses are empty, except as an expression of her profound grief.

Coriolanus promises Volumnia that he will either exceed what is expected of him "or be caught/ With cautelous baits and practices," meaning deceitful cunning and trickery. His words are prophetic because he will suffer as a result of his own questionable actions and because of Aufidius' fulfilling his earlier vow to defeat Coriolanus by any means available. Coriolanus evaluates his banishment on strictly personal terms. He can ignore the past rewards from his country, the patriotism he once felt for Rome, his friends, and even his family in his desire to revenge what remains an affront to his character, albeit a very serious one. He complains that Rome has only given him the surname "Coriolanus" in recognition of his extensive service, forgetting that his gaining renown was his and Volumnia's primary goal in life.

It was only when he entered the treacherous labyrinth of democratic politics where he would be judged by standards entirely new to him and by a class of people abhorrent to him that he established goals that could not be achieved by earning an honorable surname or other official acclaim. He now blames his predicament on the people for being envious, the tribunes for being deceitful, the nobles for being cowardly, and his country as a whole for being corrupt. He accepts none of the responsibility himself, and he admits to Aufidius that his desire for revenge is motivated by "mere spite." He philosophizes on the capacity of "chance" to change friends to enemies and enemies to friends, ignoring that he is creating his own circumstances with a willful decision. His alteration from a plain-speaking man to a man willing to join his country's enemies is signified by his appearing in Antium wearing a disguise and by Aufidius' inability to recognize an enemy whom he has fought face to face a dozen times.

The sense of insidiousness that has flowed from the Roman tribunes' practice of deceit and the many spies serving both Rome and the Volscians continues as a dominant theme with the exchange between Nicanor and Adrian and with Aufidius' resolve to ultimately bring down Coriolanus. Aufidius initially accepts Coriolanus enthusiastically as a fellow warrior, one whose wrongs he is eager to help revenge, but he mistakenly gives him too much authority over the Volscian army and the strategy to be used against Rome, a mistake quickly realized by Aufidius' servants. Like the Roman nobles who revere Coriolanus for embodying traditional values more than they love him as a personal friend, Aufidius addresses him as "Thou noble thing," and his attitude toward him quickly grows more distant. He realizes that he has misjudged Coriolanus, that either pride, poor judgment, or an inability to adjust from war to peace has caused the Roman people to fear and to banish him.

Following the battles at Corioli, Aufidius swore he would use even dishonorable means to defeat his enemy, and he plans to follow that resolve, but he has allowed Coriolanus to become so essential to the

Volscian army and its campaign that he believes that he must wait until Rome falls before he can act. His conversation with his lieutenant at the end of Act IV counterbalances the preceding scene, and the peril threatening Rome has a parallel in Coriolanus' situation; he will lose regardless of the outcome of the Volscian war with Rome.

## ACT V

### Summary

In Rome, Menenius tells the tribunes that he will not go to plead with Coriolanus, and he suggests that they go instead. Cominius describes Coriolanus' earlier rejection of him on the grounds that Rome is not worth sparing for the few friends whom Coriolanus has there. Menenius, however, takes some comfort in knowing that he and a few others are still in Coriolanus' thoughts. Sicinius pleads for Menenius to intervene. At first, he refuses, but he finally agrees after Sicinius promises that all Romans will appreciate his effort. Thus, he leaves to visit Coriolanus, but Cominius predicts that Menenius will fail because Rome's only real hope lies with Volumnia and Virgilia.

In the Volscian camp, two sentinels stop Menenius and tell him that he may not see Coriolanus. He argues to no avail that he is a special friend of Coriolanus. They answer that the weak pleas of elderly women, virgins, and old dotards such as he cannot be expected to have an effect on the man whom they, the Romans, have banished. They advise him to return prepared to perish with the city, and they refuse his further entreaties with insults and threats. Coriolanus and Aufidius enter then, and Menenius asks Coriolanus, after an elaborate greeting, to spare Rome. Coriolanus tells him to go away because he has only the power to *revenge*; the power to *pardon* lies with Aufidius and the Volscians. He acknowledges their former friendship, but he gives Menenius a prepared letter and asks him again to leave. Coriolanus and Aufidius exit, and the sentinels ridicule Menenius, who leaves for Rome, totally dejected.

Inside his tent, Coriolanus tells Aufidius that they will attack Rome the next day, and he asks that his conduct of the war be reported to the Volscian lords. Aufidius compliments him for being successful and for being loyal to the Volscian cause. Volumnia, young Marcius, Virgilia, and Valeria then arrive to plead for Rome, and Coriolanus finds it very difficult to deny them. He begs forgiveness of Virgilia, but he repeats that he *cannot* forgive Rome. He kneels before his mother, who tells him to rise; then she kneels before him. Coriolanus is touched and speaks lovingly to his wife and son, asking them all not to take his refusal personally. He asks Aufidius to note that he is undertaking no private conversations.

Volumnia says the women and young Marcius are the most unfortunate of people because they will lose regardless of which side wins – should Coriolanus attack – and young Marcius pledges to run away so that he can fight when he is older. Coriolanus starts to leave, but Volumnia reminds him that peace will benefit both parties and that he will be branded a traitor if he continues. She accuses him of never having shown proper appreciation for her role as his mentor and of being dishonorable and unfilial in dismissing her. The women and young Marcius then kneel before him, and Volumnia charges him with being excessively proud; in addition, she calls him a true Volscian. The women and young Marcius then prepare to depart, and Coriolanus capitulates.

Coriolanus tells Volumnia that while she has won a victory for Rome, she has also placed his life in dire jeopardy. He promises Aufidius that he will conclude a just and fair peace, and he asks for Aufidius' advice. Aufidius admits that he has also been moved by Volumnia, but in an aside he confesses that he is happy that Coriolanus has given him a chance to raise his own fortunes. Coriolanus invites the women to drink with him while the treaty is being written, and he suggests that a temple should be built to honor them for their victory for Rome.

In Rome, Menenius tells Sicinius that he has little hope for the women's visit because Coriolanus has devoted himself totally to living as a warrior. But at that moment, a messenger enters, informing them that a mob has captured Brutus and that Brutus will be killed if the women fail. A second messenger enters with news of the women's success, and celebration breaks out. Menenius leaves to welcome the women, and Sicinius is greatly relieved. Two senators escort the ladies through the streets of Rome and proclaim Volumnia as the savior of the city.

In Corioli, Aufidius plans to bring charges against Coriolanus. Some "conspirators" enter and encourage Aufidius to let them murder Coriolanus. Aufidius claims Coriolanus has used flattery to win the favor of the Volscian lords and thereby replace Aufidius as one of the chief military leaders. He also wants to punish Coriolanus for betraying Volscian honor by yielding to the pleas of Volumnia and Virgilia. The conspirators refer to Coriolanus' triumphant return from Rome, to the lack of welcome extended to Aufidius, and to the necessity for Aufidius to kill Coriolanus. The Lords of Corioli enter, and they also agree that Coriolanus has betrayed the Volscian cause.

Coriolanus arrives and proudly announces his success in the war, his capture of spoils, and an honorable peace. Aufidius accuses him of being a traitor and, refusing to honor him any longer with the name of "Coriolanus," he calls him "boy." Enraged, Coriolanus calls Aufidius a liar and a slave, and he asks the lords to proclaim Aufidius a liar. He then challenges the Volscians to kill him, boasting of his feats of Corioli. Aufidius asks if the lords will endure Coriolanus' bragging, and the people shout for his immediate death, but one of the lords judges that Coriolanus deserves a fair hearing.

Coriolanus wishes he were free to fight Aufidius, but before he can act, the conspirators kill him, and Aufidius stands on his body. The lords reproach Aufidius for the murder and the desecration of the body, and Aufidius asks to be allowed to delineate Coriolanus' offenses in the Senate. One of the lords orders an honorable funeral for Coriolanus, and another says that Coriolanus' fiery nature somewhat justifies Aufidius' actions. Somewhat calmed, Aufidius helps carry out the body of Coriolanus in a stately procession through Corioli.

## Commentary

The plebeians of Rome remain consistently inconstant in their allegiances. For example, they rashly capture Brutus and threaten to torture him to death for his role in causing Coriolanus to join the Volscians, and they welcome Volumnia's return after she has managed to stop the Volscian advance on Rome. Their joyous tumult of welcome for her is reminiscent of their welcome of Coriolanus when he returned from the victories at Corioli. The Volscian citizens, likewise, are shown to be as inconstant in their loyalties as are the Roman citizens. Seemingly, fickleness is universal among the lower classes. One of the Volscian citizens advises Aufidius that the people will remain uncommitted until either he or Coriolanus shows clear evidence as to which of them is the prevailing leader; then the people will rally behind the man who seems to be the stronger. They do exactly this. When Aufidius publicly has the endorsement and support of the Volscian lords and when he has Coriolanus on the defensive, the Volscian citizens suddenly remember that the man whom they have recently welcomed among them is the same man who slaughtered their cousins, sons, wives, and fathers in the past.

Coriolanus, in contrast, has remained constant – especially in his contempt for the plebeian class, and he still feels strongly that revenge is the best way to satisfy a personal affront, but Coriolanus has affected a regal bearing that reflects both his insecurity and his pride. He tells Volumnia, for instance, that he will never capitulate to "Rome's mechanics"; on the other hand, however, he is ready, if necessary, to sacrifice his family and friends, whom he refers to unemotionally as "one poor grain or two," in order to gain his revenge. His rejection of basic human compassion is further emphasized when he vows to be ungrateful rather than merciful and when he rebuffs Menenius, who has appealed to him as a "son." The Volscian guards believe that nothing can shake their new general's resolve to defeat Rome.

It is Volumnia who ultimately is able to change Coriolanus' resolves; first, she falls on her knees before him; the mentor has become suppliant.

Volumnia then confronts her son with a subtle argument, the type which Coriolanus is least prepared to resist. She shifts the blame away from Rome and away from its nobility and places it upon him. If he rejects her arguments, she claims it will be because of his "hardness" and not because justice is on his side. Echoing Menenius' figurative rhetoric, she blames Coriolanus for desiring a war which will tear "his country's bowels out." She reminds him that his family and friends have been placed in the unenviable position of being losers—no matter which side wins; they will either see their country devastated or else they will see a loved one beaten and dishonored. Furthermore, she tells him that his past renown will be forgotten and that he will be branded a traitor forever. She ridicules him for wanting to act like a god, she accuses him again of being too proud, and she even charges him for neglecting to show proper gratitude and courtesy to her in the past—a charge obviously not consistent with previous events in the play. Ironically, she asks the son whom she has trained to be the superior warrior to become a peacemaker. Then, after she wins his consent, the irony is compounded when Coriolanus' role of peacemaker leads directly to his slaughter by Aufidius, who previously failed to defeat Coriolanus in combat. Coriolanus' last hopes are for his son; he hopes that young Marcius will follow in his footsteps, but only as a warrior—not as a politician. His experiences have confirmed his belief that war and warriors are noble, but that peace and politicians are ignoble.

Before Aufidius kills Coriolanus, he notes that Coriolanus is not "subtle"—that is, Coriolanus is not wily; thus Aufidius can defeat his old enemy in any way he can. Coriolanus does not have the insight to realize that Aufidius is working to turn the Volscian people and nobles against him. Aufidius' most decisive act in arousing Coriolanus' ire occurs when he provokes Coriolanus by calling him a traitor, a "boy of tears," and refusing to refer to him by his honorary title "Coriolanus." Coriolanus flares into a rage, offending the Volscian citizens and giving Aufidius a chance to claim that he had no alternative, that he was forced into having the conspirators murder Coriolanus. In fact, Aufidius carefully manipulates events so that Coriolanus will appear dangerous; then Aufidius arouses the people and then, to satisfy his own envious and resentful drive for revenge, he defeats Coriolanus—decisively and finally. Significantly, it is Coriolanus' pride and sense of social rank which dominates his life and interferes with his ability to function effectively when he is not on the battlefield. It is dramatically fitting that these factors should contribute to his death.

1607

# timon
# of athens

# A BRIEF SYNOPSIS

The drama begins as a crowd of people—a merchant, a painter, a poet, a jeweler, and others—awaits the arrival of the rich and generous Lord Timon. Timon enters, and he is everything we expected to see; he is exceedingly gracious and he is also exceedingly generous. Everyone *seems* to hang onto his every word—and *does* accept every gift which Timon dispenses freely. Two key incidents occur in the midst of this massive outpouring of feigned affection, however, which are inserted to impress upon us that Timon is generous—to a fault. The first incident occurs when he reassures a worried messenger that the debts of Ventidius, a friend of Timon's, will be paid; therefore, Ventidius will be released from prison. The other incident occurs when one of Timon's many "friends" makes an entrance. Unlike the rest of Timon's fawning flatterers, however, Apemantus is no materialistic parasite. He attends Timon's gatherings in order to feed his disgust for the rampant fraud which he sees Timon surrounded by. Apemantus has a sharp tongue, a keen wit, and an open hatred for most of mankind. He mocks Timon's guests, calling them liars and knaves, but the naive Timon is so generous with his time and his hospitality that he is able to overlook Apemantus' "bad manners," and he treats him simply as another guest and hopes that his friends will also overlook Apemantus' bad temper.

After Ventidius is released from prison, he attends a great feast at Timon's house and tries to repay him with some money from a large fortune that he has just inherited, but Timon refuses the money. His assistance was a gift—not a loan. Flavius, Timon's steward, tries repeatedly to curb Timon's rash generosity, as does Apemantus—with different tactics, of course. Apemantus, for example, refuses all money and all gifts offered to him by Timon; in this way, he can feel free to banter and bitterly denounce Timon for his senseless philanthropy.

Matters change, however, when Timon realizes that his coffers are empty and that debtors are at his door. Flavius does his best to pacify and turn away the crowd of creditors, but he fails—as does Timon. And finally Timon admits to Flavius that his "flaw" lies in his irrational generosity: "Unwisely, not ignobly, have I given." But he fiercely denies what Flavius fears—that Timon's friends will desert him, now that *he* needs loans. Thus he sends his servants, in turn, to Lucius, to Lucullus, and to Sempronius to ask each of them for money. In each case, his servants return empty-handed, and in each case, Timon's former "friends" are haughty in their refusal to lend money to Timon.

Timon's house continues to be besieged with creditors and their servants. Flavius quits his post, and Timon appears and tells them all that they can cut his "heart to sums" and "count out his blood," he is broke. Yet Timon suddenly has an idea. He tells Flavius to go quickly and invite all of his "friends" to a grand banquet. Flavius agrees to do so, but he is frankly puzzled; he knows that there is no money nor is there any food in the house.

In the meantime, one of Timon's friends, Alcibiades, pleads in the Athenian Senate for mercy for one of his friends who murdered not "with cowardice [but with] honor [and] with a noble fury." The senators are not impressed, and they refuse Alcibiades' pleas and exile him because he tried "to make an ugly deed look fair," and because he made them angry. Alcibiades accepts the judgment of banishment but privately vows revenge on Athens by waging war on the city.

When Timon's "friends" have gathered merrily around the banquet table, Timon offers grace and thanks to the gods, and, in his prayers, he slowly reveals the depths of his fierce hatred for all of those assembled around him. These men, he says, are suitable for one thing only—destruction. With a flourish, he uncovers the silver dishes and commands the men to eat: "Dogs," he rails at them, "lap!" The guests are dumbfounded; the dishes contain only warm water. Releasing all of his pent-up fury, Timon seizes the dishes and flings them at his guests. This is his "last supper," and he hopes, sarcastically, that it washes off some of his so-called friends' "reeking vanity."

The lords flee from Timon's house and Timon leaves also. He has decided to become a hermit. He finds a cave in a woods near the seashore and lives there for a time with no companionship; he exists on roots and enjoys the quietude of nature. One day, however, he discovers a great cache of gold; he hides it, and not long afterward, Alcibiades happens upon Timon. He does not recognize him at first, but after he does, he asks if he can help Timon. Timon, of course, refuses. Instead, he offers gold to Alcibiades in order to help him destroy Athens. Alcibiades accepts the gold and promises to return.

Apemantus enters and chides Timon for playing at being a misanthrope. Apemantus admits that he himself is a true misanthrope, but he says that Timon is incapable of being a true misanthrope. The two men argue and finally engage in a rock-throwing fight before Apemantus flees. Shortly thereafter, several thieves enter and ask for Timon's gold; Timon gives it to them, and it is then that Flavius appears. He is appalled at Timon's appearance. Timon recognizes Flavius' genuine concern, and his facade of misanthropy crumbles. Afraid, ashamed, and embarrassed, he flees, pleading with Flavius to flee also—from him and from mankind.

The play ends with Timon's refusing two Athenian senators who have come to ask for Timon's help in defending the city. He is bitter in his refusal; he hopes with all his heart that Alcibiades is successful. Later, a soldier finds a crudely fashioned grave; it belongs to Timon. Obviously, he found someone to bury him, or else he was murdered and buried.

Back in Athens, the Senate pleads for mercy from Alcibiades. He relents—finally—and agrees to kill only Timon's "friends" and his own. The soldier who has found Timon's grave reports what he has found, and Alcibiades reads the epitaph. Then he grieves for the noble, misunderstood Timon, vowing to marry, for Timon's sake, "the olive with [his] sword" and "make war breed peace."

# LIST OF CHARACTERS

## Timon

An Athenian lord and a former military leader. He is very generous to his friends while he is wealthy, but those same friends refuse to assist him when he becomes bankrupt as a result of his irresponsible generosity. Disillusioned with humanity, Timon leaves Athens to live in a cave in the woods, where he discovers a large cache of gold. He gives gold to Alcibiades to help finance the army threatening Athens, and he gives gold to all whom he meets in the belief that it will further corrupt their already degenerate natures. He dies in the woods, and he is buried (by whom, we never know) in a grave by the sea.

## Lucius

An Athenian lord and a "friend" of Timon's. He sends Timon a gift of four richly harnessed horses when Timon is still supposedly wealthy, but Lucius pretends to be without funds when Timon requests a loan from him.

## Lucullus

An Athenian lord and a "friend" of Timon's who sends a gift of four greyhounds when Timon is still believed to be rich, but, like Lucius, he refuses to loan Timon some money when Timon is in need.

## Sempronius

Another Athenian lord who refuses to loan Timon money because he is "affronted" that Timon has insulted him by requesting loans from other lords before approaching him.

## Ventidius

An Athenian lord and another "friend" of Timon's. When Ventidius is imprisoned because of debts, Timon gives him enough money to pay off his creditors and thereby gain his freedom. During Timon's theoretically solvent period, Ventidius offers to repay his old friend with money he has inherited. Timon refuses to accept the money; later, when Timon is greatly in need of funds, he asks Ventidius for some money, but Ventidius refuses the request, proving that he is the most ungrateful of all the men whom Timon has befriended.

## Alcibiades

The commander of the Athenian army and a friend of Timon's. When the Senate rejects his plea to spare the life of a friend of his who has been condemned to death for murder, Alcibiades decides to use his army to conquer Athens in revenge. He meets Timon in the woods, and Timon gives him some gold, hoping that Alcibiades will decimate the city. Alcibiades, however, enters the city (at the conclusion of the play) with plans to establish a government built on honorable principles.

## Apemantus

An extremely cynical misanthrope. He is the only person who does not flatter or lie to Timon while it is believed that Timon is a very prosperous man. Timon, at first, rejects Apemantus' vile opinion of human nature, but after his monetary reversal, Timon adopts a similar attitude himself and goes to live alone in the woods. Significantly, Timon gains a measure of satisfaction by believing that despite his poverty, he is still superior to Apemantus as a human being.

## A Poet and a Painter

These two men call on Timon when he is still thought to be prosperous and present him with their works, of which he is the chief subject. They hope to please him so much that he will feel obligated to become their patron. After learning that Timon is again rich, they visit him in the woods. He curses them for being villains, but he gives them gold and beats them as they leave.

## Flavius

Timon's honest steward. He tries to tell Timon that his resources are rapidly being depleted and that Timon should cease his reckless spending, but Timon refuses to listen to him. Flavius shares his meager supply of money with Timon's other servants after their master has left Athens.

Later, he visits Timon in the woods and offers to be his servant in adversity; it is then that Timon becomes convinced that Flavius is the only honest man alive.

### Flaminius

Another of Timon's servants; he calls on Lord Lucullus to request a loan for his master, Timon. Lucullus attempts to bribe Flaminius to tell Timon he could not be located, but Flaminius refuses and continues to be faithful as long as he remains in Timon's service.

### Lucilius

Another servant of Timon's. Timon befriends him by giving him enough money to make him an acceptable son-in-law to the rich father of the young woman whom he loves.

### Servilius

Another servant of Timon's; he unsuccessfully solicits Lord Lucius for a loan, but remains faithful to Timon until the servants disperse, following Timon's departure from Athens.

### Caphis

A servant of an Athenian senator who realizes that Timon is financially irresponsible. The senator sends Caphis to Timon's house to plead with Timon to pay his debts, but by then all of Timon's fortune is exhausted.

### Philotus, Titus, and Hortensius

Servants of Timon's creditors; they call on Timon with requests for money for their masters.

### Phrynia and Timandra

Two harlots accompanying Alcibiades when he finds Timon in the woods. Timon gives them gold and encourages them to remain prostitutes so that they will continue to corrupt youth and spread diseases.

## CRITICAL COMMENTARIES

### ACT I

*Timon of Athens*, for reasons that remain unknown, is an unfinished play. It was probably not acted in Shakespeare's lifetime, and it appeared first in print in the collected edition of Shakespeare's plays, which was published in 1623, over seven years following his death.

The play opens in a hall in Timon's house in Athens. A poet, a painter, a jeweler, a merchant, and others enter and wait for an audience with Timon, a noble Athenian famed for his generosity. The poet and the painter strike up a conversation in which they agree that the matters of the world are growing worse, and the poet comments on the power of Timon's generosity to draw an audience. Attention shifts momentarily to the jeweler, who tells the merchant that he has a fine jewel which he hopes to sell to Timon. The poet then recites some of his verses, and the painter asks if he is currently absorbed in creative concentration on a poem intended for Timon. The poet contends that his poems grow out of an inspiration which feeds upon itself, not from a conscious effort to create. He adds that he will publish his book shortly after Timon sees it, indicating that he is here to seek Timon as a patron. The painter then shows the poet a portrait of Timon which he is carrying with him, and the poet praises it lavishly for being even more realistic than life. The painter, feigning modesty, agrees that it is a good representation.

Some Athenian senators pass through the hall as they leave Timon's chambers, and the poet remarks that they are "happy men" because they have access to Timon. He then describes his poem briefly. It is an allegory in which the goddess Fortune once favored Timon above all other men but, without warning or reason, abandoned him to a friendless misfortune; as such, it presents in miniature the main dramatic theme of the play. The poet asserts that the moral to be drawn from his "rough work" is applicable to a wide range of people and is not intended to injure any specific person. The painter asks for a more complete explanation. The poet replies that because Timon is acknowledged to be a good and generous man, he is fawned upon by people of all social stations and temperaments, from deceitful commoners to solemn noblemen, from false flatterers to the cynic Apemantus, who rants about self-hatred, but who nevertheless enjoys the attention which Timon bestows on him.

In his fable, the poet has placed the goddess Fortune on the top of a hill, and at the base of the hill is a group of men of all types and social ranks, all seeking financial gain. Fortune looks with the most approval upon Timon, whose grace and nobility are so apparent that all who are with him appear to be servants and slaves by comparison, and she motions for him to climb the hill.

The painter interrupts to say that the poet's conception has a parallel in their own endeavor to gain Timon's patronage. The poet listens to the comment, then continues: when Timon begins to mount the hill, the other people, including some of even higher social status than he, begin to follow him with flattering compliments, referring to him in godlike terms, even blessing him for the air which they breath. However, when Fortune casts Timon backward down the hill, none of the people return with him nor offer him assistance. The painter says that the poet's story is consistent with human nature, but he argues that he could create a thousand paintings depicting the reverses of Fortune even better. He does, however, compliment the poet for presenting Timon as a man who, like everyone, is subject to the caprices of Fortune.

Accompanied by a messenger from Lord Ventidius, his own servant Lucilius, and other servants, Lord Timon enters and speaks courteously to everyone present. The messenger reports that Ventidius has been imprisoned for a large debt and that he deeply hopes that Timon can pay off his creditors. Timon declares that he is not a man to abandon a friend in need, and he agrees to pay Ventidius' debts. He instructs the messenger to have Ventidius come to him after being freed to receive more money if he needs it.

The messenger exits, and an old Athenian enters and entreats Timon to forbid Timon's servant Lucilius from courting the old man's daughter. The old man argues that Lucilius is too poor to be either an acceptable husband for his expensively educated daughter or a deserving inheritor of his great estate. Timon argues that Lucilius is honest, but the old man maintains that honesty alone is not enough to gain his consent for a marriage. Timon asks whether or not the old man's daughter loves Lucilius; the old man answers that the girl is too inexperienced to understand her own passions. Timon then asks Lucilius if he loves the girl, and Lucilius replies that he loves her with her approval. The old man insists that he will dispossess his daughter should she marry against his will, but he answers Timon that he is prepared to give his daughter an immediate dowry and make her sole inheritor of his wealth and property if she marries a man of wealth equal to her own. At that point, Timon promises to match the father's dowry and legacy with equal gifts to Lucilius, and the father then agrees that the young people may marry with his consent. Lucilius thanks Timon profusely and swears that he will be in his debt for all that he may ever possess. Timon's dealings with Ventidius and Lucilius demonstrate that he is simultaneously both genuinely generous and extravagantly irresponsible in dispensing his wealth.

After Lucilius and the old man leave, the poet gives his manuscript and the painter his portrait to Timon. Timon praises the painting for its representation of the ideal inner nature of man, which he finds more pleasing than the actual outward countenances that experience in the corrupt, real world has forced men to adopt. He promises to reward the painter for the gift. He then accepts a jewel from the jeweler for approval, but he says that it has been appraised so highly that he cannot afford to buy it. The jeweler insists that the advertised value is correct, but he adds that objects gain or lose true value according to their owners, and he contends that Timon will enhance the value of the jewel by wearing it. Timon compliments the jeweler on his ability to flatter, but the merchant assures Timon that the jeweler is only repeating what everyone says about him.

Apemantus enters, and Timon asks those soliciting him if they are ready to be chided. The jeweler and the merchant reply that they are willing to endure Apemantus' churlishness if Timon can endure it. Timon ironically greets "gentle" Apemantus, and Apemantus snarls that he will become "gentle" only when Timon becomes a dog and the "knaves" present become honest. (There are many references to dogs in the play, and one reason for this is that Apemantus is a cynic, and Timon, after his rejection by his false friends, becomes a cynic; significantly, the word "cynic" is derived from the Greek "kynikos," meaning "doglike.") Apemantus declares that those presently soliciting Timon, and in fact all Athenians, are dishonest scoundrels.

Timon asks Apemantus if he is not proud, and Apemantus retorts in terms that will be reflected later by Timon: "Of nothing so much as that I am not like Timon." Apemantus then ridicules both the painting and the painter, and he answers Timon's request to join him for a meal with this biting comment: "No; I eat not lords," implying that all the others present are parasites, gathered here to gain at Timon's expense. Timon jokingly says that eating lords would anger the ladies, and Apemantus returns the banter by referring to ladies who get pregnant by eating lords. The two men continue to exchange wordplay with sexual connotations, and then Apemantus turns and dismisses the jewel as worthless and chides the poet for answering to his salutation of "poet" and for claiming to be that which he is not. Apemantus claims that Timon is worthy of the poem, however, because those who accept flattery deserve to be misled by flatterers. He then exclaims, "Heavens, that I were a lord!" And he answers Timon's inquiry as to what he would do—if he were a lord—by asserting that he would hate himself for having no more sense than to desire to be a lord. Then, discovering that he has neglected to insult the merchant, Apemantus curses the fellow for being a slave to trade.

A trumpet sounds, and a messenger enters to announce the arrival of Alcibiades and a company of twenty soldiers. Timon tells the messenger to escort them in, and he entreats the solicitors to remain to dine with him. Apemantus prays that their joints will be wracked with pain, and he ridicules the excessive courtesy customarily expressed by scoundrels who detest each other. He ends with the observation that mankind has degenerated into a race of baboons and monkeys. Timon and Alcibiades greet each other, and all but Apemantus leave the hall.

Two lords enter, and Apemantus accuses them of being dishonest, but he agrees to go to Timon's feast so that he can "see meat fill knaves and wine heat fools." The Second Lord says farewell to Apemantus twice, and Apemantus calls him a fool to "waste" a farewell since he, Apemantus, will not give one in return. Apemantus then leaves, trading curses with the lords. The First Lord suggests that they attend Timon's feast, and the Second Lord observes that Timon is more extravagant than Plutus, the god of gold, never accepting a gift without rewarding the giver seven times over – an insight into Timon's behavior that a senator will elaborate on further at the beginning of Act II. Agreeing that Timon is the most noble-minded man who has ever lived, they leave to join the feast.

Scene 2 is set in a banqueting room, where Timon, Alcibiades, Ventidius, several nobles, and Apemantus enter to enjoy a lavish meal. Ventidius, newly released from prison, informs them that his father has died, leaving him a very large inheritance. He offers to repay his debt to Timon, but Timon refuses, insisting that he intended for the money to be considered a gift, not a loan. Ventidius thanks him, and Timon postulates that courtesy was invented to accompany *in*sincere acts of generosity; true acts of friendship need no accompaniment. He declares that he would rather share his wealth with those present than keep it to himself. A lord "confesses" that they have long known and spoken of Timon's liberality, eliciting a curse from Apemantus, because of the word "confess." Timon tells Apemantus that he is welcome, but Apemantus says that Timon will have to throw him out for what he will say later.

Timon accuses Apemantus of having an especially rude manner and of belying the old saying "anger is a brief madness" because Apemantus is *always* angry. Timon then calls for a separate table to be set for Apemantus, but Apemantus asks to remain at Timon's table where he can comment more pointedly on the activity. Timon again tries to soothe Apemantus by welcoming him as an Athenian, and he hopes that the food will silence him.

Apemantus rejects the food, asserting that he will never flatter Timon and lamenting that Timon encourages so many men to take advantage of his generosity. He questions why wealthy men dare to dine with men holding knives, since the wealthy are always in danger from false friends. He ends his brief tirade by advising the wealthy to wear more armor on their throats when dining in company. Timon proposes a toast to health, and a lord asks to second it, again eliciting a curse from Apemantus; he criticizes the lord for using flattery and chides Timon for letting his estate be eaten up by irresponsible extravagance. Apemantus then raises a toast of water and offers a grace, in which he prays for nothing nor for no man but himself. He prays that he will trust no man, even a supposed friend, and he concludes with the observation that he will avoid the rich man's gluttony and will, instead, eat roots.

Timon shifts attention away from Apemantus by turning to Alcibiades and asking him if battle is not preferable to the banquet table. Alcibiades answers in the affirmative, and Apemantus interjects a wish that the flatterers around Timon were Alcibiades' enemies in the field so that he could kill them. A lord requests that Timon give his friends an opportunity to express their great friendship for him, a speech which will prove to be ironic in light of later events.

Timon answers with a short speech on friendship, and he assures these men present, his particularly close friends, that the gods will provide means for them to express their friendship. He believes friends are like unused musical instruments if others do not call on them when in need, and he believes that people should consider their friends' property their own. He then falls to joyous weeping because he is blessed by being among so many worthy friends who are willing to share each other's fortunes. A lord proclaims that the same joy has brought the guests to tears, and Apemantus derides Timon for weeping only to solicit more flattery and mocks the lord for lying.

A trumpet sounds, and a servant enters to inform Timon that a group of ladies and their "forerunner" have arrived and their desire is to enter (they turn out to be entertainers provided by the guests). Timon bids them enter. The forerunner, an actor dressed as Cupid, salutes Timon and his guests. He announces that the five human senses, in recognition of Timon as their chief benefactor, have come to entertain him. Timon welcomes them and calls for music, as a lord tells him that the provision of the masque demonstrates how much his friends love him.

Cupid returns with a group of women dressed as Amazon warriors, playing stringed instruments and dancing before the diners. Apemantus is overjoyed by the vain extravagance of the display and enters into a diatribe comparing the "insane" dance to the insanity of life in general and especially to the insanity of Timon's feast. He maintains that men make fools of themselves in order to prosper by flattery, but that, in the end, men become only spiteful and envious. He asks if there is anyone alive who is not depraved, or if there is anyone who has died who truly appreciated a gift from a friend.

The lords rise, display an exaggerated affection for Timon, and dance with the Amazons. At the end of the dance, Timon thanks the ladies for their performance and thanks his guests for providing the entertainment. Apemantus suspects that exacting discourse would label the ladies for what they are – harlots. Timon ignores the comment and tells the women to partake of the banquet. They thank him and, along with Cupid, exit.

Timon asks his steward, Flavius, to bring in his jewel case. In an aside, Flavius regrets that he cannot stop Timon from giving away all he owns, and he speculates that before long, Timon's irresponsible generosity will lead him into debt. While Flavius is gone, the lords put on a show of pretending that they are in a great bustle to leave. Timon takes his jewels and pleads with one of the lords to accept a jewel, and in unison the lords acknowledge their indebtedness to Timon for earlier gifts.

A servant enters to announce the arrival of several senators, and Timon sends his welcome. Flavius tries to draw Timon aside to explain that his master's wealth is rapidly running out, but Timon puts him off until after he has received and entertained his new guests. Another servant enters to report that Lord Lucius has sent four horses harnessed in silver as a gift for Timon. Timon accepts the gift and commands that gifts be bestowed on his guests. A third servant enters to bring word that Lord Lucullus has sent Timon four greyhounds and an invitation to go hunting on the following day. Timon accepts and orders that the servant be generously rewarded.

In an aside, Flavius anguishes over Timon's continuous spending and his refusal to acknowledge his impending ruin. Flavius knows that Timon has no money left and that his present expenses are driving him deeper into debt and into the necessity of mortgaging his lands to those who are even now benefiting from his bounty. He states proverbially that a man is better off with no friends than with friends who do more harm to him than his enemies do. With a deepening sadness, he exits.

Timon accuses the lords of unjustly undervaluing their merits, and he continues to pass out gifts, to which the lords respond with flowery thanks. Timon gives one of his horses to a lord who praised it a few days earlier. The lord acts as though he will decline it, but Timon insists, promising that he will ask the lord for assistance one day. In unison, the lords assert that they would welcome a request from Timon. Timon wishes that he had kingdoms to reward the lords who please him so much with their visits. He tells Alcibiades that since he is a soldier of little means, he must interpret Timon's gift as having been motivated solely by friendship. Timon and the lords thank each other for their mutual generosity, of which Timon's has been significantly greater. Timon then calls for lights, and after the lords exit, Timon and Apemantus are left alone.

Apemantus mocks the exaggerated gestures of courtesy made by the departing lords. He curses them for being dishonest and comments that "honest fools," of which Timon is one, will willingly exchange money for such courtesies. Timon says that he would be good to Apemantus if he were not so obstinate, but Apemantus insists that he alone – of Timon's friends – refuses to be bribed. One man, says Apemantus, must be left to point out Timon's error and to curb his wasteful spending. Otherwise, Timon will soon give away all he has on useless ostentation. Timon refuses to listen any longer and leaves. Alone, Apemantus threatens not to advise Timon later if he will not listen now, but he laments that Timon, who is so susceptible to flattery, steadfastly refuses to listen to sound advice.

## ACT II

The first scene of this act puts into dramatic motion the events that Flavius foresaw at the banquet. In Athens, a senator is at home, examining records of Timon's debts to him, and he affirms for us that Timon is still carelessly giving his money away even though he is deeply in debt. The senator says that if he himself should need money, he would only have to steal a beggar's dog and give it to Timon to get gold, or give a horse to Timon to get enough money in return to buy twenty better horses. He can see nothing but disaster for Timon in the future. He calls his servant Caphis and instructs him to go to Timon and to insist that he be paid what is due the senator, taking care not to be put off by pleasantries but to demand the money and say that the senator's credit is being damaged because Timon's repayment is past due. He realizes that when all demands have been met, Timon will be completely broke. The senator's final instructions to Caphis include a command to collect all *interest* due on the loans as well, demonstrating that Timon's creditors will be relentless toward Timon now that they have no more to gain from his generosity.

In the next scene, Timon finally realizes the full extent of his financial problems, and he begins to suspect the true nature of man. In a hall in Timon's house, Flavius is studying a large number of bills from Timon's creditors, all demanding payment. He is frustrated because Timon will neither cease his exorbitant giving nor will he take the time to understand the reality of his situation. Flavius resolves to force Timon to listen as soon as he returns from hunting. Caphis, along with a servant of Isidore and a servant of Varro enter, and they learn from each other that all have been sent by their masters to collect from Timon. However, none of them actually expects to receive payment.

Timon, several lords who have accompanied him on the hunt, and Alcibiades enter, and Timon announces that they will resume the hunt after they have eaten. Caphis approaches Timon, but Timon refers him to his steward. Caphis retorts that Flavius has put him off repeatedly before and that his master is now in desperate need of money and expects Timon to follow his noble precepts and to pay immediately. Timon asks Caphis to return the next morning. The servants of Varro and Isidore rush to present their bills to Timon, and Caphis joins them in pleading for payment. Timon asks them all to excuse him for a moment, and he asks Flavius why so many people are accosting him for money. Flavius begs the departing servants to hold off their demands until after dinner and after he has talked to Timon; he and Timon then exit.

Apemantus and a jester, on an errand for a harlot, enter. Caphis thinks that it would be great sport to tease them, and the other servants agree, although apprehensively. Apemantus and the jester exchange insults immediately with the servants, each calling the others fools. The jester claims that the servants will soon become infected with venereal disease, and he derides them for not being able to afford his mistress' prices. A page of the jester's mistress enters and greets the jester and Apemantus, who remarks that a whipping is the only appropriate answer for the page. The illiterate page asks Apemantus to read the addresses for two letters which he has been sent to deliver, and Apemantus tells him that they are for Timon and Alcibiades; after a further exchange of banter, the page exits, and Apemantus offers to accompany the jester to see Timon.

The two men joke about serving usurers, with overt sexual connotations involving the jester's mistress' use of her body to make money. The jester wonders why men who visit usurers leave happy while men who visit their mistresses leave sad. Varro's servant offers an answer, then asks what is a "whoremaster"—that is, what is someone who frequents prostitutes? The jester answers that a whoremaster can be someone like Varro's servant or someone like a lord, a lawyer, a philosopher, a knight—or any male from fourteen to eighty. Varro's servant compliments the jester for not being a complete fool, and the jester compliments the servant for not being completely wise. Apemantus, in turn, compliments the jester for answering with wit that could have been uttered by Apemantus himself.

Timon and Flavius enter, and Apemantus, the jester, and the servants exit. Timon is astounded to realize the seriousness of his financial plight, and he asks why Flavius did not inform him earlier so that he could have lived within his means. Flavius refers to his many attempts, but Timon argues that his steward deliberately approached him at times when he was preoccupied. Flavius points out that Timon has continually escaped studying his accounts by insisting that he trusts his steward. He states further that he has seen Timon returning expensive presents for trifling gifts, and he believes that he overstepped his bounds in the past as steward when he advised Timon emphatically to spend less freely, advice for which Timon reproved him severely.

He then tells Timon that there is not enough money and property left to pay half the debts. Timon orders him to sell land, but Flavius reports that some land has already been sold, some mortgaged, and what remains will not go far toward satisfying Timon's current debts. He questions how the estate can be run and how Timon's affairs can be settled permanently with debts continuing to mount. Timon refers to the vast extent of his former lands, but Flavius reminds his master that had he owned the entire world he would have given it away, and Timon finally accepts his predicament for what it is.

Flavius requests that auditors be called in if Timon suspects mismanagement, swearing that for a long time he has wept to see such excessive waste of food, drink, and entertainment. Timon asks him to say no more, but Flavius calls on the heavens to witness the waste of this very night, and he predicts that those who fawn so effusively upon Timon will abandon him totally when all his wealth is gone. Timon beseeches Flavius to preach no more because he has been unwise, not dishonest, in his spending. He tells the steward to dry his tears; Timon is sure that his friends will freely open their coffers to him if he asks them for loans. Flavius can only hope that Timon's faith will be confirmed.

Timon envisions a blessing in his need since it gives him reason to test his friends, and he calls his servants and sends them to the Lords Lucius, Lucullus, and Sempronius to borrow large sums of money from each. After the servants leave, Flavius questions whether the Lords Lucius and Lucullus, in particular, will respond. Timon tells him to go to the senators of Athens and to ask for an immediate loan. Flavius says that he has already contacted the senators, to no avail, and Timon is astounded. Flavius reports that the senators have refused unanimously, some claiming to be low in funds, others wishing that they could help an honorable friend, still others alleging that Timon's dealings may have been dishonest. But all gave short, ungracious answers and went on with what they said were more important things to be considered. Timon urges Flavius to cheer up since it is only natural for old men to lack generosity. He sends another servant to Ventidius to ask for the return of the money which Timon paid to have him released from jail. Timon instructs Flavius to use the money from Ventidius to pay the most demanding bills and to rest assured that his friends will assist him. Flavius hopes they will repay Timon's generosity with their own; otherwise, people will cease to be generous.

## ACT III

Timon's servant Flaminius enters the house of Lord Lucullus, and Lucullus, in an aside, expresses joy at seeing him because he is sure that Flaminius has come to deliver an expensive gift from Timon. He sends for wine and asks about Timon's health. Flaminius reports his master is well, and Lucullus asks with exaggerated politeness what he is carrying beneath his cloak. Flaminius answers that it is an empty box—which Timon is sure that Lucullus will fill with money. Lucullus immediately insults Timon for expecting money from him after spending so lavishly on entertainments. Lucullus ironically recounts his dining with Timon for the express purpose of counseling his friend to spend less, but Timon would not heed his warning.

A servant brings wine, and Lucullus hands Flaminius a cup, offering a toast and flattering him for the wisdom which he has displayed so often. Leading up to an attempt to bribe Flaminius, Lucullus continues to praise him for his intelligence and industry. He sends his servant out and privately tells Flaminius that he is wise enough to know that this is no time to loan money secured only by friendship, even though Timon has been generous.

Lucullus then offers money to Flaminius to say he could not be located. Flaminius damns Lucullus for being thoroughly unprincipled and hurls the money back at him. Lucullus responds that Flaminius is obviously as great a fool as his master. Angered, Flaminius "prays" that Lucullus will be scalded with molten money and that he will grow sick from the food he has eaten at Timon's and that he will die a lingering death.

In Scene 2, set in a street in Athens, Lord Lucius is speaking of Timon's nobility with three strangers. One of them says that he has heard rumors that Timon is nearing bankruptcy, but Lucius denies such a possibility. Another of them relates the urgent request which Timon sent to Lord Lucullus and Lucullus' subsequent refusal. Lucius protests that he is shamed by Lucullus' action, and, referring to the many gifts which he himself has received, he swears that *he* would not deny a similar request from Timon, even though his own gifts were less expensive than those given to Lucullus. Timon's servant Servilius enters, seeking Lucius, and Lucius greets him with commendations for his "very exquisite" friend Timon. He then interrupts Servilius' statement, "My lord hath sent . . ." to inquire eagerly what Timon has sent, expecting another gift. When Servilius answers that Timon has sent a request for a loan, Lucius declares that such a request is not possible since Timon possesses a fortune. Servilius says that Timon's need could not be considered a fortune, but that it is a need so great and so honest that Servilius must insist on Lucius' honoring the request. Lucius asks if he is serious, and when Servilius answers in the affirmative, Lucius pretends to curse himself for having made an excessive, recent expenditure which left him short of funds. He tells Servilius that these fellows to whom he was talking can attest that he was just about to send for a loan from Timon. He sends his best wishes to Timon, and he also sends his regret that he cannot send the money requested, but he hopes that Timon will continue to think well of him anyway. Servilius leaves, and Lucius tells the strangers that Timon is indeed broke, but that he will probably not make another request from someone (meaning himself) who has denied him once.

After Lucius leaves, one of the strangers states that all flatterers are like Lucius. He says that Timon has been like a father to Lucius, providing money to sustain his credit, to run his estate, and to pay his servants' wages. Yet Lucius has refused to give Timon a sum of money no larger than most charitable men willingly give beggars. The last stranger holds Lucius' behavior to be an offense against religion. Although he himself has received no gifts from Timon, the first man declares that had he been asked, he would have gladly given Timon over half his wealth out of respect for his honor, nobility, and generosity. He quickly demonstrates the falsity of his generous sentiment, however, by saying that experience has taught him that self-interest is more to be valued than conscience.

Scene 3 is set in Sempronius' home in Athens, and Sempronius is telling a servant of Timon's that his master should have first asked for loans from the Lords Lucius, Lucullus, and Ventidius, all of whom owe their estates to Timon. The servant answers that all *have* been approached and *all* have denied Timon. Sempronius seems incredulous that all three lords have refused, but he suddenly realizes how he can refuse as well. He acts as though he is offended that Timon did not come to him first, *he* who was the first man ever befriended by Timon. He contends that people will think him a fool if he sends money now – after being insulted so grievously, and he vows never to loan money to any man who has so dishonored him. Left alone, the servant calls Sempronius a villain, and he theorizes that the devil made an error when he made man deviously cunning because it gave man a capacity for villainy that will eventually make the devil appear good by comparison. Noting that Sempronius has acted with the zeal of a religious fanatic, the servant reveals that Sempronius was Timon's best hope; now, all that Timon can do is trust in the gods. All the doors in Athens have been shut against Timon, and thus he must remain a prisoner in his own house to avoid arrest for nonpayment of his debts.

In Scene 4, in a hall in Timon's house, shortly before nine o'clock in the morning, a group of Timon's creditors' servants have gathered, and they discuss the fact that their missions are all the same – money. Philotus, another servant of a creditor, enters and wonders why Timon has not yet appeared since he customarily arises at seven. Lucius, a usurer's servant, speculates that Timon's days are shorter now because his extravagance has brought him to bankruptcy. Another usurer's servant, Titus, comments on the "strangeness" of Hortensius' master's having sent for money while he still wears jewels given him by Timon. Hortensius admits that he does not like what he is doing since he personally considers ingratitude to be worse than stealing.

The servants are adding up the total amount which they have come to collect when Flaminius enters, and they ask if Timon is ready to meet them. Flaminius answers that Timon is not ready, and he tells them sarcastically that he "knows [they] are too diligent" to leave. Flaminius leaves then, and Flavius walks in with his cloak pulled over his head. The servants recognize him and call to him. He asks what they want, and they answer that they have come for money. Flavius asks why they did not demand money when their "false masters" were enjoying Timon's bounty; he tells them that they are wasting their time now because Timon is broke. The servants refuse to accept this answer, and Flavius agrees that it is inappropriate since it is not *undignified* enough for the servants of scoundrels. He goes on his way, and two servants of Varro remark about their satisfaction in knowing that Flavius is as poor as Timon. Servilius enters, and Titus asks if Timon will answer them. Servilius asks them to come later because ill health is keeping Timon in his room. Lucius' servant observes that many choose seclusion who are not sick, and he suggests that if Timon is ill, he should prepare himself for heaven by paying his debts. Servilius is revolted by the servants' insensitivity.

Flaminius calls from within for Servilius to help him with Timon, who now enters in a rage, questioning why his house has become a prison for him. The creditors' servants rush to present their bills, and Timon angrily encourages them to keep up their assaults on him. He leaves, and Hortensius expresses doubt that the creditors will ever regain their money now that Timon has become insane. All the servants leave, and Timon returns with Flavius. Timon blames the servants for making him so angry that he cannot speak; then he conceives a plan to gain revenge upon his creditors, but he keeps the details to himself. He instructs Flavius to invite Lucius, Lucullus, Sempronius, and his other friends to a feast. When Flavius protests that they cannot afford to provide even a modest meal, Timon says that he and his cook will make adequate provisions.

In Scene 5, Alcibiades appears before the Athenian Senate to plead for a pardon for a friend who killed a man in self-defense and who is now condemned to die. In many ways, his situation parallels Timon's in several ways. Alcibiades is being generous with what he has most of, renown and honor, to benefit a friend. His pleas, however, will be rejected by the elderly senators just as Timon's requests were refused by elderly lords and senators. The "friends" of Timon practice usury; here, Alcibiades accuses the senators of having grown rich on usury while he has remained poor in service to Athens. The Senate will finally be ungracious to a man who has benefited them enormously, just as Timon's "friends" have been ungracious to him. However, Alcibiades readjusts quickly when the Senate banishes him, gaining fortitude from the knowledge that he has the means to right the wrongs done him.

In the Senate House, arguing that mercy encourages crime, a senator adds his approval to a decision that an unnamed man be executed for murder. Alcibiades greets the Senate and speaks on behalf of his friend, the condemned man, one who remains anonymous. He proposes that the greatest virtue of law is pity and that only tyrants use law in a cruel manner. He admits that his friend is guilty of a crime of passion, but he argues that the man is essentially virtuous. He did not kill in a cowardly manner, but fairly and honorably to defend his reputation. He fought his enemy not in a fury of passion, but in a detached anger to defend his honor.

A senator claims Alcibiades' defense is merely a rationalization intended to make a bloody crime appear noble, proper, and valorous. Manslaughter, says the senator, is, in fact, valor misdirected, and it has always been accompanied by arguments involving "sects and factions." The senator then argues that the truly valiant man is one who can endure wrongs dispassionately without becoming angry or seeking revenge. Alcibiades tries to interject a response, but the senator cuts him short, saying that Alcibiades cannot justify heinous crimes by making "gross sins look clear."

Alcibiades then asks permission to speak like a soldier. If the greatest honor and wisdom lie in suffering, he asks, why do men engage in battle rather than allow their enemies to cut their throats while they sleep, and why are women not considered more valiant than soldiers, and, finally, why are bound convicts not considered wiser than their judges? He agrees that cold-blooded murder is abhorrent, but he is defending murder in self-defense since all men are subject to anger. When a senator tells him that he argues in vain, Alcibiades tries a new tactic and refers to the battles in which his friend distinguished himself. A senator responds that the man is well known for his past recklessness and drunkenness in which he allowed his passion to overcome his valor, leading him into violence, out-rageous behavior, and membership in factions. Another senator declares that the death sentence is final.

Alcibiades appeals for the Senate to combine his own service to Athens with that of his friend. He pledges his military reputation and his honor as surety, and he asks that the sentence be commuted to combat duty against the enemies of Athens. A senator warns Alcibiades not to risk anger-ing the Senate by arguing further because the man has committed mur-der and thus must be executed. Alcibiades again pleads that the Senate owes him a debt for the protection he has given it on the battlefield, and he suggests that it is poor memory, brought on by old age, which has caused the senators to be so ungracious to him. In anger, a senator banishes Alci-biades. He responds, "Banish me!/ Banish your dotage! Banish usury,/ That makes the Senate ugly!" One of the senators gives Alcibiades two days to leave Athens, and he orders the immediate execution of Alcibiades' friend.

The senators then file out of the Senate House, and Alcibiades delivers a soliloquy. He prays that the already aged senators will be damned to an even longer life of misery, and he repeats his conviction that he has remained a poor soldier protecting Athens while the senators have grown rich on usury. However, he becomes heartened when he realizes that his command of the army gives him the power to gain revenge. He ends with a declaration that soldiers, like the gods, should endure no wrong.

Scene 6 takes place in the banquet room of Timon's house, where a group of unnamed lords have arrived for a feast. They discuss the requests for money which Timon has made of them lately, and the First Lord says that he hopes Timon's finances are not as bad as his messengers have implied. The Second Lord points out that the present preparations for a feast belie the idea that Timon is broke. Both lords claim to have put off other important engagements in order to attend Timon's banquet, and all the lords express regret for recent events. Timon enters with his attendants and greets the lords with feigned enthusiasm. The lords return the greeting, and the Second Lord compares their devotion to Timon with the swallows that follow summer. In an aside, Timon notes that they also abandon him as quickly in the winter of his adversity. Aloud, he tells the lords to enjoy the music in anticipation of a splendid dinner. The lords apologize for not sending money when he requested it, but Timon acts as though he has dismissed their refusals without a second thought. He calls for food to be brought in, and the lords exclaim that the covered dishes promise a fine, expensive meal indeed. They begin to discuss Alcibiades' banishment, but they agree to delay the subject when Timon invites them to the table.

The lords gather around the table and comment that Timon is still as extravagant as ever. Timon bids them to find their places as quickly as they would rush to kiss their mistresses, and he invites them not to stand on protocol but to begin eating as soon as they wish. However, he radically changes his tone when he begins to say the grace. He asks the gods to be plentiful, but he reminds them to be careful that they save something to give in the future or men will come to despise even them. He also asks the gods to give every man enough so that he will not have to borrow, because men will forsake even the gods should the gods become indebted to men. He prays that men will love food more than the hosts who provide it, that all men will become villains, that all women will become harlots, and that the gods will make preparations to destroy the senators along with the remaining citizens of Athens.

After stating that the worthless guests deserve nothing, he ends his bitter grace by shouting, "Uncover, dogs, and lap!" as his attendants uncover the serving dishes, which are filled with lukewarm water. The lords are amazed. Timon is sure that they will never enjoy a better meal, because "smoke and lukewarm water" are precisely what he thinks they deserve. Promising that this is his final feast, he throws water on the lords and curses them all with long, unpleasant lives. He calls them parasites, fair-weather friends, and obsequious slaves to the well-to-do. Proclaiming that he will lend them money but borrow none, he pelts them with the dishes. He prays that his house will burn and that Athens will sink into the ground, and he leaves, announcing that from this time forward he will hate all mankind. Another group of lords and senators enters and asks the cause of the disturbance. Looking for articles of clothing which they have lost in the melee, the confused guests declare that Timon has gone mad.

## ACT IV

As he leaves Athens, determined to become a hermit, Timon looks back on the walls of the city and vents his anger in a lengthy soliloquy. He prays that the walls will sink into the earth and leave the city defenseless. He hopes for social order and government to break down, for innocent youth to become morally corrupt, for bankruptcy to ruin all creditors, for servants to steal from their masters, and for young men to murder their fathers. He hopes that piety, peace, justice, honesty, domestic peace, sleep, human fellowship, education, manners, crafts, trades, social distinctions, customs, laws, and all other civilized ceremonies will decline into destructive chaos. He hopes that diseases and sicknesses will poison the entire population. He prays for crop failures and he cries out proudly that he takes nothing away from the city but his nakedness; he will live in the woods, and there he expects the most ferocious beast to be more kind to him than men have been. He calls on the gods to damn all Athenians, both inside and outside the city, and he beseeches the gods to increase his hatred for all classes of men. Timon has become a misanthrope.

Scene 2 returns us to Timon's house, where a servant asks Flavius where Timon has gone and what, if anything, has been left to pay the servants; Flavius answers sympathetically that he is as poor as the rest. The servant laments the fall of Timon, who has been left without a single friend to accompany him. Another servant criticizes Timon's former friends for having dismissed him as completely as men customarily bid farewell to the dead. A third servant says that they are still comrades and still wear Timon's livery, but now their strongest bond is their mutual sorrow. He compares himself and the others to sailors abandoning a sinking ship; they must go their separate ways "into this sea of air." Flavius, however, offers to share what money he has, and he proposes that they continue the bond they established by being fellow servants of Timon. The servants at first refuse his money, but when he insists, they partake, embrace, and go their separate ways.

Alone, Flavius reveals his decision to follow Timon. He declares that the misery brought on by wealth should lead all to avoid riches. He sees the irony in Timon's having destroyed himself through acts of goodness, and he wonders if Timon's example will prevent everyone from doing good deeds in the future. He knows that Timon has gone into the woods without food or the means to purchase necessities, but he plans to continue in his service as long as he has any money remaining.

The third scene begins near a cave in a woods, next to the seashore; it is here that Timon has come to live as a misanthrope. He asks the sun to draw infectious vapors from the earth with which to infect mankind. He notes that even an identical twin will scorn a brother who is less fortunate financially; this, he says, is a trait common to human nature. If a beggar becomes wealthy and a senator becomes poor, Timon maintains that the beggar will reap honor, but the senator will reap only contempt. He believes that society is permeated with flattery, causing scholars to be forced to cater to rich fools, and forcing all social intercourse (excepting villainy itself) to accept all sorts of false practices. He swears that he will never again live in the accursed society of mankind, which he hopes will be destroyed. Incensed at the injustice he has suffered, he begins furiously digging for roots and—to his amazement—he discovers a large hoard of gold. He tells the gods that he wants only *roots*, not gold, which can alter every concept and condition of humanity, which can cause murder, inspire widows to remarry, restore the most grievously ill to full health, create and destroy religions, make the accursed blessed, the leper adored, and make thieves into senators. However, he does keep the gold and promises to put it to its proper use. Distant drums announce the approach of an army, and Timon buries the gold, keeping a bit, however, for present use.

Alcibiades and two prostitutes—Phrynia and Timandra—enter. Alcibiades sees Timon and asks him to identify himself. Timon declares he is a "beast," similar to Alcibiades, and he hopes that Alcibiades will become afflicted with cankers for bringing inhumanity into Timon's presence again. Timon then says that his name is Misanthropos, meaning one who hates mankind, and he wishes Alcibiades were a dog so that he could have at least a little affection for him. They admit that they recognize one another, and Timon urges Alcibiades to continue his military profession, but, becoming sarcastic, he says that he has full confidence that Phrynia can cause more destruction as a prostitute than Alcibiades can as a soldier. Phrynia is furious, and she and Timon curse one another, and Alcibiades asks, with concern, what has caused Timon to change so drastically. Timon answers metaphorically that unlike the renewing moon he now lacks "light to give." Alcibiades inquires what he can do to aid Timon, and Timon answers that Alcibiades can follow nature and falsely promise to be a friend. Alcibiades admits to having heard rumors of Timon's condition, and Timon counters that Alcibiades was familiar with his miseries when he was prosperous. Alcibiades refers to that as "a blessed time," and Timon states that it was a time very much like what Alcibiades is experiencing now, accompanied as he is by two harlots; Timon is equating the harlots following Alcibiades to the parasites who once flattered him.

Timon encourages Timandra to continue her profession so that she may infect the young with wealth-destroying diseases, and Alcibiades entreats her to forgive the offensive statements of a madman. He regrets that the financial demands of his campaign against Athens will not allow him to be as generous with his resources as he would like, but he assures Timon that he, himself, is very aware of the fact that Athens has forgotten her indebtedness to Timon for his successful leadership in war and his generosity in peace. Timon interrupts to beg Alcibiades to continue on his march, and Alcibiades expresses renewed friendship and pity for Timon. He even offers Timon some gold, but Timon rejects everything. However, when Alcibiades again alludes to Timon's hatred toward Athens, Timon excitedly calls for confusion to fall first on the Athenians and, second, on Alcibiades. Alcibiades asks why Timon has cursed him, and Timon replies that he does so because Alcibiades will conquer his country by killing villains. He then tells Alcibiades to keep his gold, and he gives him more, hoping that it will assist him to visit Athens like a plague, sparing neither the elderly, mothers, virgins, babes, nor priests because all are inwardly evil. Alcibiades takes the gold but rejects the advice; Timon states he does not care what Alcibiades does and curses him in any event.

Phrynia and Timandra, greedy at the sight of Alcibiades' gift, also ask for gold. Timon brags that he has enough to make a whore either give up her trade or become the madam of her own brothel, and he orders them to hold up their aprons to receive the gold. He is confident that the two whores will continue to spread diseases even though they themselves may have to resort to wearing wigs to disguise venereal disease-induced baldness. He concludes by shouting for them to remain whores until the time when they must use so much makeup that a horse will mire down in it. The women respond only by asking for more gold, admitting that they will do anything for it. Timon continues to curse the harlots, telling them to spread corruption, to destroy the lawyer's false-pleading voice, to give leprosy to the false priests, to rot the noses of those who abandon duty for personal gain, to make pimps bald, to infect cowardly soldiers, and, in summation, he charges them to infect the whole of Athens, giving them even more gold as he damns them. The women ask for more advice— so long as he accompanies it with money—and Timon promises to give them even more after they have done their "mischief."

Alcibiades calls for his drummer to signal the resumption of the march to Athens, and he promises to visit Timon again if he is successful. Timon hopes never to see Alcibiades again. Alcibiades insists he has never harmed Timon, but Timon disagrees, maintaining that Alcibiades has spoken well of him, a thing which men daily find to be harmful. Alcibiades, his army, and the two women leave, and Timon resumes his digging for roots. He prays that mother earth, who provides for all and who is responsible for the creation of all animal life, will yield one poor "root" who is universally hated. He beseeches the earth to cease producing ungrateful men and to produce only fierce animals and "new monsters." After suddenly coming upon a root and giving thanks to the earth, he asks nature to dry up the fruit, vines, and pasturelands which provide the produce which ungrateful men use for their own corruption.

Apemantus enters, causing Timon to curse the presence of another man. Apemantus has come to confirm a rumor that states that Timon has started to act like Apemantus. Timon attributes his behavior to Apemantus' not having a dog he can imitate. Apemantus blames Timon's alteration on depression, caused by his change of fortune, and he asks Timon why he lives as he does while the flatterers who have forgotten him live in splendor.

He tells Timon not to shame the woods by pretending to be a cynic but, instead, to thrive by becoming a dedicated flatterer, deeming it to be only just that a man who once believed flatterers should now become one himself. However, he admits that Timon would only give any wealth he might again possess to flatterers, and he suddenly demands that Timon quit acting like *him*. Timon cuttingly responds, "Were I like thee, I'd throw away myself."

Apemantus counters with the assertion that Timon has degenerated from being a longtime madman into now being a fool. He questions if Timon believes that wild nature will take care of him and assume the duties once performed by servants, and he sarcastically asks him to solicit flattery from the animals of the woods. Timon interrupts; he orders Apemantus to leave, but Apemantus vows that he now cares for Timon more than ever. Timon declares that he hates Apemantus more than ever for flattering misery. In answer, Apemantus says that he has searched out Timon only to chide him. He argues that it would be fine if Timon had assumed his own personal role of a cynic in order to repent having once been proud, but he contends that Timon plays his own role reluctantly, really wanting to live again in luxury. He alleges that people who genuinely accept misery as the lot of mankind are happier than those who prefer the pomp of high station, which consistently promises but never delivers contentment. He thinks that Timon should desire to die since he is so miserable.

Timon asserts that he will not listen to someone who is even more miserable than himself, someone who has been so shunned by Fortune that he has been a "dog" since birth. He speculates that if Apemantus had ever enjoyed Timon's one-time good fortune and authority, he would have succumbed totally to lascivious living and would have ignored reason altogether. Timon reminisces about his former position of wealth, respect, and power, and he compares the many who once attended him in numbers to the leaves on a tree. Citing his own experience, he can attest that it is indeed a severe burden for one to endure severe want, especially one who has known only plenty previously. He avers that Apemantus has become hardened to suffering because that is all he has ever known; it is not surprising that Apemantus cannot curse men for not flattering him — he has never given anyone anything. Apemantus can logically curse only his father for begetting him a beggar's life and condemning him to a life of depravity. Apemantus wonders whether Timon can still be proud, and Timon answers, "Ay, that I am not thee." This echoes Apemantus' insult in the first scene of the play. Apemantus then responds sharply that he is proud that *he* is not a spendthrift, and Timon again asks him to leave; he says that if Apemantus could contain all the "wealth" which Timon has now, Timon would tell the cynic to hang himself. Timon then eats a root, and Apemantus offers him another, but Timon says that he only wants

Apemantus to leave. He shows Apemantus some gold and asks him to hurry to Athens with the news that he is again wealthy.

Apemantus can see no use for gold in the woods, but Timon argues that it is put to its best use there, for it can do no harm in the woods. Apemantus asks where Timon sleeps; Timon answers that he sleeps in the open, and he asks where Apemantus eats. Apemantus answers that he eats wherever he finds food; Timon says that he wishes Apemantus' food were poisoned. Apemantus tells Timon, "The middle of humanity thou never knewest, but [that he has known] the extremity of both ends," emphasizing that the once sophisticated Timon now associates with only the most base. He asks Timon if he likes sour medlars (apple-like, decaying fruit), but Timon says he "hates" medlars—even though they look similar to Apemantus. Apemantus then asks if Timon has ever known a spendthrift who was genuinely loved; Timon answers by asking if Apemantus has ever loved anyone who was not a spendthrift. Apemantus answers "Myself," and he asks what is most comparable to the men who once flattered Timon. Timon answers that women are similar but that "men are the things themselves." He asks what Apemantus would do if he had the power to change the world; Apemantus says that he would rid it of men and give it to the beasts. Timon asks Apemantus if he would like to remain as one of the beasts after the destruction of men. Apemantus answers, "Ay," and Timon hopes that Apemantus' "beastly ambition" will be fulfilled because all animals have natural enemies, possess evil traits, and live in danger. Timon cites a long list of animals, combining each with an enemy or an obnoxious trait, and he asks Apemantus to name an animal that is not prey to another, declaring that Apemantus is already a beast without realizing it. Apemantus admits that this cynicism would be pleasing, were it possible for Timon to please him with any conversation, because all the citizens of Athens have become beasts. Timon wonders if a donkey has broken the wall of Athens to let Apemantus escape. Apemantus announces the approach of a poet and a painter and offers to leave (they do not, in fact, appear until the next act). Timon contends that he could welcome Apemantus' presence only if nothing else were left alive, and Apemantus accuses Timon of being the "cap of all the fools alive" (the greatest fool living). They continue to hurl increasingly insulting invectives at each other, provoking Timon to finally throw a stone at Apemantus.

Timon reaffirms that he is "sick of this false world," and he decides that it is time to prepare a grave by the sea and to write an epitaph expressing his belief that death is preferable to life. He sings a sarcastic paean to his gold, praising it for defiling human nature, disrupting human order, and uniting things that should remain apart. He prays that gold will finally set men at odds and bring about the destruction of humanity. Apemantus agrees with Timon's curse, vowing to spread the word that Timon is again rich so that people will throng to see him. Timon once more asks Apemantus to leave; Apemantus wishes Timon a long life in which to enjoy his misery. Timon returns the wish for long life, but he judges his own life to be nearly finished. Announcing that more men are approaching for Timon to be disgusted with, Apemantus leaves.

Three bandits enter, discussing Timon and his rumored gold. The First Bandit thinks that perhaps Timon has retained only a small portion of his former wealth, but the Second Bandit says that reports indicate that the amount is large. The Third suggests that if they ask Timon for it he will give it to them willingly if he does not value it or else he will lead them to its hiding place if he does. They greet Timon, who salutes them as thieves. They claim to be soldiers, however, but this makes no difference to Timon, who equates soldiers and thieves. The bandits state that they are men who desire a great deal. Timon claims that their greatest desire is meat, and he questions why they are not content with the fresh water and fruit which nature abundantly provides in the woods. The First Bandit answers that they cannot live like beasts. Timon notes they cannot live by eating beasts either; they should eat men, he says, although he admits that there is at least some honesty in their being professed thieves. He gives them some gold and tells them to use it to drink themselves into a stupor. He advises them not to trust doctors, since doctors kill more people with poisonous antidotes than the thieves rob, and he urges them always to kill their holdup victims. Timon philosophizes on everything's being in a sense a thief, including the sea, the earth, and human law. Hoping that his gift will spur them to even greater thievery, he gives them more gold and advises them to continue their profession in Athens, where they will be stealing only from other thieves. Commenting on Timon's extreme hatred of mankind and on his speech encouraging thievery, the bandits depart for Athens.

Unnoticed by Timon, Flavius enters; he is clearly saddened by the sight of his former master ruined in wealth and declining in health, and he construes Timon's plight to be a good example of the folly of bestowing good deeds on those who do not deserve them. He questions if anything on earth can be more evil than the "friends" who have brought Timon to his present condition, and he hopes that he will never allow himself to be deceived by people who pretend to be friends. At this point, Flavius vows to continue to serve Timon faithfully and steps forward. Timon asks who he is and orders him to go away. Flavius asks if Timon has forgotten him; Timon replies that he has forgotten *all* men. When Flavius identifies himself as an honest servant, Timon answers that he has always been served by dishonest scoundrels. Flavius swears that he genuinely grieves for Timon, and Timon confesses that he can love Flavius, after all, because Flavius' tears prove that he is a woman and not a hardhearted male, inherently incapable of weeping. Flavius dismisses the sarcasm and begs Timon to accept him again as a steward and allow him to share his modest supply of money. Timon is moved by Flavius' offers, and he asks the gods to forgive him for not realizing that there were exceptions when he damned all mankind for being ungracious and evil, but he insists that Flavius—a lowly steward—is the only honest man alive. He believes Flavius to be foolish not to realize that he could get a better position by taking advantage of his wretched master, for such is customary, and he asks if Flavius has any ulterior motives for being kind. Flavius answers that he does not and that he wishes Timon had developed a suspicious nature earlier, when he was spending extravagantly. He swears that his only concern is for Timon's well-being and for his becoming prosperous again.

Timon realizes that Flavius is sincere, and he gives him a large amount of gold advising him to live richly and happily but to hate all men, to live apart from them, and to give charity to no one—no matter how terrible his plight might appear. He hopes that all men will eventually be imprisoned, consumed by debt, and infected by disease. He commands Flavius to leave, and when Flavius expresses a desire to stay, Timon confesses that he would only curse him if he stayed. He repeats his wish for Flavius to live a free and happy life, but a life apart from men in general and from himself in particular.

## ACT V

The first scene of this act is set in the woods, outside Timon's cave. The poet and the painter who presented their works to Timon in Act I have heard of his new wealth, and they are now seeking him in the woods. Unknown to them, however, he observes them from within his cave. They are sure that he is rich again because of the gold which he has reportedly given Alcibiades, Phrynia, Timandra, and Flavius. The poet postulates that Timon has feigned bankruptcy to test his friends. The painter agrees, adding that Timon will surely be a great man once again in Athens. He theorizes that it will look honorable on their part if they befriend him in his need, and he speculates that Timon will no doubt reward them with gold.

The poet asks what the painter has brought to present to Timon, and the painter replies he has brought only the promise of an excellent future work. The poet says that he also will have to rely on a promise, evoking a comment on current trends from the painter. He explains that mere promises are fashionable, arouse expectations in the patron, and are far more interesting than the dull work of actual production. He concludes by observing that only foolish artists actually deliver their creations since the more sophisticated patrons do not expect anything beyond promises.

Unseen, Timon leaves his cave and muses on the villainy of the two men. The poet plans to promise Timon a satire on flattery, but he contends that they would do well to find Timon before he gives all his gold away. Speaking to himself, Timon says that he is confident that he can match their deviousness. He contemplates the power of gold and prays that all who worship it will become diseased. He steps forward, and the poet and the painter greet him respectfully. Timon asks if he has lived long enough "to see two honest men." The poet informs him that they have heard of the "monstrous" ingratitude with which his noble and generous nature has been repaid, an ingratitude beyond their powers to express adequately. Timon flatters them again for being honest.

The painter acknowledges that he and the poet profited from Timon's generosity, and he offers their services to Timon, who continues to flatter them for being honest men and asks casually if they can live on roots and water. Both say that they can, and Timon again flatteringly refers to their honesty and asks pointedly if they are truthful and honest. The painter affirms that they are, but in an unintentional irony he adds, "but therefore/ Came not my friend nor I." With intentional irony, Timon flatters the painter for being able to "counterfeit" (that is, to paint portraits *and* to deceive) better than any other Athenian, and he praises the poet for succeeding so well in his composition that his verse reflects his true nature.

Timon seemingly interrupts his praise to suggest that both of them suffer from a minor fault which he wishes that they would try to correct. They beg him to tell them what it is, promising not to become upset by his reply. Timon tells them that they trust a rascal who greatly deceives them, and they are eager to learn who it is. He tells them that they listen to a knave's lies, see his pretenses, and realize his clear dishonesty, yet they hold him in dearest friendship even though they know him to be an archvillain. They deny knowing such a person, but Timon promises them gold now—and more later—if they will rid themselves of their villainous acquaintance with this man by stabbing, drowning, or by any other deadly means—and then return to him. They cry for him to name the villain. Cryptically but pointedly referring to their individual and collective dishonesty, Timon tells them that each of them always carries an "archvillain" with him wherever he goes, no matter how alone he may be. He then gives them gold, curses them, and beats them away from his cave, calling them "rascal dogs."

Timon returns to his cave, and Flavius enters, escorting two senators from Athens. Flavius tells the senators that their mission to seek Timon's assistance in the defense of Athens is hopeless because Timon has become a misanthrope. The First Senator wants to see Timon anyway to fulfill his promise to the Senate; the Second Senator believes that Timon may revert to his former self when he learns that they bring word that he will have his former fortune and position restored in return for his assistance. Flavius accompanies them to the cave and announces them to Timon. Timon curses them, hoping that the sun will burn them and that each word will raise a blister on their tongues.

When they tell him that they have been sent by the Senate, he says that he wishes he could send the plague back to Athens with them without endangering himself. The First Senator says that the Senate, in unanimous resolution, decreed that "special dignities" be bestowed on Timon when he returns. The Second Senator reports that the Senate's current need of Timon has made it aware of its past ungracious treatment of him and that the Senate has sent them to make amends and to offer recompense even greater than its acknowledged great offense warrants. He hopes that his offer will erase the Senate's wrongs and reconcile Timon to Athens.

Timon tells them that they have bewitched him "to the very brink of tears," and he sarcastically concedes that he would weep over the Senate's offer if they could give him "a fool's heart and a woman's eyes." The first Senator invites Timon to return to Athens as commander of the army with absolute power and with his reputation and wealth restored. Then, he asserts, they will defeat Alcibiades. Timon answers that it matters not to him if Alcibiades sacks Athens totally. He insists that nothing can arouse his pity for his former country. However, he values his own life even less than that of any Athenian, and he bids them farewell with a sarcastic prayer calling on the gods to protect them.

Flavius calls for him to stay, but Timon says that he must finish the epitaph which will be needed tomorrow, and he hopes again that Alcibiades will destroy them. The First Senator realizes that all entreaties are in vain, but Timon suddenly decides to feign that he has relented. He declares a love for his country and a desire to prevent its destruction. He sends his greetings to his "loving countrymen," and the senators rejoice in their success. Timon says he will show them how to oppose Alcibiades. The First Senator naturally interprets this to mean that Timon will return to lead the defense, but Timon has led them into a rhetorical, philosophical trap which he now prepares to spring. He says that he has a tree outside his cave which he must shortly cut down (to use for his coffin), and he tells the senators to tell everyone in Athens that if anyone wished to put a stop to his misery, then he should come and hang himself from the tree. Flavius tells the senators to leave ("all's in vain"), because Timon is always in this humor. Timon then asks the senators to report that he is in a grave, washed daily by the tides. He wants his gravestone to become an oracle which will proclaim the evil and the futility of life. Telling the sun to hide its beams, he leaves. The First Senator suggests that because their mission has failed, they should hurry to Athens to prepare alternate defenses.

Scene 2 opens outside the walls of Athens. A messenger reports to two senators that Alcibiades is ready to attack Athens in full force. One of the senators expresses fear that a successful defense of the city will be lost if the emissaries fail to bring Timon back. The messenger tells of meeting another messenger carrying letters from Alcibiades seeking Timon's help in his attack on Athens. The senators return from their mission to Timon to announce their failure. One of them also reports that Alcibiades and an eager army are near, and he expects the worst to befall.

The third scene takes place in the woods near Timon's cave. A soldier comes across a crudely constructed tomb. He knows that this is the place where Timon has been living, and therefore he suspects that the tomb is Timon's. He cannot read, so he takes a wax impression of the inscription to deliver to Alcibiades.

Scene 4 begins as a trumpet heralds the approach of Alcibiades and his army before the walls of Athens. Alcibiades orders the trumpeter to announce their arrival "to this coward and lascivious town." Some senators appear atop the walls, and Alcibiades shouts that the days of their unrestrained power and their arbitrary disposal of justice are over. Those who have endured Athenian tyranny have finally cried "No more"; they now intend to overthrow the Senate. The First Senator informs Alcibiades that the Senate has long ago sent messages to him offering to compensate for its act of ingratitude. The Second Senator adds that they have also tried to reach a reconciliation with Timon, demonstrating that they are neither without kindness nor deserve war. The First Senator argues that it will not be proper for Alcibiades to revenge himself by destroying walls, monuments, and schools built by a different generation of Athenians than those who offended him. The Second Senator relates that those who offended Alcibiades are all now dead; they have died from shameful remorse over their shameful treatment of Alcibiades. He invites Alcibiades and his army to enter the defenseless city and to satisfy his revenge by slaughtering one-tenth of the population. The First Senator argues that it would be unjust to kill those not responsible. The Second Senator tells Alcibiades that no matter what course he decides to follow, they hope he will do it peacefully, and the First Senator tells him that if he will come in friendship, the gates to the city will be opened readily. The Second Senator asks him to give them a sign that he intends peace, and Alcibiades throws down his glove and asks for the gates to be opened, agreeing to punish only those who have been unjust to Timon and himself. He promises that if any of his soldiers violate established law, they will be punished by that law.

As Alcibiades prepares to enter the gates, the soldier who visited Timon's grave enters and reports Timon's death. He gives to Alcibiades the wax impression which he made from the inscription on the tomb. Timon left two epitaphs, both of which are distinctly different. One states that the tomb holds an unnamed corpse, it asks passersby not to seek the name of the occupant, and it hopes that all who are left alive will contract diseases. The second epitaph states that the "hated Timon" lies within the grave, it asks all observers to "curse thy fill," but to be sure not to linger. Alcibiades says that the inscription expresses Timon's opinions well. He speaks imaginatively to Timon, telling him that even though in life he hated his friends' expressions of grief, he has taught those friends to weep forever on his humble grave. Alcibiades turns to enter the city, promising to use his military power to ensure peaceful ends and promising that he will heal the civic wounds of Athens: "I will use the olive with my sword . . ."

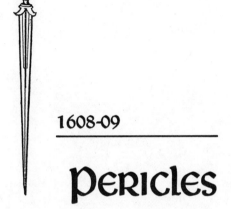

1608-09

# pericles

# INTRODUCTION

This play was popular in Shakespeare's time, but since then, it has fallen into relative obscurity. There may be good reason for this since it does not compare favorably with Shakespeare's usually tightly constructed and highly dramatic plays. Additionally, there is also some doubt about whether or not Shakespeare wrote all of the play himself, although many critics agree that he wrote all or most of the last three acts of the play.

The play's basic theme is about loss and recovery, and the death and rebirth which they resemble. This notion of loss and renewal appears as the central theme in later plays of Shakespeare, such as *Cymbeline* and *The Winter's Tale*. It is also significant that these plays focus on familial relationships as being of central importance in an ordered world; therefore, much of the conflict in the plays involves parents and children, or husbands and wives. Unlike *Cymbeline*'s plot, however, where the conflict is between a father and his daughter, and between a husband and his wife – in *Pericles*, outside forces create the divisions which separate the family members. However, in both plays, the resolution of the conflict is achieved by reuniting the family unit as it should be.

In the following brief synopsis of the action in *Pericles*, the character of John Gower plays a minor, but not unimportant role. As the narrator or "chorus," he introduces each act. Not only does he summarize what is to occur in the next act, but he also fills in what has happened in the time that has passed between one act and another. Shakespeare apparently found this device of a narrator useful, considering the period of time spanned by the play (about twenty years).

Gower wrote his *Confessio Amantis* in the fourteenth century, which is the main source of the plot in *Pericles*, and it is possible that Shakespeare used the character of the medieval poet to create an impression of romance and antiquity for his audience, as well as to help tie together the rather loosely connected events of this play.

# A BRIEF SYNOPSIS

The play opens in Antioch, where Pericles meets King Antiochus and his daughter. The visiting prince is challenged to solve a riddle – if he succeeds, he wins the princess' hand; if he fails, he dies. Other suitors have tried and failed, but Pericles discerns the solution to the riddle, which describes the incestuous relationship existing between the king and his daughter. Pericles, however, realizes that giving the correct answer would be as dangerous as failing to give an answer, so he responds in an equivocal manner that merely hints that he knows the true solution to the riddle. The king gives him forty days to answer the riddle or lose his life, and Pericles wisely decides to leave Antioch.

The king, of course, realizes that Pericles has deciphered the secret of the riddle, and he plans to have him killed. Meanwhile, Pericles, having returned to Tyre, decides that it would be unsafe for him or his city if he were to remain there. So rather than risk bringing Antiochus' wrath upon his city, he embarks upon a long voyage, leaving Tyre in the hands of a trusted nobleman, Helicanus.

As he begins his travels, Pericles' first stop is at Tarsus, a city which is experiencing a terrible famine. He rescues the city with a shipload of grain, earning the gratitude of the governor and his wife, Cleon and Dionyza. They vow to be his friends forever, although they later betray that friendship.

Pericles then continues his travels until his ship is capsized in a fierce storm, and he is washed ashore at Pentapolis, ruled by a good king, Simonides. After some fishermen aid Pericles and rescue his suit of armor from the sea, they inform him that there is to be a tournament to celebrate the birthday of Simonides' daughter, Thaisa.

Although he is somewhat bedraggled in appearance, Pericles decides to enter the tournament anyway, and he is victorious. (The reader might note at this point that although the romance is set in ancient times, it follows many of the conventions of medieval romances rather than those of ancient literature. Clearly, the Elizabethan audience was not overly concerned with anachronisms.)

As the victor, Pericles wins the hand of Thaisa, who has fallen in love with him. At first, Simonides appears reluctant to let the two lovers marry, but eventually he agrees to the union. As the months pass, the lords of Tyre demand that Helicanus agree to be their king, for Pericles has been gone for so long that it is possible that he is dead. But Helicanus refuses, and he asks the lords to wait one more year; they agree, and Helicanus tells them to set off to search for Pericles in the interim.

Meanwhile, Pericles and his wife embark for Tyre. Unfortunately, she is expecting a baby, and she goes into labor during a violent storm at sea. During the course of the storm, Thaisa dies while giving birth to a daughter, who is named Marina. Thaisa is then placed in a sealed coffin and is buried at sea, and Pericles, continuing on toward Tyre, decides to leave his child and her nurse at Tarsus, to be cared for by Cleon and Dionyza, for he feels that the tiny baby cannot survive the rough journey back to Tyre.

Although Pericles thinks his wife is dead, an unusual event occurs which he doesn't learn about for nearly twenty years. Thaisa's coffin is washed ashore at Ephesus, and, there, a wise man, Cerimon, revives her through his knowledge of many of the lost secrets of medicine. Afterward, Thaisa becomes a priestess at the temple of Diana in Ephesus, and she stays there until Pericles is led to Ephesus and finds her there.

Years pass, and Marina grows up in the household of Cleon and Dionyza and becomes a beautiful woman. Dionyza, however, is jealous because Marina is so much more beautiful and gifted than her own daughter, Philoten, and so she orders her servant, Leonine, to kill Marina. He is about to carry out her orders on a deserted beach when he and Marina are attacked by pirates, who carry her off.

The pirates take Marina to Mytilene and sell her to the owner of a brothel, where she is able to resist all the customers' advances and remain virtuous.

Back in Tarsus, Cleon regrets what has happened to Marina, but Dionyza is unrepentant, and, as a result, they build a monument to Marina, so that Pericles will think that his daughter died of natural causes. Pericles, of course, is deeply saddened by this second loss, and he vows never to stop mourning for his lost wife and child.

More time passes, and Marina continues to preserve her honor at the brothel by refusing to have anything to do with the customers, including the governor of the city, Lysimachus. She explains to them all why she refuses them, and rather than being angry with her, they admire her goodness and virtue. The brothel owners, of course, aren't getting any richer, but Marina eventually persuades them to help her get honest work.

It is at this time that Pericles arrives in Mytilene, dressed in sackcloth. He is despondent, and he refuses to speak to anyone. Lysimachus meets Pericles, likes him, and tells Helicanus, who has come to Mytilene, that there is a maiden in the city who can make Pericles, the noble knight, speak—if anyone can. She is Marina, and when she meets Pericles, she tries to cheer him by telling him a little about herself and her own tragic life. Marina's manner reminds Pericles of Thaisa, but more important, Marina's story has details in it which at first shock Pericles, but they then cause him to rejoice, for he recognizes Marina as the daughter whom he lost. He feels as though he has been reborn, and he makes plans to take her with him when he goes to Tarsus to avenge himself upon Cleon and Dionyza.

Before that happens, however, Pericles' joy turns into drowsiness, and he falls into a deep sleep. He then has a dream in which the goddess Diana tells him to, first, go to her temple at Ephesus and to worship there. He awakens and, out of gratitude, he leaves for Ephesus, accompanied by Marina and Lysimachus, who wishes to marry her. At Ephesus, Pericles meets Thaisa, and she is reunited with him. Although much has been suffered by all, things turn out well.

# LIST OF CHARACTERS

### Pericles

The prince (king) of the city of Tyre. His travels through the cities on the eastern end of the Mediterranean Sea form the main story of the play, which is set in ancient times. Although Pericles is a good ruler, he suffers various misfortunes—such as the loss of his wife and daughter. But after many years, they are restored to him. He is the hero of the play, not so much because of what he does, but because of the evil that he does not do. He stands in contrast to such evil characters as Antiochus, Cleon, and Dionyza.

### Helicanus

A lord of Tyre. Helicanus is made Pericles' deputy, and he rules in Pericles' place during the years that Pericles is abroad. Helicanus is loyal to Pericles, and he refuses to let the lords of the city name him as king in Pericles' place.

### Antiochus

The evil king of Antioch. Pericles solves a riddle put to him by the king, revealing the king's incestuous relationship with his daughter. Knowing that Pericles guesses his secret, Antiochus sends an assassin after him, but Pericles escapes. Antiochus and his daughter are later killed while riding in their chariot.

### Simonides

The king of Pentapolis. Like Pericles, he is a good king. Pericles arrives at Pentapolis, unexpectedly, when he becomes the victim of a shipwreck; later, he becomes Simonides' son-in-law when he marries Simonides' daughter, Thaisa.

### Thaisa

The daughter of Simonides and the wife of Pericles. While returning to Tyre with her husband, Thaisa dies at sea after giving birth to a daughter. She is buried at sea, but she is retrieved, and later, she is miraculously revived by Cerimon of Ephesus.

### Marina

The beautiful and virtuous daughter of Pericles and Thaisa. As an infant, she is left with the governor of Tarsus and his wife to be cared for until Pericles can return for her. As a result of a series of misfortunes, however, she is kidnapped by pirates and sold into a brothel. Nevertheless, she maintains her chastity and her honor and, eventually, she finds her father and mother again.

### Cleon and Dionyza

The governor of Tarsus and his wife, who have a daughter of their own, **Philoten**. Pericles gains their friendship when he rescues Tarsus from a famine. But when he later entrusts them with the care of his infant daughter, Marina, they betray his trust. Cleon is reluctant to kill Marina, but Dionyza, jealous of Marina's beauty, plots to have her murdered anyway.

### Cerimon

Lord of Ephesus. He is skilled in medicine, and perhaps in more arcane arts as well. He retrieves Thaisa's coffin from the sea, and he is able to revive her. Thaisa lives peacefully in Ephesus until Pericles is led to her by the goddess Diana.

### Lychorida

Marina's nurse.

### Lysimachus

Governor of Mytilene; he eventually marries Marina.

### Escanes

A lord of Tyre.

### Thaliard

A lord of Antioch; Antiochus assigns him the task of murdering Pericles, but he is never able to catch up with him.

### Philemon

Servant to Cerimon.

### Leonine

Servant to Dionyza. Dionyza orders Leonine to kill Marina, but at the last moment, he is prevented from doing so by pirates, who attack them and carry her off.

## A Pandar, A Bawd, and Boult

The pandar (pander) and his mistress, or wife, the bawd, own a brothel in Mytilene. Boult is their servant. Marina is sold to them by the pirates, but they never succeed in making a prostitute of her.

## Diana

The goddess who speaks to Pericles in a dream, instructing him to go to her temple at Ephesus. It is there that he will meet his long-lost wife, Thaisa.

## John Gower

Gower was a medieval poet who wrote about the Prince of Tyre in his poem *Confessio Amantis*. Although he was not a contemporary of Shakespeare, he functions as the narrator, or "chorus," and he introduces each act or new section of the play and, in addition, he provides a historical setting for the play.

# CRITICAL COMMENTARIES

## ACT I

The fourteenth-century poet John Gower opens the play by telling the audience that they are about to see a dramatization of a love story which is found in his *Confessio Amantis*. He says that he has returned from "the ashes," and then he summarizes the opening scenes, which are set in the ancient city of Antioch.

The play opens in Antioch, in front of the palace of the king, Antiochus. The mounted heads of suitors who have tried to win the hand of Antiochus' daughter are visible on the palace wall. They all failed at the task which Pericles, Prince of Tyre, will attempt to solve: a riddle posed by Antiochus. If Pericles is successful, he will win the princess in marriage.

Pericles and Antiochus agree that Pericles will attempt to solve the riddle, and the princess enters, dressed as a bride. Antiochus then hands Pericles the riddle, which he reads:

> I am no viper, yet I feed
> On mother's flesh which did me breed.
> I sought a husband, in which labour
> I found that kindness in a father.
> He's father, son, and husband mild;
> I mother, wife, and yet his child.
> How they may be, and yet in two,
> As you will live, resolve it you.

(I,i,64–71)

As is apparent both to the audience and to Pericles, the riddle describes the incestuous relationship existing between Antiochus and his daughter. Pericles realizes that Antiochus has a strong motive for not wanting him to succeed and also for not wanting Pericles to live if he does succeed in answering the riddle. Thus, knowing that he is trapped, Pericles tells the king just enough of a hint to let him know that Pericles knows the answer, but that some things are best left unsaid:

> Great king,
> Few love to hear the sins they love to act:
> 'Twould braid yourself too near for me to tell it.
>
> (I,i,91–93)

Antiochus realizes that Pericles indeed knows the answer to the riddle, and so he pretends to be merciful, granting him forty days in which to provide the answer. Then Antiochus lies and says that if Pericles can solve the riddle at that time, he will be happy to have him for a son-in-law. Pericles sees through this ruse, however, and he realizes that he must leave the city at once if he is to avoid being killed.

Antiochus orders Thaliard, a nobleman, to kill Pericles, but a messenger informs both Antiochus and Thaliard that Pericles has left the city. Thaliard is then instructed to follow Pericles and kill him. Thaliard promises to do so and swears that if he can get Pericles within "a pistol's length," he will be able to murder him. The reference is amusing, since there were no pistols at the time during which the action presumably occurs, but such anachronisms were not unusual in the plays written in the Elizabethan era.

Pericles then returns to Tyre, and Helicanus, a lord of Tyre, advises him to leave the city and travel for awhile in order to prevent Antiochus from either having Pericles assassinated or, else, invading Tyre under a false pretext aimed at achieving the same end. Pericles agrees to his friend's advice and entrusts him with ruling Tyre while Pericles travels.

Pericles' behavior so far, his disgust with the immoral behavior of Antiochus, and his loyalty and trust for his friend Helicanus, suggest that Pericles is a good man, as indeed he turns out to be. As Pericles embarks on his travels, we will see how he fares in many adventures, and although he will suffer much, he eventually will be rewarded. This is a pattern of sorrow and joy that is typical of romances, as opposed to comedies or tragedies. This play, like *Cymbeline*, is a tragi-comedy, where events occur which could be called tragic, except for the fact that, eventually, things turn out well.

By this time, Thaliard has arrived in Tyre and attempts to find Pericles. By accident, he overhears Helicanus tell some other lords of the city that Pericles has fled. Thaliard is relieved, for he need not kill Pericles if Pericles has already left.

The scene now shifts to Tarsus, Pericles' first stop on what will prove to be the first of many journeys. At Tarsus, Pericles discovers that the city is suffering from a terrible famine. Cleon (the governor) and his wife (Dionyza) bemoan their fate, but Pericles provides them with grain from his ships and, thus, the famine is ended. Cleon and Dionyza express their gratitude, which will prove to be ironic in light of their later betrayal of Pericles.

## ACT II

Gower, again introducing the act to follow, tells us that Helicanus has written to Pericles that Thaliard arrived in Tyre, hoping to murder Pericles, and he urges Pericles not to stay too long in Tarsus. Heeding Helicanus' advice, Pericles again puts out to sea, but he is caught in a storm and is shipwrecked on a beach near Pentapolis.

Washed ashore, Pericles is found by three fishermen, and in the course of their conversation, they tell him that the king of their city is Simonides, whom they call "the good Simonides." The fishermen talk with Pericles and, to his relief, he discovers that they are full of good humor and a rough sort of wit. In addition, they tell Pericles that Simonides' daughter, Thaisa, is about to celebrate her birthday the following day and that there is to be a tournament in her honor. The winner, of course, will be "her knight."

Pericles would like to enter into the contest, but as a poor shipwrecked sailor, there is not much he can do. At that moment, however, two of the fishermen net an unwieldy object that turns out to be Pericles' father's enchanted armor. Although the armor is in shabby, rusted condition, Pericles says that he will wear it and enter the tournament.

The scene now shifts to the pavilion near where the tournament will take place. The knights all parade before Simonides and his daughter, Thaisa, where they present their shields to the princess, exhibiting their coats of arms and their mottoes. Five knights pass before her, and then Pericles arrives. His armor is discolored and, as we said, badly rusted, and the coat of arms on his shield consists of only a withered branch that is barely green at the top. This symbol alludes to both the hardships which he has suffered and also to those which he will suffer before he will finally gain true and lasting happiness. His motto, *In hac spe vivo* (In this hope I live), reflects the same idea. Simonides interprets it to his daughter:

> A pretty moral;
> From the dejected state wherein he is,
> He hopes by you his fortunes may yet florish.
>
> (II,ii,45–47)

When Simonides is finished, the lords who attend him criticize the ragged appearance of this particular knight, but the wise king retorts:

Opinion's but a fool, that makes us scan
The outward habit by the inward man.

(II,ii,56-57)

That is, the outward appearance of a man will not tell one how to judge a man's inner worth. Although Pericles is a prince, his nobility is disguised here, and it must be illustrated by his inner, rather than by his outer, qualities.

A shout is heard, and it appears that "the mean knight" (that is, Pericles) has won the tournament. This is later revealed to be true.

The next scene reveals a banquet, celebrating Pericles' victory. Thaisa is quite impressed with Pericles, although he modestly attributes his victory to luck. She appears to be falling in love with him, and her father, Simonides, also likes Pericles, but he tells his daughter not to become too enthralled since Pericles is probably just like any other knight. We should note here that all that Pericles has told these people is that he is a gentleman of Tyre; thus, they do not necessarily assume that it would be appropriate for Thaisa to be courted by him—particularly, since he presents himself as being also an adventurer who was shipwrecked near Pentapolis.

This scene and the preceding scene, which describes the worth of Simonides and Thaisa, present us with an interesting contrast to the evil Antiochus and his daughter. As we shall discover later, Pericles deeply loves his only child, Marina; later, he will be an honorable and devoted parent. These images of parent-child relationships are repeated throughout the play, illustrating the good that can come from relationships that are good in themselves.

While Pericles enjoys the banquet with Simonides, Thaisa, and several knights, the scene shifts back to Tyre, where Pericles' deputy, Helicanus, tells another lord, Escanes, that the incestuous Antiochus and his daughter have been killed in a mysterious fire that burned up their chariot. (From the description, one assumes that a lightning bolt struck their chariot.)

Other noblemen of Tyre enter at this point, and they inform Helicanus that they fear that Pericles is dead; they wish to proclaim Helicanus as their official ruler. Helicanus, however, refuses the offer and asks them to wait one more year before concluding that Pericles will never return. If they cannot agree to this, Helicanus advises, then they should, first, make every attempt to find Pericles before trying to elect a new ruler. They agree to this, and they say that they will begin a search for him.

We now return to Pentapolis, where for some unknown reason, Thaisa has announced that she will not marry for a year. The full meaning of her speech is not clear, but it appears that her announcement may be a ruse to get rid of the other knight-suitors so that she will be free to marry Pericles; a letter that she has written to Simonides also seems to suggest this. Simonides, one should note, approves of Pericles, so there are no obstacles to their marrying.

Pericles enters, and Simonides tells him that Thaisa thinks highly of him—so much so, in fact, that she would like to marry him. Pericles protests that he is unworthy. Then the king shows him Thaisa's letter, and the young prince thinks that a trap has probably been set for him, since in the past he has had bad luck with fathers and daughters.

Pericles argues that he has never had an impure thought regarding Thaisa, and, on hearing this, Simonides is rather put out. He acts as if he is offended, and he makes Thaisa herself tell Pericles what she feels for the young man. She does so, and the king tells them both that they had best obey his unspoken will—which is, that they marry—or else he will be forced to make them marry one another.

> Therefore hear you, mistress: either frame
> Your will to mine; and you, sir, hear you:
> Either be ruled by me, or I'll make you—
> Man and wife.

(II,v,81–84)

The basic good humor of this scene is evident, for the father can threaten the "disobedient" daughter with that which she most wants. Here, again, is a father and daughter relationship that is somewhat idealized in the sense that the two agree perfectly that what she wants is what she should have.

Pericles is persuaded by this turn of events, and so he marries Thaisa.

## ACT III

Gower's introduction to this act explains that Pericles and Thaisa have now been married, and that she is expecting a child. At this time, a letter has arrived from Tyre, informing Pericles that unless he can return within the year, the nobles will crown Helicanus as Prince of Tyre. Simonides and his court are pleased by the news, for it reveals that Pericles is a prince in his own right, something they did not know. Pericles, Thaisa, and Lychorida, a nurse, then prepare to leave.

At sea, however, a storm rises, and the violent tempest brings on Thaisa's labor. (Most of Pericles' seafaring expeditions appear to be plagued with storms.) Pericles is on deck as waves thunder and roar, and Lychorida comes on deck carrying an infant. She tells Pericles that Thaisa has died, but that their infant daughter is alive. Pericles is stunned. And to make matters worse, the sailors tell Pericles that the storm will not abate until Thaisa's body is cast overboard. Pericles listens to their superstitious fears and, reluctantly, he has a coffin prepared for Thaisa.

A sealed coffin is thus made ready, and Thaisa is placed in it. Pericles then decides that he must sail for Tarsus, where he believes Cleon and

Dionyza can be trusted to care for his tiny infant daughter, for he fears that she will not survive the trip to Tyre. Thaisa's coffin is then thrown overboard in the vicinity of Ephesus. Fortunately, in this city, there lives a wise physician, Cerimon, who has been occupied during the storm helping the sick and injured. Cerimon is a lord in Ephesus, but he is also a student of "physic," the "secret art," by which he can perform nearly miraculous cures.

A discussion which he has at home with some visitors makes it clear that he is well known for both his knowledge and his charity. This, in turn, prepares us for his reaction to the chest, which is brought in, containing Thaisa's body. Cerimon finds a letter in the coffin that requests that anyone who finds it is to bury her with dignity, for she is a queen. Cerimon notes how fresh she looks and thinks that perhaps she is not truly dead. Thus, he applies his skill to the task of reviving her. It turns out that Thaisa has only been unconscious for a few hours, and Cerimon succeeds in reviving her.

Meanwhile, Pericles arrives at Tarsus and entrusts his baby to Cleon and Dionyza. We learn, in addition, that he has named his daughter Marina, for she was born at sea. Cleon promises that she will be well cared for, and Pericles makes the rather odd vow that he will never cut his hair – as a sign of mourning – until Marina is safely married. This seems to be an odd thing to say to the persons who have promised to care for her, but it is appropriate in light of future events, since it foreshadows the time when Pericles will deeply mourn, believing that his daughter is dead.

The act ends with a brief scene at the house of Cerimon, where we find that Thaisa remembers her illness, but does not know what happened to her, or even whether or not she actually gave birth. Consequently, since she does not think that she will see her husband again, she decides to become a vestal virgin, a priestess, at the shrine of the goddess Diana. Diana is mentioned several times in this play, and later she will play a part in reuniting Pericles and Thaisa.

Thaisa takes her vows and begins to live quietly at Diana's temple in Ephesus.

## ACT IV

Gower now fills in information concerning what happened in the intervening years since Pericles left Marina at Tarsus and returned to Tyre. As Marina grew up, she was well cared for and was educated as if she were Cleon and Dionyza's own daughter. But trouble soon began, however, because they already had a daughter of their own, Philoten, who was about Marina's age. The two girls were always together, but whatever they did, Marina was always the more graceful. It is not clear whether or not this bothered Philoten, but it certainly bothered her mother,

Dionyza, whose emotions finally grew to the point that she decided to have Marina murdered.

Act IV opens with Dionyza conferring with Leonine, the man to whom she has assigned the task of murdering Marina. Marina enters, mourning her mother, whom she thinks has long since died. For once, Philoten is not with her, so Dionyza advises her to take a walk along the beach with Leonine. At this point, compare this scene with those in *Cymbeline*, in which the outwardly good stepmother cares nothing for the stepchild but only for her own child. Here again, we have a foster mother who expresses the same relationship.

Leonine and Marina talk for a bit, and she tells him of the circumstances of her birth at sea, and then, abruptly, he says to her, "Come, say your prayers." This is the first time that Marina realizes that Leonine intends to kill her. She begs him for mercy, but he feels that he must do the deed. Yet before he can kill her, pirates enter and seize her. Leonine flees.

This whole scene is very weak, for events pile up in an improbable manner, and what should be dramatic events seem often to be merely silly. Nevertheless, it is important—for the plot—to get Marina away from Tarsus, and the device of the pirates accomplishes this.

Once the pirates have taken Marina away, Leonine returns to make sure that she is gone. So long as there is "no hope she'll return," Leonine feels safe in assuming that his work is done. But, first, he must wait to see what they will do, for if the pirates leave her on the beach, he will have to come back and kill her. However, the pirates do not rape her or leave her on the beach. Instead, they take her to the city of Mytilene and sell her into a brothel.

The second scene opens in Mytilene, where the brothel owner is discussing with his servant, Boult, the problem of acquiring new women. Much of the dialogue of these crude characters in Act IV is quite funny and is typical of the bawdier strain of Elizabethan humor. Boult leaves, and the owner remains, talking to another character, a woman, called only "Bawd," about the poor condition of the women in the brothel. Boult then returns, followed by the pirates and Marina.

Because she is a virgin, Marina fetches a high price. What the brothel owner does not know, however, is that Marina intends to *remain* a virgin. The deal is closed, and the owner turns Marina over to the bawd to instruct her in what she is to do.

Feeling utterly forlorn, Marina laments that Leonine did not have the chance to kill her before this fate could befall her. The bawd does not understand, and she assures Marina that she will live a life of luxury and pleasure, but Marina is not comforted.

In the meantime, Boult has gone throughout the town advertising their new acquisition in order to ensure that some wealthy customers will arrive that night.

The bawd turns to Marina and advises her to act shy and fearful, for Marina is to be marketed as a virgin. Of course, the irony lies in the fact that this is *precisely* how Marina feels. The exchanges between the two women make it apparent that the bawd has no idea that such a thing as virginal innocence can exist in a young woman.

Boult returns, then, and goes out again to advertise their new acquisition. Marina is dismayed at their matter-of-fact commercialism, and she vows that she will die before she becomes a party to their business. Thus, she prays to Diana, the goddess of chastity, to aid her:

> If fires be hot, knives sharp, or waters deep,
> Untied I still my virgin knot will keep.
> Diana, aid my purpose!
>
> (IV,ii,159–61)

The scene then shifts to Tarsus, where Cleon is dismayed and remorseful at the crime that was committed because of Dionyza's jealousy. He asks what they will say when Pericles returns for his daughter, and Dionyza, still unrepentant, says merely that they will tell Pericles that Marina has died; after all, they only promised to *care* for her – they did not *guarantee* that they could protect her from all harm whatsoever. Cleon is not satisfied; he feels guilty, but Dionyza, clearly the villainess here, calls him a coward. There is no way, she says, that Pericles will ever know that his daughter was murdered. Here, one should remember that they mistakenly assume that Marina is dead – at the hands of pirates.

The next events are narrated by Gower, who enters to tell us that Pericles, accompanied by Helicanus, has set sail to retrieve Marina. He arrives at Tarsus, where Cleon and Dionyza sadly show him Marina's tomb. Pericles is devastated, and he vows never to wash his face, cut his hair, or wear anything but sackcloth for the rest of his life. He sets out to sea again and eventually arrives at Mytilene.

In the meantime, Marina is busily reforming the brothel's customers with her goodness and purity; we learn this from the conversation of two gentlemen who are discussing Marina after leaving the brothel. This, naturally, upsets the brothel keepers, and the bawd says:

> Fie, fie upon her! She's able to freeze the god
> Priapus and undo a whole generation.
>
> (IV,vi,3–4)

While the brothel keepers argue over what is to be done about Marina, the governor of the city, Lysimachus, comes to the brothel in disguise. He asks for a healthy wench, and the bawd tries to warn him that Marina is pretty enough, but that Marina is also adamant in her refusal to play her part. Lysimachus does not let the bawd finish, and Boult enters with Marina.

The bawd scolds Marina and tells her that this is an important man whom Marina should treat well. Her admonitions are ignored, of course, and they leave Marina and the governor alone. The governor then asks Marina how long she has been at this trade, but her answers do not interpret "this trade" to be prostitution. She thoroughly confuses him and increases his confusion by saying that if he were a man of honor, he would not come to such a place. She then explains who she is, and he understands her, gives her some money, and wishes her well.

> For me,
> That am a maid, though most ungentle fortune
> Have placed me in this sty . . .
> O, that the gods
> Would set me free from this unhallowed place,
> Though they did change me to the meanest bird
> That flies i' th' purer air!
>
> (IV,vi,102–9)

The brothel keepers are outraged at her treatment of Lysimachus, and they tell Boult to rape her, the rationale being that once she is no longer a virgin, she will be less reluctant to engage in their trade.

Left with Boult, Marina berates him for being part of such an awful business. Boult, rather humorously, it seems, replies:

> What would you have me do? Go to the wars,
> Would you? Where a man may serve seven
> Years for the loss of a leg, and have not
> Money enough in the end to buy him a
> Wooden one?
>
> (IV,vi,180–84)

Marina answers that any occupation is better than what he does here. She offers all of her money to Boult and tells him to use it to find her honest work, for she can teach the finer arts which she learned as a child: weaving, sewing, and music. Boult agrees to this, and he says that he will persuade the brothel owner to let her go. Marina's goodness and integrity have at last triumphed over evil.

## ACT V

Gower now relates what has happened as a result of Marina's powers of persuasion. She has found honest work, and now, she can earn something for the brothel owner, to whom she gives her earnings. It is not a perfect situation, but she is far better off than she was. In the meantime, Pericles arrives in Mytilene, driven ashore by adverse winds.

The first scene opens on Pericles' ship, where he sits silent, dressed in sackcloth. Lysimachus comes aboard to greet Pericles, and Helicanus tells him of Pericles' grief, and says that there is nothing and no one who can comfort him; he has neither eaten nor spoken for three months. Lysimachus observes Pericles and tells Helicanus that there is a maiden in the city who can, if anyone can, persuade Pericles to speak.

A lord goes to fetch Marina and returns with her. This passage contains the painful and dramatic recognition scene between Marina and her father. Marina meets Pericles and, of course, she does not know him, for she was only a newborn baby when he left her at Tarsus. She tells him the story of her tragic life and something in the story stirs Pericles to speak. He feels as if he knows her:

> Pray you, turn your eyes upon me.
> You're like something that—What countrywoman?
> Here of these shores?
>
> (V,i,102-4)

Marina tells him that she is not of these shores nor of any others. Pericles realizes that she reminds him of his wife, and he asks her to tell him more about herself. At first, Marina hesitates, but then she tells him that her name is Marina. Pericles is shocked. He thinks that she jokes with his misery, though how anyone in Mytilene would know his wife's or his daughter's names does not occur to him.

As Marina tells her story, it of course matches perfectly with what Pericles knows happened soon after his own daughter's birth. Finally, Pericles comes to a full recognition that this girl *is* his daughter; his daughter did *not* die at Tarsus. She is alive. Pericles is so happy that he fears that he will die from happiness:

> O Helicanus, strike me, honour'd sir!
> Give me a gash, put me to present pain,
> Lest this great sea of joys rushing upon me
> O'erbear the shores of my mortality,
> And drown me with their sweetness. O, come hither,
> Thou that beget'st him that did thee beget;
> Thou that wast born at sea, buried at Tarsus,
> And found at sea again!
>
> (V,i,192-99)

This speech is one of the most moving speeches in this often awkward play, and it is reminiscent of many of the other recognition scenes in Shakespeare's romances. Pericles is sure that the young woman is his daughter, but he asks her, just to make absolutely certain, what her mother's name was, and when Marina answers, "Thaisa," Pericles is overjoyed and embraces his daughter. Now he is finally ready to dress himself in his royal robes again and take upon himself the role of ruler, but suddenly, he hears strange music. No one else hears it except Pericles, and it causes him to fall asleep. Everyone present seems to think that the tumultuous emotions of the day have exhausted him, and they all leave.

While Pericles is in a swoon, as it were, he is visited by Diana, who tells him to come to her temple in Ephesus; there, he will learn what happened to his wife. Pericles awakens and tells Lysimachus and the others, who have reentered, that although he intended to go to Tarsus to seek revenge for Cleon and Dionyza's betrayal, he must first go to Ephesus.

Lysimachus then mentions that he has a matter to discuss with Pericles (the hand of Marina in marriage), and Pericles is receptive. The proposal, however, seems to come almost too quickly after the emotion of the recognition scene, but the idea of a good marriage is a fitting end for the heroine of a comedy or a romance.

Gower also tells us that Lysimachus and Marina are engaged to be married, but first, Pericles must obey Diana's command. Consequently, Pericles, Lysimachus, and Marina go to Diana's temple at Ephesus. When they arrive, Pericles enters the temple, and he worships Diana, telling her why he came. Thaisa, a priestess in the temple, overhears his voice, listens to his life story, and realizes who he is. She cries out to him, and at first, Pericles cannot believe that his long-lost wife is alive. But Cerimon explains what happened, and Pericles recognizes Thaisa at last. Her appearance, of course, has changed, but Pericles remembers her voice, and she recognizes the ring which her father gave him. In addition, Marina meets her mother for the first time, and all are overjoyed.

The play ends here, followed by a brief epilogue in which Gower explains that Good prevails, and Evil is punished. Clearly, the play has a basically simple story line; however, it reminds one more of a fairy tale than a story with any degree of realism. But, despite all of its flaws, it reminds one of the other, later romances which Shakespeare wrote in which death and rebirth play important parts. Also too, the use of the imagery of the sea foreshadows the more well-known fantasy play, *The Tempest*, in which another virtuous daughter, Miranda, finds happiness even though she is marooned with her father and yet another shipwrecked group on an island. *Pericles*, however, is a play where the characters overcome their plights with patience and endurance. It may seem slow-moving at times, but, like many other tales, one can assume that Pericles, Thaisa, and Marina lived "happily ever after."

1610

# Cymbeline

# INTRODUCTION

By their very nature, romance and comedy demand that readers suspend their critical faculties during the play and give themselves wholly over to the story, accepting its conventions. This is particularly true when the setting, characters, plot, or natural laws of the world which are presented in the play differ to any extent from what we call reality.

Shakespeare's *romantic comedies* do not operate under the same assumptions as realistic or satiric comedies do. The *comedy of manners*, developed by Ben Jonson and his followers, requires that the audience accept an illusion as reality for a short while. The assumption behind this illusion is that it approximates reality to some degree. However, the difference between the two types of comedy quickly becomes apparent. Shakespeare creates a self-contained fantasy world that is not wholly intended to represent a comic picture of Elizabethan England. This is not to say that the play does not have satiric elements in it, as exemplified by the buffoon Cloten in *Cymbeline*, and the scenes involving the brothel in *Pericles*. In general, the romances of Shakespeare's later career were not meant to be a mirror of the real world. If they mirror anything, they reflect the eternal truths of human nature which comprise their main themes, and they are not dependent upon historical accuracy or social verisimilitude.

*Cymbeline* and *Pericles* are generally very accurate in their portrayal of certain aspects of human nature. They resemble the archetypal patterns of folktales in which events that would seem incongruous if taken literally are the very substance of the stories themselves. In this way, the play, although stylized and unrealistic according to one set of standards, does not violate its own basic assumptions. It is precisely what Shakespeare intends it to be. The point-of-view which such comedies suggest is, in fact, one much less structured than the heavily plotted realism of the comedy of manners. For example, the narrative moves with the rhythm of a dream. It is interesting that the important recognition scenes in these two plays strongly echo the imagery and thought patterns of a dream as well. Since the dream state is a repository of much that is mythic or archetypal in human consciousness, it is important that a drama dealing with such mythic themes might also be styled in a manner that would universalize rather than particularize the events. In essence, both *Cymbeline* and *Pericles* can be said to derive their basic plots from a folklore tradition, from myths of death and regeneration.

In both plays, people and qualities which were thought to be lost forever are regained, a theme which Shakespeare uses more elaborately in *The Winter's Tale*. Cymbeline has lost his two sons, and his daughter disappears. Posthumus believes that he has lost his wife (symbolically, at first) because of her infidelity. Later, he thinks that he has actually lost her because he believes that his servant has followed Posthumus' orders to kill her. Imogen sees the headless body of Cloten wearing Posthumus' clothes and thinks that the corpse is Posthumus. While the play veers close to being tragic at times, all ends well when Imogen and her brothers, Arviragus and Guiderius, are restored to their loved ones.

Similar events also occur in *Pericles*; there, the king believes that he has lost his wife and, later, his daughter. But in the end both are miraculously restored to him; good triumphs over evil, and harmony is re-established.

The *masque*, an elaborate form of courtly entertainment, appears to some extent in both plays. It is used more elaborately in Shakespeare's last play, *The Tempest*, but in these plays there is also a strong element of the pageant and the masque, along with magic, dreams, and mythic divinities.

*Cymbeline*, like many typical masques, relies on thematic associations to help unify the plot. The social stereotypes of English nobility and Italian corruption, the lost children, and the deceived husband all echo throughout the palaces, as well as in the humble shelters of Britain, Wales, Italy, and Rome. The anachronisms of time and place, while sometimes detracting from the realism of the history, do ultimately help universalize the story for all times. Like a folk tale, the story of Cymbeline is not a particular story of one person alone; it approaches an allegory of human nature.

In both *Cymbeline* and *Pericles*, the dreams of Posthumus and Pericles respectively are presented in the style of the masque. In *Cymbeline*, the masque of Jupiter is modeled on the traditional masque form, during which the characters perform a set series of speeches protesting the fate of Posthumus at the hands of Jupiter. This follows the form of the dialectic in some masques, wherein two opposing principles meet, represented by mythical figures, and one is ultimately victorious. As the masque progresses, Jupiter descends and explains the ultimately good purpose of Posthumus' trials. Shakespeare shows a tremendous amount of psychological insight when he uses the device of the masque-dream to represent the expression of Posthumus' troubled conscience.

During the masque scene, the ghosts of Posthumus' family enter, accompanied by solemn music, and they talk with the despondent hero in a dream. It is interesting that Shakespeare made this concession to realism in order to aid in creating a convincing illusion. Instead of presenting the masque as such, without explaining the physical presence of ghosts and deities, he set it within the context of a dream so that its stylized and mythical elements would be logically explicable.

In *Pericles*, the goddess Diana appears to Pericles as he sleeps and tells him to go to her temple at Ephesus, where his wife, Thaisa, is to be found. Thus, again, a supernatural force (more direct than the psychological proddings received by Posthumus) aids the hero in regaining the love which he thought that he had lost.

*Cymbeline* and *Pericles* present to their audiences visions of other worlds, where the edges of myth and reality are blurred. But the processes of human degeneration, discovery, and forgiveness are recognized by the playgoers as universals for all times and places.

The fantastic settings and unlikely events of the plays tend to draw the audience away from reality, but they do so on purpose. The plays are not meant to show a true-to-life romance between two human beings, but rather, they are an ideal story of a romance, in which conflicting forces play as much of a role as the human beings do. A play such as *Cymbeline* is enhanced and deepened by the abstract and mythical implications which dream and fantasy give, and *Pericles'* story of loss and restoration can have significance only in a mythical context.

When Shakespeare wrote his great tragedies, he was always truthful to the workings of human nature in terms of individuals. In his later romances, he appears to be more concerned with the workings of the human mind in a general sense. *Cymbeline* and *The Tempest* are almost allegories. They describe motifs of human feeling in a wider sense than the individual fate of one single character. The individuals and their actions, while human and real to a point, are somewhat subordinated to the theme. Shakespeare, however, never loses sight of human nature when he does this; rather, he simply presents the same truths in a different form.

# A BRIEF SYNOPSIS

There are two basic stories and a subplot in this play which Shakespeare weaves into a complex tale of loss and recovery. The first story involves a "wager plot." The king's daughter, Imogen, has married Posthumus, a man whom her father disapproves of, and so Posthumus is exiled to Italy. While in Rome, he meets an Italian, Iachimo, who is skeptical of Posthumus' praise for his wife's fidelity. They wager that if Iachimo goes to Britain, he will *not* be able to seduce Posthumus' wife.

Iachimo thus goes to Britain, and in fact he cannot seduce Imogen, but by means of a trick he is able to get into her bedroom while she is asleep. He doesn't touch her, but he sees enough to be able to describe her and the room in detail, thus convincing Posthumus that his wife has been unfaithful.

Enraged, Posthumus writes to his servant in Britain and orders him to kill Imogen. However, the servant cannot do this, and so he comes up with another plan. Imogen, dressed as a boy, is to hide in the woods near the coast until she can gain passage to Rome. There, she can safely observe her husband and can figure out why he is so angry with her. Their plans don't quite conclude in this way, however, for Imogen never goes to Rome; instead, Posthumus returns to Britain. The two eventually meet, but Posthumus doesn't recognize his wife until she reveals herself. The true villain, Iachimo, then confesses, and Posthumus and Imogen are reunited. Their reconciliation is, in part, possible because Posthumus has, for a long time, regretted his hasty order to kill Imogen and has, in fact, forgiven her of any wrong which she might have done, although as it turns out, she was wholly innocent.

The second story involves the king's two other children, Guiderius and Arviragus. Belarius, a nobleman, having been falsely accused by the king of forming an alliance with the Romans, escapes from court, and in order to avenge himself for having been deprived of his title and his lands unjustly, he kidnaps Cymbeline's two infant sons.

However, Belarius is not evil at heart, and he takes the children's nurse with them so that they will be properly cared for. As it turns out, he and the nurse rear the boys as their own. Although the two boys grow up in the forest and know nothing of their ancestry, their foster father perceives that their nobility is expressed in their every word and deed.

When the two boys are grown, they meet their sister, Imogen, who is hiding (in disguise as a boy) in the woods. Although they do not know that she is their sister, eventually they will all be reunited with their father and, soon afterward, with each other.

The Romans invade Britain, and it is the bravery of Guiderius, Arviragus, and Belarius that enables Cymbeline, King of Britain, to be successful in battle and thereby be reconciled with his family.

These are the two basic plot lines in the play, but they are also connected with a subplot which involves the queen's son, Cloten, Imogen's stepbrother. Cloten wants to marry Imogen and gain the throne, and his attempts to court Imogen, along with the schemes of his mother to get rid of Imogen, form an undercurrent of suspense that is sometimes humorous in its absurdity and sometimes frightening.

Cloten fails in his courtship attempts, and thus he decides to find Imogen and rape her, after he has killed her husband. Instead, he meets Guiderius, who kills him. The queen eventually dies also, despairing because her son will never become king.

In the end, all the major characters are brought together. Cymbeline learns that his wife was evil, but his loss and horror are compensated for by the fact that he regains his long-lost sons and his daughter, as well.

Imogen is reunited with her husband, so she is happy. Good triumphs over evil, and everything works out for the best. Some of the characters, Cymbeline and Posthumus, for example, have had hard lessons to learn about trust and love, but they succeed and regain the love of those people whom they did not know how to love.

# LIST OF CHARACTERS

## Cymbeline

The king of Britain during the Roman occupation. He has three children by his first wife, who is dead. They are Imogen, Guiderius, and Arviragus. The latter two have been missing for some twenty years. Cymbeline has remarried – to an evil queen – whose equally evil son desires to gain the throne. For most of the play, Cymbeline is influenced by the schemes of his wife and does not realize what her true character is.

## Posthumus Leonatus

The son of Sicilius, an old friend of the king. When Sicilius died, Posthumus was reared at Cymbeline's court. However, Cymbeline becomes angry when Posthumus marries Cymbeline's daughter, Imogen, and he banishes Posthumus from court. Posthumus is a good man, basically, but he allows his faith in Imogen to be corrupted by a liar's tricks. Later, he forgives his wife, and they are reunited.

## Imogen

Cymbeline's daughter and Posthumus' devoted wife. She never stops loving Posthumus, even though he rejects her because he believes her to be unfaithful.

## Cloten

The queen's son and Cymbeline's stepson. He combines stupidity with arrogance and eventually comes to a bad end.

## The Queen

She pretends to be fond of Imogen but, secretly, she plots to kill her, since she has had no luck in convincing Imogen to marry Cloten. The queen wants power, and she hopes to see her son inherit the throne.

## Guiderius (Polydore) and Arviragus (Cadwal)

Cymbeline's sons who were kidnapped as infants and were reared in the forest by Belarius. Although they know nothing of their origins, their goodness, courage, and nobility are apparent.

## Belarius (Morgan)

He was once loyal to Cymbeline, but when Cymbeline falsely accused Belarius of treason, Belarius stole the king's children. He was wrong to do this, but he reared them like a father and, eventually, they are reunited with Cymbeline.

## Iachimo

A lesser villain than Cloten; all he intends is trickery, and, in addition, he is remorseful at the harm he appears to have done. He and Posthumus wager that Iachimo cannot seduce Imogen, but by means of a ruse, he convinces Posthumus that he has done so. He is a bit like the cynical schemer, Iago, in *Othello*, but he is not nearly so evil.

## Philario

A friend of Posthumus' father, with whom Posthumus stays in Rome. When Posthumus is too quick to be convinced by Iachimo's lies, Philario is the voice of reason, counseling against snap judgments.

## Cornelius

The court physician. The queen asks him for poison, but he suspects her motives and substitutes a sleeping potion instead.

## Philarmonus

A soothsayer. He erroneously predicts that Rome will win the war against Britain, but he later correctly interprets the prophecy left with Posthumus by Jupiter.

## Caius Lucius

A Roman general. He is honest and forthright. When he finds Imogen in the forest disguised as Fidele, he makes her his page.

## Helen

A lady attending Imogen.

## Jupiter

A god worshipped by both the Romans and the Britons; he appears to Posthumus in a dream, along with the ghosts of his family.

# CRITICAL COMMENTARIES

The basic elements of the intertwined plots of the lost children and the faithful wife are established in the first act.

The play opens at Cymbeline's palace in Britain. Two gentlemen meet and discuss recent events that have occurred at the king's court. One of the gentlemen is unfamiliar with the history of the loss of Cymbeline's sons, nor does he know about Imogen's recent marriage to Posthumus, so the first gentleman explains what has happened. He reveals that Imogen, Cymbeline's daughter, has angered her father by marrying his foster-child instead of her stepbrother, Cloten. The king has declared that Posthumus is to be banished from the kingdom and Imogen is to be imprisoned at the palace. The gentleman explains further that Imogen is heir to the throne, and, additionally, he tells how Imogen's brothers, Guiderius and Arviragus, disappeared twenty years earlier, when Guiderius was about three years old and Arviragus was a baby. No one ever found out what became of them, he says.

He then goes on to describe Posthumus, "a poor but worthy gentleman." Posthumus, he says, was given the surname Leonatus because of his courage. As the orphaned son of a loyal friend of Cymbeline's father, he was dependent upon Cymbeline's generosity in his youth. Cymbeline reared Posthumus as his own son, but Cymbeline's affection ended when Imogen married the young man in defiance of Cymbeline's plans.

At this time we know little about either Imogen or Posthumus, but it becomes clear that both are admired for their goodness. One reason that Posthumus is believed to be worthy (as, in fact, he is) is that Imogen chose him for her husband, incurring the wrath of her father in doing so.

Concerning the two lovers, the gentleman says of Posthumus:

> To his mistress,
> For whom he now is banish'd – her own price
> Proclaims how she esteem'd him and his virtue;
> By her election may be truly read
> What kind of man he is.

(I,i,50–54)

The imagery of commerce is evident here for Posthumus' value is spoken of in terms of "her price." Such references to trade and money or jewels occur throughout the play, echoing the theme of one of the major plot-lines, the story of the wager involving Imogen's faithfulness.

At this point, the queen, Imogen's stepmother, enters, along with Imogen and Posthumus. She tells them that they will have a few moments alone to say goodbye. At this point, we do not know that the queen will soon be revealed to be the stereotype of the evil stepmother, which, ironically, she specifically denies. For example, she tells Imogen:

> No, be assur'd you shall not find me, daughter,
> After the slander of most stepmothers,
> Evil-ey'd unto you.

(I,i,70–72)

We learn later, however, that the queen intends to murder Imogen if she cannot persuade the young woman to marry the queen's boorish son, Cloten, in order for him to be heir to the throne.

In the few minutes that they have together, Posthumus and Imogen exchange tokens of their love. Imogen gives Posthumus a diamond ring that once belonged to her mother, and he, in turn, gives her a bracelet. He likens the exchange to a trade—an exchange for value—and he also compares the bracelet to their love that makes her a prisoner.

> As I my poor self did exchange for you,
> To your so infinite loss; so in our trifles
> I still win of you; for my sake wear this.
> It is a manacle of love; I'll place it
> Upon this fairest prisoner.

(I,i,119–23)

Cymbeline enters and is outraged at seeing them together. He upbraids Imogen, accusing her of making him old before his time. He tells her that in marrying Posthumus she has deprived herself of having a prince for a husband; she retorts that she made the better choice in choosing an "eagle" rather than a "puttock" (a bird which the Elizabethans also referred to as a "kite"). That is, Imogen chose the truly noble man over the fraudulently noble man. This idea of true or hidden nobility continues throughout the play, as we shall see later when we encounter Guiderius and Arviragus, who do not know that they are sons of a king. Thus, Imogen defends Posthumus' worthiness, and, again, using the language of commerce, she states that he is:

> A man worth any woman; overbuys me
> Almost the sum he pays.

(I,i,146–47)

Posthumus' servant, Pisanio, enters and reports that Cloten, the queen's son, has attacked Posthumus, but that the fight was stopped without anyone's being hurt. Pisanio also explains that Posthumus didn't take Cloten's offensive behavior seriously, and Imogen's attitude reveals that no one—except the queen—thinks highly of Cloten.

In the next scene, Cloten and two lords appear, and we hear Cloten's version of the fight. Here, he is revealed to be a braggart, a coward, and a fool, and the lords' remarks also reveal their skepticism about his value. They all leave, and Imogen and Pisanio appear.

Pisanio has witnessed Posthumus' departure, and he describes to Imogen how he watched the ship sail away. She explains to Pisanio that before she could give Posthumus a last kiss, her father interrupted them and that Posthumus had to leave before they could truly say goodbye. Another important use of imagery appears here—that of nature and growing things, imagery which is repeated throughout the play. In describing her father's anger, Imogen compares him to the north wind that blows away the buds of love before they can blossom.

The scene now shifts to Rome, where Posthumus has arrived at the house of Philario, a friend of Posthumus' father. Philario, Iachimo, and three other men (a Frenchman, a Dutchman, and a Spaniard) are at Philario's house and are discussing Posthumus' past life and his present, unfortunate, banishment.

Posthumus enters, and the conversation turns into a debate concerning what apparently occurred the night before—when each of the men praised the character of the women of his own country. Iachimo claims that there is no such thing as a truly faithful woman, and, of course, Posthumus disagrees. Iachimo wagers half his wealth, "the moiety of my estate," against Posthumus' diamond ring that Iachimo can seduce any woman in the world—including Imogen. Specifically, Iachimo says:

> I will lay you ten thousand ducats to your ring
> that, commend me to the court where your lady is, with
> no more advantage than the opportunity of a second
> conference, and I will bring from thence that honour of
> hers which you imagine so reserv'd.

(I,iv,138–43)

Stung by Iachimo's confidence, Posthumus agrees to the wager. However, Posthumus imposes one further condition: if Iachimo succeeds, they will remain friends, for Imogen would not be worth arguing over. Conversely, if she is *not* seduced by Iachimo, Posthumus vows to avenge the insult to her chastity with his sword. This bargain may seem unusual to modern readers, who might perhaps think that Posthumus should be angry if Iachimo succeeds, *not* if he fails. But the issue at stake here is Imogen's honor, and it is perceived as an insult to her honor that Iachimo would even think that he could seduce her. This is no longer the case, however, for if Iachimo succeeds, he will have proven that she has no honor, according to Posthumus' definition. Thus the bargain is sealed, and Iachimo prepares to go to Britain to claim, if he can, the honor of Posthumus' wife, Imogen.

In the next scene, we return to Britain and Cymbeline's palace. Here, the true character of the evil queen is revealed. Shakespeare makes certain that we have no doubt that she is evil, for in this scene we find her conferring with a physician, Cornelius, about poisons and how they work. When the scene ends, we realize that Shakespeare is cleverly showing his audience just how deeply evil the woman is. We realize also that it is possible that Shakespeare knew that there would be many people in the audience who were fond of pets, for we are absolutely convinced of the queen's villainy when she attempts to persuade Cornelius to give her some poisons so that she can experiment on dogs and cats.

The physician's suspicions about the queen's villainous nature are aroused, and, as a result, he provides her with a sleeping potion, whose effects give the appearance of death, but which permit the sleeper to eventually awaken, with no side effects.

Before Cornelius hands over the box with the supposed poison in it, Pisanio enters, and the queen beckons him aside. She drops the box, and Pisanio picks it up. She tells him to keep it, that it is a powerful "medicine"; she hopes that at some time he himself will swallow it, leaving Imogen without an ally or a reminder of her husband. Ironically, the queen thinks she has given Pisanio poison, but she has, in fact, given him only a sleeping potion, one which will figure later in the plot.

The scene ends with Pisanio's vow of loyalty, a vow contrasting his virtue with the queen's scheming attempts at manipulation. He leaves then, and Imogen enters alone, grieving at her lot:

> A father cruel, and a step-dame false;
> A foolish suitor to a wedded lady
> That hath her husband banish'd.
>
> (I,vi,1–3)

Soon, Pisanio, along with Iachimo, who has just arrived from Rome, enters and greets her. Note that although the play is set in ancient Britain during the time of the Roman occupation, the characters of the Britons and Romans resemble those of Renaissance Englishmen and Italians more than they do the peoples of the more ancient countries. Thus, the people of Cymbeline's court are described as proud and nationalistic, and the Italians of Rome are described according to the Shakespearean stereotype of the Renaissance Italian—sophisticated but crafty. Iachimo is that, plus more than a bit Machiavellian, and he has several alternate plans to seduce Imogen's honor—or to appear to, as we shall later see.

When Iachimo first sees Imogen, he is astounded by her beauty, and he says to himself that if her mind matches her appearance, he has already lost the wager.

> All of her that is out of door most rich!
> If she be furnish'd with a mind so rare,

> She is alone, th' Arabian bird, and I
> Have lost the wager.
>
> (I,vi,15–18)

Iachimo then decides to put his first plan into effect. He hopes to weaken Imogen's will by making the suggestion that Posthumus is not pining with grief in Rome, but, rather, is enjoying himself. Iachimo begins by pretending to talk to himself, wondering in amazement that a man who has such a beautiful wife could ever be contented with less:

> The cloyed will—
> That satiate yet unsatisfi'd desire, that tub
> Both fill'd and running,—ravening first the lamb,
> Longs after for the garbage.
>
> (I,vi,47-50)

Thus, Iachimo implies that Posthumus cannot distinguish between the beautiful and the ugly, and consequently seeks after other women who are far inferior to Imogen's beauty. He strengthens this impression by assuring Imogen that Posthumus is indeed well; in fact, he is called, according to Iachimo, "the Briton reveler." He then says that he pities Imogen because of the unworthy behavior of her husband; this further upsets her. But Iachimo fails to convince Imogen that she should take her revenge by doing the same.

When Iachimo offers himself, Imogen realizes that he has been lying, and she becomes highly indignant. She calls Pisanio and is about to have Iachimo punished for his insults to both her and Posthumus, but Iachimo quickly says, in effect, that he was "only testing her." He begs her pardon and praises Posthumus so well that she relents and forgives him.

Now, Iachimo decides to put his second plan into effect. He perceives that he cannot seduce Imogen, so he must find a way to make it appear to Posthumus that he *has* seduced her. He asks Imogen if she will do him a favor by storing a box containing priceless jewels and other treasures, supposedly the result of contributions made by her husband and others, to be presented to the Roman emperor. She agrees and says that she will store the box (which is, coincidentally, large enough to hold a man) in her room overnight. Iachimo is delighted and tells her that he must leave very soon. Sadly, Imogen does not realize that Iachimo plans to hide in the box after she thinks that he has left.

As we have seen, Iachimo is quite villainous. He will cheat and lie in order to win his wager concerning Imogen's honor. But one should note that Iachimo is not the most despicable character in the play. That role belongs to Cloten, who appears again in Act II.

## ACT II

This act opens, as did Act I, with a scene set in front of Cymbeline's palace in Britain. Cloten and two lords are talking about gambling and swearing, both subjects that Cloten appears to relish. The scene has two purposes. In the beginning, we get to see more of Cloten's character, and we learn that no one in the court is deceived by him *or* his mother—except Cymbeline. Toward the end of the scene, we receive a quick summary of the main plot of the play, involving Cloten's struggle to possess Imogen, as well as news of her efforts to keep her honor, in spite of the plots of Cloten and Iachimo.

Cloten discusses honor and gentility with the lords, yet even in his discussion of these virtues (which he thinks he possesses), he couches his phrases in coarse language. Cloten learns that Iachimo, said to be a friend of Posthumus, is at court, and he asks whether there would be any abasement if he were to go meet the man. The second lord, in an aside, comments, "You are a fool granted, therefore your issues, being foolish, do not derogate." That is, Cloten is already so low in everyone's esteem that he cannot possibly sink any lower.

This point is summed up by the same lord, who says after Cloten and one of the lords have left:

> That such a crafty devil as is his mother
> Should yield the world this ass! A woman that
> Bears all down with her brain; and this her son
> Cannot take two from twenty, for his heart,
> And leave eighteen.
>
> (II,i,57–61)

Apparently, Cloten is also not very bright.

The lord continues, but now he addresses his speech to the absent Imogen, succinctly summarizing her plight, one of the main issues to be resolved in the play:

> Alas poor princess,
> Thou divine Imogen, what thou endur'st,
> Betwixt a father by thy step-dame govern'd,
> A mother hourly coining plots, a wooer
> More hateful than the foul expulsion is
> Of thy dear husband, than that horrid act
> Of the divorce he'd make! The heavens hold firm
> The walls of thy dear honor, keep unshak'd
> That temple, thy fair mind, that thou mayst stand,
> T' enjoy thy banish'd lord and this great land!
>
> (II,i,61-70)

Little does this man know that Cloten is not the only one after Imogen's honor. But he aptly sums up her problems which must be overcome if order in England (a favorite theme of Shakespeare's) is to be restored. The natural order of things is perverted when an evil queen rules the king, and when base men try to separate an honorable man from his wife.

The scene now shifts to Imogen's bedroom, where she is about to go to bed. She has been reading the tale of Tereus' rape of Philomel, a story which (ironically) comments on the situation at hand. In the corner sits a large trunk containing the crafty Iachimo. Imogen prays to the gods for protection and then falls asleep. Quickly, Iachimo crawls from the trunk and goes over to the sleeping Imogen.

He does not touch her, but, rather, he makes a note of all of the details of her room, for it is unlikely that anyone but a family member or a lover would have access to it. However, such evidence *could* be purchased from servants, so he needs more evidence to present to Posthumus. Carefully, he removes the bracelet which Posthumus placed on Imogen's arm. As he does so, Iachimo notices that she has a tiny, flower-shaped ("cinque" or five-spotted) mole on her left breast. This is indeed the evidence that he will use to convince Posthumus that he, Iachimo, was Imogen's lover. As the clock strikes, Iachimo returns to his trunk, presumably to be carried away the next day, when he will return to Rome and convince Posthumus that he has "pick'd the lock, and ta'en/ The treasure of her honor."

The next morning, Cloten attempts to serenade Imogen with his music. As usual, he is crude and boorish–even in his attempts to be romantic. Apparently, someone has advised him to try to charm her with music. But all that really seems to be on his mind is sex, as is proven by his obvious double entendres.

Cymbeline and the queen enter, and Cloten tells them that Imogen ignored his music. Cymbeline assures him that the memory of Posthumus is too fresh. Once Imogen has forgotten Posthumus, the king says, "then she's yours." The queen reminds her son that it is a good thing that the king approves of Cloten's courtship of his daughter, and she advises him to persist–even though Imogen presently refuses him.

Everyone but Cloten leaves, and he wonders whether or not he will gain admittance to her room (a symbol of her fidelity and chastity) if he bribes one of her ladies-in-waiting. Like a Judas, he thinks that gold will answer all questions of ethics: "What can it [gold] not undo?"

A waiting-lady of Imogen's appears, and Cloten asks her if Imogen is "ready." In an aside, the woman says, "Ay, to keep her chamber." Cloten offers her gold if she will sell her "good report." This vague request is precisely answered. The lady says that she will neither sell her good name by accepting a bribe, nor will she offer any but her honest report of her opinion of Cloten. Just then, Imogen enters, and Cloten greets her, "swearing" that he loves her. Imogen is honest with him and replies that it does not matter how he feels; she does not love him. Cloten persists, and Imogen is forced to be plain – to the extent of being blunt with him. She tells him that she does not, cannot, and will not, love him:

> By th' very truth of it, I care not for you,
> And am so near the lack of charity
> To accuse myself I hate you; which I had rather
> You felt than make 't my boast.
>
> (II,iii, 113–16)

But Cloten foolishly persists, trying to tell her that her marriage with Posthumus, "that base wretch," is invalid because she is of royal blood and he is not. Of course, Cloten's use of "wretch" and other epithets to describe Posthumus is ironic, for it is *Cloten* who is the wretch – as Imogen explains to him:

> Profane fellow!
> Wert thou son of Jupiter and no more
> But what thou art besides, thou wert too base
> To be his groom.
>
> (II,iii,129–32)

She finally convinces Cloten of her anger when she states that Posthumus' "meanest garment" is dearer to her than Cloten can ever be because it touched Posthumus' body. Taken aback, Cloten can utter only, "His garment . . . His meanest garment!" For the rest of this scene, all Cloten can do is to continue to mutter, "His garment." One might compare, in modern language, Cloten to a lover's dirty underwear and achieve a similar effect. Cloten, stung to the quick, vows revenge.

In the meantime, Imogen notes that her bracelet is missing, and she sends Pisanio, who has just entered, to look for it. She does not realize that she did not simply mislay it.

The scene now shifts to Philario's house in Rome, where Philario and Posthumus are discussing Posthumus' unfortunate exile. They are also discussing the increasing tension that exists between Britain and Rome concerning whether or not Cymbeline will pay tribute to the emperor. Although Posthumus says that he is not a statesman, he fears that there will be war over the issue. He learns, however, that the Roman general Caius Lucius is about to go to Britain to *demand* the tribute.

At this point, Iachimo enters, having since returned to Rome, and Posthumus tells him that he hopes that "the briefness of your answer made/ The speediness of your return." However, Iachimo tells him that the "briefness" of his trip is not because Imogen refused his advances so quickly; on the contrary, she consented – and quickly. Naturally, Posthumus doesn't believe him, so Iachimo sets out to prove his point.

First, he describes Imogen's bedroom. He is careful to deny that he slept there, but his modest disclaimer of what he did *not* do there makes the implication of what he did do all the more painful to Posthumus. But Posthumus is still not convinced, so Iachimo goes further and produces the bracelet. Iachimo suggests that Imogen gave it to him, but Posthumus counters that she might have entrusted it to him to send to Posthumus. However, since she did not write a letter saying so, Posthumus is convinced of Imogen's infidelity, and so he removes his ring. At that moment, Philario intervenes and assumes the role of calm and reason. He suggests that Imogen's bracelet could have been stolen from her.

Posthumus agrees and demands that Iachimo give him "some corporal sign" (bodily proof) that he was intimately acquainted with her. Iachimo cleverly denies that this is necessary; the bracelet is evidence enough. Posthumus is again convinced, but Philario again persuades him that the bracelet is not enough to prove Imogen's infidelity.

Iachimo quickly adds that if further proof is needed, he has it, and he mentions the flower-shaped mole under her left breast. Posthumus recalls the mark, and it, more than anything else, convinces him that Imogen has succumbed to Iachimo's seduction.

Two points should be noted here. First, how quickly Posthumus is willing to believe that Imogen has been seduced. The relative ease with which Iachimo convinces Posthumus suggests that Posthumus' faith in his wife is not so great as one might suppose. This flaw compounds the second flaw in his character; that is, that Posthumus can believe that Imogen can be unfaithful. He succumbs to bitterness and anger, but he says that he will not see his wife again until he has forgiven her for whatever she may have done. His love must become as pure as hers was before whatever she may have done before he can be reunited with her.

Even Philario is convinced by the revelation made by Iachimo, and, at this point, Posthumus begins a diatribe against women that might offend many people, but we know that he is mistaken. Nevertheless, for the time being, Posthumus has nothing good to say about women.

## ACT III

Caius Lucius has arrived in Britain, and he demands tribute on behalf of the Roman emperor. Interestingly, it is Cloten and the queen who speak in favor of Britain and refuse to pay the tribute. Cloten, as usual, is rather boorish and crude in his refusal, and even Cymbeline has to finally interrupt him to smooth things over. Cymbeline then finishes with a decorous refusal, and Caius Lucius regretfully says that war is inevitable. Nevertheless, as ambassador, Caius is treated politely and is made welcome.

Later, Pisanio receives a letter from Posthumus accusing Imogen of adultery and commanding him to kill her. Pisanio is shocked (not knowing of Iachimo's trickery), for he knows that Imogen is faithful, and he reads part of Posthumus' letter to her. The first part of the letter tells us that Posthumus is now in Cambria (Wales), at Milford-Haven. Imogen says that she will go there at once. Pisanio is reluctant to take her there, and she asks him why, but he won't tell her. Imogen, however, is determined to leave and prepares to do so.

The scene now shifts to Wales and the cave of Belarius, where he and his two foster sons live. They are, of course, Guiderius and Arviragus, Cymbeline's sons, whom Belarius kidnapped when he left the court in vengeful anger many years before. Belarius and the two young men live simply and honestly in harmony with nature, and although Belarius was wrong to take the two boys, it is apparent from earlier scenes that he has treated them well. They, in turn, think that he is their real father.

Belarius compares the joys of living close to the land with the false rewards of living at the palace, but Guiderius (called Polydore) and Arviragus (called Cadwal) take exception to his words; they say that they have no experience on which to base a similar judgment. Guiderius says:

> Out of your proof you speak; we poor unfledg'd,
> Have never wing'd from view o' th' nest; nor know not
> What air's from home. Haply this life is best . . .
> That have a sharper known. . . .
>
> (III,iii,27–30)

Arviragus agrees, but Belarius chides them; they do not know the "city's usuries," nor its treachery. Belarius explains to his "sons" about the false accusation of treachery that caused him to be banished (however, he does not tell them how he took them with him). But when he is alone, he adds:

> These boys know little they are sons to th' King,
> Nor Cymbeline dreams that they are alive.
> They think they're mine, and, though train'd up thus
>       meanly,
> I' th' cave wherein they bow, their thoughts do hit
> The roofs of palaces. . . .
>
> (III,iii,80-84)

Belarius (called Morgan) further recalls that he kidnapped the children, thinking to deprive Cymbeline of his heirs, as Cymbeline deprived Belarius of his lands and title. Yet Belarius, without meaning to, came to love the young boys and therefore married their nurse, Euriphile, whom the boys thought was their mother.

As the next scene illustrates, it just happens, coincidentally, that Belarius and Cymbeline's sons live near Milford-Haven, where Imogen is going, hoping to find Posthumus.

Pisanio and Imogen arrive at Milford-Haven, and she immediately reveals how much she longs to see Posthumus; therefore, Pisanio is forced to explain his unwillingness to have her see Posthumus. He gives her the letter, so she can read for herself the part which he omitted. In the letter, Posthumus accuses Imogen of infidelity and claims that he has proof. He then orders Pisanio to kill her. Pisanio realizes that the letter deeply wounds Imogen because of its false accusations. She remembers how Iachimo described Posthumus' behavior in Italy, and she wonders if his descriptions of Posthumus were true.

Imogen, grieving, tells Pisanio to strike her with a sword; she draws it herself so that he may do so. But, of course, he refuses. She asks him why he brought her to this wilderness, if not to kill her, and Pisanio answers that he has a plan. He says that he will send word to Posthumus that she is dead, along with a bloodied cloth as proof. She refuses to return to Cymbeline's court and face Cloten's wooing, so she decides to hide in the forests of Wales.

Pisanio suggests, in addition, that she disguise herself as a boy and enter the services of Caius Lucius, who will at least take her with him to Rome; there, she can be near Posthumus and find out what has happened to make him hate her so. Pisanio urges her to disguise her gentleness with aggressiveness; otherwise, he says she will not survive. Pisanio, having thought ahead that such a plan might work, has conveniently brought the clothing which she will need.

Imogen gratefully accepts Pisanio's offer of help, and she also accepts the box with the sleeping potion in it (which the queen thought was poison, and which Pisanio thinks is medicine).

The scene then shifts back to Cymbeline's palace, where the king is still discussing with Caius Lucius the matter of Britain's refusal to pay tribute to Rome. Cymbeline then agrees to give Lucius safe conduct to Milford-Haven. However, they both are prepared for war.

Cymbeline then notices that Imogen has not been seen at the palace lately. He thinks that this lapse is impertinent of her, and he sends a servant to fetch her. The queen cleverly—considering her own interests—advises Cymbeline not to be angry with Imogen, for it is natural that she should be somewhat upset because of Posthumus' banishment. The servant returns and says that Imogen's room is locked and that no one answers the door. The king and Cloten go to find out what has happened, while the queen speculates: it is possible, she thinks, that Imogen ran away to be with Posthumus. Such a risky venture will either result in her death or cause her to be banished from court for disobeying her father. Either fate, the queen concludes, is to her advantage, for she desires to see Cloten inherit the throne. Cloten returns to tell the queen that Imogen has disappeared and that the king is outraged. The queen goes to comfort her husband, and Cloten is left to think about what has happened to Imogen.

Cloten's attitude towards Imogen is made clear in his soliloquy, in which he admits that she is beautiful and full of good qualities. But the fact that she prefers Posthumus makes Cloten hate her, and he vows revenge for the injury she has done him. It is his later attempt to carry out this revenge that indirectly leads to his death.

Pisanio enters, and Cloten demands that he tell where Imogen has gone. At first, Pisanio pretends that he does not know, but eventually he gives Cloten the letter from Posthumus. Cloten asks Pisanio if the letter is true, and Pisanio says that it is. Cloten then asks Pisanio to serve him and do whatever he asks him to do, no matter how villainous it may be. Pisanio agrees, but he is only pretending, for his true loyalty is to Imogen and Posthumus.

Cloten asks Pisanio to provide him with some of Posthumus' clothing so that he can go to Milford-Haven, and Pisanio leaves to do this. In his letter, Posthumus said that he would meet Imogen there, and Cloten plans to kill Posthumus and rape Imogen. He will wear her husband's clothes as a last bit of revenge, to get even with her for her slighting remark – that Cloten was unworthy of her husband's "meanest garment."

Pisanio returns with the clothes, not knowing nor caring why Cloten wants them. Cloten tells him to be silent about his knowledge of the plan and leaves. Pisanio reveals his true feelings when he is alone; that is, to be true to Cloten would be "to prove false, which I will never be,/ To him that is most true."

We return now to Wales, where Imogen, disguised in boy's clothing, camps alone in the woods. She is tired and hungry. She sees a cave and notes that it looks as if someone lives there. She calls out, but no one answers, so she draws her sword and enters the cave to see what she can find.

In the meantime, Belarius and his two foster sons return. They plan to get ready to eat, but when Belarius goes to the cave to get their food, he discovers Imogen eating.

She apologizes for taking their food and offers to pay for it, but the youths scorn her offer of gold, for money means nothing to them. (Compare this response to the love of money and gambling embodied in the character of Cloten).

She apologizes again and explains that she is headed for Milford-Haven. They ask her her name, and she says that she calls herself "Fidele," which has in it the echo of "fidelity." She says that she has a kinsman, referring to Caius Lucius, whom she hopes to meet, for he will be leaving for Italy from there.

Belarius and the two boys are impressed by her and ask this strange but charming "young man" to stay with them and be welcome. It is a convention in Shakespeare's plays that disguises *always* work, and no one –

not even Posthumus—recognizes that Fidele is Imogen until she reveals her true identity later in the play.

Thus the princes welcome Imogen, Guiderius going so far as to say that if she were a woman, he could love her. Ironically, they welcome her as they would a brother, and she wishes to herself that had her brothers lived, they would be like these two young men. The irony, of course, lies in the fact that they *are* her long-lost brothers, and the mutual affinity that exists among the three of them is apparent for they are, in truth, related.

Imogen wishes further that she really could be their brother, since her beloved husband, Posthumus, has abandoned her. They perceive that she is troubled, but since the cause is unknown to them, they try to make her welcome as best they can.

The act ends with a brief scene in Rome, during which several senators and tribunes discuss Caius Lucius' appointment as general of the forces and his trip to Britain. The scene serves no purpose except to remind us that a potential war exists in the situation created by Cymbeline's refusal to pay tribute to Rome.

## ACT IV

Cloten arrives in Wales and, in a soliloquy, he outlines his plan to kill Posthumus and rape Imogen. He believes that while Cymbeline may be a bit angry at Cloten's "rough usage" of Imogen, Cloten's mother will eventually persuade her husband that all is well.

In another part of Wales, Belarius (Morgan), Polydore (Guiderius), Cadwal (Arviragus), and Fidele (Imogen) live in relative harmony. Belarius tells Fidele to remain at the cave while they hunt because Fidele does not seem well. Guiderius offers to stay with the young man, but Fidele says that *he* is not too ill and that *he* can stay alone. Of course, the source of Fidele's illness is grief over Posthumus' rejection.

Both Guiderius and Arviragus assert that they love Fidele like a brother, and Belarius is impressed by their nobility. They then decide to prepare to leave, and Imogen, still "heart-sick," as she says, decides to try some of the "medicine" which Pisanio left with her. She swallows it and retires to the cave. Her brothers praise her virtues—her patience, her voice, and her smile—all supposedly feminine qualities, although possessed by a "boy," Fidele.

Just as the men are about to leave, Cloten enters, and Guiderius sends the others away to see if Cloten has brought other men with him. Cloten challenges Guiderius, calling him a thief. Guiderius challenges him in return, his words echoing those which Cloten expressed in his challenge to Rome in Act III. Cloten demands to know whether or not Guiderius knows him by his clothes, possibly suggesting that either Cloten forgot that he is wearing Posthumus' clothes, or that he is simply wearing courtly garments as opposed to Guiderius' more rustic costume. At any rate, Cloten's remark is rather stupid, and Guiderius answers it with scorn. When Cloten tells Guiderius that he, Cloten, is the son of the queen, Guiderius answers that he is "sorry for it; not seeming/ So worthy as thy birth." Guiderius also makes a reasonable man's response to Cloten's question about whether or not he is afraid.

> Those that I reverence, those I fear, the wise.
> At fools I laugh, not fear them.
>
> (IV,ii,94–95)

This is too much, and Cloten determines to kill him. They exit fighting.

Belarius and Arviragus return, having found no one. Belarius is positive that he recognized Cloten, although it has been years since he has seen him. At that moment, Guiderius returns with Cloten's head. Such a victory should be no surprise, considering the lack of prowess exhibited by Cloten earlier in the play, when he attempted to best Posthumus. It is interesting that Guiderius did the deed using Cloten's own sword.

Belarius and Arviragus discover what Guiderius has done. Belarius is fearful of the consequences, yet proud of his son's courage. Shortly thereafter, they return to the cave, and Arviragus discovers Fidele, apparently dead. He carries Fidele's body to the others and explains that he found *him* apparently resting, *his* head on a pillow.

For the rest of this portion of the scene, Guiderius and Arviragus grieve over Fidele and prepare to bury him. They sing a song, "Fear no more the heat o' th' sun," for the youth.

Belarius, who left while the brothers mourned over Fidele, now returns with the headless body of Cloten, dressed in Posthumus' clothes. He lays the body down beside Fidele's, and they leave, intending to return later to bury them.

Imogen awakes, confused and disoriented. She is covered with beautiful flowers, yet lies next to a headless body. At first, she does not recognize it as anyone she knows, but merely comments on the incongruity of her situation:

> These flowers are like the pleasures of the world;
> This bloody man, the care on it. I hope I dream.
>
> (IV,ii,296–97)

The scene has an air of unreality to it, so much like a dream is it that Imogen becomes confused as to whether any of the recent events which befell her are real or not:

> For so I thought I was a cave-keeper
> And cook to honest creatures, but 'tis not so.

'Twas but a bolt of nothing, shot at nothing,
Which the brain makes of fumes. Our very eyes
Are sometimes like our judgements, blind.

(IV,ii,298-302)

At this point, she slowly comes to recognize the clothes which the corpse wears as belonging to Posthumus, and she immediately blames Pisanio and Cloten for somehow conspiring to murder Posthumus. Then she faints, falling across the body.

Taken literally, the scene creates dramatic problems, but its stylized quality causes one to focus on the significance of the case of mistaken identity, rather than on the gruesome details of Imogen's discovery. The audience is aware that Posthumus is not really dead, and, in addition, they are perhaps even aware of the irony when Imogen swears in her distraught state that she recognizes the shape of Posthumus' leg and hand.

It is interesting that Imogen confuses Cloten with Posthumus at this point, for right now they are closer than they usually were. There is additional irony in the fact that Posthumus' actions before he repents are more worthy of a Cloten than a Posthumus. Posthumus rejected his faithful wife, disparaged her, and ordered her killed without giving her any opportunity to explain or speak in her own defense. But unlike Cloten, Posthumus goes from worse to better rather than the opposite. Before even having proof (which will come with Iachimo's confession) that Imogen is innocent, he will regret having condemned her and will forgive her. There lies the difference between the hero and the clod.

At this point, the Romans arrive, including Lucius, his captains, and a soothsayer. The Romans expect to do battle soon, and they ask the soothsayer what he foresees as the outcome. He replies that he saw the Roman eagle, the symbol of Jupiter, fly from the south toward Wales and disappear into the sunlight. The vision itself is ambiguous, since the eagle vanishing into the sun could plausibly signify victory for either side. But the soothsayer chooses to interpret his dream as signifying success for the Romans.

Suddenly, Lucius sees the headless body of Cloten with Imogen still disguised as a boy fallen on top of the corpse. They discover that Imogen, dressed still as Fidele, is alive, and they ask what has happened. She tells them that the body belonged to her master, who was slain by mountaineers, and she asks to be allowed to enter the service of Lucius, which was what Pisanio had originally planned. Lucius accepts Imogen's offer, and they prepare to bury Cloten.

Back at Cymbeline's palace, we learn that the queen is ill because of the absence of her son, an absence which has almost driven her mad. Likewise, Cymbeline grieves because Imogen, whom he loved deeply, has been gone for so long. He asks Pisanio where she is, but Pisanio swears that he does not know. This is true, after a fashion, for he does not know *exactly* where she went or how she survived.

Cymbeline is then informed that the Romans have landed on the coast, as we have just learned, and the king and his attendants leave to prepare for war. Pisanio, meanwhile, is puzzled over the fact that he has not heard from Posthumus since he informed his master that he had killed Imogen.

We return to the cave of Belarius in Wales and find the old knight and the two princes faced with an impending battle. They plan to side with Britain, but Belarius fears to do so openly because of Cloten's death. Nevertheless, Guiderius and Arviragus convince him that there is nothing else they can, or should, do.

## ACT V

This act brings Posthumus again to our attention. Shakespeare is careful to keep all the various strands of the intertwined plots connected, so in this case, he uses the Roman invasion as an occasion for Posthumus' return to England.

The act opens with Posthumus alone, expressing regret that he blamed Imogen so much and ordered her death. He blames Pisanio now, for following his orders too well. A "good servant," he asserts, does not do *all* he is told to do, but obeys only those commands which are just. Ironically, Pisanio is just such a good servant, although Posthumus does not yet know it, for Pisanio remained loyal to both his mistress *and* his master.

It is important for the purposes of the play that Posthumus forgive Imogen even though he believes her guilty of infidelity. This forgiveness helps make his happy reunion with her more plausible later on. His repentance at his order for her death is the first step toward his reformation that must occur before he will discover that she was indeed innocent.

The next scene involves a skirmish between the British and the Roman armies, and it provides the occasion for Iachimo to appear, who also suffers from guilt for having betrayed Imogen.

The battle continues, and Cymbeline is captured by the Romans. Belarius, Guiderius, and Arviragus go to rescue him and are aided by Posthumus. Their rescue is successful, and they leave together.

Lucius, Iachimo, and Imogen enter, and they comment on the strange turns of fortune in the battle and then leave. On another part of the battle-field, Posthumus and a lord discuss the battle. They note that nearly all of the Britons were driven back, except for one old soldier (Belarius) who, with two young men, bravely held the enemy off at a narrow pass. Posthumus does not mention his part in supporting the British side. Instead, Posthumus, after having favorably described the Britons' bravery, tells the lord that, although he (Posthumus) is a Briton, he is affiliated with the Romans, yet he would welcome capture. Posthumus is, in fact, taken prisoner when some British soldiers arrive, but they do not recognize him as one of the men who fought alongside Belarius.

Posthumus is now a prisoner, and he looks forward to death, as one who has lost all reason for living. Again, he expresses his feelings of repentance. He offers his own life to the gods in exchange for Imogen's, for his life is not so valuable as hers, since he is, as he believes, guilty of the gravest of sins. As he concludes, expressing his remorse, he falls asleep and dreams of his family, who are all dead.

As Posthumus sleeps, his true father, Sicilius Leonatus, appears, leading his wife, Posthumus' mother, by the hand. Two other youths then enter, who are Posthumus' brothers, bearing the wounds that killed them in battle before Posthumus was born. They stand around the sleeping Posthumus and engage in a dialogue concerning his fate.

The solemnity and unreality of Posthumus' vision is emphasized by the appearance of these ghosts from his past and their speeches, which are, except for the songs, rhymed verses set in a different meter from the dialogue of the rest of the play.

The family discusses Posthumus' basically good character and his foolishness in letting Iachimo deceive him. Then they call upon Jupiter to aid him, arguing that Posthumus has suffered for the wrong that he did and, in part, he has repaid his sins through his bravery on behalf of Britain.

Jupiter hears their pleas and descends, seated on an eagle, and he assures Posthumus' family that they should

> Be content:
> Your low-laid son our godhead will uplift.
> His comforts thrive, his trials well are spent.
> Our jovial star reigned at his birth and in
> Our temple was he married. Rise, and fade.
> He shall be lord of Lady Imogen,
> And happier much by his affliction made.
>
> (V,iv,103–9)

Thus, Jupiter tells the ghosts to fade, for all will be well with Posthumus, perhaps even more so because he has had to suffer much in order to appreciate what he had.

The structure of the preceding scene falls into the category of the masque, a form of courtly stylized entertainment still popular in Shakespeare's day. Masques were not a regular part of dramatic performances in Elizabethan plays, but Shakespeare used them on several occasions to present events that were in some way unreal or supernatural. It is typical of the playwright's sensibilities that he accounts for this interlude by placing it within a dream. The same thing occurs in *Pericles*, when the king is informed by the goddess Diana that his wife is still alive.

At any rate, Posthumus awakens from this vision and finds a booklet lying nearby. In it, he finds written the message that prophesies that he will be reunited with Imogen and that Britain will prosper.

> Whenas a lion's whelp shall, to himself unknown, with-
> out seeking find, and be embrac'd by a piece of tender
> air; and when from a stately cedar shall be lopp'd
> branches, which, being dead many years, shall after
> revive, be jointed to the old stock, and freshly grow;
> then shall Posthumus end his miseries, Britain be
> fortunate and flourish in peace and plenty.
>
> (V,iv,137–44)

At this point in the play, Posthumus does not understand what the prophecy means, nor does he think that it will have any effect on his death, which he believes is imminent. Even though he does not know it, the prophecy, as it is later interpreted, predicts that all will end well. Posthumus is the lion's (Leonatus') whelp, and Posthumus is told that he will find Imogen, although he is not seeking her because he believes her to be dead. She is the "piece of tender air," for the Latin words for "a woman" and "tender air" are almost the same—*mulier* and *mollis aer*. She is also like air to the extent that Posthumus does not recognize her when he first sees her, thinking her a boy, and so she will not become real, or solid, for him until he does recognize her.

Likewise, the "stately cedar" is Cymbeline, whose "lopped branches" are his sons, who will be restored to him. How this happy ending comes about is the subject of the final scenes in the play.

While Posthumus thinks about this prophecy, his guards return for him and ask him if he is ready to die. He says that he is, since he has lost—or so he thinks—all that he thought was worth living for.

The first of the two jailers asks Posthumus if he is "ready for death," and Posthumus replies, "Over-roasted rather; ready long ago." The jailor tells Posthumus that perhaps he is fortunate, for after he is gone there will be no more "tavern bills" to pay. This passage incorporates two sets of images—that of the meal about to be cooked and that of paying the bill of fare once the meal is eaten.

This play on words, of course, refers to the way in which one asks whether or not dinner is ready. Since Posthumus' "goose is cooked," so to speak, he is ready. (Compare this with the scene in Act IV,ii,113-15, where Guiderius describes Cloten's head as "an empty purse.") The jailor also makes a similar simile: once the tavern bill is paid, "purse and brain [are] both empty."

A messenger then enters and tells the guard to remove Posthumus' manacles and bring him to the king's tent. The guards are bleakly amused that Posthumus seems so eager to die, and despite the fact that he is a "Roman" prisoner, they have some sympathy for him.

Cymbeline, meanwhile, still looks for the ragged soldier who bravely fought with Belarius and the two brothers, and also in the meantime, he knights the young men. But Guiderius and Arviragus do not know, and Belarius has not yet told them, that they are the king's sons.

Cornelius the physician then enters to tell Cymbeline that the queen is dead by her own hand, although she had time to confess her crimes before she died. He tells Cymbeline that she admitted that she never loved him, but only sought power for her and her son. Cymbeline is shocked and only believes the news because it was a deathbed confession. Cornelius also tells Cymbeline how the queen intended to slowly poison Cymbeline so that he would gradually sicken and die. But having failed in all her attempts, she grew reckless and finally went mad.

Thus, Cymbeline has lost that which is false, although those who really love him have not yet been restored to him. At this point, various Roman prisoners, including Lucius, Iachimo, the soothsayer, Posthumus, and Imogen all enter, guarded.

Lucius does not request any leniency for anyone except his page (Imogen), who has fought no one. Cymbeline notes that Imogen/Fidele looks familiar, and he is moved to spare him. He asks what Fidele would request, and Fidele requests that he be allowed to ask some questions of Iachimo.

She asks him where he got the diamond ring he wears. Posthumus, confused, can't understand why Fidele would be interested. (Disguises, as we noted earlier, are surprisingly effective in this play.) Iachimo, remorseful, confesses to his villainy against Imogen.

Posthumus is enraged and comes toward Iachimo, ready to take revenge against the man who tricked him into murdering his wife. Imogen tries to intervene, but Posthumus still does not recognize her and slaps her. Pisanio rushes in to comfort Imogen, and everyone suddenly recognizes who she really is. Imogen then embraces Posthumus and asks her father's blessing. Cymbeline tells her that the queen is dead, but no one knows what happened to Cloten. Pisanio admits directing him to Milford-Haven, and Guiderius admits to killing him.

Cymbeline is dismayed that Guiderius killed a prince; for a commoner to do so would be a capital crime regardless of the provocation on Cloten's part. The dire situation forces Belarius to speak up to save Guiderius, and he tells the king that Guiderius is his son and that Arviragus is his son, as well. Their identities are established because Guiderius has a mole similar to Imogen's.

Miraculously, all three of the king's children are restored to him, and Imogen and Posthumus are reunited as well. Even the prisoners are to fare well. Iachimo offers the ring and bracelet to Posthumus, and he says further that Posthumus may do as he wishes with him. Posthumus forgives him.

Now Posthumus calls upon the soothsayer to interpret the prophecy of the dream which has, in fact, been fulfilled. Even the war is ended happily, for although Cymbeline is the victor, he tells Lucius that he will make his peace with Rome. Thus the numerous story lines of the play all converge and for everyone—except the two unrepentant villains, Cloten and the queen—happiness reigns.

1613

# henry VIII

# THE HISTORICAL BACKGROUND

When Henry VIII became king, England entered a new era. Henry was less interested in the details of government than had been his father, so he relaxed the reins on royal control and permitted a new sense of liberalism to sweep the country. He was a man of numerous interests and, because he was young (eighteen years old), he enjoyed the pleasures of mind and body for all that they offered him.

This period of national renaissance, or rebirth, for England was hailed by many as the dawn of a golden age. Artists, writers, craftsmen, and actors found new freedoms of expression and reveled in the excitement of a growing, cultured society. Indeed, Henry himself was an accomplished scholar, linguist, musician, and athlete.

Perhaps this national renaissance was made possible by the political climate. Henry VIII was the first monarch in more than a hundred years to succeed to the throne with an undisputed title. The first Tudor king had held the throne by conquest (and by his Lancastrian blood), and this was further secured by a marital alliance with the Yorkists. Henry was the child of that marriage.

Henry's reign, therefore, can be seen as the transition from the medieval period to modern history. The term "renaissance" suggests everything positive about the process: England had grown beyond the confines of medieval society and was ready for unprecedented growth. Feudalism had more or less run its course during the Wars of the Roses. With the nobility strangled, it had been possible for Henry's father to fortify the kingdom. In addition, similar changes were occurring across the channel in France.

Feudalism was destroyed by the elevation of monarchical influence within the government. This was a period of tremendous imperialism; kings and queens had never been so arbitrary in their conduct. A succession of tyrants took control of the throne, continuing all the way from Henry VIII to Elizabeth I.

In former monarchies, bloodline counted for a nobleman's success. Only the most aristocratic nobles were permitted near the royalty. But with Henry VIII, matters changed; the most powerful man in Henry's court was of humble origin. Wolsey was a low-born commoner who rose through the ranks of the church to become the king's chief minister. This is but another sign of the dramatic changes afoot in renaissance England.

In a gesture of power, Henry married his brother Arthur's widow, Catherine of Aragon (daughter of King Ferdinand and Queen Isabella of

Spain). This marriage, in 1509, represented the beginning of Henry's reign, which was to last until 1547. His father-in-law, King Ferdinand, played an important role in the young king's military decision-making. In 1511, Henry entered into war with France, crossing the channel in 1513 to take part in the successful sieges of Thérouanne and Tournai in the battle of Guinegate.

Ferdinand deserted him, so Henry made peace with Louis XII and permitted him to marry Henry's sister Mary in 1514. There was even rumor that he might divorce Catherine in favor of a French wife, but he made no indication of this. When Francis I became king of France in 1515, hostilities between the two countries broke out once again, forcing Henry to seek a renewed alliance with Ferdinand.

Ferdinand died in 1516 and was succeeded by Charles V, soon to become head of the mighty Holy Roman Empire (his official name was Charles I of Spain, but he was officially known as Charles V of the Holy Roman Empire). Charles and Francis I would become lifetime rivals; both would seek the support of England, and this placed Henry in an advantageous position.

In 1520, Henry and Wolsey put on a show of friendship to Francis at the so-called Field of the Cloth of Gold (see *Henry VIII*, Act 1), yet in 1521 they joined with Charles in a war against France. Charles, however, was busy in Italy and provided little real help in the war. This meant that England achieved nothing during 1522 and 1523, and secret peace negotiations were begun soon thereafter.

Francis was defeated by a sudden burst of Charles' forces at Pavia (February 1525), thus leaving Charles within reach of total control over the realm of Christendom. Charles then promptly rejected his engagement to Henry's daughter Mary and married the infanta Isabella of Portugal. Meanwhile, Henry worried about the problem of having a successor for the English throne. Catherine had not been able to produce a healthy male heir, and this worried Henry; he knew that something must be done about it. He toyed with the idea of summoning his only illegitimate son and making him Duke of Richmond, thereby giving him precedence over his legitimate daughter Mary. But he decided to try and prove that the theological blessing given to his marriage to his brother Arthur's widow was null and void. He felt that there was surely a biblical curse against it, for all but one of the children produced by Catherine had died.

What's more, Henry loved Anne Boleyn (Anne Bullen in the play), one of Catherine's court ladies. He expected the Pope to comply with his divorce wishes, but Clement VII was reluctant: Charles V had become very powerful and was, after all, the nephew of Henry's wife, Catherine. The Pope needed Charles' support against the Lutherans in Germany, so he refused to go along with Henry's pleas. He recalled Lorenzo, Cardinal

Campeggio (Cardinal Campeius in the play) to Rome after having sent him to join Wolsey in assessing Henry's divorce proposal. Clearly the Pope was becoming wary.

To Henry's good fortune, the Parliament thought there was too much papal control over the government. The lords resented Wolsey's use of papal authority to proclaim law in certain jurisdictions. Wolsey was not popular, and this provided a chance for a rise in anticlericalism. Early in 1533, an act was proclaimed which declared England to be an empire ruled by *one person only*—the king. The act dictated that spiritual events must be "finally and definitively adjudged and determined within the king's jurisdiction and authority."

Thomas Cranmer became the new Archbishop, and he hastily pronounced Henry's marriage to Catherine null and void. Henry had already married Anne Boleyn secretly; now, she was able to become queen (May 1533). Four months later, she gave birth to a daughter, the future Elizabeth I. By early 1534, the bond with Rome was irrevocably severed and payments to the Pope were discontinued. Henry resolved the problem of his heirs by vesting the succession to the throne in his children by Anne. This brief history, then, covers the period of Henry VIII's reign as depicted in Shakespeare's play, which was a time (1534–40) of radical, ongoing reform within the church.

## BACKGROUND FOR *HENRY VIII*

Shakespearean critics have divided Shakespeare's career into four major periods: (1) *apprenticeship* to the London Theatre (which began with Shakespeare's arrival in London around 1586 and lasted until he joined the Lord Chamberlain's Men in 1594); (2) *growing mastery*, from 1594 to 1601, when the Globe Theatre was opened (1599); (3) *maturity*, during which time the great tragedies were written; this period began with his shareholding of the Globe Theatre and continued until his shareholding of the Blackfriars' Theatre in 1609; and (4) *the final retrospect*, from 1609 until Shakespeare's death in 1616.

*Henry VIII* belongs to this last period, the final retrospect. It stands out from the rest of Shakespeare's plays, especially the history ones, as an example of a loosely structured play; it was likely written on request, as part of the marriage celebration for James I's daughter, Princess Elizabeth (who is not, of course, Elizabeth I). The other plays written during this period (1607–13) are *Pericles, Cymbeline, The Winter's Tale,* and *The Tempest.* This shows the range of talent evident even during the last years of Shakespeare's life.

*Henry VIII* is, according to most critics, Shakespeare's last play. Probably written in 1613, two years after *The Tempest,* it is a work quite different in tone from the bulk of Shakespeare's other plays. For this reason, many critics have postulated that he did not write it. But then this conjecture raises an entirely different question about whether a man named Shakespeare ever existed, whether he wrote the plays attributed to him, and so on. These are rather hopeless scholarly pursuits and are best left to the dust pile. The point is, *Henry VIII* exists as a play and has been permanently associated with the canon of Shakespearean creations.

The play was written slightly more than half a century after the events of Henry's actual reign. They were still relatively fresh in the mind of the playwright. Thus, Shakespeare clearly excelled in his task and penned a drama which reflects the historical reality in an eminently faithful manner, even if it lacks the poetic inspiration which is so vibrant in many of his earlier works.

One might label *Henry VIII* as a "competent" drama. It is adequately, though not brilliantly, structured and tighter than, say, his earlier *Henry VI* plays. He used as his sources the chronicles of Holinshed and Halle, rearranging events only slightly in order to suit his dramatic needs. For the story of Cranmer, he relied principally on Foxe's *The Book of Martyrs* or *Actes and Monuments.* He knew that his audiences would recognize most of the people and the events, even if they had learned of them from their fathers and grandfathers. In the Prologue, he states: "Think ye see/ The very persons of our noble story/ As they were living."

Coleridge said of *Henry VIII* that "it is a sort of historical masque, or show-play" (*Literary Remains,* vol. ii. p. 91). Perhaps he was referring to the pomp and display of scenes such as the opening one in which the Duke of Norfolk and the Duke of Buckingham are discussing King Henry's meeting with Francis I of France, the latter glittering in gold. The play takes us from this stunning moment to the christening of Queen Elizabeth, but the tragic misery that permeates the play is more noteworthy than any of the attendant pomp or glory—the misery, that is, of human monarchs caught up in the quest for preservation and honor, and of individuals anxious to impose their political vision on the world. Grandeur and debasement interplay freely with one another throughout the drama.

Katherine is one of Shakespeare's most impressive female characters. Repudiated as a wife and degraded from the throne, she undergoes all imagined human emotions in her attempts to maintain her dignity as a wife, a mother, and as a queen. As the daughter of Spain's powerful Ferdinand and Isabella, she first arrived in England betrothed to Henry's brother Arthur. Her dowry was splendid, her pride was strong, and her background impeccable. Now, after reigning as Queen of England for over twenty years, she is confused and angered by the actions of her husband. All of this serves to justify her comments to Wolsey:

Sir,
I am about to weep; but, thinking that
We are a queen, or long have dreamed so, certain
The daughter of a king, my drops of tears
I'll turn to sparks of fire.

(II.iv.69–73)

Here she is, proud of her birth and position, aware of her utmost purity, anxious about the wrongdoings done to her, lonely in a foreign land – and she finds herself ostracized by the king and nation whom she has served. Her downfall seems terribly unjust.

And then there is Wolsey. While not exactly a tragic figure, Wolsey nonetheless attracts to himself a disastrous downfall. This worldly, ambitious man has pulled himself up the ladder of success through sheer lust for power. No obstacle was too large for him, yet his final defeat grew out of an obstacle of which he was unaware: himself. His desire to impose his will became an obsession and, like most obsessions, it was beyond relief. Nothing satisfied him; there were always new areas to conquer. So, when he tried to prevent the king's divorce from becoming a reality, he committed the great error of his life. *No one* dominated Henry VIII, as Katherine might well have acknowledged.

Wolsey has been unscrupulous in his drive for power. In attempting to stop the flow of Henry's desires, he resorts to deceit. The ultimate justice? Fate catches him at his own game. Note that Henry VIII is *not* Wolsey's killer; rather, Wolsey dies of natural causes. He is not the victim of physical harm or the gallows.

This is one of Shakespeare's history plays and, as such, must be considered in that vein. It contains many references to life at the court, including the ins and outs of who-what-where-when, and so on. Shakespeare apparently wrote it in celebration of Princess Elizabeth Stuart's marriage to the Elector Palatine. For this reason, Shakespeare uses the occasion to remind his audience of the many important events which preceded the birth of Elizabeth I. She was, after all, the most extraordinary Elizabeth ever, and of that Shakespeare had no doubts. The ideas of Katherine's trial, Anne's coronation, Elizabeth's christening, and Wolsey's death – all of these were important to theater-goers and citizens of the day, and especially significant for monarchs-to-be.

As usual, Shakespeare shows interest in the human drama of royalty. The pomp and ceremony are not his domain, though there are, of necessity, moments of such pageantry. The grandeur of the soul is far more intriguing to him and, in this light, we can see his portraits of Katherine, Wolsey, Henry, and the others as natural extensions of his greater, more famous characters.

As a historical footnote, this play was being performed when the Globe

Theatre burned on June 29, 1613. In less than thirty minutes, the house was a pile of cinders. Miraculously, no one perished.

# A BRIEF SYNOPSIS

*Henry VIII*, set in the period of 1520–33, is a play about power and the struggle to obtain it. Cardinal Wolsey is of humble birth and has inherited nothing which would place him in a position of influence. Through ambition and political maneuvering, however, he has positioned himself close to the king and is now one of Henry's most intimate advisers.

One obstacle in his way is the Duke of Buckingham. The duke, who has been charged by Wolsey of high treason, is defended by Henry's wife, Katherine, the former widow of Henry's brother. Wolsey needs to get rid of Buckingham so as to consolidate his power with the king. To this end, he produces a surveyor who once worked for the duke and who claims that the duke harbors intentions to kill Henry.

Buckingham is thus sentenced to execution and his son-in-law, the Earl of Surrey, is shipped off to Ireland. With the duke out of the way, Wolsey begins work on his final obstacle: Queen Katherine. He plants doubts in Henry's mind about his marriage to Katherine and arouses in him a curiosity about Anne Bullen, whom he met at a ball.

Wolsey then requests the Pope to sanction a royal divorce. His case is furthered by the fact that Katherine has provided Henry with no male heirs. Cardinal Campeius arrives from Rome and, shortly, Katherine is expelled from court. She sequesters herself at Kimbolton.

Wolsey has now obtained the desired level of power, but his tragic flaw is greed: he lusts for ever more control and, in so doing, he sets his own trap. He has become very wealthy indeed—much more so than the king. Fearing that the king will marry Anne Bullen instead of seeking a royal alliance with France, Wolsey writes a letter to the Pope asking that the marriage be delayed.

By mistake, the letter is delivered to Henry. Seeing what has happened, Henry is appalled at the actions of his adviser; Wolsey is now a broken man and has no choice but to leave the court. Later, he is arrested in York and dies en route to London before having to face the indignity of a trial.

Henry divorces Katherine, marries Anne Bullen, and chooses as his new adviser Cranmer, the new Archbishop of Canterbury. But things are still awry; Gardiner, the Bishop of Winchester, seeks to destroy Cranmer by accusing him of heresy. The king, sympathetic to Cranmer's plight, offers him the royal signet ring. In the event that Cranmer's prosecutors refuse to accept his arguments, he is to produce this ring.

The trial takes place as Henry listens from behind a curtain. Cranmer is found guilty, but, on producing the ring, discovers that the nobles are repentant for their actions. Henry enters, condemns them for their errors, and then blesses them. He beseeches them to join forces in a unified and loving way.

Henry and Anne have a new little daughter to whom Cranmer becomes godfather. Her name is Elizabeth, and, at her christening, Cranmer predicts that she will be wise and wonderful, strong and feared, and that she will rule long throughout the kingdom and will accomplish many good deeds.

# LIST OF CHARACTERS

### Henry VIII

King of England; married to Katherine of Aragon, then to Anne Bullen (historically spelled "Boleyn"); father of Elizabeth I.

### Duke of Buckingham

An opponent of Wolsey's; he is accused of high treason against the king and is executed.

### Cardinal Wolsey

An ambitious commoner who manipulates his way up the hierarchy of power and becomes the king's most powerful adviser; he dies before he can be brought to trial.

### Queen Katherine

The daughter of King Ferdinand and Queen Isabella of Spain; wife of Henry VIII; a noble, elegant, dignified woman who is victimized in a foreign country by a system in search of a male heir for Henry VIII.

### Earl of Surrey

The Duke of Buckingham's son-in-law; before the duke is executed, Surrey is sent off to Ireland by Wolsey so as not to present a threat; he returns to see Wolsey's downfall.

### Gardiner

The Bishop of Winchester; a petty, ambitious man who attempts to drive Cranmer out of favor.

### Cromwell

A servant to Wolsey; he is instructed by Wolsey to serve the king well;

Henry makes him Master of the Jewel House and of the Privy Council; he becomes Henry's new secretary.

### Cardinal Campeius

The Pope's emissary from Rome; he arrives in London to assess Henry's proposed divorce from Katherine.

### Anne Bullen (Boleyn)

A knight's daughter; lady-in-waiting to Queen Katherine; Henry falls in love with her and secretly marries her before his divorce from Katherine; Anne gives birth to the future Queen Elizabeth I.

### Cranmer

The newly appointed Archbishop of Canterbury; he becomes Henry's closest adviser at the end of the play.

# SUMMARIES AND COMMENTARIES

## PROLOGUE

In a Prologue before the play begins, the playwright tells his audience that he no longer comes to make them laugh (note: Shakespeare's most recent play had most probably been the comedy *The Tempest*). His subject in this new production is "sad, high," and "full of state and woe." Nobility is what he intends to present, in a way which will command pity. Most assuredly, he stresses, this play is *not* a comedy or even an "entertaining" play; anyone who expects such a piece "will be deceived." Shakespeare urges his audience to be sad and to consider the people on stage as if they were real beings, not fictitious characters.

The Prologue is used to shape the audience's emotional frame of mind before the drama begins. Here, Shakespeare's primary point is: be prepared for a sad story in which noble people do un-noble things. *Henry VIII* is by no means a coherent drama; it is a succession of fine dramatic moments, but it lacks unity. An awareness of this fact will help readers move more easily through the various scenes.

## ACT I—SCENE 1

### Summary

The Dukes of Buckingham and Norfolk discuss their last meeting in France. Buckingham was in his room, ill, but Norfolk witnessed the rendezvous between King Henry VIII and King Francis I of France. It was a stunning moment of earthly glory when the kings saluted one another on horseback and grew close in an embrace. Everyone was resplendent with sparkling gold, "like heathen gods"; even the dwarfish pages resembled gilt cherubs.

The kings were "equal in lustre" ("no discerner durst wag his tongue in censure"). Cardinal Wolsey arranged this royal meeting, and Buckingham expresses open disdain for the man: "No man's pie is freed from his ambitious finger." He recalls that Wolsey is the son of a butcher, not a nobleman, and that he monopolizes the king at everyone else's expense.

The dukes analyze the much-hated Wolsey: he has no noble ancestry which might have given him such a position in society; he has accomplished nothing spectacular for the crown; and he has no connections with high-ranking officials. He is a self-made man ("Spider-like, out of his self-drawing web, he gives us note; the force of his own merit makes his way"). Foremost, he suffers from the excess of pride, a poison which seeps through every part of him. He even took it upon himself to appoint the officials who attended the king in his meeting with Francis I.

Buckingham knows of many people who ruined themselves by spending their estates on expensive clothing for the event. Norfolk believes that the trip cost more than the peace they sought. Moreover, the storm which followed their arrival in France foreboded a breach in the peace: "France hath flawed the league and hath attached [that is, seized]/ Our merchants' goods at Bordeaux."

The fact that the peace was aborted by the French emphasizes the superfluousness of Wolsey's actions: at a very great expense, the English have ruined themselves in the plan and have nothing to show for it. But Wolsey is powerful and has the ministers in his control.

Wolsey enters, stays but a moment, and exchanges contemptuous glances with Buckingham. After Wolsey leaves, Buckingham becomes angry and starts to follow him, but Norfolk convinces him to be reasonable: "Heat not a furnace for your foe so hot/ That it do singe yourself." Buckingham agrees, but insists on exposing Wolsey to the king. He resents the fact that Wolsey "does buy and sell his honour as he pleases/ And for his own advantage."

Brandon and a Sergeant-at-Arms arrive to arrest Buckingham for *high treason.* The duke knows that his days are numbered: clearly Wolsey is behind all this and will scheme to bring harm to the duke. A word from Wolsey is enough to end anyone's life, and so Buckingham says to Brandon:

> The net has falled upon me!
>
> *   *   *   *   *   *   *
>
> I am the shadow of poor Buckingham,
> Whose figure even this instant cloud puts on
> By darkening my clear sun.

(I.i.203–26)

## Commentary

Like many opening scenes, this is a time of exposition during which Shakespeare quickly sets the stage for future action. We learn of King Henry VIII's trip to France to meet with Francis I and that a storm has augured badly, hovering above a breach of peace, suggesting that Wolsey is to be feared.

The pomp and glory associated with the king's entourage soon fade into the distance as Shakespeare punctures the facade and bears open the heart of his drama: the battle against the evils of power-hungry individuals. The expensive clothing has cost the English nobles dearly, and the cost may have ruined their meager fortunes. Shakespeare's message is this: external possessions are less significant than internal peace. All the money in England cannot purchase Henry's freedom or happiness; the latter will be obtained only by resolution of mind and determination. And, by the same token, the money spent by the spectators of Henry's encounter with Francis is ultimately meaningless. The meeting accomplishes little and their lavish expenditures serve no real and lasting purpose.

The contempt for Wolsey is clear from the very start. He has manipulated his way into the chambers of power through unscrupulous, self-centered means. No one is sacred to him, not even the king, and the people of England resent this deeply. Moreover, Wolsey is a commoner like them, and jealousy is no small factor in their emotions toward him. Now, Wolsey is seemingly responsible for Buckingham's arrest – before Buckingham can expose Wolsey's evil, ambitious designs toward Henry.

## ACT I – SCENE 2

### Summary

The king enters, leaning on Wolsey's shoulder. He prepares to hear testimony concerning Buckingham's treason, but Queen Katherine enters with Norfolk and Suffolk (note: Katherine's name was spelled "Catherine" historically). She is there to defend Buckingham. She explains that Henry's subjects are "in great grievance" over Wolsey's policies, that he has damaged the citizens' loyalty to the crown, and that rebellion is at hand. Wolsey is present as she presents her arguments, and she is careful to point out that the people are equally angered by their king – mostly because he gives such power to Wolsey.

Norfolk cries out that the taxations are intolerable and that tradesmen of all sorts are desperately poor. The king claims no knowledge of such taxes ("What taxation?") and requests an explanation from Wolsey. The latter suggests that he knows only about "a single part," one small aspect of the taxes. Katherine, however, argues that the taxes "are devised by you." One sixth of the common people's earnings is levied by the government, apparently to support the wars in France.

Henry is not pleased with what he hears. But Wolsey is shrewd to point out that he himself has only a single vote and that all such matters must pass through the hands of learned judges. His scorn for the people is clear: he insists that the government must not stint on quality or in its plans simply because a group of critics wishes to protest. Already it is obvious that Wolsey seeks to impose his own desires on the king, but Henry shows signs of independence. He does not want his subjects to be treated unfairly: "We must not rend our subjects from our laws/ And stick them in our will." The idea of such taxation horrifies Henry. There is no precedent for such taxation, he says; thus, he orders that *free pardons* be given to every man who has denied the validity of Wolsey's taxation. The commissions shall be heeded. In an aside, Wolsey tells his secretary to word the letters so that the people will think that he, Wolsey, intervened on their behalf.

Katherine then returns to the subject of Buckingham's arrest. She regrets that such an event has occurred, and Henry agrees with her, but he says that he thinks that Buckingham's noble features have turned sour. He fears that the duke poses a threat to the monarchy:

> He, my lady,
> Hath into monstrous habits put the graces
> That once were his, and is become as black
> As if besmeared in hell.

>                                        (I.ii.121–24)

A surveyor who once worked for Buckingham is brought into the room and told to recount what he knows about Buckingham. The man begins with: "It was usual with him, every day/ It would infect his speech, that if/ The King should without issue die, he'll carry it so/ To make the sceptre his." In other words, Buckingham is believed to want the throne. The surveyor adds that Buckingham has sworn to seek revenge on Wolsey.

Katherine sheds light on the surveyor's character: he was once hired by Buckingham and was fired because of his unpopularity with the tenants. But Henry wants to hear more; he is angered by the possibility that Buckingham may have uttered threatening or treasonous statements about himself or Wolsey. He has made up his mind: Buckingham is guilty of treason. Henry orders the duke to stand trial: "If he may/ Find mercy in the law, 'tis his; if none,/ Let him not seek it of us."

## Commentary

In Scene 1, we see Wolsey through the eyes of other people (Norfolk and Buckingham, for example). They find him despicable and vile. In

Scene 2, we see Wolsey in person and discover that he is all that the others have described him as being. He manipulates and contorts reality to suit his own purposes, such as with the fraudulent letter to the citizens. He is low, common, and bereft of dignity. He has exerted himself in ways which the king does not fully realize the seriousness of (the taxation), and this is proof of Wolsey's evil interests: money and power.

Henry, on the other hand, is clearly to blame for not knowing more about his governmental affairs. His father, Henry VII, was notorious for his interest in the details of political events around him. Henry VIII, in contrast, is more of a renaissance man in that he finds excitement in a wide variety of pursuits unrelated to politics. But if Henry is somewhat misinformed about his government's policies, he is nonetheless a humanitarian: he stands up for the fair treatment of his people and orders an end to the outrageous taxation in effect at that time.

Katherine makes her first appearance in this scene. Her regal entrance is announced by a chorus chanting: "Room for the Queen!" and when she arrives, her composure and dignity fill the air. She is something to behold— a moving presence whose aristocratic demeanor offers a bold contrast to the lowly Cardinal Wolsey. Katherine is a noble. He is not. And since she represents justice and human rights, she immediately earns our respect and admiration.

## ACT I – SCENE 3

This small scene serves only one purpose: it tells us that there is to be a large supper at Cardinal Wolsey's York Place that evening and that many lords and ladies will be in attendance.

## ACT I – SCENE 4

### Summary

The scene takes place in York Place, where there is a small table for Wolsey and a longer table for the guests. Sir Henry Guildford announces that good fun—good company, good wine—is to be had by all. Lord Sandys jokes lightly that good fun is "as easy as a down-bed." Sir Thomas Lovell notes that Sandys ought to be their confessor—and Sandys remarks that he would grant "easy penance." Lord Chamberlain then begins to seat people at the table and places Sandys between two women.

Anne Bullen (Anne Boleyn's surname, as we have pointed out, is spelled "Bullen" in this play) is seated beside Sandys. When she makes a comment concerning Sandys' father's "madness," he impulsively kisses her.

Wolsey enters then and decrees that pleasure will be the rule of the evening: "That noble lady or gentleman that is not freely merry/ Is not my friend."

A drum and trumpet sound. Wolsey learns that, seemingly, a barge of French ambassadors has arrived, and so he sends Lord Chamberlain (since he speaks French) to greet them. Within moments, the king enters with others, all disguised as shepherds, and salutes the Cardinal, pretending not to speak English. They claim to have chosen this party since it is reputed to be an exciting event. The "ambassadors" select ladies to dance with and, significantly, the king chooses Anne Bullen.

Wolsey guesses that the king is present, and so Henry unmasks for him and asks about Anne Bullen. He is told that she is one of Katherine's attendants. Henry is obviously taken with her: "By heaven, she is a dainty one." Thus, he takes full advantage of the epicurean theme of the evening – "eat, drink and be merry" – dancing feverishly and enjoying his drink.

## Commentary

In the absence of the king, Wolsey plays his "pseudo-royal" role to the fullest. He commands total devotion and enters the room as if he were royalty. But there is an aura of viciousness about him, and one suspects that the guests nearby are no doubt intimidated. They refer to him as "my lord," yet when King Henry enters the room, this is, ironically, the very term which Wolsey uses with him. There is no question that Wolsey would like to be the most powerful man in the kingdom. But Wolsey has flaws and will make error after error in his attempt at ascension.

Henry is quick to notice Wolsey's ambitions: "You hold a fair assembly; you do well, lord./ You are a churchman, or, I'll tell you, Cardinal,/ I should judge now unhappily." In other words, the king expresses an awareness of Wolsey's grand style, and there is a hint of warning against Wolsey's growing authority. Clearly, the king *alone* reigns victorious, and anyone attempting to supplant him should be aware of the consequences.

## ACT II – SCENE 1

### Summary

Two gentlemen in a street in Westminster discuss the fate of Buckingham. One of them was present at the trial and announces that the duke was found guilty; Buckingham, he says, was condemned to execution after his surveyor, his chancellor (Sir Gilbert Peck), and his confessor (John Car), and that "devil-monk," Hopkins, all "accused him strongly." Not surprisingly, his peers found him guilty of high treason.

But Buckingham held up well under the strain; he pleaded not guilty. It was not death that he feared, but rather the idea of dying for such an injustice.

It is conjectured that Wolsey is behind Buckingham's indictment. Certainly he wasted no time in arresting the Earl of Kildare, Deputy of Ireland, for maladministration. In his place, he sent off the Earl of Surrey, Buckingham's son-in-law (lest he would help Buckingham); with the latter in Ireland, perhaps Wolsey will not be threatened by an attempt to reverse what he has done to Buckingham.

The second gentleman protests openly about Wolsey: "All the commons hate him perniciously and, o' my conscience,/ Wish him ten fathom deep." Moments before his death, Buckingham now appears before the people. He explains to them that he is innocent of the alleged crime. It is not the law, however, which he condemns since the process of law has been duly followed. On the contrary, it is those who manipulated the law whom Buckingham resents. Yet he departs in peace, asking his supporters to help elevate his soul to heaven. "I forgive all. . . . No black envy shall mark my grave."

Buckingham says that he has nothing but praise and love for the king. He wishes him many long years of successful rule. But he says that eventually truth will avenge this wrongdoing. His father, Henry of Buckingham, had revolted in protest against King Richard, the usurper. He was found guilty without the benefit of a trial, but Henry VII restored the Duke of Buckingham to his present position, thereby making his name noble again. Now Henry VIII, by "one stroke," has taken him "forever from the world."

Ironically, both Buckinghams have fallen by their servants, "by those men we loved most." The duke advises his listeners not to be too liberal with their love and trust in others. People tend to remain faithful only when the fortunes are vast.

When the duke is led off, the two unnamed gentlemen resume their conversation. The second one whispers the rumor that Henry and Katherine are about to separate; it seems, though, that when Henry heard the rumor, he sent a command to the Lord Mayor that it be stopped. The gentleman suspects that Wolsey has planted the desire for separation in the king's mind "out of malice." In order to confirm the rumor, Cardinal Campeius has arrived. The first gentleman concludes that it was indeed the plotting of Wolsey that is at stake here: he is angry with the Emperor (Charles V of Spain, Emperor of the Holy Roman Empire) for not bestowing on him the archbishopric of Toledo.

### Commentary

This scene is vital for two reasons: it depicts the Duke of Buckingham as an honest, righteous man whose death is unjust and whose destiny, it seems, will be revenged; but it also assumes as a fact that the Cardinal will have his will and that Katherine "must fall." Her marriage to Henry is no small matter, however, and if Wolsey thinks himself powerful enough to manipulate the lives of royalty, then he must prepare for the worst: destiny will deal its own blow and, now, it is only a question of time before true justice reigns.

Let us recall the notion of cause and effect – that is, when evil is done, evil returns to the doer. Wolsey has now scored two evil victories – he thinks – over potential adversaries. He has eliminated Buckingham (but not the Earl of Surrey, his son-in-law), and he has made plans for the removal of Katherine. Katherine's nephew is Emperor Charles V of the Holy Roman Empire, an immensely powerful figure of the day. When Wolsey was overlooked for an important archbishopric position, he used the occasion to get even with Charles. But since the act was initiated out of malice, not justice, only malice can result from it.

Early in Act II, the stage is set for a devastating blow to Wolsey. It graphically shows the fragility of English power and the deceptiveness which can grow out of deceit: seemingly, Wolsey is extremely powerful, whereas in fact his days are numbered.

Note that Buckingham remains faithful to the king until his final moments. This is typical of the times: royalty was at the very center of people's lives.

Katherine has already made an appearance and we have seen her to be sympathetic, justly outraged, and noble. Let us now watch for her reactions to the idea of divorce, for herein lies the most moving thrust of the drama.

## ACT II – SCENE 2

### Summary

Lord Chamberlain meets with the Dukes of Norfolk and Suffolk to discuss Wolsey. Wolsey, they say, has ruined England's relationship with the Emperor and has now succeeded in governing the king's thoughts. Norfolk refers sarcastically to Wolsey as "the king-cardinal." Only when the king gets Wolsey out of his life, says Suffolk, will he be able to think rationally.

The king is worried about his marriage, and Wolsey makes things worse by planting fears and suspicions. According to Norfolk, Wolsey "dives into the King's soul, and there scatters/ Dangers, doubts, wringing of the conscience,/ Fears, and despairs; and all these for his marriage."

Norfolk is supportive of Katherine; she has been a loving wife to Henry for twenty years and hardly merits this kind of treatment. He suggests that something must be done about Wolsey before the latter reduces everyone "into what pitch he please." Suffolk is neither afraid nor enamored of Wolsey. He believes that eventually Wolsey will be dealt with by the Pope.

Norfolk and Suffolk then enter the king's chambers, hoping to cheer him as he meditates. Henry, however, is disturbed – and angry – that they have dared to come on business while he is trying to relax and read. Just then, Wolsey arrives and is welcomed; hopefully he can soothe his (the king's) "wounded conscience"; Norfolk and Suffolk are ordered away.

Cardinal Campeius has accompanied Wolsey, and Henry thanks the cardinal for coming, and Campeius responds by saying that his commission to investigate the divorce will provide an "unpartial judging of this business." As for Katherine's defense in the trial, Wolsey has "arranged" for scholars (that is, lawyers) to argue her case; Henry agrees. He wants the best. When Gardiner, the king's new secretary, is called into the room, Wolsey beckons him aside and reminds him that he is "the king's now." Gardiner understands, but vows to remain faithful to Wolsey's wishes, despite his new link to the king.

## Commentary

Notice the swift transition from Buckingham's death to the divorce trial. The death helps us see clearly the injustices attendant in Wolsey's "regime," and the upcoming process of divorce will serve to undo everything that Wolsey has contrived.

Wolsey ever more deeply immerses himself into trouble in this scene. We discover that he intends to further sabotage the trial of Katherine and Henry's divorce hearings by selecting lawyers who will not defend Katherine properly.

The scene also reveals Henry in a slightly new light. He is annoyed and irascible when the two dukes – Norfolk and Suffolk – approach his chambers; he is not the lighthearted, affable renaissance man of whom we often read. In particular, his dependence on Wolsey is a mystery. He shows no signs of intellectual awareness or objectivity about this relationship, and he seems completely vulnerable to Wolsey's wishes.

It is this vulnerability which Shakespeare seeks to highlight. Henry is still young, and he must learn to analyze personal and political intrigues for himself. Dependence on anyone – especially on a man (Wolsey, here) with misguided religious importance – can be fatal to a national leader. Quite obviously, self-respect and clarity of thought are necessary in order to establish a firm reign. Elizabeth I will show this to be true.

## ACT II – SCENE 3

### Summary

In an ante-chamber of the queen's apartments, Anne Bullen and a character simply designated as an old lady talk glowingly about Katherine. They believe that it is a crime that anyone so flawless should be tossed aside after twenty years of marriage. Anne thinks it is better "to be lowly born" and happy than to be noble and miserable and "wear a golden sorrow." Says Anne, ironically: "By my troth and maidenhead, I would not be queen." But the old lady snaps back at her that she is being a hypocrite, that she would gladly be a queen if given the opportunity for she has a "woman's heart" which, by nature, sets great store for eminence, wealth, [and] sovereignty.

But Anne still claims that she would want nothing to do with being a queen, "not for all the riches under heaven." The old lady scoffs, and Anne repeats her vow.

The Lord Chamberlain passes by and relates to Anne that the king is very much interested in her:

> . . . the King's Majesty
> Commends his good opinion of you, and
> Does purpose honour to you no less flowing
> Than Marchioness of Pembroke; to which title
> A thousand pound a year, annual support,
> Out of his grace he adds.
>
> (II.iv.60–65)

Anne is not sure that she is worthy of a king's favors ("More than my all is nothing"), but she sends her "thanks" and "obedience" to Henry. In an aside, Chamberlain confesses that he has examined Anne closely and that she is both beautiful and honorable, one from whom "may proceed a gem to lighten all this isle"—that is, the infant Elizabeth I.

## Commentary

This scene advances the plot by practically naming Anne Bullen as the chosen favorite of the king for his next queen. Of note here is the fact that Anne is genuinely uncomfortable with the idea of accepting the role of Henry's queen. But she is dutiful toward Henry, and she accepts with gratitude the praise which Chamberlain offers her. Anne is a sympathetic young woman whose devotion to Katherine is real. There is no sign of envy, malice, or social climbing; Anne is simple and beautiful—and she is about to become Henry's new queen.

## ACT II—SCENE 4

## Summary

This scene takes place in a hall in Black-Friars. It is the courtroom which will house the divorce hearings. Several people, including the Archbishop of Canterbury, the two Cardinals (Wolsey and Campeius), some noblemen, bishops, and the royal couple enter the chamber.

When the proceedings begin, Katherine kneels at Henry's feet and begs that he do her justice:

> . . . bestow your pity on me; for
> I am a most poor woman, and a stranger,
> Born out of your dominions, having here
> No judge indifferent, nor no more assurance
> Of equal friendship and proceeding.
>
> (II.iv.14–18)

Quite clearly, Katherine does not understand how she has offended Henry. She has been a true and humble wife, faithful at all times to the king. Whenever Henry wanted to make love to her, she was willing. Her marriage to Henry has been deemed lawful by a wise council, so why should he now choose to abandon her?

Katherine pleads for time to consult with her friends in Spain. Wolsey tells her that she doesn't need to; the lawyers present for her defense are "reverend fathers" of her own choice. He is, of course, lying since it was *he* who chose them. To this, she replies:

> Sir,
> I am about to weep; but, thinking that
> We are a queen, or long have dream'd so, certain
> The daughter of a king, my drops of tears
> I'll turn to sparks of fire.
>
> (II.iv.69–73)

She reproaches Wolsey for being arrogant and asserts openly that he is her enemy. She condemns him for spreading this turmoil through the land and for bringing about the separation between Henry and herself.

> I utterly abhor, yea, from my soul
> Refuse you for my judge; whom, yet once more,
> I hold my most malicious foe, and think not
> At all a friend to truth.
>
> (II.iv.81-84)

Wolsey tries to cheapen her by casting doubt on her character, by suggesting that she has lost touch with herself. He plays the solemn, pious man of God, but she rejects his words and retorts that his "heart is crammed with arrogancy, spleen, and pride." Wolsey's meek and humble behavior do not fool Katherine. She requests that her case be reviewed by the Pope.

Katherine leaves then, despite attempts to keep her there. Henry admits that she is a lovely wife and queen, "the queen of earthly queens." He confesses that she has carried herself nobly in this difficult task. He then turns to Wolsey and frees him from all responsibility for this divorce matter. To conclude the scene, he pronounces a lengthy explanation of his original reasons for considering a divorce: he was determined to have a male heir ("I weighed the danger which my realms stood in by this my issue's fail") and realized the necessity for marrying another woman. The Bishops (Lords) of Lincoln and Canterbury give him their support.

In a final aside, Henry utters contempt for the entire process. He abhors the power of Rome and welcomes the return of Cranmer (who will eventually become Henry's chief adviser as Archbishop of Canterbury); Cranmer, he feels sure, will be able to bring him the right decision.

## Commentary

Katherine presents her own defense in a logical and moving fashion. Her arguments are neither maudlin nor unreasonable; she wishes, very simply, to know why she has been rejected after so many years of fidelity. She is a noble, beautiful woman with admirers throughout the land. There is no question that the theatre audience is in full support of her and empathizes with her struggle for dignity. Significantly, Katherine's pride is a healthy, worthy pride, unlike that of Wolsey. Pride, for Wolsey, amounts to little more than unlimited ambition.

Henry is quite wrong about Wolsey. In a speech when he excuses Wolsey from all involvement in the plan to divorce Katherine, he states:

> You ever
> Have wished the sleeping of this business; never desired
> It to be stirred; but oft have hind'red, oft,
> The passages made toward it.
>
> (II.iv.162–65)

We know, however, that the opposite is true, that Wolsey has manipulated the divorce from the very beginning. So now we have both Henry and Katherine as victims of Wolsey's malice: Katherine is victimized by Wolsey's choice of lawyers, and Henry is duped by a sophisticated scheme of which he has no awareness. If Henry is not up-to-date on the country's taxation policies, it is not likely that he would know much about Wolsey's involvement in the divorce, a highly sensitive and secretive sort of negotiation.

Wolsey is a hypocrite par excellence. Katherine discerns his evil, but he cleverly parries with a woe-is-me approach. His appeal to those around him takes place on an emotionally subtle level: he seeks their sympathy and wants them to identify with him in this moment when he hopes that they will see an obviously disturbed woman making blind accusations about his hypocrisy. Yet, which man in the room is not also guilty of hypocrisy? It is not difficult for them to lend support to their "role model."

This scene offers a vivid study in human trust, pitting Henry's faith in Katherine against his dependence on Wolsey. Both "competitors" for the king's favor appeal to his sense of equity and justice, yet this is done in two different ways: Katherine is clearly honest, while Wolsey is very clearly dishonest. Katherine's arguments are based on truth; Wolsey's on desire and ambition. Since Henry is inclined to believe the arguments offered by a man, Wolsey, he is thus blinded by the man's lies. The more Wolsey distorts the truth, the more thoroughly Henry sides with him. Shakespeare's message is obvious: even kings can be idiotic fools—and they have a responsibility to know what is going on in their kingdom and look out for the best interests of their people.

Henry seems still to be in love with Katherine, but he is desperate for a male heir and, thus, he is attracted to Anne Bullen. But this does not prevent him from recalling the past and admitting to Katherine's virtues:

> That man in the world who shall report he has
> A better wife, let him in nought be trusted
> For speaking false in that. Thou art alone
>
>      *   *   *   *   *   *   *
>
> The queen of earthly queens.

(II.iv.134–41)

Ironically, Wolsey thinks he has selected a better wife for Henry—and, if we can believe Henry's words in the above passage, he ought not to trust Wolsey. Yet trust him he does.

Act II advances the plot, for the most part, emotionally; the audience feels protective of Katherine, bitter about Wolsey, and disapproving of Henry's actions, and Act III will expand these feelings even further.

## ACT III—SCENE 1

### Summary

In the queen's London apartments, Katherine asks a maiden to play a song on a lute for her; she is sad and needs cheering up. But no sooner has the maiden begun to sing than a messenger interrupts and says that two cardinals—Wolsey and Campeius—await her. Wolsey and Campeius enter, claiming to bring peace and counsel to her. Katherine, however, believes they have come to betray her ("Alas, I am a woman, friendless, hopeless!"). Campeius asks her to cooperate with Henry instead of forcing the divorce case further; he says that she should think of the king's protection (that is, Henry must protect the royal lineage by having a male heir). Katherine has little choice; if she balks at this idea, she will be banished in disgrace.

But Katherine sees through their ploys. She knows that these are the wishes of the two cardinals rather than what her husband desires: "Is this your Christian counsel? Out upon ye!" She scolds them for their unchristian behavior and says they should mend their hearts. She is determined *not* to be debased by these creatures. She has spent most of her adult life dedicated to Henry's needs – having compromised, slaved, and remained obedient to him all these years. Now, she refuses to give up her royal title: "I dare not make myself so guilty to give up willingly that noble title your master wed me to. Nothing but death shall e'er divorce my dignities."

Campeius warns her to act more nobly, to forget about her tears and remember her virtues; he says that the king still loves her, but that she might lose Henry's love if she carries on like a fool. This jars Katherine into assuming a different pose: she becomes subservient to the two cardinals and begs them to counsel her.

## Commentary

This scene portrays Katherine in full despair. She has fallen as low as she can and fears the worst: she is friendless and without hope. No one dares befriend her; to do so would mean violating the will of the king. When the cardinals arrive, they innundate her with more hypocrisy and propaganda about their (fraudulent) good will. Clearly, they seek to manipulate her – absolutely. When they tempt her with a possible reconciliation with Henry ("The King still loves you; beware you lose it not"), she finally complies with their wishes. Katherine is a broken woman and anxious to find peace – the former peace of royal dignity alongside her husband.

The tragedy of this scene is twofold: on the one hand, we see a proud, noble woman taken advantage of by two conniving men of the church; on the other hand, we witness her unwilling surrender to them, *on their terms,* and thus we know that she has given up her last strength – that is, her pride.

## ACT III – SCENE 2

### Summary

In an ante-chamber to the king's apartment, the Dukes of Norfolk and Suffolk assemble, along with the Earl of Surrey and Lord Chamberlain. Norfolk wants everyone to unite in their complaints about Cardinal Wolsey so that he will no longer be a threat. The Earl of Surrey is especially anxious to avenge his father-in-law's memory (the Duke of Buckingham). But Chamberlain cautions that nothing must be attempted against Wolsey unless they can bar the cardinal totally from the king because "he hath a witchcraft over the king."

Norfolk then relates a story of key importance: Henry has become aware of Wolsey's treacheries and is not likely to place too much credence in him anymore. The messy divorce affair, in retrospect, is seen by Henry as being wholly the doings of Wolsey. In the cardinal's attempts to communicate *privately* with the Pope (trying to discourage Henry's marriage to Anne Bullen by citing the king's divorce from Katherine), Wolsey wrote a letter destined to the Pope. But the letter was accidentally delivered to Henry, who was outraged to learn of his adviser's duplicity.

Chamberlain announces furthermore that Henry has *already* married Anne Bullen. What's more, Cardinal Campeius has returned to Rome, leaving the king's divorce case unresolved and vowing to support Wolsey's plot.

Meanwhile, not only does Cranmer support the king, but all the famous colleges of Christendom support the king's decision, and Cranmer will soon be made Archbishop of Canterbury. Katherine will no longer be called queen, but rather Princess Dowager and widow to Prince Arthur.

Wolsey enters with Cromwell, demanding to know whether the packet was given to Henry and whether he has read its contents. Cromwell replies positively to both questions. Obviously Wolsey does not yet know the extent of the damage done because, in an aside, he speaks of his desire for Henry to marry the Duchess of Alençon, the French king's sister. Wolsey wants nothing to do with Anne Bullen. She is a Lutheran and would not fit in with the scheme of things.

Moreover, Wolsey defines Cranmer as yet another threat ("one hath crawled into the favour of the King and is his oracle"). Clearly he is jealous about this recent development.

Henry enters, studying a document which contains information about the amounts of money accumulated by Wolsey for his own use. Henry is livid with anger toward the cardinal and cannot imagine how such vast sums of money were accumulated by him. Wolsey has become too dangerously wealthy for safety, and the king realizes that religion seems to be the *last* thing on the cardinal's mind.

Henry summons Wolsey and confronts him with the truth. He gives him a packet of papers – including the incriminating letter to Rome – and an inventory of his wealth, and then exits, disgusted. The cardinal, confused by the king's sudden anger, examines the materials and discovers two items: (1) an account of Wolsey's wealth and (2) the letter which he wrote to the Pope. He realizes immediately that there is no way that he can extricate himself from this entanglement; he says to himself:

> Nay then, farewell!
> I have touched the highest point of all my greatness;
> And, from that full meridian of my glory,
> I haste now to my setting. I shall fall
> Like a bright exhalation in the evening,
> And no man see me more.

> (III.ii.222–27)

There is no pity or sympathy for Wolsey. He has destroyed himself, and others in the process, and he seems worthy of no positive human emotion.

Norfolk and the others return and demand that Wolsey surrender the great seal. He has instructions to retire promptly to Asher House until hearing further from the king. Wolsey resists, accusing them of envy. The Earl of Surrey, however, succeeds in goading Wolsey with a series of pointed criticisms. He reminds the cardinal of various crimes committed in the name of loyalty to the crown.

Suffolk terminates the session by informing Wolsey that he must surrender and forfeit all his goods, lands, tenements and chattels to the throne and that he is no longer under the king's protection. As they prepare to leave Wolsey, Norfolk says in contempt: "So fare you well, my little good Lord Cardinal."

Alone and left to his thoughts, Wolsey finally sees himself for what he is:

> I have ventured . . . far beyond my depth. My high-
>     blown pride
> At length broke under me, and now has left me.
>                                    (III.ii.358–62)

When Cromwell arrives on the scene, Wolsey tells him that he has never felt better—now he knows himself fully: "I feel within me/ A peace above all earthly dignities,/ A still and quiet conscience." Cromwell announces that Sir Thomas More has been chosen Lord Chancellor in Wolsey's place, that Cranmer has been installed Lord Archbishop of Canterbury, and that Anne Bullen has been officially recognized as Henry's wife and queen.

In a surprising reversal of mood, Wolsey makes a moving and truthful speech to Cromwell. This, seemingly, is the first time that his words have been absolutely genuine and when he actually utters a Christian message:

> Cromwell, I charge thee, fling away ambition!
> By that sin fell the angels; how can man, then,
> The image of his Maker, hope to win by it?
> Love thyself last. Cherish those hearts that hate thee;
> Corruption wins not more than honesty . . .
>     Be just and fear not.
> Let all the ends thou aim'st at be thy country's,
> Thy God's, and truth's; then if thou fall'st, Cromwell,
> Thou fall'st a blessed martyr! Serve the king!
>                                    (III.ii.440–49)

Wolsey then resigns himself to death and asks Cromwell to lead him away.

### Commentary

For an extremely long scene, its message is quite simple: truth conquers all. Wolsey's hypocrisy and lies have come to a quick halt as soon as the king discovers the evil truth about his once-trusted cardinal. It comes as no surprise, really, to learn that Wolsey lies almost to the end. Yet when left to himself, Wolsey realizes that only truth will rescue him. He despises himself for what he has done and comprehends at last that heaven is his only hope.

This, then, is the key scene of crisis in this act. Henry realizes what Wolsey has done to him, and Wolsey discovers his villainy is no longer secret. The dénouement begins as we see Wolsey learn, point by point, that Henry has made several key changes in high-level positions. Wolsey has at last learned his lesson and can now prepare to die.

## ACT IV–SCENE 1

### Summary

The mood of the play has changed to gaiety as two gentlemen discuss the forthcoming coronation of Anne Bullen. Pageants, shows, and "sights of honour," it is decided, will take place everywhere.

Katherine has now been moved to Kimbolton; the divorce has been completed. She is reported to be sick, however, possibly from the discovery that a reconciliation with Henry is impossible.

Henry and Anne's coronation procession passes across the stage, with two judges, the Lord Chancellor, choristers, the Mayor of London, and an assortment of nobles. When the new queen arrives, she is a picture of beauty in her stunning robe, her hair richly adorned and entwined with pearls. All of the gentlemen admire her beauty, comparing her to an angel. They understand full well why Henry has chosen her as his new wife.

A third gentleman enters then to relate the events of the wedding. The crowd was so enraptured of Anne, he says, "such joy I never saw before." Clearly, the entire kingdom has fallen in love with her. Already, however, trouble has begun, for the two bishops on either side of Anne are Stokesly and Gardiner (the latter being the Bishop of Winchester, who is anxious to become Henry's new secretary). Already the rumor is out that Gardiner despises Cranmer, the newly appointed Archbishop of Canterbury. Plainly, trouble looms between these two.

### Commentary

The purpose of this scene is to emphasize the affection felt by the English people toward Queen Anne, but also to set the stage for conflict between Cranmer and Gardiner. Political intrigue is omnipresent in every monarchy, and Henry's court is no exception; but curiously enough, Henry is the first monarch in more than a century whose claim to the throne is undisputed. Yet there is seemingly no peace in the orbit surrounding him. It is as if the tensions formerly associated with selecting the "correct" (legal, blood-line) monarch have now been shifted to the circle of the king's advisers. It would seem, however, that Henry pays little attention to detail—though indeed he should, especially after the Wolsey scandal—and this treachery should alert him to the possibility for more grappling for power in the ranks beneath him.

## ACT IV—SCENE 2

**Summary**

An ailing Katherine asks her servant to relate the details of Wolsey's death. He was arrested by the Earl of Northumberland in York and was being transferred to London when he became too sick to travel. There, they arranged for a room in the abbey in Leicester, where Wolsey told the abbot:

> An old man, broken with the storms of state,
> Is come to lay his weary bones among ye;
> Give him a little earth for charity!
>
> (IV.ii.21–23)

Three nights later, about eight o'clock, he died "in peace." Katherine assesses his character, and her gentleman attendant, Griffith, speaks about Wolsey's virtues, particularly about his expertise in the area of education. Griffith's speech causes Katherine to readjust her opinion of Wolsey: the man she hated when he was still alive, she now, ironically, honors in death. She sees the truth of Griffith's words: "Men's evil manners live in brass; their virtues we write in water."

Sad music lulls Katherine to sleep, and she witnesses a vision wherein six personages clad in white robes exchange curtsies to one another and hold garlands above her head. Katherine awakens and cries out for "these spirits of peace," but no one else in the room has seen them. Griffith and the servant Patience suddenly notice that Katherine's face has grown pale and drawn. She appears to be near death.

Capucius, an ambassador from Katherine's nephew Charles V (Emperor of the Holy Roman Empire), arrives with the message that Charles sends his condolences. She says that the Emperor's condolences are "like a pardon after execution," and gives the messenger a letter for King Henry. In it, she requests that her servants be well looked after; she also tells Capucius to give Henry her best wishes and to tell him that she is about to die and that he will no longer have the burden of her presence to tolerate: "Tell him, in death I blessed him, for so I will."

Katherine then outlines details of her funeral which she wishes done for her: the flowers, the embalming, and an honorable, queenly treatment.

## Commentary

While it is not absolutely clear in this scene whether Katherine is actually close to death, or only imagining herself to be, we can nonetheless see her total despair about life. She is no longer a queen, though royalty is in her genes, and now she has shifted the focus of her thoughts from life to death. She amends her opinion of Wolsey and sees him as a man of honor.

She realizes that, on a symbolic level, Wolsey and she have led similar existences. They have both reached extraordinary heights of power, and each has been humiliated in a rapid procession of changes. The difference is that Wolsey's downfall was due entirely to his own actions, whereas Katherine was wholly victimized by Henry's decisions.

Act IV functions primarily as a dénouement: it provides two quite separate emotions as part of the unraveling of the drama. First, there is joy and ecstasy in Scene 1 when Anne becomes the new queen, yet there is also sadness and pity in Scene 2 for the dethroned Katherine. Since Shakespeare has structured the act so that sadness and pity follow the joy, it is possible that he meant to stress the tragedy of Katherine's debasement. Royalty, though exalted, is nonetheless human and subject to the same range of emotions as everyone else is. The psyche of a king or queen is no less fragile or vulnerable than that of a commoner. Love, self-esteem, and respect from others are important factors in monarchs' lives. For this reason, Katherine is a tragic figure about whom one can only say: she did her best, but was destroyed in the process.

## ACT V–SCENE 1

## Summary

In one of the palace galleries, Gardiner meets with Sir Thomas Lovell, who is on his way to see the king before the latter goes to bed. Gardiner wonders why Lovell must see the king at such a late hour, and Lovell reveals his errand: Queen Anne is in labor and is likely to die before her baby is born. Gardiner cares nothing for Anne but hopes the baby will survive.

Lovell indicates a fondness for Anne, but Gardiner insists that all will not be well until Anne, Cranmer, and Cromwell are all dead. Gardiner continues by saying that he has incensed the lords of the council against Cranmer, claiming that the latter is "a most arch heretic." In fact, he is to appear before the council-board in the morning to answer for alleged "mischiefs."

The king discusses Anne's critical labor pains with Suffolk and Lovell, who then leave. Cranmer arrives, and Lovell lingers to listen to Cranmer and the king, but Henry notices Lovell and orders him away.

Henry tells Cranmer that he has heard many grievous things about him lately. He has arranged with the council to meet Cranmer in the morning. But Henry has no fears; he knows that Cranmer has integrity and will stand up well to the council. Henry also knows that Cranmer has many enemies who have a way of distorting truth: "You are potently opposed and with a malice of as great size."

Henry then gives him a signet ring which he must produce during the council if the members vote to condemn him. By this ring, he will demonstrate to them that the king is on his side.

## Commentary

Henry has been wrong before about his advisers, but this time he is convinced that Cranmer is a decent man. There is no evidence that Cranmer has done evil or that he has violated his duty to the crown. So Henry decides to give his full support to the man. The fact that Gardiner seeks to get rid of Cranmer is but one more incident of jealousy among the ranks. With Wolsey gone, Gardiner takes the fore and assumes this pretense to try and gain power. But Cranmer's ultimate victory will underscore Wolsey's warning to Cromwell: give up ambition and serve the king. Service to one's self amounts to nothing.

## ACT V–SCENE 2

## Summary

In a lobby before the council chamber, Cranmer is abandoned to wait until the council has called for him. They had rushed him there, and now he worries about the reason for such haste. He confesses to himself that he never sought the council's malice, especially not in activities which were self-serving or ambitious.

Henry enters near a window above and sees Cranmer down below. He is appalled at the way in which the council members are treating the Archbishop of Canterbury, and he is glad "there's one above 'em yet. . . . By holy Mary, there's knavery."

## Commentary

Henry intends to hear the process from above, behind a curtain. It annoys and angers him that the council members have such little regard for his choice of archbishop and that their manners are so lacking. Justice will be done, however, since Henry holds the final trump.

## ACT V–SCENE 3

### Summary

This scene takes place in the council chamber. The Lord Chancellor tells Cranmer that his teachings and opinions reflect heresy which, if uncorrected, may prove to be dangerously pernicious. At this point, Gardiner suddenly bursts forth in open protest about Cranmer and insists that he be ousted immediately from his position. Cranmer, however, defends himself well, claiming that *he too* despises those who agitate public peace. Not knowing that the king is listening above, Gardiner announces that it is Henry's will that Cranmer be sent to the Tower of London. Cranmer realizes that Gardiner is the real "voice" behind this nonsense, and so he thanks him for being "so merciful" and for being both judge and juror. He clearly sees that Gardiner wishes to ruin him, but as a man of the church, he is more interested in love and meekness than ambition.

Cromwell interrupts Gardiner and defends Cranmer by suggesting that the prosecution arguments are a bit too sharp. Despite an exchange of criticism between Cromwell and Gardiner, the members agree to send Cranmer to the Tower. In exasperation, Cranmer produces the king's ring and removes the discussion from merely the council level to that of the *monarch.*

Henry enters then, frowning on the members, and Gardiner realizes that he must do something quickly in order to save himself, so he lapses into a maudlin show of praise for the king:

> Dread sovereign, how much are we bound to Heaven
> In daily thanks, that gave us such a prince;
> Not only good and wise but most religious . . .
>
> (V.iii.114–16)

His speech continues in this gushing vein, but Henry calls his bluff: "You were ever good at sudden commendations, Bishop of Winchester. But know, I come not to hear such flattery now." He declares that Gardiner has a cruel, bloody nature and that he is not interested in conversing with him. To Cranmer, Henry offers comfort and praise, daring the council members to object openly to the archbishop. His fury with the council mounts as he scolds them harshly for being incompetents.

Henry orders them to accept Cranmer as a worthy, respectable man; then he softens his tone somewhat and asks them to embrace Cranmer: "Be friends, for shame, my lords!" He then announces that his infant daughter requires a baptism and that he has chosen Cranmer as her godfather.

### Commentary

The scene is pleasant because justice comes to pass. We see the uselessness of flattery and dishonesty when truth prevails, and we witness the workings of a strong, just king whose love of equity for all is a major priority. He does not hold a grudge against the council members for being nasty with Cranmer. But there is no question that he understands their true motives and that he will monitor them closely in the future: Cranmer surfaces as a man of integrity and as an archbishop in whom everyone will place their trust.

## ACT V–SCENE 4

### Summary

This is a humorous scene of noise and tumult and includes a porter who orders his man to keep the merrymakers quiet. The christening is an important event, and the porter is not going to permit a bunch of lusty beer-drinking rascals to ruin things. People push from every direction to attend the event, and the porter finally shouts in despair: "This one christening will beget a thousand."

### Commentary

This is a robust scene, typical of many Shakespearean comedies. The beer-guzzling men are down-to-earth, bawdy, and unsophisticated, and they have no pretenses; they are – very simply – what they are. And because of this, they offer a sharp contrast with the *phony nobles* who assume airs of importance well beyond their birth or position. Shakespeare was used to this kind of boisterous crowd at the Globe Theatre. Thus, he portrays them as ecstatic human beings, anxious to see an important event in the royal family. As always, the populace is exceedingly interested in their royal leaders.

## ACT V–SCENE 5

### Summary

Cranmer blesses the newborn child and announces her name to Henry: she is to be called Elizabeth. Cranmer makes a very touching speech in which he expresses a premonition of Elizabeth's future talents: she will bring "a thousand blessings" to the kingdom; she will be a model to royalty everywhere and to future monarchs, and she will have wisdom and virtue, truth and respect from others:

> She shall be loved and feared: her own shall bless her;
> Her foes shake like a field of beaten corn
> And hang their heads with sorrow.
>
> (V.v.31–33)

Cranmer's speech moves Henry to great emotion. He has had no luck with siring children to this point, and now he has a strong heir:

> This oracle of comfort has so pleased me
> That when I am in heaven I shall desire
> To see what this child does, and praise my Maker.
>
> (V.v.67–69)

He then thanks the mayor and everyone else for being present, and they leave to see Queen Anne.

### Commentary

The play ends on a positive, promising note: the newly christened baby, the future Queen Elizabeth, will be an heir of whom Henry can be proud. Henry has now come full cycle from the days in Act I when he was anxious about his divorce, dependent on Wolsey for advice, and uncertain for his country's future. Gardiner, who is a vengeful, petty man, is of no importance now that Henry has openly favored Cranmer, and it is Cranmer's final speeches about Elizabeth which confirm in our mind the correctness of Henry's thinking. As a king, Henry seems to hold true promise and can teach his daughter many fine lessons about the monarchy which will be one day hers.

### EPILOGUE

At the play's end, there is a brief epilogue whose purpose is to tie up loose ends, speak directly to James Stuart's audience, and to offer the playwright's opinion of what spectators are likely to say about this drama.

## CRITICAL ANALYSIS

### Unity in *Henry VIII*

There is very little central conflict in this play, other than perhaps that of Henry's gradual emergence from dependence to independence as a king. But even that is not a critical conflict. It is more a state of affairs represented by a succession of events which are often not integrally related.

The play begins after the young king's meeting with the young Francis I of France at the famous "Field of the Cloth of Gold"—a designation which refers to the opulent and brilliant display of color, fabric, and wealth of the royalty and spectators. The play ends with the christening of Elizabeth, an event which has nothing to do with Henry's meeting with Francis. The line tracing these unrelated events is a meandering one, with only Henry as the common denominator.

For this reason, the play is not a dramatically well-made play; rather, it is a loose assembling of stories which give us an idea of the multiple personalities at court, the strong temperaments of Henry's advisers, and so on.

The first three acts are more or less dedicated to the story of Wolsey. We learn of his rise to power, his unfair use of power, and his ultimate downfall. To show us Wolsey's abuse of power, Shakespeare sketches in the episode of villainy surrounding the Duke of Buckingham's death. Wolsey is shown to be unscrupulous, ambitious, and politically greedy. He is never satisfied with his rank and seeks always to better himself. But "bettering himself" generally means "worsening" the lives of other people. That is why he falls in disgrace, and with a speed proportionate to his malice.

Essentially, the play seems over by the end of Act III. Wolsey is dead, Buckingham is dead, and Queen Katherine has been humiliated in her position as queen, wife, and mother. Henry has achieved his controversial divorce and is well on his way to leading a new life. Act IV provides two contrasting ceremonies which prepare us for Act V: there is an elaborate narration of Queen Anne's coronation, and, in contrast to this, we have the death scene of Katherine, in which she sees a vision of peace, with white-robed figures.

The play, thus, might be divided into three movements: the story of Wolsey, the simultaneous fall of Katherine and the rise of Anne, and then the fifth act presents the third movement of the play: the rise of Cranmer to Archbishop of Canterbury and the subsequent attempts to control his power. In a sort of allegorical manner, we might call Cranmer's success a victory of good over evil: Gardiner has attempted to defame the new archbishop with cries of heresy, yet justice (that is, Henry) prevails and the council members are turned into a unified group devoted to supporting Cranmer. The same allegory was true with Wolsey, only it was Wolsey himself who brought about his own downfall. Wolsey was evil, but in him lay the contrasting forces of good and evil which exist in all human beings.

This is a summation, then, of the various stories contained within *Henry VIII:* Wolsey, Buckingham, Katherine, Anne Bullen, Cranmer, Henry, and finally the infant Elizabeth. It is a group of people rather than a unified action. Their lives brush past those of other people and, as an ensemble, they make up the drama surrounding King Henry VIII. This is why it is not a truly unified play, but rather a collection of crises and human interactions. Unlike even the earlier *Henry VI* dramas where there is the concerted action of obtaining the crown, *Henry VIII* offers more of a personality gallery than a structured drama.

## Symbolism

Symbolism is not widespread in this drama. At the end of the play, Henry gives Cranmer a signet ring to use during the council's "trial" if the members decide to vote against him. The ring symbolizes the king's kin-ship with Cranmer and is something of a talisman: with this ring, no harm can come to the bearer. When the council members vote to send Cranmer to the Tower, he produces the ring, a symbol of justice, demonstrating the power of this virtue: a roomful of blustering men can be silenced by the sight of something as fragile and delicate as a ring.

## Pomp and Circumstance

Shakespeare knew that his audiences were tremendously interested in their royal families. This is one of the reasons why he chose history as a subject for a number of his dramas. But he was not a history teacher, nor did he seek to cram vast sums of data into a spectator's head. His pur-pose was to show the human drama of royal figures – the behind-the-scenes conflicts which tormented them, the ins-and-outs of the court, and so on. Because he was not interested in external facades, he generally spent less time in his history plays describing gowns, crowns, banquet tables, and jewelry than in painting the emotions of the heart.

In *Henry VIII*, the same phenomenon occurs. He takes more of an inter-est in the psychology behind Wolsey, Cranmer, Gardiner, Katherine, and the others than in telling us about their possessions. But there are some scenes in *Henry VIII* where he uses pageantry to his advantage, mostly to show the profound contrast between what is truly important (the inter-nal feelings) and what is merely passing fancy (the external facade).

That is why the ceremonial aspects of *Henry VIII* are important: not because they implicitly intrigued Shakespeare, but because by their very presence, they run counterpoint to the major psychological crises. For example, when we know the despair and hurt suffered by Katherine, we find it somewhat difficult to become too enthusiastic about the corona-tion of Anne Bullen, even though it is not something for which we blame Anne. Likewise in the pious death scene of Katherine: when the white-robed figures descend on her room, curtsying and dancing around her, this is no cause for celebration or delight. We are not interested in the outer show of costuming (that is, pomp), but rather in the tragic state of a dying Katherine (that is, circumstance).

For this reason, we can safely state that Shakespeare maintains his usual stance concerning the flashy gaiety of the court, preferring to expose human beings in all their complexity. The internal fascinates him more than the external, and that is why we have a King Lear, a Macbeth, and a Hamlet.

## Some Final Questions

There are a number of unresolved questions in *Henry VIII*, most of which relate to the nature of the characters and to their motivation. What, for example, is the true nature of Buckingham? Is he an honest man of integrity who happens to see through Wolsey and is thereby victimized by him? Or is he truly culpable and worthy of the gallows? What is Anne Bullen really like? Do we believe her when she says that she never wishes to be queen? Or does she harbor a deep-seated desire for power, disguised by this facade of humbleness? How about Cranmer? Can we really trust him, or does Gardiner know something which we do not?

The only character whose true motivations we understand is Katherine. She has been wronged by her husband and by the council members, and she strives to bring justice to the situation. Her attempts to restore her honor and dignity are genuinely motivated: she is noble, well-bred, has brought a generous dowry to England, and she has been undeniably patient with Henry for more than twenty years. She exemplifies the Spanish matriarch in her sense of devotion to the husband, her silence throughout years of pain, and her willing compliance with an authority figure's wishes. But this final outrage of divorce is more than she can accept—and her struggle to regain self-respect is the focal point of the drama.

Shakespeare's authorship of this play, as we have seen, is questioned by many scholars. One of the reasons is its loose structure and cavalier treatment of conflict. Perhaps Shakespeare's purpose in writing *Henry VIII*, other than simply as an entertainment for James Stuart's daughter, was to show the fundamental mystery surrounding human beings. Do we really know what people are thinking? Do we understand their motivations in life or do we judge them based on a facade, rather than on intimate knowledge of their intentions?

There is no question that this drama is less sophisticated than Shakespeare's earlier plays. But it has a place nonetheless in the flow of history plays from *King John* to *Henry VIII*, a cycle which covers the period from 1167 to 1547 and which highlights many of the principal historical figures of this period. If *Henry VIII* is less than perfect, we have at least a memorable description of Queen Katherine, and we realize the importance for England of the future Queen Elizabeth's reign. In addition, we have here many moments of beautiful language and a dramatization of one of England's more stable monarchs. As Shakespeare's last play, it is a positive, optimistic way of bidding farewell to the dramatic world.

# a Chronology of
# english Monarchs

## 👑 THE NORMAN CONQUEST

| | |
|---|---|
| 1066–87 | William the Conqueror |
| 1087–1100 | William II |
| 1100–35 | Henry I |
| 1135–54 | Stephen |

## 👑 PLANTAGENETS

| | |
|---|---|
| 1154–89 | Henry II |
| 1189–99 | Richard I |
| 1199–1216 | John |
| 1216–72 | Henry III |
| 1272–1307 | Edward I |
| 1307–27 | Edward II |
| 1327–77 | Edward III |
| 1377–99 | Richard II (mother a Plantagenet; father a Lancastrian) |

## 👑 HOUSES OF LANCASTER AND YORK

| | |
|---|---|
| 1399–1413 | Henry IV (Lancaster) |
| 1413–22 | Henry V (Lancaster) |
| *1422–61 | Henry VI (Lancaster) (1455–87 Wars of the Roses) |
| 1461–70 | Edward IV (York) |
| *1470–71 | Henry VI (Lancaster) |
| 1471–83 | Edward IV (York) |
| 1483–85 | Richard III (York) |

*Henry VI had a split reign*

## 👑 THE TUDORS

| | |
|---|---|
| 1485–1509 | Henry VII |
| 1509–47 | Henry VIII |
| 1547–53 | Edward VI (father Henry VIII; mother Jane Seymour) |
| 1553–58 | Mary I (father Henry VIII; mother Catherine of Aragon) |
| 1558–1603 | Elizabeth I (father Henry VIII; mother Anne Boleyn) |

## 👑 THE EARLY STUARTS

| | |
|---|---|
| 1603–25 | James I |
| 1625–49 | Charles I |
| 1649–60 | The Civil Wars and Interregnum |

## 👑 THE LATER STUARTS

| | |
|---|---|
| 1660–85 | Charles II |
| 1685–88 | James II |

## 👑 THE REVOLUTIONARY SETTLEMENT OF 1688

| | |
|---|---|
| 1689–1702 | William III |
| 1689–94 | Mary II |
| 1702–14 | Anne |

## 👑 THE HANOVERIAN KINGS

| | |
|---|---|
| 1714–27 | George I |
| 1727–60 | George II |
| 1760–1820 | George III |
| 1820–30 | George IV |
| 1830–37 | William IV |
| 1837–1901 | Victoria |
| 1901–10 | Edward VII |

## 👑 THE HOUSE OF WINDSOR

| | |
|---|---|
| 1910–36 | George V |
| 1936 | Edward VIII (abdicated) |
| 1936–52 | George VI |
| 1952– | Elizabeth II |

# themes for further Study

## HENRY VI, PARTS 1, 2, 3

- Shakespeare's poetic style in the trilogy, compared to that of his great plays in the 1599–1608 period
- Causes of the Wars of the Roses
- The various kinds of love found in the trilogy
- Shakespeare's use of fact and fiction to fit his dramatic purposes
- The role of Good and Evil in the trilogy

## TITUS ANDRONICUS

- The consequences of Titus' failing to heed Tamora's pleas for Alarbus' life
- Titus' refusal to become Emperor of Rome
- Marcus' role in *Titus*
- Aaron's contribution to the decimation of the Andronicus family
- Tamora's use of power as empress

## KING JOHN

- Positive qualities of King John
- The seige of Angiers
- The personality and character of the Bastard
- Pandulph's role in *King John*
- Unity through religious issues

## MERRY WIVES OF WINDSOR

- The "realistic" aspects of this "contemporary" drama
- The significance of disguises and costumes
- The function of the masque in *Merry Wives*
- Two Falstaffs? His character in *Merry Wives* vs. that in the *Henry VI* plays
- The role of wealth in *Merry Wives*

## ALL'S WELL THAT ENDS WELL

- The effect of the "gloomy mood" in the first scene of *All's Well*
- Shakespeare's use of sexual wordplay
- The role of honor in *All's Well*
- Helena's two "tasks"
- The resurrection theme in *All's Well*

## TROILUS AND CRESSIDA

- Elements of tragedy in *Troilus*
- Cressida's manipulation of the "love plot"
- Patroclus' loyal, perceptive friendship
- The function of Thersites' foulmouthed cynicism
- The metaphor of "infection" in *Troilus*

## TIMON OF ATHENS

- The absence of women in *Timon*
- Causes of Timon's cynicism
- Apemantus as choral commentator
- The role of revenge in *Timon*
- The philosophy of art, as espoused by the poet and the painter

## CORIOLANUS

- Volumnia as mother
- The flaw in Coriolanus' patrician character
- The function of the "gown of humility"
- Duplicity in *Coriolanus*
- Aufidius—a three-dimensional villain?

## PERICLES

- The relationship between Simonides and Thaisa, compared to that of Antiochus and his daughter
- The love for one's child in *Pericles*
- The role of the sea in *Pericles*
- Dionyza in *Pericles* and the queen in *Cymbeline:* a comparison
- Disguises in *Pericles*

## CYMBELINE

- Cymbeline's relationship with Imogen
- Iachimo and Cloten: a comparison of characters
- The imagery of trade, commerce, and money in *Cymbeline*
- Posthumus' eventual metamorphosis
- The role of coincidence in *Cymbeline*

## HENRY VIII

- Katherine's dominant qualities
- The role of the commoners in *Henry VIII*
- The manifestations of ambition in *Henry VIII*
- Wolsey: a good man or an evil man?
- Cause and effect in *Henry VIII*

# Selected
# Bibliography

# GENERAL

BENTLEY, GERALD EADES. *Shakespeare, a Biographical Handbook.* New Haven: Yale University Press, 1961.

BOYCE, CHARLES. *Shakespeare A to Z.* New York: Facts on File, 1990.

BRADLEY, A.C. *Shakespearean Tragedy.* London: The Macmaillan Co., 1904.

CHUTE, MARCHETTE. *An Introduction to Shakespeare.* New York: E.P. Dutton, 1951.

CRAIG, HARDIN. *An Interpretation of Shakespeare.* New York: Dryden Press, 1948.

FRYE, NORTHROP. *On Shakespeare.* Robert Sandler, ed. New Haven, Connecticut: Yale University Press, 1986.

GIBSON, H.N. *The Shakespeare Claimants.* New York: Barnes & Noble, Inc., 1962.

KNIGHT, G. WILSON. *The Wheel of Fire.* Oxford University Press, 1930.

PAPP, JOSEPH, AND ELIZABETH KIRKLAND. *Shakespeare Alive!* New York: Bantam, 1988.

SITWELL, EDITH. *A Notebook on William Shakespeare.* London: Oxford University Press, 1928.

WATKINS, RONALD. *Moonlight at the Globe.* London: Michael Joseph, 1946.

WEBSTER, MARGARET. *Shakespeare Without Tears.* Cleveland: World Publishing Company, 1965.

WILSON, J. DOVER. *The Essential Shakespeare.* New York: Cambridge University Press, 1932.

# HISTORIES

BECKER, GEORGE J. *Shakespeare's Histories.* Ungar, 1977.

HOLDERNESS, GRAHAM. *Shakespeare's History.* St. Martin, 1985.

THOMSON, W.H. *Shakespeare's Characters: A Historical Dictionary.* Folcroft, 1972.

TILLYARD, E.M.W. *Shakespeare's History Plays.* London, 1956.

# COMEDIES

ANDERSON, LINDA. *A Kind of Wild Justice: Revenge in Shakespeare's Comedies.* University of Delaware Press, 1987.

FRYE, NORTHROP. *A Natural Perspective: The Development of Shakespearean Comedy and Romance.* Peter Smith, 1988.

MUIR, KENNETH, ED. *Shakespeare, the Comedies: A Collection of Critical Essays.* Prentice Hall, 1965.

# PROBLEM PLAYS

MUIR, KENNETH, AND STANLEY WELLS, EDS. *Aspects of Shakespeare's "Problem Plays":* All's Well That Ends Well, Measure for Measure, Troilus and Cressida. Cambridge University Press, 1982.

# HENRY VI, PARTS 1,2,3

ALEXANDER, PETER. *Shakespeare's* Henry VI *and* Richard III. Arden Library, 1978.

CALDERWOOD, JAMES L. *Metadrama in Shakespeare's Henriad:* Richard II *to* Henry V. University of California Press, 1979.

GAW, ALLISON. *Origin and Development of* One Henry Six *in Relation to Shakespeare, Marlowe, Peele & Greene.* Borgo Press, 1982.

RIGGS, DAVID. *Shakespeare's Heroical Histories:* Henry VI *and Its Literary Tradition.* Harvard University Press, 1971.

# TITUS ANDRONICUS

HARDIS, G. *Titus Andronicus.* Garland Publications, 1985.

ADAMS, J.C. "Shakespeare's Revisions in *Titus Andronicus,*" *Shakespeare 400.* Holt, Rinehart and Winston, Inc., 1964.

# KING JOHN

ELSON, J. "Studies in the *King John* Plays," *Adams Memorial Studies* (1948).

WARREN, W. "What Was Wrong with King John?" *History Today* (VII) (1957), 806-812.

MCDIARMID, M. "Concerning the Troublesome Reign of King John," *Notes and Queries* IV (1957), 435-538.

# THE MERRY WIVES OF WINDSOR

ROBERTS, JEANNE A. *Shakespeare's English Comedy:* The Merry Wives of Windsor *in Context.* University of Nebraska Press, 1979.

FORSYTHE, R.S. "*The Merry Wives of Windsor:* Two New Analogues," *Philolgical Quarterly* VII (1928), 390-398.

SCHUCKING, L. "The Fairy Scene in *The Merry Wives of Windsor* in Folio and Quarto," *Modern Language Review* XIX (124), 338-40.

# ALL'S WELL THAT ENDS WELL

WILSON, H.S. "Dramatic Emphasis in *All's Well That Ends Well,*" *Huntington Library Quarterly* XIII (1950), 222-240.

LEECH, C. "The Theme of Ambition in *All's Well That Ends Well,*" *Journal of English Literary History* XXI (1954), 17-29.

KING, W.N. "Shakespeare's Mingled Yarn," *Modern Language Quarterly* XXI (1960), 33-44.

# TROILUS AND CRESSIDA

ADAMSON, JANE. *Troilus and Cressida.* G.K. Hall. 1988.

CAMPBELL, O.J. *Comicall Satyre and Shakespeare's* Troilus and Cressida. 1938.

# TIMON OF ATHENS

SOELLNER, ROLF. Timon of Athens: *Shakespeare's Pessimistic Tragedy.* Ohio State University Press, 1979.

DRIVER, T.F. *The Sense of History in Greek and Shakespearean Drama.* New York: Columbia University Press, 1960.

# CORIOLANUS

BLOOM, HAROLD, INTRO. *Coriolanus.* Chelsea House, 1987.

GIVEN, CHRISTOPHER. "Shakespeare's *Coriolanus:* The Premature Epitaph and the Butterfly." *Shakespeare Studies* 12 (1979), 143-58.

GRANVILLE-BARKER, HARLEY. *Prefaces to Shakespeare:* Coriolanus. David & Charles, 1982.

HOLT, LEIGH, AND JAMES HOGG. *From Man to Dragon: A Study of Shakespeare's* Coriolanus. Longwood, 1976.

PHILLIPS, JAMES EMERSON, JR., ED. *Twentieth Century Interpretations of* Coriolanus. Englewood Cliffs, N.J.: Prentice-Hall, 1979.

POOLE, ADRIAN. *Coriolanus.* G.K. Hall, 1988.

ZOLBROD, PAUL G. "Coriolanus and Alceste: A Study in Misanthropy," *Shakespeare Quarterly* 23, (1972), 51-62.

# PERICLES

HOENIGER, F.D., ED. *Pericles.* London: Methuen & Co., Ltd., 1963.

MUIR, KENNETH. "The Problem of *Pericles," English Studies* XXX (1949), 65-83.

# CYMBELINE

ABARTIS, CAESAREA. *The Tragicomic Construction of* Cymbeline *and* The Winter's Tale. Longwood, 1977.

GRANVILLE-BARKER, HARLEY. *Prefaces to Shakespeare:* Cymbeline, The Winter's Tale. David & Charles, 1985.

MARSH, D.R.C. *The Recurring Miracle: A Study of* Cymbeline *and the Last Plays.* Lincoln: University of Nebraska Press, 1962.

## HENRY VIII

MICHELI, A. *Henry VIII.* Garland Publications, 1986.

TILLYARD, E.M.W. *Shakespeare's Last Plays.* London: Chatto & Windus, 1938.

TRAVERSI, D.A. *Shakespeare: The Last Phase.* New York: Harcourt Brace, 1955.

# To understand great authors, you need to read between the lines.

## Cliffs Complete Study Editions

The more you learn about the classics, the richer your enjoyment and the deeper your understanding become. These easy-to-use Complete Study editions contain everything a student or teacher needs to study works by Shakespeare or Chaucer. Each illustrated volume includes abundant biographical, historical and literary background information, including a bibliography to aid in selecting additional reading.

The three-column arrangement provides running commentary for the complete Cambridge edition of the Shakespeare plays, plus glossary entries explaining obscure Elizabethan words. The Chaucer titles contain running commentary, individual lines of the Middle English text, followed by literal translations in contemporary English, and glossaries.

### Complete Study Editions
8½ × 11

| Shakespeare | Qty. |
| --- | --- |
| 416-5 Hamlet | |
| 419-X Julius Caesar | |
| 425-4 King Henry IV, Part 1 | |
| 422-X King Lear | |
| 428-9 Macbeth | |
| 431-9 Merchant of Venice | |
| 434-3 Othello | |
| 438-6 Romeo and Juliet | |
| 441-6 The Tempest | |
| 445-9 Twelfth Night | |
| **Chaucer's Canterbury Tales** | |
| 406-8 The Prologue | |
| 409-2 The Wife of Bath | |

Prices subject to change without notice.

## $6.95 each

Available at your booksellers, or send this form with your check or money order to **Cliffs Notes, Inc., P.O. Box 80728, Lincoln, NE 68501**
**http://www.cliffs.com**

☐ Money order ☐ Check payable to Cliffs Notes, Inc.

☐ Visa ☐ Mastercard Signature_____

Card no. _____ Exp. date_____

Signature _____

Name _____

Address _____

City _____

State _____ Zip_____

# Legends In Their Own Time

$A$ncient civilization is rich with the acts of legendary figures and events. Here are three classic reference books that will help you understand the legends, myths and facts surrounding the dawn of civilization.

*Cliffs Notes on Greek Classics* and *Cliffs Notes on Roman Classics*— Guides to the idealogy, philosophy and literary influence of ancient civilization.

*Cliffs Notes on Mythology*—An introduction to the study of various civilizations as they are revealed in myths and legends.

Find these legendary books at your bookstore or order them using the form below.

---

## Yes! I want to add these classics to my library.

*Cliffs Notes on Greek Classics*   ISBN 0566-2 ($7.95) . . . . . . . . . . . . . . . . . . _____

*Cliffs Notes on Roman Classics*   ISBN 1152-2 ($7.95) . . . . . . . . . . . . . . . . . . _____

*Cliffs Notes on Mythology*   ISBN 0865-3 ($7.95) . . . . . . . . . . . . . . . . . . _____

Total $_____

Available at your booksellers, or send this form with your check or money order to **Cliffs Notes, Inc., P.O. Box 80728, Lincoln, NE 68501**
**http://www.cliffs.com**

☐ Money order   ☐ Check payable to Cliffs Notes, Inc.
☐ Visa   ☐ Mastercard   Signature_____

Card no. _____ Exp. date_____

Signature _____

Name _____

Address _____

City _____ State_____ Zip_____

*Get the Cliffs Edge!*

**Cliffs NOTES INC.**